W. P. Butler

Irrigation Manual

Containing useful Information and Tables, appertaining to Irrigation by Artesian

Waters, in the States of North and South Dakota

W. P. Butler

Irrigation Manual
Containing useful Information and Tables, appertaining to Irrigation by Artesian Waters, in the States of North and South Dakota

ISBN/EAN: 9783337186067

Printed in Europe, USA, Canada, Australia, Japan

Cover: Foto ©Andreas Hilbeck / pixelio.de

More available books at **www.hansebooks.com**

IRRIGATION MANUAL,

CONTAINING

Useful Information and Tables

APPERTAINING TO

Irrigation

BY

Artesian Waters,

IN THE STATES OF

North and South Dakota,

TOGETHER WITH

Many Tables, Rules, and Items of Miscellaneous Information,

OF VALUE TO

Farmers and Business Men.

BY W. P. BUTLER,

Civil and Irrigation Engineer, Aberdeen, S D.

1892.

" *Let things that have to be done be learned by doing them.*"

HURONITE PRINTING HOUSE,
HURON, S. D.

PUBLISHERS' CERTIFICATE.

HURON, S. D., June 1st, 1892

The publishers of this book hereby certify that, in accordance with the orders of the author, they have printed and bound 3500 copies of the same.

SHANNON & LONGSTAFF,

Publishers.

A

INDEX TO TABLES.

Index to Tables—Continued.

INDEX TO FIGURES.

C

GENERAL INDEX.

General Index – Concluded.

INDEX TO ADVERTISEMENTS.

See Index to articles advertised on
next page.

H

INDEX TO ARTICLES ADVERTISED.

PREFACE.

The idea in presenting this little book to the public is to supply, in part, a demand for such tabulated and general information as is needed by many, at the present time, who are becoming interested in the matter of irrigation. Few have access to books of tables and rules and fewer still are able, without them, to figure out the problems involved, and hence, many abandon the subject because unable to cultivate an interest sufficiently satisfactory to themselves to warrant the taking of some definite step in the direction of a practical trial of that which, if properly managed, must open up the road to fortune to all who choose to enter. The idea is not to present an exhaustive treatise on irrigation, or to treat at length any of the matters presented, but simply to *suggest* them and, by giving many rules and tables, to supply the information needed, so that each may, for himself, make such estimates as the circumstances of his own case may require; and further, to put the investigator in the way of obtaining such desired information as circumstances would not permit of being given here.

In the selection of many rules and tables the following standard works have been freely consulted and properly credited:

Haswell's Engineer's Pocket Book, (Harper & Bros., New York.)
Trautwine's Engineer's Pocket Book, (John Wiley & Sons, New York.)
Engineer's Pocket Book, 1876, (Lockwood & Co., London.)
Useful Information, (Jones & Laughlin, Pittsburgh.)
The Measurement and Division of Water, (L. G. Carpenter, Ft. Collins, Colorado.)
Pocket Companion, (Carnegie Phipps & Co., Pittsburgh.)
The trade cataloges of the Chapman Valve Mfg. Co., National Tube Works, James Leffel & Co., Addyston Pipe Co., Pelton Water Wheel Co., Reading Iron Co., and others.
State and government reports, and all other available and reliable sources, such as the Engineering News, Irrigation Age, and Scientific American.

Besides the matter thus compiled, many entirely new tables have been computed to answer the special requirements of those to whom this matter is addressed.

If the matter presented is instrumental in creating any new, or in fostering any present interest in irrigation, or in aiding any in need of such information as is presented, then will the object of the compiler have been accomplished.

In the hope that hereby a demand has been partially satisfied this little book is inscribed to the advocates of irrigation in the Dakotas, by

W. P. BUTLER,
Compiler.

THE SUBJECT.

Much valuable time is wasted in the preparation and printing of articles on irrigation the burden of which seems to be to remove a doubt as to whether irrigation will pay, if practiced in the Dakotas.

The chief object accomplished by such articles is to keep alive the very doubt they aim to overcome, and at a time when, and in a place where, a doubt will do the most harm. The only good accomplished is that the subject is kept open and before the public.

THERE IS NO DOUBT

as to irrigation paying in Dakota, and this may be abundantly shown by a study of the history of irrigation in this and other lands.

Irrigation is as old as the race and it has been both the heritage and the legacy of every tribe and nation. The dawn of history dimly reveals the practice by those ancient peoples, and history, both sacred and profane, has recorded its onward march, as it has the march of armies. In Palestine, in Egypt, in Assyria and in India it was, as it still is, the life of the people. As irrigation developed, empires arose, and with its fall they fell; and where was once the verdant homes of countless millions there is, to-day, a desert waste.

The legions of Rome may be said to have been supported by irrigation; for the Roman Empire was but a union of irrigated nations. The subject in that day having the sanction and fostering care of every monarch. As the world has developed so has irrigation—until to-day, a large percentage of the products of the world are raised by that means; and now, as in all past ages, those who till the soil under a system of irrigation are the most prosperous of their class, and their lands the most valuable of all devoted to purposes of agriculture.

Irrigation has developed during these ages, as has everything else; now progressing, and again declining, with the progress or decline of the arts and peoples of each age and nation. The system of Spain was not that of Italy, nor is the system of to-day the same as that of a century ago.

The literature of irrigation is most interesting, and every irrigator in the Dakotas should "read up" to the fullest extent.

The system of irrigation practiced in every country has been a development, not alone in its engineering sense but in its legal sense also; for the questions of water rights and appropriations have always been most intricate and have demanded most studied treatment.

Irrigation in the United States was first practiced in the Salt Lake valley and in lower California, although very extensive systems of irrigation works built by the aborigines

were in ruins when the earliest settler went into the country.
The ancient inhabitants of Mexico and of Peru had vast
systems of canals, aqueducts and tunnels for the purpose of
water supply and irrigation, so that the industry of the
white man is but a revival, on this western continent, of the
older irrigation system of the ancients.

From the crude beginnings of the pioneers who lacked
both capital and labor, and were forced to begin anew, without previous knowledge of the subject, and under new conditions, there has developed in our western states a system
of irrigation so vast that its worth is measured by the tens
of millions, and so perfect as to bear most favorable comparison with the older and highly developed systems of
Spain, Italy and India. Each state has done all in its power
to foster the industry, to encourage investment in plants
and securities, and, by systems of law best suited to their
special conditions and requirements, to surround the industry with all needed protection.

IN DAKOTA

the day was, when to have spoken of irrigation as necessary
to *our* wellfare, would have been to have uttered heresy.
That day has passed. The bitter experience of a series of
dry years—when the hot wind was all we reaped—has taught
the lesson that, to live in prosperity and pleanty in Dakota,
we must irrigate. *It is no crime; it is no disgrace;* for the
most fruitful lands on the earth are such as are irrigated
and such as would be a barren waste were it not for irrigation. Such lands are in the deserts of Arabia, Africa and
our own western states. No better soil or climate exists on
this continent than that of Dakota and, with water at our
bidding, none on earth will be more fruitfull.

No country in the world, so far as known, possesses what
Dakota does—a soil of unmatched fertility, a climate suited
alike to the best needs of plant and animal life, a topography,
or surface, best suited to a system of general irrigation, and
at the minimum of cost, and a supply of water as general
in its distribution as it is inexhaustable in its volume and
powerful in its flow.

What a combination is this? Soil—climate—topography
—water and power. Each perfect; each in accord with the
other; and *all* to be had and controlled by him who wills it.

A Dakota farmer need not wait for a rich company to
build a dam to impound the clouds and then beg life on
such terms as the company may care to fix.

He has but to prick the soil and a fountain of wealth
pours forth to do his bidding. A servant as powerful as the
elements, yet as subject to control as the child; more bur-
dened with wealth than the summer shower and less bur-
dened with disaster than the summer torrent. A servant
perfectly trained to the performance not alone of one duty
but of many, and a servant the like of which nature has not
vouchsafed to the service of the men of any other land."

THE FARMER.

Has he had abundant crops? No!
Does he need, and must he have, a well? Yes!

HOW WILL HE GET IT?

No solution is offered as to the *means*, but it is giving good advice to say—*Adopt any means.* Some will be more advantageous than others yet to most farmers it will not be a matter of choice.

ANYTHING TO GET A WELL!

The " Melville " law, providing for township wells, has not been a success for, although 115 wells were located by the State Engineer during 1891, and bonds voted for them, no market (except in two cases) has yet been found for these bonds because of the manifest injustice of the law, which provides for the assessment of property not in the least benefited, or needing any benefit, in order that other private properties may be developed. Investors look askance at securties having so strong a taint of unconstitutionality and, as a result, there are few such wells being drilled; the activity being confined almost wholly to purely private enterprises.

A more equitable law must be passed to give relief. If the present law can be made to work, well and good, take that means. If a mortgage company, or an individual, stands ready, under any one of an infinite number of plans, to put down a well for you, take it at once. Raise the money in any way—only raise it!

If you can't own a whole well, own part of one. If you can own it all, do so by all means, for joint ownership means joint responsibility and its attendent evils.

Part of a well is better than no well, and 40 acres "under water" is better than 640 acres under a hot wind. Loose no time in stopping to figure—as many are continually doing—whether irrigation will pay or not, for *it never did anything else but pay, here or elsewhere.* If you want a life job take that of trying to prove that irrigation ever *failed* to pay and pay *well.* Let the first task be to get the money, figure on that and then when it is obtained there will be time to figure on its use.

The details of an irrigation plant in Dakota are very simple as compared with those in most other sections, where the sourse of water supply is at a great distance and where heavy dams, long and expensive flumes, tunnels and bridges must be built either to store or to convey it. These great engineering works entail a vast expense and preclude any individual ownership or controll. Here, however, the whole system of supply and distribution may be created upon, and limited to, ones own garden patch and at but nominal cost.

Where other systems prevail there enters in the very complex questions of water rights, which, to a great extent, cannot find a place here where the system is so different and essentially individual. If a farmer owns a well he can use it when and as he chooses, and to any extent, so long as he does not trespass upon his neighbor; and he may sell the water on such terms as he may be able to make. Nor can he prevent his neighbor seeking a supply from the same source, for whence the supply comes and what its volume may be can never be other than conjecture.

That questions of water rights as between individuals, and as between the State and individuals, will arise there can be no question, but what questions will arise and what their solutions will be, may be safely left to the future.

After the question of money supply, the first consideration is as to the well.

THE WELL.

About 200 wells have already been put down in the two Dakotas, varying in size from 2 to 8 inches. The popular and common sizes being 4½ and 6 inch wells. On the whole, very little is yet known of our wells because of lack of systematic study and experiments. Then, too, very many erroneous ideas prevail as to the wells and, unfortunately, any amount of wilful exageraation which will, in the end, result in more harm than good.

A few facts will be stated and explained.

The volume of a well does not depend upon its size, that is, an 8 inch well will not, necessarily, discharge more water than a 6 inch well. The volume discharged by a well of any size will depend entirely on the depth of the well and the character of the rock in which the water is found. If the rock is hard and fine in texture the flow of water through it will be less than if the rock is soft and coarse and filled with pores and open channels. Again—the volume need not be great because the pressure is high, as many suppose. This is shown by a comparason of the southern with the northern wells. The southern wells having in some cases a very large flow and a low pressuxe while the northern wells have a lesser volume and a much higher pressure. The former are not so deep, either, as the latter.

When the well is closed the pressure is said to be a STATIC or standing pressure. This is absorbed in throwing out the water when the well is opened. If the pipe is 6 inches all the way down, more water will get into the bottom in a minute than if the opening at the bottom is but 4 inches, and that at the top 6 inches, yet the *pressure* of the water will be the same when closed in. So, too, the rock may be so hard as to prevent a large supply reaching the pipe per minute, so the volume will be small although the pressure may be high.

In this case the supply fails to meet the duty of the pressure. Other wells have a very large volume and comparatively low pressure. In this case the rock is soft and open, permitting of a large and free flow all, or only a part of which, is thrown out. The condition is here reversed, *i. e..* the duty of the pressure fails to meet the volume of the supply. In sinking a well it is wholly a matter of conjecture as to what the volume and pressure will be. The chances are in favor of getting a larger volume from a larger well, but the pressure will not (as above explained) increase in the same proportion as the volume; nor will the velocity of discharge keep up, under a given pressure, if the well is larger and the volume only proportionately greater.

The matter of *relative economy,* as between wells of different sizes, has yet to be determined, and it can only be determined by the sinking of many wells and their careful study.

In other countries a man having 160 acres figures *in advance* on just what water he needs In Dakota a man figures on as big a well as he can pay for and is hankful for whatever water the well brings him—the more the better. In figuring on what kind of a well to put down do not figure too fine, that is, do not get a small well because its estimated volume (judging from others of its size in the neighborhood) will answer your purpose, because of two important reasons.

FIRST, a small well will clog or stop up more easily than a larger one and will be more costly and more difficult to clean out.

SECOND, in case of accident during the drilling or after completion, a small well, may be spoiled if recased, while a larger well could be recased and still leave a serviceable well. The smaller one might have to be abandoned under circumstances which would permit of the larger well being rendered serviceable.

The larger well has thus substantial advantages in its favor aside from the mere matter of volume, and a few dollars extra, in the matter of cost, ought not to stand in its way. The increased service of the increased volume from the larger well would, in many cases, pay not only the increased cost but for the whole well.

Stated generally, it would appear to be poor economy to put down a well of less than 5 or 6 inches diameter. What the economical limit above this size will be remains to be demonstrated.

Having decided upon a well, of say 6 inch bore, then comes the details of getting it. Some will contract with a well-driller near at hand; others will advertise for bids, and, *of course,* accept-the *lowest,* whether it be *best* the or not; others will seek the county rig, while still others will, either alone or by clubbing together, buy a rig and drill the well themselves. Some will favor one process and some another; while some will favor one make of rig which another person may condemn.

By reason, therefore, of this diversity of circumstances, opinion, and preferences, and the fact that, up to date, very little systematic work has been done and no one process or rig has demonstrated its superiority over all others, no definite instructions can be given as to the *best* course to pursue or the *best* method to adopt. If a CONTRACT is entered into for the drilling it is usually as a result of bidding. In this case the chief consideration to the farmer is as to size, material, cost and time, and not as to the *method* or *system* used by the contractor. He may use poles, cables, or the hydraulic process, as he prefers so long as he gets a well in proper manner and time.

The *details* of the contract are very important and it should be drawn up by some one who understands the value and importance of these details, so that there is contained all that should be, and in proper form, so that the rights of both parties will be protected.

If all goes well the contract is a mere ornament, but if trouble arises the contract comes out and then every word has a value. The contract is to the controversy what the safe is to the fire,

From the information contained herein it is expected that any man, familiar with business forms and customs, may draw up his own contract if he prefers to run the chance of doing it properly.

In case the farmer, alone, or associated with others, desires to do his own work, and with his own rig, then the choice of *methods* and *rigs* enters into first place and the matter of *contract* is eliminated.

KINDS OF MACHINES. As previously stated, no statement of general preference will be risked. Each class of machines has its special advantages or is undoubtedly the *best* under certain circumstances. The conditions of drilling here, however, differ from those of most other sections. Old eastern drillers declare work here to be far harder than work in the east where the rock is more solid, where the casing may be omitted in many or most cases, and where the formations are better known and understood. Here the formations are principally shale and the drilling very difficult and heavy casing always necessary.

POLE MACHINES. The earlier wells in Dakota were all drilled by pole rigs, that is, rigs using wooden drill-rods. Aside from the matter of *time* taken up in the coupling and uncoupling of the rods in putting the tools into, and taking them from, the well, these rigs have proved most satisfactory under all circumstances and have, without doubt, performed the best, cheapest and most rapid work.

The uncoupling of the rods or their breaking are disadvantages which tend to frequent accidents but these risks are largely overcome by the use of efficient grappling tools

The special advantages of the pole rigs lie in the certainty
of their drilling action. The revolution of the rods is uni-
formly in the direction of tightning the screw threads of the
joints, thus aiding in preserving the tightness of all the connections. Again—the rods forming a rigid connection between the drill and the hand of the driller, the action and
position of the drill is under perfect controll. If the rods
turn it is certain that the drill turned also and that the hole
is being drilled circular and not oblong. In this certainty of
control over the action of the tools lies the chief great advantage, in this state, of the pole rig over all others. Again—the
rigidity of the string of poles makes it possible to tell exactly where the bottom of the hole is and to better controll the
blows of the drill. This advantage tends further to an increase in the number of blows delivered per minute for the
rods have greater weight than the cable ond sink more rapidly, the friction of their smooth surfaces is less than with
the corrugated surface of a cable and the rigidity makes it
certain that if the upper end of the string of rods sinks that
the lower end has done the same—there being no kink, or
bending, or looping, as with a cable.

CABLE MACHINES. Cable rigs; that is, rigs using either rope or wire cables in the place of drill rods, are very largely used now because, principally, of the facility of operation.
In letting down the tools and in removing them much time
is saved by having a continuous run instead of having to
stop every thirty feet to couple or uncouple a rod or pole.
The danger due to the uncoupling of a joint is done away
with, In these features lie the chief advantages of the cable
rig. The disadvantages are many and well worth considering. The danger of breaking the cable, under strain, or if a
tool becomes fast, is greater than with poles. The cable is
rotated both to the right and to the left thus making it possible to readily uncouple a joint at the tools, if, perchance,
the joint became loose by the jar of the drilling. There is
danger that the rotation of the cable will not always cause
a corresponding rotation of the drill and the hole not be
drilled truly circular thus causing trouble in sinking the
pipe. This is especially noticable in the important operation
of reaming. which is the enlargement of the hole by scraping
away its sides, an operation requiring care and a tool so
worked as to cut away the full circle and not merely part of
it. With the cable the rotation may have the effect of merely twisting the rope instead of rotating the tool. With the
pole rig this cannot be. Again, when the hole is several hundred feet deep, and where the drilling is done in water which
may be flowing out with considerable velocity and pressure,
the velocity of the drill blows must be slow. If the motion is
rapid the walking-beam returns to the lifting motion before
the tools have had a chance to fall and drag down the cable
against the upward motion of the water.

In this way the energy expended may be absorbed not in effective drilling but in merely churning on the cable. With poles this is otherwise, as explained. On occount of these manifest disadvantages several drillers have abandoned the use of cables in the drilling work and have constructed what are called *"combination"* rigs, that is, rigs using poles for drilling and the cable for operating the sand pump, and for other purposes requiring rapid action. This arrangement has proved most satisfactory for it combines the advantages and eliminates the disadvantages of both 'ystems. There may, in the cable rigs, be a choice as to cables. In most cases the 2 inch rope is used because it is cheaper than wire, but the wire possesses the advantage of answering all the conditions of stength required in heavy service, and, it is said, the elasticity of the wire, when under the tension of the lift, aids materially in the important operation of twisting the drill, thus, to a great extent, neutralizing the effect of possible carelessness on the part of the driller.

HYDRAULIC OR JETTING MACHINES.

These rigs are of many patterns and workon quite dissimilar plans but all pass by the common name of "jetting" or "rotary" rigs. In one class of rig the drilling is done with a very short drill-bit having a hollow shank through which a jet of water is forced from the hollow drill rods (pipe-rods.) This creates an upward current which carries out the drillings, thus doing away with much pumping and permitting the almost continuous operation of the drill. These rigs are almost untried here but much is claimed for them.

The rotary hydraulic rigs are among the latest in the Dakota field and hence are the most untried. They have in other sections, and especialy in the shallower wells proved vastly superior to other rigs. In several cases here they have had phenmoinally successful runs, down to depths of 500 to 700 feet, but for greater depths they have not proved a uniform success, yet the *process* could not, in most cases, be blamed for the failure.

Judging from the very flattering successes met with in a few cases, one may safely predict a very wide field of usefulness for these machines, and especially when their operation in our peculiar formation is better understood. Even these rigs—like both the pole and cable rigs—are already undergoing the ordeal of rearrangement and modification to better suit them to the conditions here met. The lastest advices are to the effect that very important modifications have but recently been made, by the American Well Works, which promise to make the rig as nearly suited to Dakoia as mechanical ingenuity can at present approach.

The elements of watchfulness, mechanical ability, quick and accurate judgment, and, above all, extreme care necessary to success with any rig or any system apply particularly to this class of rigs.

It may be said (as the result of ten years of experience and observation in Dakota) that a very large majority of the many accidents in the well-drilling operations of this state have been due, not to any fault in the process or the rig, but to sheer ignorance or carelessness on the part of the drillers, many of whom have been without knowledge of, or experience in, the well business, hired as mere helpers yet placed, often times, in full charge of the work and with no responsibility as to its safe and proper conduct

This being undeniably true, it may be further stated that the exercise of care and judgment is of more importance to the owner of a rig than the mere mechanical details of the rig itself; for *a poor tool, in the hands of an expert, will do better work than a fine tool, in the hands of a careless and ignorant workman.*

TOOLS.

In the selection of drills, reamers, pumps, grappling-tools and other accessories of a drilling outfit select with reference to the size and style of the rig, and in matters of detail rely upon the advice of some responsible manufacturer; bearing in mind one thing—get *enough* tools. Do not work "short handed," for it will not pay in the well business.

If a rod or cable breaks, or a tool is dropped into the well, be prepared to handle the case AT ONCE, for any delay may cost hundreds of dollars. Have the tools to treat all cases, have them where they belong, and don't allow a meal, a circus or even cold or darkness to interfere with prompt action and invaribly leaving the work so it is safe.

Be prepared for accidents for they are sure to come!

The machinery having been selected, and the well begun. the next consideration is as to the pipe.

PIPE.

LAP-WELD. The selection of a suitable pipe is a matter of importance upon which depends, very largely, the success or the failure of the well. In the past, pipe of all sorts of makes and weights has been used, and with varying success.

Wrought iron pipe is of two classes— the BUTT-WELDED and the LAP-WELDED. Fig. 1 shows the great difference between these welds, and the superior strength of the lap-weld which h s BUTT-WELD. ior strength of the lap-weld which h s Fig. 1. about 4 times as much surface in contact at the weld as is had in the butt-weld.

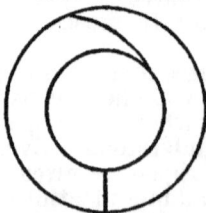

It is clear that butt-welded pipe would not be safe to use in our wells, yet some has been used and with disastrous effect.

All pipe should be lap-welded.

The thinner the pipe the shorter and weaker is the weld; the thicker the pipe the longer and stronger is the weld. Wrought iron pipe (like most other things these days,) is, in its different classes, made on standard models; that is, the thickness, area, weight, etc., per foot, for any given size will vary but little as between different makers, and certain standard brands are listed by nearly all. Thus, there is what is known as "Standard" pipe, x or extra strong, xx or double extra strong, casing pipe, line pipe, drive pipe, tubing, etc.

Most of these brands will not be used here. The standard pipe is that which is commonly used and is a brand sufficiently heavy for every use unless it be that of very heavy driving for which purpose drive-pipe is designed, it being of a better grade of iron and hence stronger. For lighter work—as for the casing used in starting a w ll, or the pipe used in recasing an old well—the lighter or casing pipe is the grade used.

Table No. 1, on the next page, gives the dimensions, weights, etc., of "Standard" pipe.

Some drillers are of the opinion that drive pipe should be used in all Dakota well work because of the liability of getting the pipe fast and being obliged then to subject it to very heavy driving, or pulling with jack-screws, in order to loosen it. There is, of course, much ground for this opinion and it goes without proof that if the stronger pipe* is used the well will be the better for it and the operation of sinking it the safer; but it were useless to use heavier pipe if a lighter grade would answer every purpose.

The opinion is, therefore, repeated that if the drilling and reaming are properly and sufficiently done, the "standard" grade of pipe will serve every purpose, at any rate in wells of 8 inches or less in size. The wear and tear on the pipe is greatly lessened by sufficiently reaming out the hole under the pipe, by the use of expansion or other reamers. Frequently this is overlooked, or insuffiiently done, and the pipe, after hard driving, becomes fast and days, or even weeks of delay are consumed in an effort to loosen it and to do over again what should have have been done well in the first place. Too great care cannot be used in this part of the work. If the reaming is well done the pipe will settle easily and rapidly, or with but light driving, and a lighter grade of pipe might safely be used; but if the reaming is insufficiently done, and heavy driving resorted to, then standard or drive pipe should be used.

It shauld be noted that the *external* diameters of pipe must remain the same in order to fit to standard couplings. If the pipe is made heavier the extra metal is added to the *inside* and the *internal* diameter thereby reduced.

*Drive and line pipes are of standard sizes and weights, but being of a better grade of iron they are stronger and more expensive.

TABLE NO. 1.

READING IRON COMPANY.

WROUGHT IRON PIPE FOR STEAM, GAS, OR WATER.

TABLE OF STANDARD DIMENSIONS.

Nominal Inside Diameter	Actual Inside Diameter. Inches.	Actual Outside Diameter. Inches.	Thickness. Inches.	Internal Circumference. Inches.	External Circumference. Inches.	Length of Pipe per sq. ft. of Inside Surface. Feet.	Length of Pipe per sq. ft. of Outside Surface. Feet.	Internal Area. Inches.	External Area. Inches.	Length of Pipe containing One Cubic Foot. Feet.	Nominal Weight per Foot. Pounds.	Number of Threads per In. of Screw.	Contents in Gallons per Foot.
⅛	0.270	0.405	0.068	0.848	1.272	14.15	9.44	0.0572	0.129	2500.	0.243	27	.0006
¼	0.364	0.54	0.088	1.144	1.696	10.50	7.075	0.1041	0.229	1385.	0.422	18	.0026
⅜	0.494	0.675	0.091	1.552	2.121	7.67	5.657	0.1916	0.358	751.5	0.561	18	.0057
½	0.623	0.84	0.109	1.957	2.652	6.13	4.502	0.3048	0.554	472.4	0.845	14	.0102
¾	0.824	1.05	0.113	2.589	3.299	4.635	3.637	0.5333	0.866	270.	1.126	14	.0230
1	1.043	1.315	0.134	3.292	4.134	3.679	2.903	0.8627	1.357	166.9	1.67	11½	.0408
1¼	1.380	1.66	0.140	4.335	5.215	2.768	2.301	1.496	2.164	96.25	2.258	11½	.0638
1½	1.611	1.9	0.145	5.061	5.969	2.371	2.01	2.038	2.835	70.65	2.694	11½	.0918
2	2.067	2.375	0.154	6.494	7.461	1.848	1.611	3.355	4.430	42.36	3.667	11½	.1632
2½	2.468	2.875	0.204	7.754	9.032	1.547	1.328	4.783	6.491	30.11	5.773	8	.2550
3	3.067	3.5	0.217	9.636	10.996	1.245	1.091	7.388	9.621	19.49	7.547	8	.3673
3½	3.548	4.0	0.226	11.146	12.566	1.077	0.955	9.887	12.566	14.56	9.055	8	.4998
4	4.026	4.5	0.237	12.648	14.137	0.949	0.849	12.730	15.904	11.31	10.728	8	.6528
4½	4.508	5.	0.247	14.153	15.708	0.843	0.765	15.939	19.635	9.03	12.34	8	.8263
5	5.045	5.563	0.259	15.849	17.475	0.757	0.629	19.990	24.299	7.20	14.504	8	1.020
6	6.065	6.625	0.280	19.054	20.813	0.63	0.577	28.889	34.471	4.98	18.767	8	1.469
7	7.023	7.625	0.301	22.063	23.954	0.544	0.505	38.737	45.663	3.72	23.41	8	1.999
8	7.982	8.625	0.322	25.076	27.096	0.473	0.444	50.039	58.426	2.88	28.348	8	2.611
9	9.001	9.688	0.344	28.277	30.433	0.425	0.394	63.633	73.715	2.26	34.077	8	3.300
10	10.019	10.75	0.366	31.475	33.772	0.381	0.355	78.838	90.762	1.80	40.641	8	4.081
11	11.00	11.75	0.375	34.55	36.91	0.34	0.32	95.03	108.43	1.50	45.	8	4.93
12	12.	12.75	0.375	37.70	40.05	0.32	0.30	113.	127.67	1.27	48.98	8	5.87

* The standard U. S. gallon of 231 cubic inches.   Taper of Threads—1 to 32 on each side.

1¼ in. and below proved to 300 lbs. per sq. in. hydraulic pressure.   1½ in. and larger proved to 500 lbs. per sq. in. hydraulic pressure.

TABLE NO. 2.

READING IRON COMPANY.

_____STANDARD._ ____

WROUGHT IRON LAP-WELDED PIPE,
FOR STEAM, GAS, AND WATER.

MANUFACTURERS' PRICE LIST.
REVISED AND ADOPTED SEPT. 18, 1889.

To take the place of all previous lists and subject to change without notice.

Nominal Inside Diameter.	Price per Foot, Plain.	Price per Foot, Galvan'z'd	Nominal Weight per Foot.	Thickness.	No. of Thread per inch of screw.
Inches.	$ c.	$ c.	Pounds.	Inches.	
1½	.23	.26	2.68	.145	11½
2	.30	.34	3.61	.154	11½
2½	.47	.53	5.74	.204	8
3	.62	.68	7.54	.217	8
3½	.74	.88	9.00	.226	8
4	.88	1.03	10.66	.237	8
4½	1.06	1.31	12.34	.246	8
5	1.28	1.60	14.50	.259	8
6	1.65	2.00	18.76	.280	8
7	2.10		23.27	.301	8
8	2.75		28.18	.322	8
9	3.75		33.70	.344	8
10	4.75		40.06	.366	8
11	6.00		45.02	.375	8
12	7.00		49.00	.375	8
13	8.00		54.00	.375	8
14	9.50		58 00	.375	8
15	11.00		62.00	.375	8

Prices of Standard Pipe.

Discount on galvanized pipe *about* 55 per cent.
"   "   plain   "   "   62½ "   "
(See table No. 3.)

The same prices are quoted by all makers and as the marbet price fluctuates the rate of discount changes. Current discounts can be had from the makers. Those given herein are not the latest but will fully answer the purpose of approximate estimates.

For selected pipe, or pipe cut to special length the discount is usually 5 per cent. less.

18

TABLE NO. 3.

The following prices are also quoted.

NET PRICES.

Size of pipe.	Tubing.	Line pipe.	Drive pipe.	Standard pipe.	
1½ inches.	.12			.08½	Discount of 62½ per cent from list prices of plain pipe stated in table 2.
2	.14	.12		.11¼	
2½	.19	.17		.17½	
3	.28	.21	.28	.22¼	
3½		.26		.27¾	
4	.39	.30	.40	.33	
4½		.36		.39½	
5		.44		.48	
6		.56	.76	.60¾	
7		.72		.78¾	
8		.90	1.20	1.07	
9		1.30		1.40½	
10		1.55	1.95	1.78	
12		2.30	2.53	2.62	

This table is arranged so as to show comparative prices of different grades of pipe. The prices for standard pipe being the *net prices* resulting from the discount and list prices given in table 2, for plain pipe.

The prices here given will fully answer the purpose of *estimate*. Exact prices can only be had by correspondence with the manufacturers, who will quote the latest lists and discounts.

That feature of the pipe which is of the greatest concern to the well driller is the thread and it is chiefly on account of the thread that heavier pipe is needed. If the pipe is thin and light so much of the body of the metal is cut away in the operation of threading as to leave a thin shell not sufficiently strong to withstand the driving blows without danger of stripping the thread.

If the pipe is heavy the body of metal back of the threads is stronger and the pipe therefore more able to withstand heavy work.

COUPLINGS. (See table No. 7.)

The common form of coupling is straight threaded, that is, the line of the threads is parallel to the outer surface of the coupling. An improved form gives greater strength to both pipe and coupling and distributes the strain more evenly over the line of the thread. This is known as the patent TAPER COUPLING. From the illustrations of this form of coupling, shown in connection with the advertisements on the front and back covers and by Fig. 2 on page 20, it will be seen that the inner face, or threaded surface of the coupling, has the form of a funnel to fit a corresponding conical taper on the pipe. In drive-pipe the ends of the pipe meet at the middle of the coupling.

TABLE NO. 4.

READING IRON COMPANY.

X STRONG AND XX STRONG

WROUGHT IRON LAP-WELDED PIPE.

X STRONG.

Size.	Price per Foot.	Actual Outside Diameter.	Nominal Inside Diameter.	Thickness.	Nominal Weight per Foot.
Inches.	$ c.	Inches.	Inches.	Inches.	Pounds.
1½	.46	1.90	1.494	.203	3.63
2	.60	2.375	1.933	.221	5.02
2½	.94	2.875	2.315	.280	7.67
3	1.24	3.50	2.892	.304	10.25
3½	1.48	4.00	3.358	.321	12.47
4	1.76	4.50	3.818	.341	14.97
4½	2.12	5.	4.25	.35	17.60
5	2.56	5.563	4.813	.375	20.54
6	3.30	6.625	5.750	.437	28.58
7	4.20	7.625	6.62	.50	37 60
8	5.50	8.625	7.50	.56	47.85

XX STRONG.

Size.	Price per Foot.	Actual Outside Diameter.	Nominal Inside Diameter.	Thickness.	Nominal Weight per Foot.
Inches.	$ c.	Inches.	Inches.	Inches.	Pounds.
1½	.92	1.90	1.088	.406	6.40
2	1.20	2.375	1.491	.442	9.02
2½	1.88	2.875	1.755	.560	13.68
3	2.48	3.50	2.284	.608	18.56
3½	2.96	4.00	2.716	.642	22 75
4	3.52	4.50	3 136	.682	27 48
4½	4.24	5.	3.56	.72	32.45
5	5.12	5.563	4.063	.75	38.12
6	6.60	6.625	4.875	.875	53.11
7	8.40	7.625	5.98	.82	60.34
8	11.00	8 625	6.88	.87	71.52

Discount *about* 62½ per cent.
Not the most recent quotation.

TABLE NO. 5. CASING, NET PRICES.

Nominal Inside Diameter.	Price Per Foot.	Actual Outside Diameter.	Nominal Weight Per Foot.	No. Threads Per Inch of Screw.
3¼	20	3½	4.27	14
3½	21	3¾	4.60	14
3¾	24	4	5.47	14
4	25	4¼	5.85	14
4¼	27	4½	6.00	14
4¼	35	4½	9.00	14
4½	30	4¾	6.50	14
4½	36	4¾	9.00	14
4¾	33	5	7.58	14
5	35	5¼	8.00	14
5	41	5¼	10.00	14
5	48	5¼	13.00	11½
5	58	5¼	17.00	11½
5 3/16	39	5½	8.50	14
5 3/16	50	5½	13.00	11½
5⅝	45	6	10.00	14
5⅝	50	6	12.00	11½
5⅝	55	6	14.00	11½
6¼	59	6⅝	11.15	14
6¼	64	6⅝	13.00	14
6¼	74	6⅝	17.00	11½
6⅝	68	7	13.00	14
6⅝	78	7	17.00	11½
7⅝	83	8	15.00	11½
7⅝	95	8	20.00	11½
8¼	95	8⅝	16.15	11½
8¼	1.05	8⅝	20.00	11½
8¼	1.15	8⅝	24.00	11½
8⅝	1.00	9	18.00	11½
9⅝	1.25	10	21.00	11½

10 inch Light Pipe for Well Purposes.............................Net, 1.50

As made by the Oil Well Supply Co., Pittsburg, Penn.—See advertisement

Fig. 2 shows sections of pipe joints and the patent taper coupling referred to on P. 18.

Fig. 2.

PATENT SLEEVE COUPLING.

FLUSH JOINT.

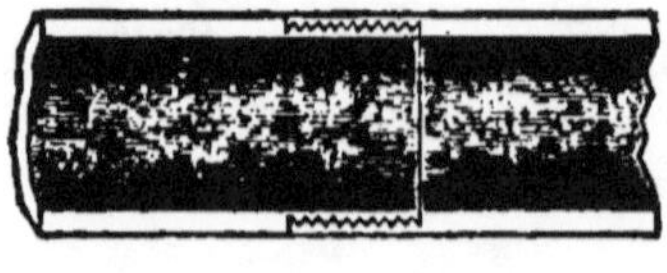

INSERTED JOINT.

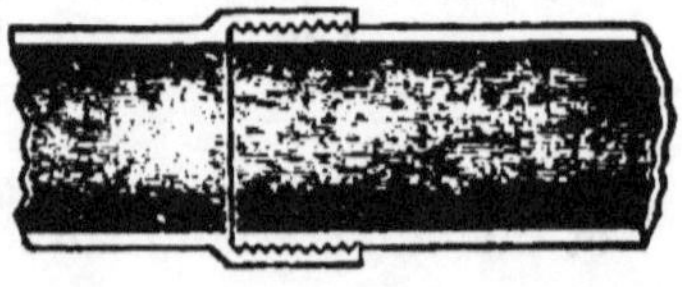

EXPLANATION OF FIG. 3.

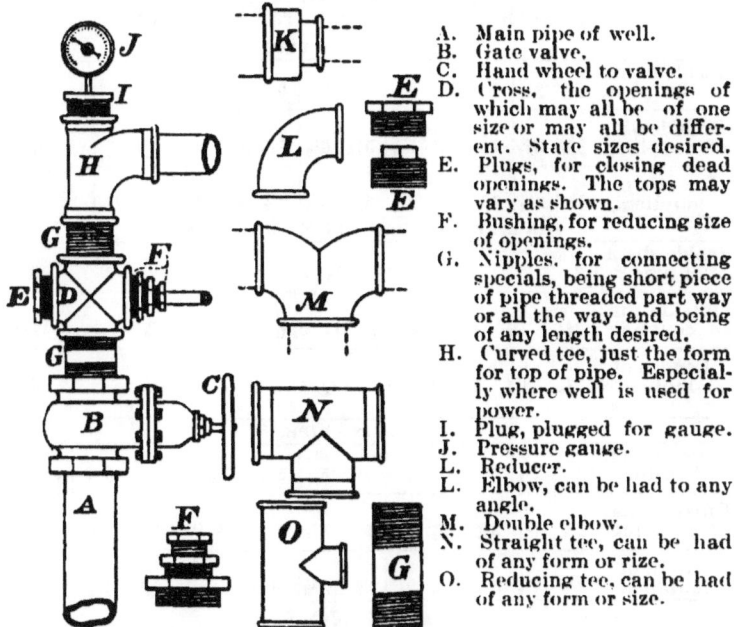

A. Main pipe of well.
B. Gate valve.
C. Hand wheel to valve.
D. Cross, the openings of which may all be of one size or may all be different. State sizes desired.
E. Plugs, for closing dead openings. The tops may vary as shown.
F. Bushing, for reducing size of openings.
G. Nipples, for connecting specials, being short piece of pipe threaded part way or all the way and being of any length desired.
H. Curved tee, just the form for top of pipe. Especially where well is used for power.
I. Plug, plugged for gauge.
J. Pressure gauge.
L. Reducer.
L. Elbow, can be had to any angle.
M. Double elbow.
N. Straight tee, can be had of any form or rize.
O. Reducing tee, can be had of any form or size.

Fig. 3. Specials and fittings for pipe. (See page 29.)

TABLE NO. 6.

TABLE OF COMPARATIVE WEIGHTS OF DIFFERENT KINDS OF WROUGHT IRON PIPE.

Size of pipe.	Casing pipe.	Standard pipe.	X. Strong P.	Drive pipe.
2	2.23	3.61	3.63	
3	3.95	5.74	7.67	
3½	4.27	7.54	10.25	Drive pipe is of standard weight and size but more expensive, stronger and better on account of its being made of a better quality of iron. Then, too, the threads are cut longer to fit a longer and stronger coupling (see table 7) and of sufficient length to permit the ends of the pipe to butt together when coupled—this it not the case in standard pipe—thus very greatly adding to the strength of the pipe in the operation of heavy driving, the pipe being practically continous and not separated at each joint. This is the distinguishing feature of drive pipe.
4	5.33	9.00	12.47	
4½	6.00	10.66	14.97	
5	7.25	12.34	17.60	
5¼	7.66	......	......	
5½	8.08	14.50	20.54	
6	9.35	......	......	
6⅝	10.06	18.76	28.58	
7	12.45	......	......	
7⅝	13.50	23.27	37.60	
8	15.10	......	......	
8⅝	16.15	28.18	47.85	
9	17.25	......	......	
9⅝	......	33.70	......	
10	20.00	......	......	
10¾	......	40.06	......	

Size—outside diameter, weights—pounds per foot.

TABLE NO. 7.

Dimensions of Wrought Iron Couplings.

FOR STANDARD PIPE.

Inside diam. of the pipe.	2	$2\frac{1}{2}$	3	$3\frac{1}{2}$	4	$4\frac{1}{2}$	5	6	7	8	9	10
Outside dia. of coupling.	$2\frac{7}{8}$	$3\frac{9}{32}$	4	$4\frac{17}{32}$	$5\frac{1}{16}$	$5\frac{11}{16}$	$6\frac{1}{4}$	$7\frac{7}{16}$	$8\frac{13}{32}$	$9\frac{3}{8}$	$10\frac{29}{32}$	$11\frac{31}{32}$
Length of coupling.	$2\frac{3}{4}$	$3\frac{1}{8}$	$3\frac{3}{16}$	$3\frac{3}{8}$	$3\frac{1}{4}$	$3\frac{5}{8}$	$3\frac{5}{8}$	$3\frac{1}{2}$	4	4	$6\frac{1}{16}$	$6\frac{1}{16}$

FOR LINE PIPE, DRIVE PIPE AND TUBING.

Inside diam. of pipe.	2	$2\frac{1}{2}$	3	$3\frac{1}{2}$	4	$4\frac{1}{2}$	5	6	7	8	9	10
Outside dia. of coupling.	$2\frac{31}{32}$	$3\frac{3}{8}$	$4\frac{1}{16}$	$4\frac{31}{32}$	$5\frac{1}{8}$	$5\frac{25}{32}$	$6\frac{11}{32}$	$7\frac{25}{64}$	....	$9\frac{9}{16}$	......	$11\frac{31}{32}$
Length of coupling.	$3\frac{3}{4}$	$3\frac{3}{4}$	$3\frac{5}{8}$	4	4	$4\frac{1}{16}$	$4\frac{1}{8}$	$4\frac{3}{4}$	....	$5\frac{15}{16}$	......	$6\frac{1}{16}$

FOR CASING PIPE.

Inside diam. of casing.	2	$2\frac{1}{2}$	3	$3\frac{1}{2}$	4	$4\frac{1}{2}$	5	$5\frac{5}{8}$	$6\frac{1}{4}$	$6\frac{5}{8}$	$7\frac{1}{4}$	$8\frac{1}{4}$
Outside dia. of coupling.	$2\frac{3}{4}$	$3\frac{1}{4}$	$3\frac{3}{4}$	$4\frac{9}{32}$	$4\frac{25}{32}$	$5\frac{3}{8}$	$5\frac{7}{8}$	$6\frac{9}{16}$	$7\frac{1}{4}$	$7\frac{39}{64}$	$8\frac{3}{8}$	$9\frac{3}{8}$
Length of coupling.	$2\frac{5}{8}$	$3\frac{1}{8}$	$3\frac{1}{16}$	$3\frac{1}{16}$	$3\frac{1}{4}$	$3\frac{5}{8}$	$3\frac{5}{8}$	$3\frac{1}{2}$	4	$4\frac{1}{16}$	$4\frac{1}{16}$	$5\frac{3}{16}$

TABLE NO. 8.

Dimensions, &c. of Special, Lap-Welded, KALAMEIN PIPE, for water and gas works, As made by the National Tube Works Co., Chicago.

Outside diam.	Weight of lock joint.	Weight of lead, one side.	Nominal weight per foot complete.	Aproximate price per foot.
Inches.	Pounds.	Pounds.	Pounds.	\$ Cts.
2	4	1	1.80	.17
3	8	$1\frac{3}{4}$	3.35	.30
4	12	$2\frac{1}{2}$	5.00	.42
5	17	$3\frac{5}{8}$	7.15	.55
6	21	5	8.60	.67
7	30	6	11.25	.87
8	33	$6\frac{1}{8}$	12.80	1.00
9	38	$7\frac{1}{4}$	15.10	1.25
10	40	8	16.60	1.45
11	50	$10\frac{1}{2}$	20.35	1.70
12	56	$11\frac{3}{4}$	24.50	1.87
13	65	$12\frac{1}{2}$	27.60	2.25
14	71	$13\frac{1}{4}$	30.00	2.50
15	100	$15\frac{1}{2}$	36.40	2.80
16	120	17	46.25	3.30

TABLE NO 9.

TABLE SHOWING RELATIVE AREAS OF STANDARD PIPE.

Size of Pipe	¾	1	1½	2	2½	3	3½	4	5	6	7	8
¾	1.00	1.77	4.00	7.11	11.10	16.00	21.70	28.10	44.4	64.00	87.10	113.70
1	....	1.00	2.25	4.00	6.25	9.00	12.20	16.00	25.00	36.00	49.00	64.00
1½	....	....	1.00	1.77	2.77	4.00	5.44	7.11	11.10	16.00	21.70	28.40
2				1.00	1.56	2.25	3.06	4.00	6.25	9.00	12.25	16.00
2½					1.00	1.44	1.96	2.56	4.00	5.76	7.84	10.24
3						1.00	1.81	1.77	2.77	4.00	5.44	7.11
3½							1.00	1.30	2.04	2.93	4.00	5.22
4								1.00	1.56	2.25	3.06	4.00
5									1.00	1.44	1.96	2.56
6										1.00	1.81	1.77
7											1.00	1.30
8												1.00

From Wm. J. Baldwin, M. E. in "Steam Heating for Buildings."

Explanation of table: The relative areas of any two sizes of pipes given in the table will be found at the intersection of the horizontal and vertical lines representing the given sizes. Thus, a 6-inch pipe = 1.00 6-inch pipe, 1.44 5-inch pipes and 4 3-inch pipes; an 8-inch pipe = 4 4-inch pipes, 16 2-inch pipes, 113.7 ¾-inch pipes. etc.

Application—It is desired to supply 50 three quarter inch pipes with a constant flow, what size of supply pipe should be used? Take top horizontal line and run to the right, it will be seen that a 5 inch main will supply but 44.4....¾ inch pipes; but a 6 inch main will supply 64.00....¾ inch pipes, hence, a 6 inch pipe must be used. An 8 inch well is as large as 7.11 three inch wells, a 7 inch well as large as 3.06....4 inch wells.

As to Relative Dircharging Powers of Pipes, see Table No. 27.

TABLE NO. 10.

WEIGHT OF STANDARD CAST IRON PIPE.

(Including Bowl and Spigot ends.)
Cast iron weighs 450 lbs. per cubic ft. and .2604 lbs. per cubic inch.

Diam. of Pipe.	Weight per foot for following thicknesses.								Length Feet.
	⅛	¼	⅜	½	⅝	¾	⅞	1	
2	3	6	9.3	14	19				8
3	4	9	13	18	23	29			12
4	5	11	17	23.5	30	37	44	52	12
5	6.5	13.5	21	29	36	45	53	62	12
6	8	16.5	25	34	43	53	63	73	12
8	10	21.5	32.5	44	56	68	81	93	12
10	14	27	40.5	55	69	84	99	114	12
12	15	32	48	65	82	100	117	135	12

As made by Addyston Pipe & Steel Co. (See adv't P. 216.)

This table incudes all of the sizes and weights likely to find a place in water and gas works plants in Dakota, where the use of cast iron for water works is on the increase.

(See also the advertisement of Dennis Long & Co. P. 217.)

TABLE NO. 11.

DIMENSIONS, PRICE, ETC., OF SPIRAL RIVETED PIPE.
No. 18 Wire Guage.   Thickness .049 inch.

Diam. in inches.	Price per ft. Black. NET.	Price, tarred and asphalted. NET.	Price per ft. Galvanized. NET.	Approx. weight per 100 feet. lbs.	Approx. bursting pressure lbs per sq in.
3	$ .17	$ .19	$ .23	185	1300
4	.21	.23	.29	245	1000
5	.25	.28	.35	300	800
6	.29	.32	.43	360	700
7	.32	.35	.45	400	600
8	.37	.40	.52	460	500
9	.41	.45	.59	525	450
10	.45	.50	.65	575	400
11	.48	.53	.70	625	360
12	.58	.64	.82	750	330
13	.62	.69	.90	800	300
14	.67	.75	.98	900	280
15	.75	.83	1.05	950	260
16	.80	.88	1.13	1000	250
18	.88	.96	1.28	1125	220
20	1.00	1.10	1.45	1250	200
22	1.10	1.21	1.55	1350	180
24	1.20	1.32	1.67	1460	160

In lengths of 25 feet and less, with plain or crimped ends.
As made by Abendroth & Root Mfg. Co.   (See adv't P. 238.)
The weights given are for the black pipe, other grades are from 10 to 20 per cent. heavier.

This class of pipe is very extensively used in the west for conveying irrigation waters, and in many places for water works use. Its strength is very great while the weight is very light, and the cost low. On account of its strength, lightness and cheapness it will be especially adapted to use in Dakota, where water must be piped on or near the surface.

The following table will show the comparative weight of the three classes of pipes—Spiral, Standard wrought iron and Cast iron:

WEIGHTS.

Heaviest Spiral Pipe.	Standard Wrought Iron Pipe.	Cast Iron Pipe, ¾ inch
3 inch....2 lbs	7½ lbs	13 lbs
4 " ...2½ "	10¾ "	17 "
6 " ...5 "	18¾ "	25 "
8 " ...8 "	28 "	32 "
10 " ..10 "	40 "	40 "
12 " ..13 "	49 "	48 "
14 " ..15 "	58 "	56 "
16 " ..18 "		64 "
18 " ..20 "		72 "
20 " ..22 "		79 "
22 " ..24 "		
24 " ..26 "		95 "

Pipes of this class in California have been in use since 1853 and have given great satisfaction, many having done useful service for 25 and 30 years.

TABLE NO. 12.

READING IRON COMPANY.

STANDARD SIZES OF AMERICAN AND ENGLISH WIRE GAUGES.

Number of gauge.	American gauge in decimals. Inch.	American gauge in fractions. Inch.	English gauge in decimals. Inch.	English gauge in fractions. Inch.	Number of gauge.	American gauge in decimals. Inch.	American gauge in fractions. Inch.	English gauge in decimals. Inch.	English gauge in fractions. Inch.
0000	.46		.454	$\frac{15}{32}$	18	.0403		.049	
000	.4096		.425	$\frac{13}{32}$	19	.0359	$\frac{1}{32}$	.042	$\frac{3}{64}$
00	.3648		.380	$\frac{3}{8}$	20	.0319		.035	$\frac{1}{32}$
0	.3248		.340	$\frac{11}{32}$	21	.0284		.032	
1	.2893		.300	$\frac{3}{64}$	22	.0253		.028	
2	.2576		.284	$\frac{9}{64}$	23	.0225		.025	
3	.2294		.259	$\frac{3}{32}$	24	.0201		.022	
4	.2043		.238	$\frac{1}{4}$	25	.0179	$\frac{1}{64}$	.02	$\frac{1}{64}$
5	.1819		.220	$\frac{15}{64}$	26	.016		.018	
6	.1620		.203	$\frac{13}{64}$	27	.0142		.016	
7	.1443		.180	$\frac{13}{64}$	28	.0126		.014	
8	.1285		.165	$\frac{5}{32}$	29	.0112		.012	
9	.1144		.148	$\frac{9}{64}$	30	.0102		.01	
10	.1019		.134		31	.01		.009	
11	.0907	$\frac{7}{64}$	.120	$\frac{1}{8}$	32	.0079		.008	
12	.0808	$\frac{5}{64}$	.109	$\frac{7}{64}$	33	.007		.007	
13	.0719		.095	$\frac{3}{32}$	34	.0063		.005	
14	.0641	$\frac{5}{64}$	.083		35	.0056		.004	
15	.057		.072	$\frac{5}{64}$	36	.005			
16	.0508		.065		37				
17	.0452	$\frac{3}{64}$	.058	$\frac{1}{16}$	38				

Inadvertently the text for this page was overlooked but
two suggestions may be here inserted with profit, no doubt,
to some.

The first suggestion is prompted by the abundant rain-fall
of the early months of 1892 which has been far greater than
that of any former year within the history of the state.
Some are heard to say that "irrigation will now be overlooked." Such will not and should not be the case, for, although 1892 may be a year of great productiveness without
irrigation, it will still—however good it may be—fall far
short of accomplishing what irrigation would accomplish. ·

Through any given series of years Dakota's rain-fall cannot be relied upon to be sufficient for remunerative farming; so irrigation must be resorted to by all who desire certainty of return for each season's labors. If all who can
will, during this favorable season, prepare for the unfavorable seasons which are sure to come, they will exercise wise
forethought by hastening to improve the opportunity so
fortunately offered of preparing in advance. This promis-
ing season will no doubt aid many financially to in whole or
in part prepare for irrigation in the future.

It is said of an Arkansas farmer that he refused to mend
his leaky roof during fair weather because it was not necessary, and during foul weather he couldn't because it was
wet. It is hoped that our farmers will not emulate such un-
thrift by refusing to prepare for irrigation during wet seasons, because it is then unnecessary, and being compelled to
put it off during dry seasons because too poor.

A second suggestion will be risked, although somewhat
outside of the scope of this work. It is:

Do not be deceived by so-called **Rain Makers!** Do not follow so intangible a will-o-the-wisp as this latest *"fake"* with
which scheming sharpers are attempting to delude the people. The U. S. government spent several thousand dollars
in a vain attempt to produce rain; an attempt which was an
acknowleded failure, except that it awakened in the breasts
of certain shapers an *idea* which they have enshrouded in
mystery, and on the strength of which they seek to extort
money from a too credulous public. Rain-making has not
been a success as yet—we hope it may be in the future.

Water we have below us. We know it is there, and that
we can get it. Seek it, therefore, and do not delay in the
vain hope that the secret of rain-making has been vouchsafed to men of whom the world has never heard, men unknown in the sphere of science, men whose investigations
were never heard of and whose successes are but hearsay or
newspaper reports, men who want pay in advance and will
not exhibit the powers which they claim thus suddenly to
have acquired to the light of scientific investigation; men
who work in the dark and who seek their own interests and
not yours. Some wit has wisely said that, as yet, "the har-
ness-maker is the only successful rein maker."

SPIRAL WELDED PIPE.

This pipe is very similar to the spiral riveted pipe, the joint being welded instead of riveted. The weights are about the same as the weights of riveted pipe, but, by reason of the welded joint, the pipe is claimed to be stronger, more durable, smoother internally. Both possess the same great advantages of lightness and cheapness and are equally well adapted to use in irrigation whenever a light, durable and inexpensive pipe can be used. (See distribution of water, P. 122.)

From the foregoing tables it will be possible to select a quality or kind of pipe suited to the needs of the well, the water-works plant, or the conveyance of water over the surface for irrigation. More detailed information may be had by correspondence with the manufacturers or dealers in pipe whose advertisements appear herein.

The proper grade of pipe having been selected, the plan of the well must be decided upon, for it may be on several plans.

A large outer casing may be first used and sunk as deep as thought desirable, then a smaller size sunk inside of the first, and, possibly, still a smaller size within the second pipe; the latter being carried to the bottom. The two outer pipes may then be pulled up, leaving a continuous pipe from top to bottom. In some cases, as where the outer casing has become fast and cannot be lifted, the outer pipe is left in the well thus making a double string of pipe. In other cases, all the outer casing is removed, but 2 or 3 lengths, the space between the two casings being then calked.

In some wells the *telescope* plan is used, In this case the well may start with an 8 inch pipe carried down say 300 feet; then a 6 inch pipe is carried down say 400 feet lower, or to a depth of 700 feet, and, by the use of a left-handed thread at the 300 foot level, the upper 300 feet of the 6 inch pipe is removed, leaving the lower 400 feet in the well as permanent casing. In like manner a 4½ inch pipe may be sunk within the six inch pipe and carried to water; the upper 700 feet being then removed. Such a well, in section, would have the appearance shown in Fig. 4.

Most of the earlier wells were of this class and many are still drilled on this plan, but the practice now appears to tend more in the direction of wells with a continuous line of pipe from top to bottom, and such wells no doubt have many marked advantages over wells of other classes.

Fig. 4.

PERFORATED PIPE.

Nearly all of the northern wells throw out more or less shlae mud, clean sand, or lumps of sand-rock or iron pyrites. These hard bodies have, in city water systems, caused much trouble by clogging the fire nozzles or water pipes. To prevent the throwing out of such masses many wells have been filled with lengths of perforated pipe dropped to the bottom of the well. The lengths of pipe thus inserted are perforated with ½ or ¾ inch holes which, while admitting the water or sand, prevent the admission of the larger solid bodies. The consequence of thus shutting off free access to the well is that large quantities of loose rock accumulate about the base of the pipe, as shown in Fig. 5, thus gradually shutting off the water supply and diminishing the volume and efficiency of the well; besides which, the effective erea of the base of the well pipe is reduced by the insertion of this smaller pipe thereby still further decreasing the capacity of the well. Additional disadvantages of this inserted pipe lie in the fact that it is out of reach and control, it becomes a loose and independent feature of the well, not under control or subject to needed repairs, and it is apt to become out of line with the main pipe —if not entirely disconnected from it—thus forming a possible and unmanageable obstruction at the base of the well.

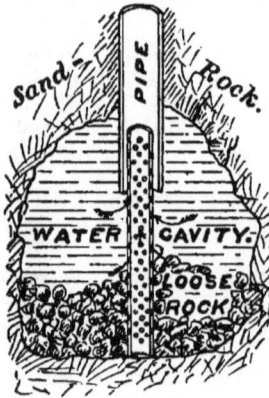

Fig. 5.

Showing a perforated pipe in the bottom of a well.

If the perforated pipe is left out, the well, at the bottom, will be clean and free to receive whatever comes to it. If rock is thrown, *care for it at the sruface* where it may be collected and disposed of. Put in a settling reservoir to receive it, *or*, in case of water works, where the pressure must stand in the pipes, run the water through a large sand drum which will collect the heavy matter and permit only the water and lighter sediment to pass to the mains.

It is, indeed, safer to collect the rock at the surface, where it may be cared for, than to permit it to accumulate at the base of the pipe where it cannot be cared for and may ruin the well.

If the well becomes stopped up by an accumulation of sand or by other causes the pipe may be more easily cleaned out if it has a uniform diameter from top to bottom and it is unobstructed by the presence of a section of loose perforated pipe. Usually the services of a well driller will be needed to open up a well which has become clogged. The objections urged against the use of perforated pipe in wells are not founded on theory alone but upon actual experience

in a number of the more important wells, of the state.
VALVES, HYDRANTS AND SPECIALS (See Fig 3 p 21)
Every well should have at le ist one gate valve in order
that it may be shut off in whole or in part, for otherwise no
control could be exercised over the flow by the person in
charge.

The kind of valve to buy is a matter of importance, for
all are not equally good, either as to pattern, workmanship,
or material. Of the many makes of valves the Ludlow and
the Chapman are among the best and are the most used in
the Dakotas. (See adv't Chapman Valve Co., P. 210; of the
Ludlow Valve Co. P. 224; of the National Tube Works Co.
front cover; of the Brass & Iron Works Co. P. 225; and of
Robinson & Cary Co. P. 242.)

The greatest care is necessary in the selection of a hydrant
for water works service. Almost any hydrant will work
well in clear water but few, however, will prove satisfactory
in case sand or gravel is held in suspension by the water.
A hydrant having a rubber or leather face or cone will need
frequent repairs, owing to pieces of sand or gravel becoming imbedded in the soft surface. These, too, tend to wear
the surface of the metal ring, and thus leaks are caused and
the hydrant frequently freezes and becomes unserviceable.

Where there is much grit in the water a metal faced hydrant should be selected. Where the water is clear the
others will prove as good. A gate valve should be handled
carefully. Do not close it suddenly for the "Water Ham-
mer," due to the sudden checking of the velocity of a rapidly moving column of water, under heavy pressure, is very
great and tends to injure the pipe and its connections.

The arrangement of the valve, or valves, will depend upon
the circumstances surrounding the well and its uses.

Usually the main valve is placed horizontally on the main
pipe and all connections are made above the valve. In this
position the valve is usually put on before the main flow of
water is struck, the drilling being continued *through* the
opened gate—care being taken to protect the face plates of
the valves by a thin nipple set into the top of the well. If
the valve is not set until after the flow is struck much loss
of time and money may result before it is finally set to the
pipe against the force of the flow. (A notable instance of
this was that of the first "city well," at Aberdeen, where it
was found to be impossible to set the valve because of the
force of the water, and hundreds of dollars were wasted, and
special tools finally constructed. before the water was finally
shut off and the valve set.)

This danger may not be ever present, especially in the
smaller wells, but reference to it will call attention to its
consideration. Sometimes a cross is set first, on top of
the pipe, before the flow is struck. It is then an easy matter to set the gate to the top or the side opening, the stream
finding a partial outlet, meanwhile, through the other open-

ing. After the gate is set the other openings may be plugged or otherwise connected.

If the main gate—or any gate valve—is set on any line of horizontal pipe, leading from a well throwing any sand or solid matter, the valve should be set vertically, that is, with the hand-wheel at the top. This will prevent sand or stone lodging in the working parts of the valve; a danger which is ever present if the hand-wheel is at the side of, or underneath, the pipe.

Whatever may be the location of the valves, or the use to which the well may be put, one thing should be observed, which is, so arrange the specials (which is understood to mean the crosses, tees, valves and such similar features of the pipe fittings) as to leave a *vertical opening* above the main pipe, which opening may be closed by a plug if not otherwise connected.

By so doing ready access to the well is always possible, for the purpose of cleaning out, blowing off, or other purpose, without disturbing the other connections of the well.

If the well is to be used for power, in the running of a mill or other heavy plant, much power may be saved by using long curved specials instead of the short, right-angled specials commonly used. Every well driller ought to have, as a part of his outfit, a full set of specials (crosses, tees, ys, nipples, bushing, plugs, elbows and a pressure guage) so that, on the completion of a well, a sufficient test of its power and volume could be made to be of value as a matter of public record and also as a matter of value to the driller himself, who would, through the wide publicity given to all such systematic tests, derive a direct benefit, in the way of advertising sufficient to pay him for the expense and time invested.

The more such matters are observed the more will public attention be called to our artesian wells and the more quickly will capital be attracted. Properly viewed, it would be a wise stroke of business policy for every well owner and contractor to interest himself in these features of a well and to be prepared to put them to efficient tests.

Even the well owner cannot afford to be without the few specials necessary to a proper control over his well, or to its direction in such manner as may best suit his varied needs. Supposing the well to be 6 inches, what ought to be provided?

1—6-inch cross.
1—6-inch tee.
1—6-inch elbow.
2—6-inch plugs (one plugged for attachment of gauge.)
2—6-inch nipples.
2—4-inch "
2—2-inch "
1 nest of bushing for 4-inch and 2-inch connections.
1 pressure gauge.

With these few specials the well, or any connection with

it may be reduced or directed as occasion may require. At least these specials should be obtained.

LOCATION OF WELL.

As a rule, a well for irrigation will be located on or near the highest point of land to be irrigated, but considerations of convenience or economy may, at times, suggest a location at a lower point or near one's buildings from which location the water may be piped to the higher ground.

The reservoir will usually occupy the highest ground and the well may be placed at the most accessible point near it or at such a point as will best conserve the proper division of the fields or the location of the ditches. All of these things should be considered and mapped out before either the well or the reservoir is located; otherwise the location may, in the end, prove to have been badly chosen.

At whatever point the well is located let that point be OUTSIDE OF THE RESERVOIR. Some wells have been located within the reservoir where they are not accessible because of either water or mud, where, in case of needed repairs, it would be difficult to convey the machinery and supplies, or to erect or handle the same, where the well cannot conveniently be used for anything else but to supply irrigation waters and where its flow could not be easily regulated during the winter months.

If located outside of the reservoir the well would be accessible at all times and subject to control; it could be easily repaired or opened up—if stopped up;—its volume could be first used as power to run machinery, a revenue, possibly, being derived from the rental of the power, and the water then conveyed to the reservoir by a short pipe. It could be enclosed and protected from the weather *as every well should be* in order to protect and preserve the pipe and valves from rust, for the well is but a piece of machinery and should be cared for as such. It will wear out in time by rust and wear and will need recasing, but in order to preserve it as long as possible, its pipes should be painted and protected. If thus cared for it will last intact for many years and pay for itself many times. The cost for repairs being almost nothing.

LOG OF WELL.

Section 35 of the "Melville" law provides that the contractor of any township well shall keep a log of the well, or, in other words, a record of the successive strata through which the drill passes. From the very nature of the case this must be a dead-letter, for it cannot be enforced.

The driller may report such a log as he chooses, and no one else be the wiser. The truth is, it is safe to say, that no properly recorded log has ever been made of a Dakota well. The author has seen many wells drilled, and has carefully noted the methods adopted, but in only one case, within his knowledge, was there any effort made to obtain an accurate log.

Dozens of records have been published in papers pamphlets and reports, but all are subject to grave doubt, as to truth or accuracy. Some drillers will make no report—prefering to keep, as a trade secret, whatever they may have discovered—but most drillers pay no attention to the drillings, and, except for the fact that at one depth the drilling is hard and slow, and at another depth it is softer and more rapid, they know little or nothing about the character of the formations in which they have worked.

The keeping of a log involves considerable extra labor, systematic watchfulness, a certain degree of knowledge of geology, and, above all, a certain amount of expense to which the contracting driller does not care to go. He agrees to drill a well, and not to instruct in geology, and, to him, the drillings discharged are all the same.

It must be admitted that a carefully kept log, or rather series of logs, would be of much value, but how to secure them is a question each driller alone can decide. Certainly section 35, above referred to, can result in nothing more than a succession of false reports which will be worse than none at all. When the first well in the state was drilled, (the Ry. well at Aberdeen) by Mr. Swan, the author was present daily and assisted in keeping the log, preserved samples of the drillings, dried and arranged them, and finally mounted them in 3-foot glass tubes secured for the purpose.

If equal care was used with each well the logs would then approach the truth and possess some value. Each owner of a well should look to it that this is done.

Equally important—yes, far more important—is the keeping of an accurate record of the performance of each well, and as to all its dimensions, thus—depth and log, and length of each size of casing in well. Size at top or bottom, or all the way.

Pressure—When closed, and when flowing from openings of different sizes.

Volume—When open full and when throwing streams of different sizes; not guessed at but carefully measured with a weir.

Discharge—Exact height of stream thrown vertically when well is opened full, and from openings of 1, 2, 3, 4, 6 or 8 inches. Also, the exact distance these streams will be thrown horizontally,

Temperature of the water.

Whether hard or soft, clear or sandy or muddy.

The exact time occupied in drilling the well, with dates.

The quality of pipe used.

The kind of machine used in drilling.

The exact cost.

There is nothing in the above form of record that cannot be kept by any farmer or driller and nothing that is not of importance or that cannot be determined if only a few specials are at hand. The measurements of volume and height of streams are simple operations and are fully explained herein. (See measurements by weirs.) See—how to measure the height of a stream, page 93.)

A series of records kept as above suggested would have
value, but the records as heretofore kept have but little.
Even the published, official records, or reports, are far from
accurate. A record, once carefully made, ought to be preserved for future reference, for the memory alone cannot be
relied upon.

DRILLING.

Little need be said under this head for it is assumed that
an expert will be in charge of the work. If an inexperi-
enced hand is in charge he has more to learn than a book of
this size would hold. A few suggestions, however, will be
in order.

Do every part of the work thoroughly and with the greatest
care. Use great care in handling tools about the pipe
so as not to drop them in.

Make every joint of the rod or the tools fast so they will
not loosen, and cause the loss of a rod or tool.

Keep the drills and reamers in proper cutting order, and
inspect everything frequently to see that nothing is loose
or defective.

Do not work the drilling tools too long before pulling out,
for it is better to pull out more frequently, and make sure
that everything is safe and sound, than to attempt to work
longer and lose a tool by reason of a loose joint.

Above all, do the reaming well, so that the pipe will settle
easily and not stick or require heavy driving.

Keep the pipe pretty close to the bottom, in order to avoid
the caving in of the walls or the inrush of quick sands
and the possible sticking of the tools. Many drillers will
run from 20 to 100 feet without settling the pipe, and they
usually have trouble in consequence. Only room enough
is needed below the pipe to work the drill and the reamer
and usually the length of a single section of pipe will be
ample.

Do not sink a smaller hole below the main hole, for it may
endanger the latter work by causing the drill to stick or
drill a sloping hole into which the pipe cannot be forced.

Never leave a tool standing in the well, for a cave-in may
bury it and render its extrication difficult if not impossible

If any accident happens do not cease labor until it is reme-
died or until its remedy is seen to be impossible.

Arrange in advance for all supplies, in order that no delay
may endanger the continuation of the work. A "shut
down" often sets the work back more, and causes greater
expense, than though no work had been done.

Always leave the work in a safe condition and protected
from the depredations of the curious and thoughtless on-
lookers.

Cautions might thus be indefinitely extended—each founded on some costly experience of the past—but enough has
been suggested to show the necessity of an exercise of such

34

a degree of care and watchfulness as is required in but
few other callings. If no accident happens the driller deserves much praise. If one does happen he usually has
himself to blame.

COST OF WELLS.

Many thoughtless enthusiasts have raised the cry that
wells ought to be drilled for from $1,200 to $2,000 but such
persons are not authorities and do not know whereof
they speak. The cost of a well depends not upon one thing,
but upon many things. The size is, of course, the chief
factor for the pipe for a large well will cost more than that
for a small well; the rig used must, as a rule, be heavier;
the tools heavier; the coal and water used will be much
more; and the labor bill will be much greater because the
drilling will take longer. The location of the well will
effect its cost. If within the limits of a town, having a
system of water works so that the water used in drilling
may be readily secured (and under pressure), the otherwise
large water-hauling bill will be saved. If the well is on a
farm, or where no water is at hand, the hauling bill will
mount to most respectable proportions.

Add to these items the cost of moving the rig to its site,
setting it up and taking it down, hauling the pipe and fuel,
to say nothing of the many certain yet unforseen incidental
expenses and you have the well driller's bill of expense,
minus the ever-present chance of an accident which may
cost hundreds of dollars or result even in his financial ruin.

No man of good business judgment will assume these
risks for the mere chance of earning day's wages. He
claims, and is fairly entitled to receive, a generous compen-
sation for the risk he assumes, and, in addition to that, such
wages as his skill as a driller entitles him to receive.

For the purpose of illustration the following approximate
cost is given of a 6 inch farm well 1,000 feet deep:

1000 feet of 6 inch pipe @ .62 per foot		$ 620
Frieght—at reduced rates	about	50
Hauling pipe to the ground	"	40
" casing pipe away	"	10
" and transporting rig	"	50
Setting up rig	"	150
Taking down rig, and breakage	"	100
Fuel, and hauling same	"	250
Hauling or obtaining water	"	100
Wear and tear on rig and tools	"	200
One gate valve	"	30
Couplings	"	40
Interest on investment for 90 days	"	75
Labor bills @ $10 per day for 60 days	"	600
Total	"	$2,315

In this estimate it is assumed that but 60 days are consumed in the work of moving, setting up, drilling and taking

down; that there are no accidents or unusual expenses and no delays.

The incidental expenses could not safely be figured at less than $300, and most of the other items given are figured too law; so that, without any allowance for incidentals, accidents or profit, and allowing but three men on the work, and but 60 days of time, the expense still exceeds $2300 for a 6-inch well. It is not the intention to throw any unfavorable light on the matter of cost of wells, but rather to throw on the true light, and, by calling attention to the details, dispel some false light.

A well is worth all it costs,

and the driller must have some show as well as the owner. A 6-inch well costing from $3000 to $4000 is cheap, if properly put down, and is a grand investment, and one which is better, at that price, for the farmer than for the driller, for where the driller may make $500 or $1000 profit on one well he may lose it all on the next; whereas, the farmer *with the well* has a *sure thing* and a competency.

Any well will pay its cost in 5 years—whatever the cost may be—or at the rate of 20 per cent. on the investment. Some wells have paid for themselves in one year.

If a farmer has a well which enables him to raise even 30 bushels of wheat to the acre, in a dry year when his neighbors fail to get back their seed, and he has but 140 acres under water, he receives 4,200 bushels, which, at but 50 cents per bushel, nets him $2,100, or sufficient to pay for a well large enough to thoroughly irrigate his 160 acres. This is not overdrawn but underdrawn as based upon actual experiences. One well, in 1891, more than paid its cost by garden irrigation, and, besides this, supplied water to the town.

Many such examples could be given to show how serviceable a well is and how short a time it takes to return its cost. Nor need one seek a dry year in order to show the contrast, for even in the best years the service of a well is so great as to make the increased yield pay very largely on its cost.

It may be asked—what do your Dakota wells cost? The answer would be difficult to frame for lack of proper information and knowledge of all the facts entering into the matter of cost. Wells 4 or 4½ inches have cost from $1,800 to $3,000. Wells of 6 inches from $3,000 to $7,000; although about $3,000 is the common price. Wells of 8 inches have cost about $4,000 or $5,000. The expensive wells have, in all cases, been expensive by reason of delays and accidents. As drillers have become more skilled in this field, and rigs have been adapted to its formations, the price of wells has been reduced, and a still further reduction may be expected as skill and competition increase. The cost of a Dakota well ought to be considered in connection with its volume. The mere hole has no value; it is the water which it supplies on which a value is placed.

The hole costs so much, regardless of the volume of water thrown out, so that if two wells cost $2000 each, and one well throws out 1000 gallons per minute, while the other throws out but 500 gallons per minute, it may be fairly said that one well cost twice as much as the other, for the one supplies but half the service of the other, or has cost twice as much for a given return. So, too, as between Dakota wells and those of other sections of the country.

The Dakota artesian basin is the largest and the greatest in the world and the volumes and pressures of its wells greater than the volumes and pressures elsewhere. So it may be said that it costs far less here to get a given volume of water than it does any where else in the world. This basin is the nearest to the manufacturers of well machinery, pipe, tools, and other supplies which therefore cost less. The depths are but moderate, and the volumes enormous, so that the duty or service received for the money expended is greater than in any other section or country.

In Australia many wells are put down by the government at a cost of from $5,000 to $25,000, yet their best wells do not equal the average Dakota wells. Our farmers may therefore deem themselves most highly favored by nature and ought not to grumble at the expense of obtaining water, for, by no other system, and in no other section of the world, can an equal volume be obtained for the same amount of money. No reasonable man will complain of expense when he pays far less than the balance of mankind and when all the conditions are so favorable for the speedy return of the money invested.

Nor will any wise investor hesitate to put his money into Dakota wells or farm lands when the conditions, as they are here, are shown to him in comparison with the conditions elsewhere, under which conditions tens of millions have been invested to the great profit of the investor, prosperity of the settler, and glory of the state and nation.

It must further be considered that the cost of the water is but a part of the cost of the land. The well is of no value except as it supplies the water; the water is of little value except as it feeds the ground and aids in producing a crop. The cost of land, well, ditches, reservoirs and other improvements could properly be "lumped," and the total value per acre found. In this, as in the cost of the water alone, Dakota will be shown to hold the palm as against the world. This matter will be more fully considered under the head of land and water values.

Some have asked—how can I get a well the cheapest?—by contracting with a driller, or by buying a rig (either alone or by clubbing together with my neighbors) and doing my own work. Many reasons prevent a reply. Firstly, iusfficient data as to what has been done heretofore renders a reply impossible, or, at best, purely speculative. Secondly, the outcome will depend upon who *you* are, what your means

may be, what your general intelligence may be, and especially as to the amount of natural mechanical ability you
may possess. Many farmers could not drill a well with the
best of tools. Some ingenuous farmers *have* actually drilled
good wells with rigs and tools of their own make. Safety
and economy would appear to lie in the selection of a contractor who has the tools, knows the business ar.d is prepared to assume all risks. It is to be hoped, however, that
hundreds of rigs will be purchased by farmers, and that we
may soon evolve a race of practical drillers from among our
own people.

ARTESIAN WELLS, ELSEWHERE.

It is within a comparatively short time that artesian well
waters have been used for irrigation in this country, but
their value is now being appreciated and thousands are being sunk for this purpose. As above stated, there has not
yet been discovered in the world another artesian basin of
such extent as the Dakota basin nor one whose wells possess
such great volume and pressure.

Artesian wells are common to nearly all of our states and
to most countries and some few wells have been drilled
that compare very favorably with the better Dakota wells
but they are few in number and widely separated, and the
artesian basins thus far discovered are of but moderate
area. The Dakota sand-rock formations extend far to the
south so that Nebraska and Kansas have a few good wells
but most of the southern wells are shallow and the flow but
weak.

A group of 5 wells at Coolidge, Kansas, cost an average of
$400 each and have an average flow of 25 gallons per min-
ute. A like ratio between cost and volume would make a
Dakota well of 1800 gallons cost $16,000, whereas there are
several throwing a greater volume the cost of which has
been from $3,000 to $4,000. The smaller wells of the Crooked Creek Valley, numbering about 100, and costing only
about $20 each are used for irrigation and about 50 of these
serve from 5 to 25 acres each.

A new artesian basin has but recently been discovered in
Washington, in the Yakima valley, where there is one well
flowing 650,000 per day or 452 gallons per minute. This
would rank among the smaller wells of Dakota. A company has been organized to drill wells throughout this new
field wherein hundreds of thousands of dollars have been
expended in irrigation development by other systems and
where, within a decade, a barren, sage-brush desert has been
made the home of the peach and the prune, and the heart of
a vast and prosperous agricultural interest.

In Colorado several thousand wells have been drilled to
depths ranging from 100 to 1800 feet, but in most cases to
depths of from 300 to 700 feet. The water from many must
be pumped but in most other cases the flow ranges from 10
to 75 gallons per minute.

The town well at Anamosa has a flow of 495 gallons per minute. This is the largest of over 2000 wells in the San Louis valley, Bucher's well, at the same place has a pressure of 25 pounds to the square inch. The Espinosa well, about 20 miles north of Monte Vista, according to the report of the state engineer, "throws a solid three-inch column of water nearly 40 inches above the casing, and flows between 300 and 400 gallons per minute."

Compare this pigmy, which thus deserves special notice in Colorado, with such Dakota gushers as the Aberdeen, Huron, Redfield, Doland, Columbia, Woonsocket, Springfield and Yankton wells not to mention a host of others each of which would be a marvel in any other land.

In California there are 25 artesian basins of varying character and pressure but that of Kern county is the most remarkable and more nearly resembles the Dakota basin than any other yet found. Its area is only about 18 by 14 miles and it has an elevation of about 300 feet above the sea. The average depth of the many wells in this area is about 500 feet. Of these wells 54 range in flow from 150,000 to 4,000,000 gallons per day, or from 100 to 3,000 gallons per minute.

One wells has a volume of 3,000 gallons per minute, two wells flow 2,100 and 2,400 gallons, nine wells flow from 1,400 to 2,000 gallons. and seventeen wells flow from 700 to 1,400 gallons per minute. The diameters range from 6 to 10 inches.

The counties of Tulare, Los Angeles and San Bernardino have also remarkable artesian basins and hundreds of very fine wells from 150 to 500 feet in depth. About 4 miles south of San Bernardino is the Gage group of 29 wells, all within the radius of a mile, the average volume being about 389 gallons per minute, and the average depth but 150 feet.

In other parts of the United States there are many notable wells and artesian basins, as there are also in China, in the Sahara desert, and in nearly all of the countries of Europe, especially in Germany and in France. The scope of this little book will not, however, permit their consideration. It is sufficient to note that the artesian well is of world-wide interest to mankind but it is in Dakota that the *great wells* may be said to be *at home*.

DAKOTA WELLS.

The pioneer well of Dakota was begun in the summer of 1881, at Aberdeen, by the Chicago, Milwaukee & St. Paul Ry., for the purpose of supplying water for its engines. The well was drilled by Mr. Swan, and, by reason of changes in the size of pipe, and unavoidable delays, the cost was far greater than it would otherwise have been. The flow was struck early in the spring of 1882, at a depth of 920 feet. The pipe was 6 inches at the top and 4½ at the bottom. The volume was not accurately measured at the time but a very close approximate measurement placed the volume at

1,200 gallons per minute and this increased later on to over 2,000. The pressure ranged from 150 to 180 pounds to the square inch. The 6 inch pipe was carried to a height of 70 feet and, from a 2-inch nozzle at the top of this pipe, a stream was thrown 60 or 70 feet into the air against a gentle breeze.*

Encouraged by the success at Aberdeen, other wells soon followed throughout the length of the territory until, today, they stretch over an area of over 400 miles north and south by over a hundred miles east and west, and the limit of the field in any direction has yet to be found.

A complete list of Dakota wells could not be given for lack of information, but a list is given below of a few typical wells which may be taken not as exceptional wells selected for the purpose of parade but as purely representative of the wells in all parts of the state—such wells as any farmer in the state can get if he will but try, and wells which, when once obtained, will be to the owners a mine of wealth such as few at present dream of.

TABLE NO. 13.

REPRESENTATIVE SOUTH DAKOTA ARTESIAN WELLS.

County.	Town or Location.	Depth in feet	Bore in inches.	Flow in gals. per min.	Pressure in ℔s per sq. in.
Aurora	Plankinton	750	6	1000	....
Beadle	Huron well	862	5⅝	1668	120
"	" Day"	840	4	476	120
"	" Risdon"	960	5⅝	2250	175
"	Hitchcock	960	4 & 3	1240	155
Brown	Aberdeen, Cy	908	5⅝	1800	180
"	" Sewer	1000	6-4½	1215	155
"	" Beard	1050	6 & 5	1000	138
"	Columbia	966	4½	1399	160
Bon Homme	Springfield	592	8	3293	80
'	Tyndall	735	4½	552	45
Douglas	Armour	725	4½	700	
Hand	Miller	1143	3½	462	100
Hughes	Harrold	1453		150	40
Marshall	Britton	1004	4½	601	120
Sanborn	Woonsocket	725		5000	153
"	"	775	7	7000	150
Spink	Ashton	900	4	750	100
"	Mellette	910	4½	1215	165
"	Redfield	964	4½	1261	166
"	Doland	897	4½	710	112
"	Baker well	920	4½	2000	165
Yankton	Yankton	610	6	1800	56
"	"	610	6	2200	50

The author compiled the above table from previously published reports and has made such corrections as were possible. The figures given, are, in the main, correct.

*This is the first *accurate* account published as to this first well. The record was made by myself at the time and has been carefully preserved. The record published by State

Engineer Coffin was erroneous, having been obtained, no doubt, from parties who were not properly informed. Similar errors appeared as to other wells, as to which I am accurately posted. The official reports ought to be as accurate as possible and none but the best authorities accepted. It is difficult, however, to attain to great accuracy in this matter. Maj. Coffin deserves praise for attaining so nearly to it.   W. P. B.

The Dakota artesian basin, as stated, is of unknown extent. Wells are found throughout the length of the two Dakotas and far northward into the British possessions, as they are also to the south through Nebraska, Kansas and Texas. On the east the field appears to terminate within the borders of the state, where first appear the quartzite formations. Certain evidences are adduced by Maj. F. F. B. Coffin. ex-state engineer, to prove that even within the quartzite area wells may be found, and that the true limit on the east is in Minnesota where the true archaean formations appear. To the west is a domain as unknown as it is vast. If the supply of this basin, as supposed, comes from the mountains of Wyoming and Montana, then it would be possible to find wells at all points between the Missouri river and the mountains except within such areas as have been affected by igneous upheavals or other geologic disturbances.

It is sufficient, however, to know that on any section within this broad basin, extending for over 400 miles north and south by about 100 miles east and west, a well may certainly be had. The water bearing formation is the Dakota sandrock, a formation of unknown thickness in this field although of vast thickness in its far western out-croppings.

The southern wells of the state penetrate this formation at a depth of about 600 feet. The formation dips thence to the northward until, at Jamestown, on the Northern Pacific it is over 1400 feet below the surface. The dip appears to be comparatively uniform so that it is possible to determine, within very close limits, at what depth water will be struck at any point.

Overlying this soft, porous, water-bearing sand-rock there is usually a thin stratum, or cap-rock, of harder sandstone or limestone. Above this the formations are principally of blue and gray shale with occasional strata of sand or limestones. It is the drilling in these shale formations that is so difficult, for, as stated by some drillers, the shale seems to pack like putty or lead and does not mix readily with the water used in drilling.

Much has yet to be learned as to Dakota wells, as to the formatioms to be penetrated, as to the relationship—if any there be—between volume and pressure and as to the source and the volume of supply, and, especially as to the best and cheapest way of drilling wells, the best machinery or process to use and, above all, the best use to be made of the water after it is obtained. The Dakota farmer has also to learn how to use the water so as to get out of it the highest duty, when to use it on different crops and in what quantity on different soils and during different seasons. A grand work is well begun, and our farmers have but to labor and gain dollars thereby, while the scientist speculates upon the marvels of nature as they develop and gains knowledge from his speculations.

Under the head of Water, and of Reservoirs, will be found several tables relating to the duty of well waters. The volumes of wells, volumes thrown per minute and per day and volumes per minute equal to given volumes per day, volumes thrown in one and three months by wells of different volumes per minute, volumes required to cover different areas to different depths and time required by different wells to do it, equivalence of cubic feet and gallons and of gallons and cubic feet. equivalence of other units of volume or measurement, and other tables of value relating to wells.

The sequence of our subject requires that the Water follow the completion of the well, so that "Water, its properties, measurement," &c will next be briefly considered; after which will be a brief consideration of the matters of storage by reservoirs and its distribution by ditches, flumes and pipes.

COPIES OF THIS BOOK

FOR SALE BY

W. P. BUTLER,

Aberdeen, South Dakota, for 25 cents.

Also sets of detailed drawings of gates, outlets, flumes, weirs, and similar constructive details of an irrigation plant. These drawings could not be inserted in this book. Price per set 25 cents.

WATER.

Its Properties, Duty and Measurement, with tables of Weight, Pressure, Volume, Discharges, &c &c. Miscellaneous Notes.

Pure water is composed of Hydrogen and Oxygen.

By weight,	11.1	88.9	Parts.
By measure ,	2	1	"

Its greatest desity is at a temperature of from 39.2° to 39.8° from which point it expands by either heat or cold.

It boils at a temperature of 212°, and freezes at 32° Fahr.

Evaporates at all temperatures.

Is but slightly compressible.

Is not palatable when pure or distilled.

Wieght—See P. 62 & 63 Tables of weight, and notes appended.

Weight—See P. 61   "   "   "   on one acre.

Pressure—See P. 64   "   "   pressure.

"   of column per sq. in. = height of column × 4.331.

"   "   "   circ. in. = height of column × .3369.

Press. of 1 ℔ per sq. in. is exerted by column 2.311 ft. high.

Volumes—See tables under head of Mensuration , and following tables.

A cu. ft. of saturated air at 50° contains 4.09 gr's. of water.

A cu. ft. of saturated air at 55° contains 4.86 gr's. of water.

A cu. ft. of saturated air at 60° contains 5.79 gr's. of water.

A fall of snow of 11 inche.sis equal to about one inch of rain, but this varies greatly. 11 inches being for a dry snow not drifted.

Depth of water in in's. × 2,323,200=cu. ft. per square mile.

Depth of water in inches ×3,630= cubic ft. per acre.

The "CENTER OF PRESSURE" is ⅔ of the depth from the surface· Thus, in a reservoir or tank 12 feet deep the *average* pressure on the sides will be found at a point 8 feet below the surface. The amount of this pressure is equal to the depth of this point × by 62⅓ (the weight of 1 cu. ft. of water). In this case 8 ft., the depth, × 62⅓= 499 pounds=the average pressure per sq. ft. on the entire surface. To get the *total* pressure on the sides multiply the total area of the sides by the average pressure, as above found. The total pressure on sides and bottom = 3 times the weight of the fluid contained in the tank or reservoir.

The pressure on a sluice gate, in the bank of a reservoir, 2x3 feet and the center 8 feet b low the surface of the water in the reservoir=8×62⅓=499 ℔s. per foot; 2×3=6 sq. ft. ×499= 2994 pounds, or nearly 1½ tons.

The daily supply of water per capita in cities having water works systems ranges from 45 to 175 gallons, and averages about 75 gallons. In nearly all cases the per capita demand increases from year to year.

Water presses towards an orifice from all directions and diminishes the volocity it the proportion of about 63 to 100; or the quantity delivered through the orifice will be less in this proportion than the calculated amount.

DUTY OF WATER.

By the *duty* of water it is meant the amount of duty or service it will perform, or the extent of its usefulness in any given field.

Considered as a *power*, it is so many horse power for a given volume under a given head. Considered as an irrigating medium its duty is the number of acres a given volume will adequately serve; *or*, as it is usually stated, the duty of a second foot is so many acres. That is to say, a volume of one cubic foot per second, flowing constantly during the irrigation season, will serve a given number of acres.

This element of *duty* is not, of course, a subject of exact measurement for too many variable elements enter into its determination to render this possible; yet the duty may, in any particular section, be very clearly estimated. What the duty will be will depend altogether upon the crop to be served, and the nature of the sub-soil and surface soil on which the crop is grown.

The duty in one state will differ from the duty in another state, as will the duty in one section of a state differ greatly from that in another section of the same state. One crop will require more water than another, or the same crop may require more water on one soil than on another.

In Dakota little is known as to the duty of water for, as yet, no measurements have been made, no extended system of irrigation is in practice and little thought has yet been given to this matter; nor has any effort been made to arrive at the maximum duty of any one well. When the township well system becomes general, and the greatest service, or duty, is demanded of each well, then will carefully kept records of duty be required, and such records will form the basis of estimates which will closely approximate to the duty of the well waters in the several sections of the state, and lead to a knowledge of better methods of application and conservation of the supply.

Nor is duty a constant quality for it is constantly on the increase; that is, the duty increases from year to year—other things being equal—the ratio of increase being very rapid immediately after the installation of the system of irrigation This is apparent on considering that when the water is first applied its volume is very largely absorbed in placing the soil in proper condition. This having been done, the same volume will, the next year, serve to supply the prepared area and still leave a surplus for the reclamation of a further area.

So, each year, the field of duty is extended until the maximum is finally reached. As stated, the duty in any locality will depend very largely on the nature of the soil, and it will depend still more upon the mean rain fall over that section. In a locality, or during a year, where the precipitation is small and nearly the full necessary supply must be artificially supplied the duty will be low; but where the precipitation is nearly sufficient to supply the needs of agriculture, and but a small portion need be artificially supplied, then the duty will be high.

In considering, therfore, what the probable duty in Dakota will be, account must be taken of the character of the soil, the comparative precipitation and evaporation and the nature of the crop.

Hon. J. S. Greene, state engineer of Colorado, in the 1888 report states, as an approximate estimate, that the precipitation on the mountain areas west of the great continental divide is 33 inches, and on the plains areas 10.7 inches; an average over the whole of that area of 25 inches. Also that on the mountain areas east of the divide the precipitation is 30 inches, and on the plains areas 15 inches; or a total average of 18.7 inches. He states further, and, in this, is in accord with other authorities, "*that the limit of remunerative farming, without irrigation is drawn at an annual precipitation of twenty-two inches,*" that is, if the precipitation is less than 22 inches there cannot be certainty as to a remunerative return for agricultural labor. The matter of *distribution* of this precipitation enters here as a matter of the greatest importance as shown by the example cited on page 92.

In this report it is further stated, with reference to the duty of water and the distribution of precipitation—"as there is a demand for *general results* in this matter, it may be stated, relative to the duty of water on the plains of Colorado, measured where distributed to the land. that one second foot, running throughout the irrigation season, in addition to about 5 inches of rain-fall during April and May, and 4.5 during June, July and August, if distributed with fair care to diversified crops, on what might be called average land, would irrigate from 60 to 70 acres. It is noticed that, to accomplish this duty, it must be measured where placed upon the land. This is not always considered when speaking of the duty of of water." (P. 406.)

Referring to table 14, below, it will be seen that the precipitation during April and May, in Dakota, has equaled or exceeded 5 inches in past years, except during 1890 and 1891; and that, in every year the precipitation during June. July and August has exceeded 5 inches, so that the conditions of distribution above quoted are much exceeded here, and hence the duty of our well waters would exceed the duty quoted (soil, average evaporation, and average humidity being equal.)

Year	Pr. Apl. & May	Pr. June, July & Aug	Total	
1882	8.68	13.18	21.86	
1883	6.59	11.30	17.89	**TABLE NO. 14.**
1884	5.60	9.47	15.07	Table of precipitation
1885	6.26	13.84	20.10	in Dakota during Apl.
1886	5.10	9.12	14.22	and May and during
1887	5.11	15.07	20.18	June, July and Aug.
1888	5.86	7.67	13.53	(From table No. 43.)
1889	6.45	5.21	11.66	
1890	3.52	8.01	11.53	
1891	3.89	10.52	14.41	
Averages	5.70	10.34	16.04	

Then, too, the average Colorado precipitation of 18 or 19 inches is less than the Dakota average of about 21 inches, so this operates still further to increase the probable duty of water here.

In the recently published report of State Engineer J. P. Maxwell, of Colorado, (1890 report) are certain very pertinent suggestions and estimates, relative to water duty which I cannot do better than to quote.

"Water rights vested on the basis of the low duty assigned to water ten years ago, have, in instances, deteriorated lands and reduced their productiveness by as urfeit in application, while on adjoining lands through an enforced economy, a higher duty, better conditions of soil, and greater productiveness have resulted."

"Unskilled labor has a penalty of 25 to 50 per cent attached to it in the application of water, and unfortunately this class is too prevalent in the irrigation fields, in many cases, no other being obtainable."

"An abundant water supply tends to carlessness in its application and consequent waste. Where liberal and old water rights are provided, it is frequently the practice to turn the water upon the land and permit it to run without change or attention throughout the night and sometimes during the day, a large volume of water soaking into the soil without benefit to the crop."

"The duplication of ditches is another fruitful source of waste, reducing the duty of the volume of water."

"Reference to some of the maps prepared by this department, will show, in different localities several ditches paralleling each other at inconsiderable distances apart, the upper one of which could be made to answer the purposes of all with marked economy in water, as well as large saving in capital."

"Too little attention has been given to the proper preparation of the surface to facilitate the rapid spreading of the water."

"This is principally the result of too large individual ownership of land, rendering it impracticable to give close supervision and secure careful preparation of the land."

"The best results will be obtained from small proprietary rights in land, and a consequent higher state of cultivation."

The ownerships of the cultivated lands of the state should be multiplied by ten and the population increased to that extent."

All that is here stated will apply with equal force to Dakota, and he who would meet with the greatest measure of success will heed the cautions thus held out by so high an authority.

Become an expert in irrigation by studying up from all available sources. Profit by the past experiences of others. Beware of attempting more than your means or experience will fully warrant and conserve well the supply of liquid wealth so freely granted you.

The following table will serve to show the great range of duty in the same state, and as a very valuable basis of comparison with our own more favorable and less fluctuating climatic conditions.

TABLE NO. 15.

TABULATED STATEMENT OF WATER-DUTY ON STREAMS INDICATED FOR 1889 AND 1890.

STREAMS GAUGED.		Mean discharge from May 20 to September 20 in cubic feet per second.	Area cultivated in acres.	Equivalent in depth over area in feet.	Rainfall during period.	Total depth over area	Duty in acres per cubic foot
Cache La Poudre.....	1889.	735.97	139,222	1.178	0.682	1.860	189.168
	1890.	770.51	139,222	1.254	0.338	1.592	180.687
Big Thompson........	1889.	214.53	91,037	0.579	no data	.....	424.35
	1890.	425.42	89,790	1.192	no data	.....	211.06
St. Vrain............	1889.	215.46	94,013	0.563	0.532	1.095	436.33
	1890.	284.238	94,385	0.739	....	.....	332.69
South Boulder and	1889.	461.97	77,682	1.406	....	.....	168.15
Boulder Creek....	1890.	419.33	76,682	1.34	....	.....	182.86
Bear Creek..........	1889.	60.40	10,173	1.46	....	.....	168.42
	1890.	33.98	8,112	1.03	....	.....	239.02

From 1890 Report of State Engineer of Colorado.

It will be noted that, in all the above cited estimates, the water is that of a natural stream the volume of which is largely augmented by seepage water. The water having been used at a higher level, seeps through the soil and finds its way back into the stream at a lower level, there to be used again and again, thus raising the duty, over a given area, of a given original volume.

In the level lands of the Dakotas, and on the purely individual system of irrigation which will prevail here, no account need be taken of seepage waters as a source of secondary supply; although the presence of seepage water, and the power of the soil to retain it, will go far towards determining the ultimate duty of the original well-supply.

Quoting, again, from the Colorado report of 1888, Engineer Greene says, "it is thought that when distributed with the greatest care, and in sufficient quantities to be handled without great waste, during seasons of average rainfall and to crops and soils fairly conditioned to its economical use, that the duty of water should approach 90 acres to the second foot."

Also "Two cubic feet of water per second carried on to a field in *one body*, will, under conditions otherwise the same, irrigate more than *twice* the area that *one* cubic foot carried *alone* would irrigate.

What will be the conditions of the duty of water under the Dakota well-system, and what the duty that may be safely relied upon under average conditions? Note that the average rain-fall for 10 years has been 21.58 inches; the maximum 28.12 inches, and the minimum 14.68 inches.

In this level country a rain-fall of 24 inches is sufficient to give abundant returns, and even less than that, with proper distribution and provided the soil could be maintained, year after year, up to a proper standard of saturation. For the sake of conservatism, reduce the average annual rain-fall to 18 inches, instead of 21 inches, then but 6 inches need be artificially supplied to give the maximum of 24 inches required.

Thus 6 inches may be taken to fairly represent the unit of duty required in Dakota.

One cubic foot per second=448.83 gallons per minute. This amount is equaled, or exceeded, by most of the smaller wells of the state.

One second-foot=10,368,000 cubic feet in 4 months, (which may be said to cover the irrigation season, from April to July) or a sufficient volume to cover 238 acres a foot deep, or 476 acres 6 inches deep. 476 acres may, therefore, be said to be the duty of a second-foot in that period of time.

Allowing for deep seepage and evaporation, and call the actual duty 320 acres, instead of 476 acres (a loss of 156 acres), and it would appear that a second foot is amply sufficient to serve a half section of land during a poor year.

Account is not here taken of the fact that during the months prior to the beginning of the irrigation season, the land may be prepared, by flooding, to such an extent as to render further service during the irrigation season almost unnecessary; and the further fact, that, by a system of reservoirs, an enormous volume may be stored to supplement the supply of the well itself during the 4 months of irrigation service. Thus the supply of the well during eight months of the year may be utilized to swell the duty of the well during the 4 months of service, to the extent of making the duty during that period extend over fully double the area above assumed to represent the estimated duty.

The difference in the uniformity of supply of the Colorado rivers and the Dakota wells is most marked. The 1890 gauging record of the Cache La Poudre river shows that the volume discharged during March varied from 50 to 150 cubic feet per second. During April, from 75 to 500 cubic feet; increasing thence rapidly to June 2d, when the discharge was 1825 cubic feet. The decrease was then quite rapid until the first of September, when it had fallen to less than 100 cubic feet, and it so remained during the balance of the season of discharge. The same is true of all other western rivers whose waters are derived from the melting snows of the mountains.

There is therefore little chance to use the waters for purpose of irrigation except during the season of flood, *or*, in exceptional cases, where the waters are impounded in storage basins of great area. In Dakota, on the contrary, the supply is constant the year around. Winter and summer the flood pours forth with unabated energy, and the irrigator may—as he actually does—work in mid winter, with a hoe in his hand and a fur coat an his back.

By reason of this periodicity the duty of the Colorado waters is limited to the actual duty during the irrigation season, and, contrariwise, the duty of the Dakota well should be measured by what might be fairly called its *annual duty*.

I have little doubt but that the duty of the second-foot in Dakota will be found, in the end, to be nearer 640 acres than 320 acres; but if, for the present, the lesser unite be adopted abundant alowance may be claimed and the claim be entitled to fair consideration by reason of its actual conservatism.

From table No. 20, of second feet reduced to gallons per minute, the following table may be constructed on the basis of a duty of but 320 acres per second-foot.

TABLE NO. 16.

DUTY OF WATER IN DAKOTA.

(New.)

Gallons per minute from well.	Equivalent in second ft.	Duty in acres.	Gallons per minute from well.	Equivalent in second ft.	Duty in acres.
448	1	320	2692	6	1920
897	2	640	3141	7	2240
1346	3	960	3590	8	2560
1795	4	1280	4039	9	2880
2244	5	1600	4488	10	3200

THE DIVISION AND MEASUREMENT OF WATER.

It has been stated by Prof. L. G. Carpenter, in his work on the above subject, that "one of the most important, as well as one of the most difficult problems of irrigation is that of making a just distribution of water." Reference being made to the distribution of irrigation waters in Colorado and elsewhere where irrigation is carried on on a vast scale and by means of waters taken from large ditches or canals which serve a large area and are supplied from rivers or great storage reservoirs in the mountains.

Every device which the ingenuity of the centuries could devise has been used to render this division more equitable, certain and economical and to prevent waste where, as is usually the case, the economy of water is of the first importance.

The literature of the subject is voluminous, but the Dakota farmer will look far, and in vain, for any information touching upon conditions similar to his own.

We have here no vast system of canals, nor will we have in the future; no vast storage basins and no need of the many devices used in other sections for the division and measurements of water. Our system is essentially individual, but the day is at hand when certain simple devices will be required to divide the waters of our wells among the few consumers under service by each well operating under the township well law, or among those who rent water from the individual owners of a well.

With us, too, it is not wholly a matter of *device* for the mere measurement of a given volume, or a question as to the *unit* of volume; but very largely a matter of legislation based upon our peculiar conditions and needs, which legislation has yet to be evolved and put to the test of practice.

Contract, too, will enter largely into the matter of the division of water and, on the start, the terms will be more varied and uncertain than the devices necessary to carry them out. With the Dakota farmer, as with farmers elsewhere, the central idea will be to secure the greatest possible service from the water at hand; and the prevention of waste will soon demand attention.

In the irrigation operations of the west all the elements are predetermined. The water supply is known, the ditches or canals are constructed of a certain size to perform a certain service or serve a given area. This service cannot well be exceeded and great economy must be observed in order that the actual service may equal the calculated service. Here—the main chanel or source of supply is the well, the volume of which is easily determined. The fountain head may be inexhaustible but only so much can be drawn off. The farmer may have a surplus which he may waste or sell to his neighbor, in which case economy in his own use and in theirs will operate to increase his revenue from the sale of the surplus.

So, too, in the operation of the *township wells*. The greatest service will be desired for each consumer and the well will be called upon to serve as many consumers as possible. In the latter case, as in the case of an individual owner, proper service to each consumer can only be had through the medium of a storage reservoir; for if a well will not—on the instant—serve one consumer fully it will certainly fail to serve several consumers.

EACH MUST HAVE HIS OWN RESERVOIR.

Herein will arise questions as to the manner of service, priority, etc.

Suppose a well serves four quarter sections (say the E. ½ of Sec. 1 and the E. ½ of Sec. 12) and that by reason of the slope of the ground it is necessary to locate the well on the center of the N. E. ¼ of section 1. If the water is carried in a ditch to the other quarters, and the amount delivered is measured at the well, the owner of the S. E. ¼ of Sec. 12 would receive far less water than the owner of the N. E. ¼ of Sec. 1 because of the far greater loss by evaporation and seepage. His loss, too, would be his neighbor's gain.

If the water be distributed in a pipe line the loss of head due to friction in the longer pipe would operate to the same end but to a lesser extent.

Again—if each consumer measures his water at the point of delivery in his own reservoir a question will arise as to the priority of service. A may fill his reservoir first and D last, but meanwhile the water in A's reservoir has been lowered a foot or two by evaparation and seepage and, at the period when greatest service is required, A may receive 20 per cent less service than D, yet each has received and paid for the same volume of water. If the service to the several reservoirs is by pipe line and is simultaneous the inequalities will be less and more easily subject to regulation.

It is not the intention here to raise any question as to the details of distribution or the possibility of an equitable division of the water; nor the purpose to suggest remedies for anticipated controversies, but it must be known that questions of detail, such as those above suggested, will arise and demand a solution. When they do a solution will be found on lines of equity to all interests.

Notwithstanding our conditions are so wholly different from those met elsewhere, the measurement of the volume of our wells must be treated the same, however much the final divisions of the waters may differ.

Heretofore too little attention has been paid to the accurate determination of the volumes of our wells. Usually the volume has been guessed at or an approximate estimate has been made by timing the filling of a barrel, hogshead or tank. In some cases the stream has been weired and an accurate estimate made as to the volume.

In a few cases grossly exagerated reports have been circulated as to the volume of certain wells (notably the Risdon well at Huron, which has been advertised as having a volume of 10,000 gallons per minute, whereas its true volume is but 2,250 gallons per minute.)

. Such exagerations can only result in harm and should be discouraged. *The truth is sufficiently wonderful to satisfy the most exacting.*

UNITS OF MEASUREMENT.

THE STATUTE INCH, is a unit of water measurement much used in the western states and territories. It varies in different states and even in different sections of the same state. It is equal to about 45 cubic inches per second. One second foot=38.4 statute inches in Colorado. This unit is practically the same as the miner's inch it being the miner's inch in the terms of a specific statutory specification. It varies in different states.

THE MINER'S INCH Is fully explained and illustrated in tables 18 and 19 and the accompanying notes and figures. When defined by state law it is known as the statute inch.

THE ACRE FOOT is equal to 43,560 cubic feet *or* such an amount as will cover one acre to a depth of one foot (See table 21 and notes & P. 60). This unit is more largely one of *service* than of measurement.

THE SECOND FOOT, or cubic foot per second, (See table 20 and note following.) is a unit definite as to both volume and time and is the one upon which all wier tables are constructed and is no doubt the coming unit in this and other countries.

GALLONS PER MINUTE. Like the second foot this unit is definite as to both volume and time and is the one commonly used in Dakota. (See tables, 19 20, 36 and 37.)

Two general methods have been adopted in the division and measurement of water.

THE FIRST is known as the DIVISOR, the object of which is to *divide* the waters of the ditches or streams into certain proportionate parts among consumers. The idea is not to *measure* according to some fixed unit but simply to *divide* or *proportion* the water according to a certain ratio. ½ to each of two consumers; ⅓ to each of three, &c &c.

THE SECOND is known as the MODULE the purpose of which is not to *divide* but to *measure* according to some fixed unit. In Spain, Italy and India measuring devices or modules have been in use for centuries but of late years they have reached their greatest perfection in our western states

Of all measuring devices the WEIR has proved to be the most acurate and satisfactory. (See the following table of weir measurements, table 17.)

The rectangular weir wherein the crest is horizontal and the sides vertical is the common form and the one to which the tables herein given apply. The trapezoidal weir has the crest horizontal and the sides sloping; this form possesses certain advantages which will not, however, be considered here. The triangular weir or notch is likewise claimed to possess certain advantages over other forms.

THE SPILL BOX.

Among the most satisfactory devices for the division and measurement of water is the *excess weir* or spill-box, invented by Mr. A. D. Foote of Idaho and illustrated in Fig. 6, wherein A is the main ditch the flow in which may be checked by gate B thus forcing a portion of the water into the spill-box D which has an opening F in the side, the discharge through which into the lateral ditch G is regulated by a slide and graduated scale as shown. The inner edge E E of the box is lower than the ends and outer side so that all water not passing through the opening F spills back into the main ditch. The head or height of the water above the opening being regulated by the height of the edge E E.

By this means the head at the opening F is maintained constant at all stages of the water in the main ditch and the amoun of water discharged through an opening of any length is not subject to fluctuations due to change of head but remains constant. Not over a foot of fall need be lost to the main ditch by using this device. The spill edge E E should be beveled to give a sharp edge, on the box side, over which the water may flow without friction. This form of module will find a wide field of usefulness in Dakota as the practice of irrigotion becomes more general and its details more closely considered.

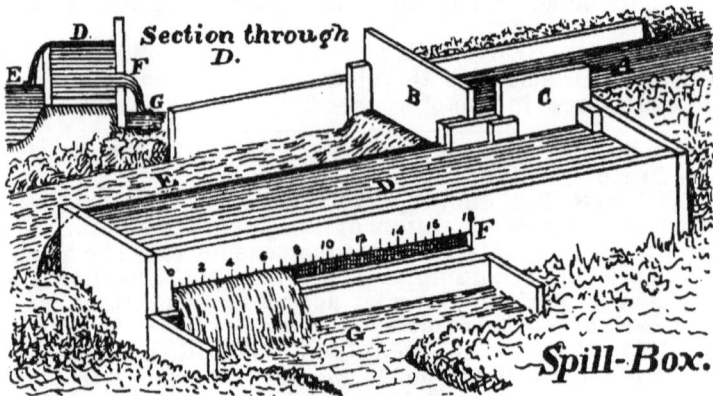

Fig. 6. Spill Box.

THE RECTANGULAR WEIR.

This form of module or measuring device having been the subject of the most exhaustive investigation, is considered to be the best suited to the accurate measurement of water.

The conditions of its proper operations are:
1st.   That the crest shall be horizontal and the sides vertical.
2d.   That the up-stream face be vertical.
3d.   That both the crest and sides be sharp edges on the up-stream side.

4th.   That the depth of water flowing over the weir be not less than 3 nor more than 25 inches.

5th.   That the depth of water flowing over the crest be not greater than 1⅓ the length of the weir.

6th.   That the weir opening be not over ⅔ the width of the stream approaching it.

7th.   That the discharge over the weir should be free and the approach of the water without velocity sufficient to produce eddies.

8th.   That the distance from the crest to the bottom of the channel—and from the ends of the weir to the sides of the channel, shall be at least twice as great as the depth of the water flowing over the weir. This is to secure complete contraction.

Weirs may have either *partial* or *complete contraction* as illustrated by figures 1 to 5 of Fig. 7.

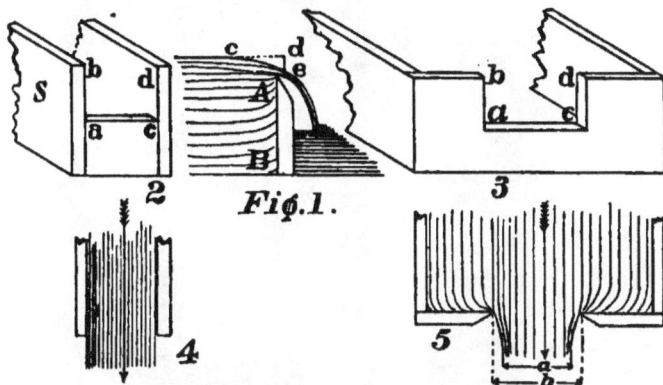

Fig. 7. Illustrating Contraction on Weirs.

In following over a weir water takes the form shown in Fig 1. The upward movement of the water toward the crest A of the weir A B causing the water to arch upward as shown. The true head, as shown at c, is reduced by the downward curve of the water, as shown at d e. This is called the contraction. If the weir has the form shown in Fig. 2 the contraction of the flow will be but partial; that is, there will be contraction at the crest a c but none at the sides a b and c d past which the water flows as shown in Fig. 4.

If the weir has the form shown in Fig. 3 the contraction is said to be *complete*, for, in addition to the contraction at the crest, there is also contraction at each side, a b and c d, as shown in Fig. 5 where it is seen that the width of the outflowing stream a is less than the width of the opening b. This will illustrate not only the action of flowing water but the meaning of the term *"Complete Contraction."* which is a requisite to the proper application of the following table of weir measurements.

TO CONSTRUCT A WEIR AND MEASURE THE VOLUME OF A WELL.

Select some convenient point where, by throwing up a low bank, a small pond may be formed by the stream from the well. Across the outlet set a board or plank out of which has been cut a rectangular piece (say 12 inches deep by 4 feet long). Support the board by nailing to stakes driven into the ground taking care that the edge of the

opening is level or horizontal. Make the bank water-tight
about the bottom and ends of the weir. Drive a stake several feet back of the weir and near the edge of the pond
making the top of the stake level with the crest of the weir
either by using a level or by driving the stake to water
level at the moment the water begins to spill over the weir.

Fig. 8. Illustrating the construction of a weir and methods of weir measurement.
Used by permission of James Leffel & Co., Springfield. Ohio. (See advertisement P. 229.)

Permit the water to rise to the full height at which it will-stand while flowing over the weir. Then measure the depth of water over the stake.

Enter the weir table with this depth (as explained in ex-amples given) and get the quantity for one inch. Multiply this quantity by the length of the weir in inches to get the total volume flowing from the well, in cubic feet per minute.

If possible have the up-stream edges of the weir lined with strips of tin or sheet iron to give a sharp edge for the water to flow over. If this is not at hand then bevel the crest and sides of the weir to a sharp edge on the up-stream side. See, in short, that ALL the conditions mentioned on page 52 have been complied with. The manner of con-structing and using a weir is illustrated on the opposite page, where A is the weir board with the beveled notch or opening B. E is the stake driven back to the side of the weir, out of the current, and from which the true depth is taken as shown.

Application of Weir Table No. 17.

This table gives the number of cubic feet of water passing per minute over *each inch in width* of a weir, and for depths from $\frac{1}{16}$ inch to 25 inches.

The top horizontal line of fractions are the fractions of an inch in depth, and the columns of figures at the right and left ends indicate the full inches of depth. The quan-tities inside the table are the cubic feet discharged.

Thus $\frac{7}{8}$ inch of depth = .11 cu. ft. per inch width of weir. ⎧ See at ⎫
10 inches " " =12.71 " " " " " " ⎰ ***** ⎱
10¼ " " . " =13.19 " " " " " " ⎰ in the ⎱
16⅛ " " " =27.43 " " " " " " ⎩ table ⎭

These examples will render clear the use of the table

Examples of Use. How many cubic feet and gallons are discharged per minute by a well the water of which, in flow-ing over a weir 5 feet long, shows a depth of 7⅜ inches?

From table the quantity of water for one inch wide by 7⅜ inches deep=8.05 cubic feet per minute; 5 feet wide=60 inches; therefore 8.05 multiplied by 60=483 cubic feet per minute. Referring to table No. 36 we find that 483 cubic feet=3612.8 gallons. Therefore by this simple process the volume of our well per minute has been found to be 483 cu-bic feet, or 3612.8 gallons per minute.

The work involved in the construction of a weir is but slight, and the calculation of the flow, as above, is a mere matter of multiplication and addition. Every well owner should see that the volume of his well is accurately deter-mined in this way; and not once alone, but every few months, in order to know whether there is any increase or diminution in the flow. A series of such systematic tests would no doubt result in furnishing valuable information leading up to a correct determination as to the source and supply of the artesian stream.

TABLE NO. 17.
WIER MEASUREMENTS.

WEIR TABLE FROM ONE-SIXTEENTH INCH DEPTH TO TWENTY-FIVE INCHES DEPTH.

James Leffel.

Inches	0	1/16	1/8	3/16	1/4	5/16	3/8	7/16	1/2	9/16	5/8	11/16	3/4	13/16	7/8	15/16	1
0		.006	.01	.03	.05	.07	.09	.11	.14	.17	.20	.23	.25	.30	.33	.36	.40
1	.40	.43	.47	.51	.55	.60	.65	.70	.74	.78	.83	.87	.93	.98	1.03	1.08	1.14
2	1.14	1.19	1.24	1.30	1.36	1.41	1.47	1.52	1.59	1.65	1.71	1.77	1.83	1.89	1.96	2.02	2.09
3	2.09	2.16	2.23	2.29	2.36	2.43	2.50	2.57	2.63	2.71	2.78	2.85	2.92	2.99	3.07	3.14	3.22
4	3.22	3.29	3.37	3.44	3.52	3.60	3.68	3.75	3.83	3.91	3.99	4.07	4.16	4.24	4.32	4.41	4.50
5	4.50	4.58	4.67	4.75	4.84	4.92	5.01	5.10	5.18	5.27	5.36	5.45	5.54	5.63	5.72	5.81	5.90
6	5.90	6.00	6.09	6.18	6.28	6.37	6.47	6.56	6.65	6.75	6.85	6.95	7.05	7.15	7.25	7.35	7.44
7	7.44	7.54	7.64	7.74	7.84	*7.94	*8.05	8.15	8.25	8.35	8.45	8.55	8.66	8.76	8.86	8.97	9.10
8	9.10	9.20	9.31	9.42	9.52	9.63	9.74	9.85	9.96	10.07	10.18	10.29	10.40	10.51	10.62	10.73	10.86
9	10.86	10.97	11.08	11.19	11.31	11.42	11.54	11.65	11.77	11.88	12.00	12.12	12.23	12.35	12.47	12.59	12.71
10	*12.71	12.83	12.95	13.07	*13.19	13.31	13.43	13.55	13.67	13.80	13.93	14.04	14.16	14.30	14.42	14.55	14.67
11	14.67	14.79	14.92	15.05	15.18	15.30	15.43	15.56	15.67	15.81	15.96	16.08	16.20	16.34	16.46	16.59	16.73
12	16.73	16.86	16.99	17.12	17.26	17.39	17.52	17.65	17.78	17.91	18.05	18.18	18.32	18.45	18.58	18.72	18.87
13	18.87	19.01	19.14	19.28	19.42	19.55	19.69	19.83	19.97	20.10	20.24	20.38	20.52	20.66	20.80	20.94	21.09
14	21.09	21.23	21.37	21.48	21.65	21.79	21.94	22.08	22.22	22.35	22.51	22.65	22.79	22.94	23.08	23.23	23.38
15	23.38	23.53	23.67	23.82	23.97	24.11	24.26	24.41	24.56	24.71	24.86	25.01	25.16	25.31	25.46	25.61	25.76
16	25.76	25.91	26.06	26.21	26.36	26.51	26.66	26.81	26.97	27.12	27.27	*27.43	27.58	27.73	27.89	28.04	28.20
17	28.20	28.35	28.51	28.66	28.82	28.98	29.14	29.29	29.45	29.60	29.76	29.92	30.08	30.23	30.39	30.55	30.70
18	30.70	30.86	31.02	31.18	31.34	31.50	31.66	31.81	31.98	32.15	32.31	32.47	32.63	32.80	32.96	33.12	33.29
19	33.29	33.45	33.61	33.78	33.94	34.11	34.27	34.44	34.60	34.77	34.94	35.10	35.27	35.44	35.60	35.77	35.94
20	35.94	36.10	36.27	36.43	36.60	36.77	36.94	37.11	37.28	37.45	37.62	37.79	37.96	38.14	38.31	38.48	38.65
21	38.65	38.82	39.00	39.17	39.34	39.52	39.69	39.86	40.04	40.21	40.39	40.56	40.73	40.91	41.09	41.26	41.43
22	41.43	41.60	41.78	41.96	42.13	42.31	42.49	42.67	42.84	43.02	43.20	43.38	43.56	43.74	43.92	44.10	44.28
23	44.28	44.46	44.64	44.82	45.00	45.18	45.38	45.53	45.71	45.90	46.08	46.26	46.43	46.63	46.81	47.00	47.18
24	47.18	47.36	47.55	47.72	47.91	48.09	48.28	48.46	48.65	48.83	49.02	49.20	49.39	49.58	49.76	49.93	50.10

Certain refinements of calculation enter into the matter
of measurement by weirs, but they have not sufficient bearing on the ordinary practice to deserve more than mention
here. Tables of weir measurements are constructed wherein these elements have been taken into account, but the
table given is sufficiently accurate for our use. In view of
the fact that the table given may not meet all the requirements of practice the formula upon which the most accurate
weir measurements are based is here given and briefly
explained.   The weir formula of Francis is as follows:

$$V = C \ (L - .2 \ H) \ H^{\frac{3}{2}}$$

Wherein V = Volume in cu ft per sec. flowing over the weir
C = The coefficient of discharge (=3.33) (or 3.3333+)
L = The length of the weir in feet.
H = The head, or depth of water over the weir.
$\frac{3}{2}$ = The square root of the cube of H.
Substituting the value of C, the formula becomes,

$$V = 3.33 \ (L - .2H) \ H^{\frac{3}{2}}$$

Which reads as follows:
*Volume per second=3.33 multiplied by (the length of the
weir less two tenths of the head) multiplied by the square
root of the cube of the head.*
This will be rendered plain by an illustration.
What will be the discharge per second over a weir 10 feet
long if the water is 1.5 feet deep?
The total length L of the weir is reduced, by reason of the
contractions at the ends, to the calculated amount of $\frac{1}{10}$ of
the depth, or head, for *each* contraction, hence the expression (L — .2H)
In the example the depth=1.5 feet, $\frac{2}{10}$ of which (there
being 2 contractions) is=.3, and ten feet—the full length—
less .3=9.7 feet, or the *effective length.*
The cube of 1.5 (the head) =3.375 and the square root of
3.375=1.837.   We now have the formula thus:

$$V = 3.33 \times 9.7 \times 1.837.$$

Which multiplied through=59.39 cubic feet per second
flowing over the weir.
The cubes and roots in these calculations may be taken
directly from the tables given elsewhere herein.   This
amount is somewhat less than that resulting from the use of
the weir table, but the table is sufficiently accurate for all
practical uses.   The use of the formula may, in some cases,
be more convenient and hence it has been given.   Ordinar-
ily the formula is given thus.

$$V = 3.33 \ L \ H^{\frac{3}{2}}$$

no account being taken of the loss to L resulting from the
end contractions.   If a weir is used wherein there are no end
contractions then this last form of formula would be used.
If the opening is obstructed by a central post there would
be 4 contractions and the expression of the formula would
be (L — .4H), and so on for any other number of contractions.

TABLE NO. 18.

TABLE OF MINER'S INCHES

Reduced to Cubic Feet and Gallons and to Cub. Ft. and Gals. per Minute.
(Corresponding with the "Colorado" inch.) *New.*

Miner's Inches.	Equivalent in Cubic Feet.	Equiv. in cu. ft. per minute.	Equivalent in Gallons.	Equiv. in Gals. per minute.
1	.0259337	1.556024	.194	11.64
2	.0518674	3.112048	.388	23.28
3	.0778011	4.668072	.582	34.92
4	.1037348	6.224096	.776	46.56
5	.1296685	7.780120	.970	58.20
6	.1556022	9.336144	1.164	69.84
7	.1815359	10.892168	1.358	81.48
8	.2074696	12.448192	1.552	93.12
9	.2334033	14.004216	1.746	104.76
10	.2593370	15.560240	1.940	116.40
20	* .52	* 31.12	* 3.88	* 232.8
30	.78	46.68	5.82	349.2
40	1.04	62.24	7.76	465.6
50	1.30	77.80	9.70	582.0
60	1.56	93.36	11.64	698.4
70	1.82	108.92	13.58	814.8
80	2.07	124.48	15.52	931.2
90	2.33	140.04	17.46	1047.6
100	25.93	155.60	19.40	1164.0
200	51.87	311.20	* 38.8	2328.
300	77.80	466.80	58.2	3492.
400	103.73	622.40	77.6	4656.
500	129.67	778.01	97.0	5820.
600	155.60	933.61	116.4	6984.
700	181.54	1089.21	135.8	8148.
800	207.47	1244.81	155.2	9312.
900	233.40	1400.42	174.6	10476.
1000	259.34	1556.02	194.0	11640.
10000	2593.37	15560.24	1940.0	116400.

* Note the change in location of the decimal point at * * * * *

Fig. 9.
Miner's Inch Measurement.

The Miner's Inch is such a quantity of water as will flow through an aperture one inch square in a board two inches thick, under a head of water of 6 inches, in one second of time and it is equal to 0.194 gallon, or 11.64 gallons per minute; and to .0259337 cubic foot, or 1.556024 cubic feet per minute. Fig. 9 shows a trough with 6 inches depth of water in it, and with a bottom 2 inches thick through which is cut a hole 1 inch square. If the depth of water is maintained at 6 inches one miner's inch per second would be discharged through the hole.

This unit of water measurement has been and is very extensively used in the west in mining operations, irrigation and the guaging of streams and ditches but it is largely giving way to more definite units. By reason of the difference in the head of water over the opening, the value of the miner's inch varies in different states from 1.36 to 1.173 cubic feet per minute. The head varies from 3 to 10 inches and in some cases it is measured from the *top* of the opening, (in the *side* of the box or flume) in other cases from the *bottom* and in still other cases—and properly—from the *center* of the opening.

Then, too, the volume discharged under a given head, and from a given area of opening, varies as the *form* of the opening is changed—thus, 36 miner's inches will be discharged through an opening one inch high by 36 inches long, and also from an opening 6 inches high by 6 inches wide, (the area of the opening being the same) yet, as a fact, more water will flow through the latter opening because it flows with less resistance from the edges of the opening. In the first case the edges of the opening measure 74 inches, while in the second case they measure but 24 in. The volume discharged is further varied by the form of the edge, i. e., whether it be square, rounded, sharp or beveled; and further still by the thickness of the edge—whether it be one inch or more. It being manifestly impossible, over any extended area, to secure any uniformity in the head of water maintained, or in the form or thickness of the edges of the outlet, or in the ratio of the area of opening to wet perimeter, it is impossible to maintain any standard of value for the miner's inch except within the limits stated. The Colorado inch most nearly corresponds with the theoretical discharge. The California inch, as usually measured, is from an aperature 2 and inches high of any desired length, though a plank 1¼ inches thick as shown in Fig. 10. The bottom of the aperature being

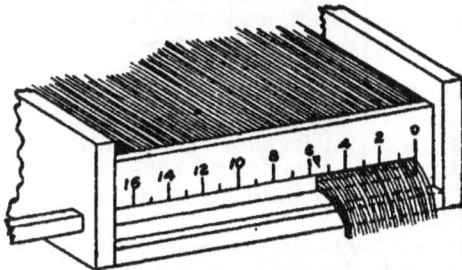

Fig. 10.   Miner's Inch Measurements.

2 inches above the bottom of the flume. This secures a complete contraction of the stream. The value of the inch will increase as the orifice is enlarged. as shown in the following table.

TABLE NO. 19.

TABLE OF MINER'S INCH MEASUREMENTS.

From Pelton Water Wheel Co.

Length of openi'g in inches.	Opening 2 inches high.			Opening 4 inches high.		
	Head to center 5 inches.	Head to center 6 inches.	Head to center 7 inches.	Head to center 5 inches.	Head to center 6 inches.	Head to center 7 inches.
	Cubic ft.	Cubic ft.	Cubic ft.	Cubic ft.	Cubic ft.	Cubic ft.
4	1.348	1.473	1.589	1.320	1.450	1.570
6	1.355	1.480	1.596	1.336	1.470	1.595
8	1.359	1.484	1.600	1.344	1.481	1.608
10	1.361	1.485	1.602	1.349	1.487	1.615
12	1.363	1.487	1.604	1.352	1.491	1.620
14	1.364	1.488	1.604	1.354	1.494	1.623
16	1.365	1.489	1.605	1.356	1.496	1.626
18	1.365	1.489	1.606	1.357	1.498	1.628
20	1.365	1.490	1.606	1.359	1.499	1.630
22	1.366	1.490	1.607	1.359	1.500	1.631
24	1.366	1.490	1.607	1.360	1.501	1.632
26	1.366	1.490	1.607	1.361	1.502	1.633
28	1.367	1.491	1.607	1.361	1.503	1.634
30	1.367	1.491	1.608	1.362	1.503	1.635
40	1:367	1.492	1.608	1.363	1.505	1.637
50	1.368	1.493	1.609	1.364	1.507	1.639
60	1.368	1.493	1.609	1.365	1.508	1.640

This table shows the discharge in cubic feet of each miners' inch of the openings given in the table. For an opening 2 inches high by 20 inches long and 5 inch lead the total discharge per minute would be 1.365×40=54.6 cubic feet. (2 inches by 20 inches=40 inches=area of opening.)

The following brief table, by C. L. Stevenson, C. E., of Salt Lake City, shows at a glance the relationship between the different units of water measurement with sufficient accuracy for ordinary calculation. It will be valuable for ready reference.

1 cu. ft. per second equals:

2 acre feet in 24 hours.	7.5 gallons per second.
60 acre feet in 30 days.	449 gallons per minute.
180 acre feet in 3 months.	50 California inches.
730 acre feet in 1 year.	38.4 Colorado inches.

100 California inches equal:

4 acre feet in 24 hours.	15 gallons per second.
1 acre foot in 6 hours.	900 gallons per minute.
120 acre feet in 30 days.	77 Colorado inches.
360 acre feet in 3 months.	2 cubic feet per second.
1460 acre feet in 1 year.	

100 Colorado inches equal:

5¼ acre feet in 1 hour.	19.5 gallons per second.
1 acre foot in 4.2 hours.	1,170 gallons per minute.
155 acre feet in 1 month.	2.6 cubic feet per second.
465 acre feet in 3 months.	130 California inches.
1,886 acre feet in 1 year.	

The unit of the miner's inch will find no place in Dakota. Mention has been made of it here because it is so extensively used elsewhere and is so frequently referred to in the irrigation literature of the day.

TABLE NO. 20.

"SECOND FEET"
REDUCED TO GALLONS.
New.

No. of second feet.	Equivalent in gallons per second.	Equivalent in gallons per min'te.
¼	1.87	112.2
½	3.74	224.4
¾	5.61	336.6
1	7.48	448.8
2	14.96	897.6
3	22.44	1346.4
4	29.92	1795.2
5	37.40	2244.0
6	44.88	2692.8
7	52.36	3141.6
8	59.84	3590.4
9	67.32	4039.2
10	74.80	4488.
20	149.61	8976.
30	224.41	13464.
40	299.22	17952.
50	374.02	22440.
60	448.83	26928.
70	523.63	31416.
80	598.44	35904.
90	673.24	40392.
100	748.05	44883.
200	1496.1	89766.
300	2244.2	134649.
400	2992.2	179532.
500	3740.2	224412.
1000	4780.5	448330.

NOTE.

The unit of water measurement known as the SECOND FOOT is very largely used in the west where it is becoming more popular because it is a unit whose value cannot be disputed. A second foot is one cubic foot per second. This is definite as to a determinable volume discharged within a determinable time, and thus is established a unit most capable of expression in the terms of ordinary calculations.

It might be well if such a unit were used to express the volume of our wells but the unit of gallons-per-minute has, by usage, become established and it will probably be retained. Some equity, too, may be urged in the retention of the *gallon* unit, as applied to wells, instead of the adoption of the larger unit of the *second foot* which is more applicable to the greater volumes to which it is applied in the greater irrigation operations of the far west.

TABLE NO. 21.

VOLUME AND WEIGHT OF WATER ON ONE ACRE.

New.

Depth in inches.	Cubic feet of water.	Gallons.	Weight, at 62.425 pounds to the cubic foot.		
			Tons	and	Pounds.
1	3630	27153	113		603
2	7260	54308	226		1206
3	10890	81462	339		1809
4	14520	168616	453		411
5	18150	135771	566		1014
6	21780	162924	679		1618
7	25410	190079	793		220
8	29040	217234	906		822
9	32670	244388	1019		1424
10	36300	271542	1133		27
11	39930	298695	1246		630
12	43560	325850	1359		1233

Note: For amounts less than 1 inch cut off one place to the right for tenths and two places for hundredths, thus—
For .1 inch Cu. ft. = 363.0 and Gals. = 2715.3.
" .01 " " = 36.3 " " = 271.53

Example: Required the volume for fall of 7.38 inches?

7. inches	= 25410	cu. ft.	190,079	gallons.	
.3 "	= 1089	"	8,146.2	"	
.08 "	= 290.4	"	2,172.34	"	
7.38 "	= 26,789.4	"	200,397.54	"	

1 ACRE FOOT = 43,560 cubic feet, or sufficient water to cover the acre to a depth of one foot.
This unit is the most recent of the units of water measurement. The element of *time* is entirely eliminated and the element of *volume* is specifically fixed in the terms of the definite unit, the cubic foot.
The unit is largely used in representing the capacity of storage reservoirs, since it conveys a definite or comprehensible idea as to the *service* of the water stored. To say that a reservoir will hold 4,356,000 cubic feet conveys but little knowledge to the average man; but to say that the reservoir will hold 100 acre feet of water conveys at once the idea as to the *service* which will be rendered by the impounded water. The unit is, therefore, what may be properly termed a SERVICE UNIT, and it fully answers this purpose.
The last column of Section A, of Table No. 34, will give the cubic feet in the number of acre-feet represented by the acres of the first column, and Section B the corresponding number of gallons, while Section C will show the time required for wells of different volumes to throw this amount of water.

TABLE NO. 22.

From Trautwine's "Civil Engineer's Pocket Book."

HYDRAULICS.

TABLE 2. Weight of Water (at 62¼ lbs. per cubic foot) contained in one foot length of pipes of different bores. (Original.)

Bore. Ins.	Water. Lbs.	Bore. Ins.	Water. Lbs.	Bore. Ins.	Water. Lbs.	Bore. Ins.	Water. Lbs.
⅛	0.005305	4	5.43234	14½	71.3843	40	543.234
¼	0.021220	4¼	6.13260	15	76.3922	42	598.915
⅜	0.047745	4½	6.87530	15½	81.5699	44	657.313
½	0.084880	4¾	7.66044	16	86.9174	46	718.427
⅝	0.132625	5	8.48803	16½	92.4346	48	782.257
¾	0.190981	5¼	9.35805	17	98.1216	50	848.803
⅞	0.259946	5½	10.27051	17½	103.9783	52	918.065
1	0.339521	5¾	11.22542	18	110.0048	54	990.044
1⅛	0.429706	6	12.22276	18½	116.2011	56	1064.738
1¼	0.530502	6¼	13.26254	19	122.5671	58	1142.149
1⅜	0.641907	6½	14.34477	19½	129.1029	60	1222.276
1½	0.763922	6¾	15.46943	20	135.8084	62	1305.119
1⅝	0.896548	7	16.63653	21	149.7288	64	1390.678
1¾	1.039783	7¼	17.84608	22	164.3282	66	1478.954
1⅞	1.193629	7½	19.09806	23	179.6067	68	1569.946
2	1.358084	7¾	20.39249	24	195.5642	70	1663.653
2⅛	1.533150	8	21.72935	25	212.2007	72	1760.077
2¼	1.718826	8¼	23.10865	26	229.5163	74	1859.218
2⅜	1.915111	8½	24.53040	27	247.5109	76	1961.074
2½	2.122007	8¾	25.99458	28	266.1845	78	2065.646
2⅝	2.339512	9	27.50121	29	285.5372	80	2172.935
2¾	2.567628	9½	30.64178	30	305.5690	82	2282.940
2⅞	2.806354	10	33.95211	31	326.2798	84	2395.661
3	3.055690	10½	37.43220	32	347.6696	86	2511.098
3⅛	3.315636	11	41.08205	33	369.7385	88	2629.251
3¼	3.586191	11½	44.90166	34	392.4864	90	2750.121
3⅜	3.867357	12	48.89104	35	415.9133	92	2873.707
3½	4.159133	12½	53.05017	36	440.0193	94	3000.008
3⅝	4.461519	13	57.37906	37	464.8044	96	3129.026
3¾	4.774515	13½	61.87772	38	490.2685	98	3260.761
3⅞	5.098121	14	66.54613	39	516.4116	100	3395.211

The weight of water in a given length (as one foot) of any pipe or other circular cylinder **is in proportion to the square of the bore,** or inner diameter. Hence the weight of water in 1 foot length of any cylinder of other diameter than those in the table can be found by multiplying that for a 1 inch pipe, 0.339521, by the square of the inner diameter of the given cylinder in inches. Thus, for a cylinder 120 inches diameter: diameter^2 = 120^2 = 14400, and weight of water in 1 foot depth = 0.339521 × 14400 = 4889.10 lbs. Similarly, $(\frac{7}{16})^2 = \frac{49}{256} = 0.191406$, and 0.339521 × 0.191406 = 0.064986 lb. = weight in 1 foot of $\frac{7}{16}$ inch pipe. Here, also, $\frac{7}{16}$ = *half* of $\frac{7}{8}$; hence, weight for $\frac{7}{16}$ inch = one-*fourth* of weight for $\frac{7}{8}$ inch = one-fourth of 0.259946 = 0.064986.

Weight of one square inch of water 1 foot high, at 62¼ lbs. per cubic foot = 62.25 ÷ 144 = 0.432292 lb.

For **further information** respecting weight of water, see pages 61 & 63

TABLE NO. 23.

TABLE OF WEIGHT OF WATER.

Maximun density is at 39.8° Fahr.   *New.*

Cubic feet.	=	Pounds.		Gallons.	=	Pounds.
1		62.425		1		8. 3216
2		124.850		2		16.6432
3		187.275		3		24.9648
4		249.700		4		33.2864
5		312.125		5		41.6080
6		374.550		6		49.9296
7		436.975		7		58.2512
8		499.400		8		66.5728
9		561.825		9		74.8944
10		624.250		10		83.2160
20	*	1248.50		20	*	166.432
30		1872.75		30		249.648
40		2497.00		40		332.864
50		3121.25		50		416.080
60		3745.50		60		499.296
70		4369.75		70		582.512
80		4994.00		80		665.728
90		5618.25		90		748.944
100		6242.50		100		832.160
200	*	12485.0		200	*	1664.32
300		18727.5		300		2496.48
400		24970.0		400		3328.64
500		31212.5		500		4160.80
600		37455.0		600		4992.96
700		43697.5		700		5825.12
800		49940.0		800		6657.28
900		56182.5		900		7489.44
1 000		62425.0		1 000		9321.60
2 000	*	124850.		2 000	*	16 643.2
3 000		187 275.		3 000		24 964.8
4 000		249 700.		4 000		33 286.4
5 000		312 125.		5 000		41 608.0
6 000		374 550.		6 000		49 929.6
7 000		436 975.		7 000		58 251.2
8 000		499 400.		8 000		66 572.8
9 000		561 825.		9 000		74 894.4
10 000		624 250.		10 000		83 216.0
100 000		6 242 500.		100 000		832 160.0
1 000 000		62 425 000.		1 000 000		8 321 600.0

(left column note, set vertically:) Note the change in location of decimal point at * * *

(right column note, set vertically:) Note the change in location of decimal point at * * *

For ordinary purposes the weight of a cubic foot of water may be taken to be 62½ pounds. The weight varies with the temperature as shown in the following table.

Temperature Fahrenheit.	Lbs. per cubic ft.	Temperature Fahrenheit.	Lbs. per cubic ft.
32° freezing	62.417	70°	62.302
40°	62.423	80°	62.218
50°	62.409	90°	62.119
60°	62.367	212° boiling	59.675

Cubic foot of ice = 57.2 lbs.
Cubic foot salt or sea water = 64.31 lbs.
35.84 cubic feet of water weighs one ton.
39.13 " " ice " " "
2.311 feet of water = 1 lb. per square inch.
1 cubic inch of water = .036024 lb. approximately.
1 " " " = .576384 ounce.
1 U. S. Pint = 1.0402 lb. of water.
1 U. S. Quart = 2.0804 lb. of water.
1 U. S. Gallon = 8.3216 lb. of water. (8½)
1 U. S. Wine barrel—31½ Gal. = 262.131 lb. of water.
                                  Trautwine and Haswell.

TABLE NO. 24:

PRESSURE OF WATER.

The pressure of water in pounds per square inch for every foot in height to 300 feet; and then by intervals, to 1000 feet head. By this table, from the pounds pressure per square inch, the feet head is readily obtained; and *vice versa.*

Feet Head.	Pressure per square inch.	Feet Head.	Pressure per square inch.	Feet Head.	Pressure per square inch.	Feet Head.	Pressure per square inch.	Feet Head.	Pressure per square inch.
1	0.43	65	28.15	129	55 88	193	83.60	257	111.32
2	0.86	66	28.58	130	56.31	194	84 03	258	111.76
3	1.30	67	29 02	131	56.74	195	84.47	259	112.19
4	1.73	68	29 45	132	57.18	196	84 90	260	112.62
5	2.16	69	29.88	133	57.61	197	85.33	261	113.06
6	2 59	70	30.32	134	58 04	198	85 76	262	113.49
7	3.03	71	30.75	135	58 48	199	86.20	263	113.92
8	3.46	72	31.18	136	58.91	200	86.63	264	114.36
9	3.89	73	31.62	137	59.34	201	87.07	265	114.79
10	4.33	74	32.05	138	59.77	202	87.50	266	115 22
11	4.76	75	32.48	139	60.21	203	87.93	267	115.66
12	5 20	76	32 92	140	60 64	204	88 36	268	116.09
13	5.63	77	33 35	141	61.07	205	88.80	269	116.52
14	6.06	78	33.78	142	61.51	206	89 23	270	116.96
15	6.49	79	34 21	143	61.94	207	89 66	271	117.39
16	6.93	80	34.65	144	62.37	208	90 10	272	117 82
17	7.36	81	35 08	145	62 81	209	90.53	273	118 26
18	7.79	82	35 52	146	63.24	210	90.96	274	118.69
19	8 22	83	35.95	147	63 67	211	91 39	275	119 12
20	8.66	84	36.39	148	64.10	212	91.83	276	119.56
21	9.09	85	36.82	149	64.54	213	92.26	277	119 99
22	9 53	86	37.25	150	64.97	214	92.69	278	120 42
23	9.96	87	37 68	151	65 40	215	93 13	279	120.85
24	10.39	88	38 12	152	65.84	216	93.56	280	121.29
25	10.82	89	38.55	153	66.27	217	93 99	281	121.72
26	11.26	90	38 98	154	66.70	218	94.43	282	122.15
27	11.69	91	39.42	155	67.14	219	94.86	283	122.59
28	12.12	92	39.85	156	67.57	220	95.30	284	123.02
29	12.55	93	40.28	157	68.00	221	95.73	285	123 45
30	12.99	94	40.72	158	68.43	222	96 16	286	123.89
31	13.42	95	41.15	159	68 87	223	96 60	287	124.32
32	13 86	96	41.58	160	69.31	224	97.03	288	124.75
33	14.29	97	42.01	161	69.74	225	97.46	289	125.18
34	14.72	98	42 45	162	70 17	226	97.90	290	125.62
35	15.16	99	42.88	163	70.61	227	98.33	291	126.05
36	15.59	100	43 31	164	71.04	228	98 76	292	126.48
37	16.02	101	43.75	165	71.47	229	99 20	293	126 92
38	16.45	102	44.18	166	71.91	230	99.63	294	127.35
39	16.89	103	44.61	167	72.34	231	100.06	295	127.78
40	17.32	104	45.05	168	72.77	232	100 49	296	128.22
41	17.75	105	45 48	169	73.20	233	100 93	297	128 65
42	18.19	106	45 91	170	73.64	234	101 36	298	129.08
43	18.62	107	46.34	171	74.07	235	101.79	299	129.51
44	19.05	108	46.78	172	74.50	236	102 23	300	129.95
45	19.49	109	47 21	173	74.94	237	102.66	310	134.28
46	19 92	110	47.64	174	75.37	238	103 09	320	138.62
47	20.35	111	48 08	175	75.80	239	103 53	330	142.95
48	20.79	112	48.51	176	76.23	240	103.96	340	147.28
49	21 22	113	48.94	177	76 67	241	104.39	350	151.61
50	21.65	114	49.38	178	77 10	242	104.83	360	155.94
51	22.09	115	49 81	179	77.53	243	105.26	370	160.27
52	22.52	116	50 24	180	77.97	244	105.69	380	164.61
53	22.95	117	50 68	181	78.40	245	106.13	390	168.94
54	23.39	118	51 11	182	78.84	246	106.56	400	173 27
55	23.82	119	51.54	183	79.27	247	106.99	500	216 58
56	24.26	120	51.98	184	79 70	248	107.43	600	259.90
57	24 69	121	52.41	185	80.14	249	107.86	700	303.22
58	25.12	122	52.84	186	80.57	250	108.29	800	346.54
59	25.55	123	53.28	187	81.00	251	108.73	900	389.87
60	25.99	124	53.71	188	81.43	252	109.16	1000	433 18
61	26 42	125	54.15	189	81.87	253	109.59		
62	26.85	126	54.58	190	82.30	254	110.03		
63	27.29	127	55.01	191	82 73	255	110.46		
64	27.72	128	55.44	192	83 17	256	110 89		

From catalogue of Chapman Valve Mfg. Co.
To find the pressure per sq. in. of a column of water of any height multiply the height of the column by .43318 (or 434, as it is usually given.)
See note on next page.

Note, as to table on last page. Many suppose that a well
having a static pressure of a certain number of pounds per
sq. in. has the same service, duty and volume of delivery as
would be obtained from a column of water falling through a
pipe of same size and with a head corresponding to the pressure of the well. Such is not the case, however. there being
no known relationship between the two so far as a well is
concerned.

To illustrate—From table we see that a head of 231 feet
will give a pressure of 100.06 pounds per square inch and
(although not given in the table) a certain volume will be
delivered per minute. If either the head, pressure or volume be known the other two may be accurately estimated.
In case of a well, however, this is not true. A well having
a pressure of 50 pounds per sq. in. may throw *more* water
than another well having a pressure of 100 pounds per sq.
inch and *either* one may throw *either* more or less than would
be delivered from a pipe of the same size having a head of
116 feet, which corresponds nearly with a pressure of 50
pounds to the inch. In other words—the volume of a well
cannot be found by knowing its pressure; nor can the pressure be found by knowing its volume. The pressure must
be measured with a gauge and the volume by weiring the
stream or by some other accepted method.

EVERY WELL SHOULD BE PROVIDED WITH A GAUGE

and a proper record preserved of the pressures during different seasons of the year, during different stages of the
weather and directions of the wind and during the several
stages of service of the well.

Systematic records thus kept would no doubt go far
toward settling the questions of source and supply. It has
been claimed, and apparently on good grounds, that the
standing of the barometer and the direction of the wind have
a marked effect on both the volume and pressure of some
wells. No systematic records having been kept of these
observations it cannot be definitely stated that the fluctuations in volume and pressure of the wells were due to the
changes in the weather, but the matter having been suggested
is one well worthy of attention because of its scientific possibilities.

TABLE NO. 25.

Diam. of pipe in inches.	Area in square feet.	Area in square inches.	Gals. in 900 feet of pipe.	Weight of water in 900 feet.
3	.0491	7.07	330	2756 lbs.
4	.0873	12.56	587	4897 "
4.5	.1105	15.90	743	6199 "
5	.1364	19.64	918	7656 "
6	.1963	28.27	1322	11021 "
7	.2673	38.48	1799	15011 "
8	.3490	50.27	2350	19598 "

An idea may be gained from this table as to the stupend-
ous energy necessary
to throw out this vol-
ume of water at velo-
cities ranging from
500 ft. to 2000 feet per
minute as is done by
Dakota's Artesian
Wells.

TABLE NO. 26.

From Trautwine's "Civil Engineer's Pocket Book."

CONTENTS OF CYLINDERS, OR PIPES.

Contents for one foot in length, in Cub Ft, and in U. S. Gallons of
231 cub ins, or 7.4805 Galls to a Cub Ft. A cub ft of water weighs about 62½ lbs; and a gallon about 8⅓ lbs. **Diams 2, 3, or 10 times as great,** give 4, 9, or 100 t'---- ---- content.
For the weight of water in pipes, see Table No. 22

No errors.

Diam. in Ins.	Diam. in decimals of a foot.	For 1 ft. in length. Cub. Feet. Also area in sq. ft.	Gallons of 231 Cub. Ins.
¼	.0208	.0003	.0025
5-16	.0260	.0005	.0040
⅜	.0313	.0008	.0057
7-16	.0365	.0010	.0078
½	.0417	.0014	.0102
9-16	.0469	.0017	.0129
⅝	.0521	.0021	.0159
11-16	.0573	.0026	.0193
¾	.0625	.0031	.0230
13-16	.0677	.0036	.0269
⅞	.0729	.0042	.0312
15-16	.0781	.0048	.0359
1.	.0833	.0055	.0408
¼	.1042	.0085	.0638
½	.1250	.0123	.0918
¾	.1458	.0167	.1249
2.	.1667	.0218	.1632
¼	.1875	.0276	.2066
½	.2083	.0341	.2550
¾	.2292	.0412	.3085
3.	.2500	.0491	.3672
¼	.2708	.0576	.4309
½	.2917	.0668	.4998
¾	.3125	.0767	.5738
4.	.3333	.0873	.6528
¼	.3542	.0985	.7369
½	.3750	.1104	.8263
¾	.3958	.1231	.9206
5.	.4167	.1364	1.020
¼	.4375	.1503	1.125
½	.4583	.1650	1.234
¾	.4792	.1803	1.349
6.	.5000	.1963	1.469
¼	.5208	.2131	1.594
½	.5417	.2304	1.724

Diam. in Ins.	Diam. in decimals of a foot.	For 1 ft in length. Cub. Feet. Also area in sq. ft.	Gallons of 231 Cub. Ins.
¾	.5625	.2485	1.859
7.	.5833	.2673	1.999
¼	.6042	.2867	2.145
½	.6250	.3068	2.295
¾	.6458	.3276	2.450
8.	.6667	.3491	2.611
¼	.6875	.3712	2.777
½	.7083	.3941	2.948
¾	.7292	.4176	3.125
9.	.7500	.4418	3.305
¼	.7708	.4667	3.491
½	.7917	.4922	3.682
¾	.8125	.5185	3.879
10.	.8333	.5454	4.080
¼	.8542	.5730	4.286
½	.8750	.6013	4.498
¾	.8958	.6303	4.715
11.	.9167	.6600	4.937
¼	.9375	.6903	5.164
½	.9583	.7213	5.396
¾	.9792	.7530	5.633
12.	1 Foot.	.7854	5.875
½	1.042	.8522	6.375
13.	1.083	.9218	6.895
½	1.125	.9940	7.436
14.	1.167	1.069	7.997
½	1.208	1.147	8.578
15.	1.250	1.227	9.180
½	1.292	1.310	9.801
16.	1.333	1.396	10.44
½	1.375	1.485	11.11
17.	1.417	1.576	11.79
½	1.458	1.670	12.49
18.	1.500	1.767	13.22
½	1.542	1.867	13.96

Diam. in Ins.	Diam. in decimals of a foot.	For 1 ft. in length. Cub. Feet. Also area in sq. ft.	Gallons of 231 Cub. Ins.
19.	1.583	1.969	14.73
½	1.625	2.074	15.51
20.	1.667	2.182	16.32
½	1.708	2.292	17.15
21.	1.750	2.405	17.99
½	1.792	2.521	18.86
22.	1.833	2.640	19.75
½	1.875	2.761	20.66
23.	1.917	2.885	21.58
½	1.958	3.012	22.53
24.	2.000	3.142	23.50
25.	2.083	3.409	25.50
26.	2.167	3.687	27.58
27.	2.250	3.976	29.74
28.	2.333	4.276	31.99
29.	2.417	4.587	34.31
30.	2.500	4.909	36.72
31.	2.583	5.241	39.21
32.	2.667	5.585	41.78
33.	2.750	5.940	44.43
34.	2.833	6.305	47.13
35.	2.917	6.681	49.98
36.	3.000	7.069	52.88
37.	3.083	7.467	55.86
38.	3.167	7.876	58.92
39.	3.250	8.296	62.06
40.	3.333	8.727	65.28
41.	3.417	9.168	68.58
42.	3.500	9.621	71.97
43.	3.583	10.085	75.44
44.	3.667	10.559	78.99
45.	3.750	11.045	82.62
46.	3.833	11.541	86.33
47.	3.917	12.048	90.13
48.	4.000	12.566	94.00

Table continued, but with the diams in feet.

Diam. Feet.	Cub. Feet.	U. S. Galls.	Diam. Feet.	Cub. Feet.	U. S. Galls.	Dia. Feet.	Cub. Feet.	U. S. Galls.	Dia. Feet.	Cub. Feet.	U. S. Galls.
4	12.57	94.0	7	38.49	287.9	12	113.1	846.1	24	452.4	3384
¼	14.19	106.1	¼	41.28	308.8	13	132.7	992.8	25	490.9	3672
½	15.90	119.0	½	44.18	330.5	14	153.9	1152.	26	530.9	3971
¾	17.72	132.5	¾	47.17	352.9	15	176.7	1322.	27	572.6	4283
5	19.64	146.9	8	50.27	376.0	16	201.1	1504.	28	615.8	4606
¼	21.65	161.9	½	56.75	424.5	17	227.0	1698.	29	660.5	4941
½	23.76	177.7	9	63.62	475.9	18	254.5	1904.	30	706.9	5288
¾	25.97	194.3	½	70.88	530.2	19	283.5	2121.	31	754.8	5646
6	28.27	211.5	10	78.54	587.6	20	314.2	2350.	32	804.3	6017
¼	30.68	229.5	½	86.59	647.7	21	346.4	2591.	33	855.3	6398
½	33.18	248.2	11	95.03	710.9	22	380.1	2844.	34	907.9	6792
¾	35.79	267.7	½	103.90	777.0	23	415.5	3108.	35	962.1	7197

TABLE NO. 27.

RELATIVE DISCHARGING CAPACITIES OF FULL SMOOTH PIPES.

Dia. in Feet.	Relative Discharg'g Power.	3	4	6	8	10	12	14	16	Diam in Inches.
d	$d^{\frac{5}{2}}$									
4.	32.000								15.59	48
3.667	25.750							17.50	12.54	44
3.333	20.235						20.23	13.47	9.85	40
3.	15.588						15.58	8.41	7.59	36
2.750	12.541				34.55	19.78	12.54	8.52	6.11	33
2.500	9.859				27.09	15.54	9.85	6.54	4.80	30
2.250	7.594			42.95	16.61	9.96	7.59	5.16	3.70	27
2.	5.657			32.00	15.58	8.92	5.65	3.84	2.75	24
1.833	4.549		70.96	25.73	12.53	7.17	4.55	3.09	2.16	22
1.667	3.588		55.96	20.29	9.88	5.66	3.58	2.43	1.74	20
1.500	2.756		42.01	15.58	7.25	4.34	2.75	1.87	1.34	18
1.333	2.052	65.77	32.01	11.60	5.65	3.23	2.05	1.39	1	16
1.167	1.471	47.14	22.94	8.32	4.05	2.32	1.47	1		14
1.	1.	32.05	15.60	5.65	2.75	1.57	1			12
.833	.6339	20.31	9.88	3.58	1.74	1				10
.667	.3629	11.63	5.66	2.05	1					8
.500	.1768	5.66	2.75	1						6
.333	.0641	2.05	1							4
.250	.0312	1								3

From J. T. FANNING's "Water Supply Engineering."

The foregoing table shows approximately the relative discharging powers of pipes of different diameters. In the second column the diameter 1 foot is assumed as a unit, and the figures show the relative discharging value of pipes whose diameter is given in the first column; for example, a pipe four feet in diameter will discharge 32 times as much water as one which is one foot in diameter, other things being equal; a pipe 3 feet in diameter 15.588 times as much, one 2½ feet in diameter, 9.859 times as much and so on.

► The numbers at the intersections of the horizontal and vertical columns from the diameters in inches give also approximate relative discharging capacities. For example, a 48-inch pipe is equal to 15.59, 16-inch pipes, or we find that a 24-inch pipe is equal to 32, 6-inch pipes or 15.58, 8-inch pipes, and that a 12-inch pipe is equal to 5.65, 6-inch pipes.

NOTE: The relative discharging power as given above is seen to equal the square root of the fifth power of the diameter. ($d^{\frac{5}{2}}$) To find, therefore, the rel. dis. power for any size not given in this table consult the table of sq. rts. of 5th powers, table No. 69, page 166.

TABLE NO. 28.
FRICTION HEADS AND DISCHARGES.

For 100 feet of pipe.   By Wiesbach's Formula.   *Trautwine.*

Diam. in Inches.

Vel. in Feet per Sec.	Vel-head in Feet.	3		3½		4		4½		5	
		Fr head Ft per 100 ft.	Cub ft per Min	Fr head Ft per 100 ft.	Cub ft per Min	Fr head Ft per 100 ft.	Cub ft per Min	Fr head Ft per 100 ft.	Cub ft per Min	Fr head Ft per 100 ft.	Cub ft per Min
2.0	.062	.659	5.89	.565	8.02	.494	10.4	.439	13.2	.395	16.3
2.2	.075	.780	6.48	.669	8.82	.585	11.5	.520	14.6	.468	18.0
2.4	.090	.911	7.07	.781	9.62	.683	12.5	.607	15.9	.547	19.6
2.6	.105	1.05	7.65	.901	10.4	.788	13.6	.701	17.2	.631	21.3
2.8	.122	1.20	8.24	1.03	11.2	.900	14.6	.800	18.5	.720	22.9
3.0	.140	1.35	8.83	1.16	12.0	1.02	15.7	.905	19.8	.815	24.5
3.2	.160	1.52	9.42	1.31	12.8	1.14	16.7	1.02	21.2	.915	26.2
3.4	.180	1.70	10.0	1.46	13.6	1.27	17.8	1.13	22.5	1.02	27.8
3.6	.202	1.89	10.6	1.62	14.4	1.41	18.8	1.26	23.8	1.13	29.4
3.8	.225	2.08	11.2	1.78	15.2	1.56	19.9	1.39	25.2	1.25	31.0
4.0	.250	2.28	11.8	1.96	16.0	1.71	20.9	1.52	26.5	1.37	32.7
4.2	.275	2.49	12.3	2.14	16.8	1.87	22.0	1.66	27.8	1.50	34.3
4.4	.302	2.71	12.9	2.33	17.6	2.03	23.0	1.81	29.1	1.63	36.0
4.6	.330	2.94	13.5	2.52	18.4	2.21	24.0	1.96	30.4	1.76	37.6
4.8	.360	3.18	14.1	2.72	19.2	2.38	25.1	2.12	31.8	1.91	39.2
5.0	.390	3.43	14.7	2.94	20.0	2.57	26.2	2.28	33.1	2.05	40.9
5.2	.422	3.68	15.3	3.15	20.8	2.76	27.2	2.45	34.4	2.21	42.5
5.4	.455	3.94	15.9	3.38	21.6	2.96	28.2	2.63	35.8	2.37	44.2
5.6	.490	4.22	16.5	3.61	22.4	3.16	29.3	2.81	37.1	2.53	45.8
5.8	.525	4.50	17.1	3.85	23.2	3.37	30.3	3.00	38.4	2.70	47.4
6.0	.562	4.78	17.7	4.10	24.0	3.59	31.4	3.19	39.7	2.87	49.1
6.2	.600	5.08	18.2	4.36	24.8	3.81	32.4	3.39	41.0	3.05	50.7
6.4	.640	5.39	18.8	4.62	25.6	4.04	33.5	3.59	42.4	3.23	52.3
6.6	.680	5.70	19.4	4.89	26.4	4.28	34.5	3.80	43.7	3.42	54.0
6.8	.722	6.02	20.0	5.16	27.3	4.52	35.6	4.01	45.0	3 61	55.6
7.0	.765	6.35	20.6	5.45	28.0	4.77	36.6	4.24	46 4	3.81	57.2

Diam. in Inches.

Vel. in Feet per Sec.	Vel-head in Feet.	6		7		8		9		10	
		Fr head Ft per 100 ft.	Cub ft per Min	Fr head Ft per 100 ft.	Cub ft per Min	Fr head Ft per 100 ft.	Cub ft per Min	Fr head Ft per 100 ft.	Cub ft per Min	Fr head Ft per 100 ft.	Cub ft per Min
2.0	.062	.329	23.5	.282	32.0	.247	41.9	.220	53.0	.198	65.4
2.2	.075	.390	25.9	.334	35.3	.293	46.1	.260	58.3	.234	72.0
2.4	.090	.456	28.2	.390	38.5	.342	50.2	.304	63.6	.273	78.5
2.6	.105	.526	30.6	.450	41.7	.394	54.4	.350	68.9	.315	85.1
2.8	.122	.600	32.9	.514	44 9	.450	58.6	.400	74.2	.360	91.6
3.0	.140	.679	35.3	.582	48.1	.509	62.8	.453	79.5	.407	98.2
3.2	.160	.763	37.7	.654	51.3	.572	67.0	.508	84.8	.458	105
3.4	.180	.851	40 0	.729	54.5	.638	71.2	.567	90.1	.510	111
3.6	.202	.943	42.4	.808	57.7	.707	75.4	.629	95.4	.565	118
3.8	.225	1.04	44.7	.892	60.9	.780	79.6	.693	101	.624	124
4.0	.250	1.14	47.1	.979	64.1	.856	83.7	.761	106	.685	131
4.2	.275	1.25	49.5	1.07	67.3	.935	87.9	.832	111	.748	137
4.4	.302	1.35	51.8	1.16	70.5	1.02	92.1	.905	116	.814	144
4.6	.330	1.47	54.1	1.26	73.7	1.10	96.3	.981	122	.883	150
4.8	.360	1.59	56.5	1.36	76.9	1.19	100	1.06	127	.954	157
5.0	.390	1.71	58.9	1.47	80.2	1.28	105	1.14	132	1.03	163
5.2	.422	1 84	61.2	1.58	83.3	1.38	109	1.23	138	1.10	170
5.4	.455	1.97	63.6	1.69	86.6	1.48	113	1.31	143	1.18	177
5.6	.490	2.11	65.9	1.81	89.8	1.58	117	1.40	148	1.26	183
5.8	.525	2.25	68.3	1.93	93.0	1.68	121	1 50	154	1.35	190
6.0	.562	2.39	70.7	2 05	96.2	1.79	125	1.59	159	1.43	196
6.2	.600	2.54	73.0	2.18	99.4	1.90	130	1.69	164	1.52	203
6.4	.640	2.69	75.4	2.31	102	2.02	134	1.79	169	1.61	209
6.6	.680	2.85	77.7	2.44	106	2.14	138	1.90	175	1.71	216
6.8	.722	3.01	80.1	2.58	109	2.26	142	2.01	180	1.81	222
7.0	.765	3.18	82.4	2.72	112	2.38	146	2.12	185	1.90	229

See exmaple of use on page 69.

Example of use of table No. 28. I have 150 lbs. pressure at well; 2000 ft. of 3 inch pipe discharging 110 gallons per minute. What is the effective pressure at point of discharge? From table 36 we find that 110 gals. = 14.7 cu, ft. From table 28, under head of 3 inch pipe, we find 14.7 cu. ft. discharge = 5 ft. velocity per sec. and a loss of 3.43 ft. head per 100 ft. 3.43 × 20 = 68.6 = ft. loss of head in 2000 ft. of pipe. From table 24 we find 68.6 ft. head to = 29.7 lbs. of pressure. 150 lbs. (given pressure)—29.7 lbs.= 120.3 lbs.= effective pressure at point of discharge.

Further example of use of table 28.

To get discharge from pipe of given size and length.

From table 28—within certain limits —may be found the volume discharged by a pipe of given size and length, under a given pressure.

Example: A well has a pressure of 78 lbs. per inch, and it is desired to convey water to a reservoir through 3000 ft. of 3 inch pipe; what will the pipe discharge per minute at the reservoir? From table 24 (P. 64.) we find that 78 lbs. = head of 180 ft. which head is to be used to force the water through 30 hundred feet of pipe, therefore $\frac{1}{30}$ of 180 = 6 ft. = the available head for 100 ft. In table 28 we find, under 3 inch pipe, the nearest corresponding friction head which is 6 02 ft. which corresponds to a velocity of 6.8 ft. per sec. and a volume of 20 cubic ft. per minute, which, from table 36 = 149.6 gallons. (No account is here taken of the *velocity head* which is less than 1 ft. and remains the same for any *length* of pipe; being dependent only upon the velocity in the pipe.)

Over column two of table No. 28 appears the heading " Vel. head in ft.", and over column three appears the heading " Fr. head ft. per 100 ft." The first is read as *Velocity head* and the second as *Friction head*. The distinction is here explained.

By **Head** is meant the vertical distance in feet between the surface of the source of supply and the centre of the orifice through which the water flows. The total head is divided into 3 parts called, respectively, **Entry Head. Velocity Head,** and **Friction Head;** the respective functions of which are as follows:

Entry Head is that portion of the total head used in overcoming the resistance to the *entry* of the water into the pipe. The entry head is less as the edges at the point of entry are rounded. It is equal to about one-half the velocity head.

Velocity Head is that portion of the total head used in maintaining a certain velocity within the pipe, assuming that there is no friction in the pipe. It is therefore equal to the height through which a body would fall —in a vacuum—to gain the same velocity as that of the water in the pipe.

Expressed as a formula Vel. Hd. $= \dfrac{V^2}{2g}$, in which $V^2 =$ the square of the velocity in ft. per sec. and g = the acceleration of gravity, or 32.2. The formula then becomes

Velocity Head $= \dfrac{V^2}{64.4}$. *or*, what is practically the same—

Velocity or } = { square of vel. } × .0155.
Theoretical Head } = { in ft. per sec. } × .0155.

The velocity head rarely exceeds 1 ft. and is constant for all lengths of pipe.

Friction Head is the remainder of the total head; or such an amount as is just sufficient to overcome the friction in the pipe leaving the remaining head to cause the entry and velocity of the flow. The smoother and shorter the pipe is the less the friction head will be and the greater the velocity head will become.

The **Theoretical Velocity** due to any given head is, if expressed in a formula—

Theor. velocity in ft. per sec. $= \sqrt{2gh} = \sqrt{64.4h}$, in which h = the given head in feet.

This is practically the same as Theor. Vel. = 8.03 times the sq. rt. of h.

Example—What is the theoretical vel. under a head of 4 ft? $\sqrt{64.4 \times 4} = \sqrt{257.6}$ which, from table of roots, = 16.05—or—by the second rule, the sq. rt. of h (4 ft.) = 2 which × 8.03 = 16.06.

The above explanation will not only explain clearly the significance of the values in table 28 but will also be of use otherwise.

Table 29 is similar to table 28, except that the velocities in the pipe are in single feet, and extend to 20 feet, instead of in feet and decimals, as in table 28. The values in table 29 differ slightly from those due to corresponding sizes and velocities given in table 28. This difference is due to calculations having been made from different formulae, but they are too slight to be material since the variations in the pipes themselves will cause as great variations—either more or less—from the quantities given in either table.

The limits of tables 28 and 29 are too narrow to suit all the conditions of our wells and practice, so a few simple rules are given to suit all conditions, these rules, and table 30 upon which they are based, being adapted from Haswell's Pocket Book.

It may be added that by reason of varying conditions whatever rules or formulae are applied the result will be in a measure approximate.

To find the Friction Head.—Wiesbach's Formula.

$$\text{Friction head in feet} = \left\{ .0144 + \frac{.01716}{\sqrt{\text{vel in ft per sec}}} \right\} \times \frac{\text{Length in feet}}{\text{Diam in feet}} \times \frac{\text{Vel}^2 \text{ in ft per sec}}{64.4}$$

The use of this formula requires a knowledge of the velocity in ft. per sec. which may be found by dividing the volume in cubic ft. per second by the area of the pipe. (See page 82.)

TABLE NO. 29.

LOSS OF HEAD BY FRICTION OF WATER IN PIPES.

CALCULATED FOR PIPES 100 FEET LONG.

Velocity of Water through Pipe in Feet per Second.	INSIDE DIAMETER OF PIPE IN INCHES.											
	3		4		5		6		7		8	
	Discharge per Min. in Cubic Feet......	No. of Ft. Loss of head due to friction	Discharge per Min. in Cubic Feet......	No. of Ft. Loss of head due to friction	Discharge per Min. in Cubic Feet......	No. of Ft. Loss of head due to friction	Discharge per Min. in Cubic Feet......	No. of Ft. Loss of head due to friction	Discharge per Min. in Cubic Feet......	No. of Ft. Loss of head due to friction	Discharge per Min. in Cubic Feet......	No. of Ft. Loss of head due to friction
1	2.95	.196	5.22	.147	8.17	.118	11.77	.098	16.03	.084	20.88	.074
2	5.89	.659	10.44	.494	16.34	.395	23.54	.329	32.05	.282	41.76	.247
3	8.83	1.35	15.67	1.02	24.51	.815	35.32	.679	48.08	.581	62 64	.509
4	11.80	2.28	20.89	1.71	32.69	1.37	47.09	1.14	64.11	.977	83.52	.856
5	14.70	3.43	26 12	2.57	40.87	2.05	58.87	1.71	80.15	1.47	104.40	1.28
6	17.70	4.78	31.34	3.59	49.05	2 87	70.64	2.39	96.18	2.05	125.28	1.79
7	20.60	6.35	36.57	4.77	57.22	3.81	82.41	3.18	112.21	2.73	146.16	2.39
8	23.56	8.14	41.79	6.11	65.40	4.89	94.19	4.07	128.24	3.49	167.04	3.06
9	26.51	10.12	47.02	7.59	73.57	6.07	105 97	5.06	144.27	4.34	187.92	3.79
10	29.45	12.32	52.24	9.24	81.75	7.39	117.74	6.16	160.30	5.28	208.80	4.62
11	32.40	14.71	57.47	11.03	89.92	8.82	129 52	7.36	176.34	6.31	229.68	5.52
12	35.34	17.31	62.70	12.98	98.10	10.38	141.30	8.65	192 37	7.41	250.56	6.49
13	38.33	20.10	67.92	15.08	106.27	12 06	153.07	10.05	208.40	8.61	271.44	7.54
14	41.23	23.12	73.15	17.34	114.45	13.87	164.85	11.56	224.43	9.91	292.32	8.67
15	44.20	26.32	78.38	19.74	122.62	15.79	176 63	13.16	240.46	11.28	313.20	9.87
16	47.12	29.72	83.60	22 29	130.80	17.83	188.40	14.86	256.48	12.74	334.08	11.15
17	50.05	33.33	88.83	25.00	138.97	20.00	200.18	16.67	272.51	14.29	354 96	12.50
18	53.00	37.14	94.05	27.86	147.15	22.29	211.96	18.57	288.54	15.92	375.84	13.93
19	55 95	41.12	99.28	30.84	155.32	24.67	223.73	20 56	304.57	17.62	396.72	15.42
20	58.89	45.32	104.50	33.99	163.50	27 19	235.51	22.66	320.60	19.42	417.60	17.00

TABLE NO. 30.

TABLE AND RULES. *From Haswell.*

Diameter inches.	Tabular No.	Diameter inches.	Tabular No.
1	4.71	7	612.32
1¼	8.48	8	854.99
1½	13.02	9	1147.61
1¾	19.15	10	1493.5
2	26.69	11	1894.9
2¼	46.67	12	2356.0
3	73.5	13	2876.7
3½	108.14	14	3463.3
4	151.02	15	4115.9
4½	194.84	16	4836.9
5	263.87	17	5628.5
6	416.54	18	6493.1

APPLICATION OF THE TABLE.

I. To Compute Volume Discharged—Length of Pipe, Diameter, and Fall or Head being given.

RULE—Divide the tabular number opposite to the diameter of the pipe, by the square root of the rate of inclination (head), and the quotient will give the volume required in cu. ft. per min.

EXAMPLE—A pipe has a diameter of 4 inches, a length of 2982 ft. and a head of 123 pounds pressure (284 ft.) What is the discharge per min.?

$$\sqrt{\frac{2982}{284}} = \sqrt{10.5} = 3.24, \text{ and tabular number for 4 in.} = 151.02.$$

then, $\dfrac{151.02}{3.24} = 46.6$ cu. ft. per min. $=$ (from table 36) 119.68 gals

If head, as in above case, is in *pounds* pressure reduce it to *feet* by reference to table 24; but if pipe is not connected with the well, and the pressure is due to gravity alone, then the head will be the vertical distance between the upper and the lower ends of the pipe. Reduce volume in cubic feet to volume in gallons by reference to table 36.

II. To compute the Diameter necessary to discharge a given Volume—the Head and Length being given.

RULE—Multiply the given volume by the square root of the ratio of the inclination—head—; take the nearest corresponding number in the table, and opposite to it is the diameter required.

EXAMPLE—A pipe has a length of 2982 feet, the head is 123 lbs., (284 ft.) What size of pipe will it require to discharge 46.6 cubic feet (119.68 gals.) per minute?

$46.6 \times \sqrt{\dfrac{2982}{284}} = 46.6 \times 3.24 = 150.98.$ The nearest tabular number $= 151.02$ opposite which is 4 inches $=$ required size.

III. To compute the Head—the Length, Diameter and Volume of discharge being given.

RULE—Divide the tabular number for the given diameter by the given discharge in cu. ft. Square the quotient, and divide the length of the pipe by it; the quotient will give the head necessary to force the given volume per minute through the pipe.

EXAMPLE—What head in ft. (or pressure in lbs) will be required to cause a discharge of 46.6 cu. ft. (119.68 gals.) of water per minute from 2982 ft. of 4 in. pipe?

$\dfrac{151.02}{46.6} = 3.24; \ 3.24^2 = 10.5; \ 2982 \div 10.5 = 284 =$ required head in feet which $= 123$ lbs. pressure.

TABLE NO. 31.

HORIZONTAL AND VERTICAL DISTANCES REACHED BY JETS.

Diam. of Nozzle.		PRESSURE AT NOZZLE.								
	Head in lbs. per sq. in. ...	20	30	40	50	60	70	80	90	100
	EQUAL = Head in feet	46.2	69.3	92.4	115.5	138.6	161.7	184.8	207.9	231.0
in. 1	Gallons discharged......	110	134	155	173	189	205	219	232	245
	Horizontal distance of jet	70	90	109	126	142	156	168	178	186
	Vertical " "	43	62	79	94	108	121	131	140	148
1⅛	Gallons discharged......	131	170	196	219	240	259	277	294	310
	Horizontal distance of jet	71	93	113	132	148	163	175	186	193
	Vertical " "	43	63	81	97	112	125	137	148	157
1¼	Gallons discharged......	171	210	242	271	297	320	342	363	385
	Horizontal distance of jet	73	96	118	138	156	172	186	198	207
	Vertical. "	43	63	81	99	115	129	142	154	164
1⅜	Gallons discharged......	207	253	293	327	358	387	413	439	462
	Horizontal distance of jet	75	100	124	146	166	184	200	213	224
	Vertical " "	44	65	85	102	118	133	146	158	169

FROM FANNING'S "WATER SUPPLY".

To calculate the altitude reached by jets.

$$A = H\left(\frac{H^2 \times .0125}{8 \times D}\right)$$ in which A = altitude required, H = head on jet in feet, and D = diameter of nozzle in inches.

EXAMPLE—What will be the altitude of a jet discharged from a 1½ inch nozzle under a head of 80 pounds pressure?

(The head being given in lbs. reduce it to feet by multiplying by 2.311— 1 pound per sq. in. equalling 2.311 ft. of head.)

$$80 \text{ lbs.} \times 2.311 = 184.88 = \text{head in feet.}$$

Then $$A = 184.88 - \left(\frac{184.88^2 \times .0125}{8 \times 1.5}\right) = 149.28 \text{ ft. altitude.}$$

To calculate discharge of jets in gallons per minute.

$$G = \sqrt{H} \times (8 D)^2 \times 0.288$$ in which G = discharge in gals. per min. H = head of jet in ft. D = diam. of nozzle in inches

Using above example. What will be the discharge per min. from a 1½ inch nozzle under a head of 184.88 feet. (=80 lbs. pressure)

$$\sqrt{H} = \sqrt{184.88} = 13.597 \text{ and } (8 D)^2 = (8 \times 1.5)^2 = 144.$$

Then formula becomes G=13.597×144×0.288 which=563.89 gallons per minute. In this way the volume of a well may be calculated very closely. Table No. 38, page 89 gives the discharges from different nozzles, under different heads, as calculated by this formula.

SOURCE AND SUPPLY.

"Where does the artesian water come from?" has been asked a thousand times, but has, as yet, received no answer, other than a purely theoretical one. Nor can any answer be given until a careful geological survey has been made of this state and those adjoining it; and until some systematic investigations are made in the field of the wells themselves. When more wells have been drilled, so that the influence of one upon another may be ascertained, or when a series of purely experimental wells shall have been drilled by the U. S. government, we may then learn something as to the direction of the flow and its source. A carefully prepared series of analyses, too, may aid in leading the way to the true source. There is infinite room for investigation, and nothing but room as yet provided for the investigator. The past season witnessed the taking of the first step leading to the determintion of the source of these subterranean waters.

Considerable work in the way of geological study and statistical investigation was done by the several members of the committee of Artesian Underflow, and Irrigation Investigation, acting, by authority of Congress, under the Department of Agriculture.

Without entering into any consideration of the many facts upon which this committee of experts based its opinion, as expressed in its reports to Congress, I state briefly the conclusion reached by them as to the probable source of this vast subterranean sea. As is well known, the water is, in all cases, found in the layers of more or less porous and soft sand-rock which underlies nearly the whole state and extends thence westward, finally to find an outcropping among the eastern foothills of the Rocky Mountains, and transverse to the courses of most of the large rivers which find a head in that vast drainage area.

Many observed facts of great weight would tend to prove that the vast quantities of water known to be lost to the Missouri, the Yellowstone and other large rivers, while flowing over the upturned edges of this outcropping sand-rock, is carried through these porous sponge-like formations to find a lodgement beneath the broad acres of Dakota, and an outlet, no one knows where. In the absence of any theory having the support of better evidence and a greater array of facts in its support this theory as to the source of the artesian waters will stand. There seems to be little doubt as to its correctness. Assuming it to be correct that the fountain head of our wells is in the vast water-shed of the Rockies and that the volume supplied to this great underground river is what it is calculated to be, the demonstration is complete that the supply is *absolutely inexhaustible* for *all time* and under whatever tax it may serve this or future generations.

In no case has a well failed

or shown any decrease in its volume, provided it has been kept clean and open. Some wells have become closed entirely but when cleaned out they have again flowed with their old time vigor.

What the thickness or depth of the water-bearing sandrock is, has not been determined for no drill has yet gone through it. Several wells have been sunk from 50 to 75 feet into this rock but the flow has then become so powerful as to prevent further drilling. It would be folly indeed to suppose that the feeble efforts of man to gain a little water for his use would have any effect upon the vast sea of water beneath us the area of which is measured by hundreds of miles and the depth by hundreds of feet. ALL THE WATER THAT ALL THE WELLS IN DAKOTA CAN THROW FOR A HUNDRED YEARS WOULD, IF GATHERED TOGETHER, EQUAL A LESSER VOLUME THAN NOW UNDERLIES A SINGLE COUNTY—BROWN. Figure it out. This is no guess.

In conclusion I quote from a letter written by Col. E. S. Nettleton (The Chief Engineer of the Department of Irrigation Inquiry, of the U. S. Department of Agriculture.) to Mr. R. O. Richards of the Consolidated Land and Irrigation Co. of Huron, S. D.

Col. Nettleton says:
"In reply to your request for an expression of opinion concerning the extent and durability of the Dakota artesian water supply for irrigation purposes, I will state that after two seasons spent in examining the artesian wells in South Dakota, and their probable source of supply, we have come to the conclusion that the supply comes from the elevated and mountainous country lying to the west (principally in Montana), where the rock strata are turned up so as to come to the surface. The water is transmitted through and is retained in the sand rock, which is estimated to be several hundred feet in thickness, and is made up of layers (more or less fractured) from one to fifteen feet in thickness, and of variable degrees of hardness and porosity. Below the strata are thin layers of impervious clay, shale, soft sand and lignite. This formation is exposed and is capable of imbibing a large amount of water from the unfailing supply from the mountains and the mountain streams and rivers, which have cut their way deeply into the artesian water bearing rock. I therefore conclude the supply will never fail. It is natural to suppose that the artesian supply can be found along the entire line between the source of supply and the present basin, which has an extent, north and south, of about 425 miles. I am of the opinion that the deeper the water bearing strata are penetrated the greater will be the volume obtained."   E. S. NETTLETON.

Artesian Water and Vegetation.

Before irrigation was thought of in Dakota, and the water
used upon grains, the opinion was frequently expressed that
artesian water would injure house-plants and trees and
would kill grass. Experience has disproved all of these
statements for the most delicate house-plants now thrive on
this water, the finest lawns in our towns are sprinkled with
it. Of field grains and garden truck the same is true. Where,
without its use the plant would die, with its use—and abundant use—there is such an abundant growth as to astonish the
grower. Plant growth is a chemical process and the plant
itself a chemical creation brought about in the laboratory of
the earth and through the agency of the air and water; the
latter being nature's great solvent and reagent. From the
air the plant derives its supply of nitrogen and oxygen, and
from the water its supply of hydrogen, and, through the solvent action of water, its supply of lime, soda, potash, mag-
nesia, iron, manganese, silica, chlorine and other chemicals
all of which are indispensable to plant life. Different plants
require different chemical ingredients in their food and ab-
sorb, of the same ingredient, different proport ons.

Many analyses have been made of artesian waters and in
no case has any showing been made of any chemical constit-
uent of the waters that would be in any way injurious to
plant life but, on the contrary, the result has shown that the
artesian water was especially well adapted to the fertiliza-
tion of our soil and the production of such plants and grains
as are best suited to our soil and climate.

The analyses of this water show

Silica	Alumina
Sulphate of sodium	Carbonate of lime
" " potassium	" " iron
" " calcium	Chloride of sodium
" " magnesia	Traces of organic matter
" " lime.	" " phosphates.

which elements are in varying quantities according to the
location of the well.

The waters of the northern wells are *very soft* and this is
true of some of the southern wells, but, as a rule, the southern well waters are harder and not so well adapted, on that
account, to household uses. The taste varies greatly but in
all cases the water is palatable when cold and it is used by
thousands of families for drinking in preference to any other
waters. When warm—as when it flows from the well—it, in
some cases, has a brackish, saline, unpleasant taste; but on
cooling this disappears. The temperature ranges from 55°
to 68°. In the winter it will run in ditches for several miles
before freezing and ponds of it will remain open where the
temperature ranges from 10° to 40° below zero for a week or
two. This warmth imparted to the soil in the spring forms
a valuable supplement to the warmth of the sun, quickens
the act of germination and aids much in the early stages of
growth.

THE POWER OF WELLS.

It is not alone for irrigation and domestic use that the artesian waters will be used but also for POWER. The first well at Aberdeen, in 1882, demonstrated the possibility of utilizing the pressure of the well for the purpose of forcing the water through water mains, thus furnishing a system of water supply and fire protection second to none in point of efficiency and equalled by none in economy of management and maintenance. No steam fire engine is necessary to force a stream through the mains and hose and over the highest buildings; nor is it necessary to provide for the care and maintenance of such an expensive plant as is necessary with a steam power plant. The first cost of the well was less than the cost of an engine, and it fills the double purpose of supplying the water and forcing it wherever it may be needed; and all this at no expense other than an occasional repair to pipe or valve.

Few there are, no doubt, in the many towns of Dakota, where there are systems of artesian water works, who ever pause to consider what these towns would have been had it not been for these wells; or what they would have done for public fire protection or for domestic consumption but for these wonderful "spouters."

There is no other source adequate, other than to the Missouri river towns, except to an occassional town, where large surface wells, in sand formations, might have supplied a very limited public service. The wells have been a Godsend indeed. The application of the well's pressure to fire-pressure service, led naturally to the idea of using it for power to run water motors.

The first application of well power to the operation of machinery was by the Aberdeen Electric Light Co. They tapped the main pipe of the city's well with a ¾ inch pipe and with this stream they ran the entire plant for some time. This power was, in the end, abandoned because the sand in the water cut out the buckets of the motor.

At this time there was a move made to build a flour mill to be operated by artesian power, but the project was abandoned upon the advice of several eastern hydraulic engineers to whom the matter was submitted by the author. Each declared it to be impracticable—impossible—to utilize the power of these wells, and such expressions of opinion are, even now, common among that class of experts; and little credence is given to what has since become a demonstrated fact.

Soon the use of small motors became quite common, and to-day scores of motors of different makers are used to run coffee mills, feed mills, printing presses, elevators and similar classes of machinery. The first application of well power to the running of a flour mill was at Hitchcock, Beadle county, S. D., where, with a small well 3⅝ inches at the bottom, they run a mill grinding from 40 to 50 barrels of flour per day. The motor is a simple, home-made wheel and the efficiency fully up to what could be desired from an expensive steam plant. The *saving* in this instance is not alone the cost of fuel, oil, engineer's salary, expensive repairs to boiler and engine, etc., etc., but also the decreased danger from fire and explosion and the consequent reduction in fire insurance rates. *The saving in insurance alone will fully cover all the expense of operation by the well power.*

This small well also supplies the domestic use and fire service of the town, and the exhaust water from the mill serves to irrigate a large farm.

Where on earth, outside of this artesian valley, can another showing be made that will compare with this? (See page 81.)

A larger mill at Woonsocket, using a Pelton wheel, runs at a capacity of 100 barrels per day. (See page 81.) Other mills at Springfield, Yankton and other points also use wells for their motive power. All the machinery in the "Huronite" publishing house, at Huron, S. D., is run by a Chicago Water Motor connected to the city water mains; and the electric light plant, operating both arc and incandescent lamps, is run by a 3 foot Pelton wheel connected directly to a $5\frac{5}{8}$ inch well, which also supplies water to the water works.

A plant, unique in this field and having, to the engineer, a greater degree of interest than any other, because of the manner of applying the water and the results accomplished, is, the *sewer plant* at Aberdeen. This was the first application of a well to the performance of heavy duty and it is the only plant of its kind on the globe. The well is $4\frac{1}{2}$ inches at the bottom and 6 inches at the top, and has a volume of about 1500 gallons per minute, under a pressure of from 140 to 160 pounds to the inch.

The water is supplied through 3-inch pipes to two Worthington water motors and pumps. The application of the water to the pistons in the cylinders being the same as with steam in the cylinders of a steam engine—the water operating the same as the steam.

When the two pumps are running at the rate of 60 strokes each per minute there is a reserve of pressure at the well of 40 pounds per inch. The pumps running at this rate have a capacity of 2,500,000 gallons per day of sewage pumped a vertical distance of 23 feet. When on their tour of inspection the U. S. Senate committee on irrigation investigation pronounced this plant to be the most wonderful adaptation of the powers of nature that had come under their observation.

Any man who believes that a well cannot be successfully harnessed to a load needs but to witness the operation of this plant to be convinced that he is in error, for when a well, through the agency of proper machinery, will lift a load of twenty millions of pounds a day through 23 feet, or 479 millions of pounds one foot high in a day, that well may be fairly said to have performed a good day's WORK.

Experts to the contrary, the artesian wells of Dakota supply the most wonderful power on the globe. The stupenduous unutilized, and to a great extent, unavailable power of mighty Niagara must pale in comparison with the power of Dakota's artesian wells.

Here no special mill site must be chosen and then purchased of the owner at his own figures, for every inch of our broad domain is as good a mill site as there is on the earth. The ground here has but to be opened in order to pour forth the flood which will serve not one purpose alone but many.

Power, domestic use, fire protection, irrigation, and even heat are but the chief among the many duties to which a well may be called. More there are which will soon find a place in the every day economy of Dakota life; and all combined will soon be the chief factors in making this the wonderland of America.

Every well owner who can afford it should have a motor, for with it much labor of the farm may be performed. A very small expense, added to a little ingenuity and home labor, will harness the churn, the feed mill, the fanning-mill, the feed-cutter, the threshing machine, the grindstone and other farm machines to the motor and thus save a vast amount of labor, expense and even life itself. Any farmer will appreciate the great advantage of having his threshing done by water power instead of by steam power, in which latter case there is the constant danger from fire and explosion.

All these things will come, in time, for Dakota's farmers are too enterprising to long delay the utilization of the forces thus gratuitously laid at their feet. Lack of means is the only obstacle to the proper utilization of that which, ere long, will transform Dakota into the most productive, prosperous, wealthy, and wonderful agricultural region in this or any other land.

Nor will capital long hold back when it has been fully assured of the successes already achieved by the pioneers in the field of irrigation and the development of artesian power. No more profitable investment can be found to-day than such as is made in Dakota lands on which wells are placed, or in the development of this inexhaustable power that flows not to wreck and to ruin but to fructify and enrich. It becomes, then, the duty of every lover of Dakota to herald the great truths (unembellished by any exaggerations) as to the wonderful possibilities that we ourselves have but just begun to appreciate.

The ear of capital will be reached if we but call long and loudly, and when reached the *means* will cease to be the obstacle to success which now awaits us.

On page 81 will be seen the reports of some of the millers of the state as to the service rendered them by artesian wells. In the face of such facts no argument need be given to prove the great value to Dakota of this great source of power. The reports are from points widely separated which shows the extent of the field.

80

TABLE FOR CALCULATING THE HORSE POWER OF WATER.

The following table gives the horse power of one cubic foot of water per minute under different heads.

TABLE NO. 32.

Adapted from Pelton Water Wheel Co.

Heads in feet.	Pressure per Sq. inch, lbs.	Horse Power.	Heads in feet.	Pressure per sq. inch, lbs.	Horse Power.
1	.43	.0016098	310	134	.499038
20	8.66	.032196	320	138	.515136
30	12.99	.048294	330	143	.531234
40	17.32	.064392	340	147	.547332
50	21.65	.080490	350	152	.563430
60	25.99	.096588	360	156	.579528
70	30.32	.112686	370	160	.595626
80	34.65	.128784	380	164	.611724
90	38.98	.144892	390	169	.627822
100	43.31	.160980	400	173	.643920
110	47.64	.177078	410	178	.660018
120	51.98	.193176	420	182	.676116
130	56.31	.209274	430	186	.692214
140	60.64	.225372	440	191	.708312
150	64.97	.241470	450	195	.724410
160	69.31	.257568	460	199	.740508
170	73.64	.273666	470	204	.756606
180	77.97	.289764	480	208	.772704
190	82.30	.305862	490	212	.788802
200	86.63	.321960	500	216	.804900
210	90.96	.338058	520	225	.837096
220	95.30	.354156	540	234	.869292
230	99.63	.370254	560	243	.901488
240	103.90	.386352	580	251	.933684
250	108.29	.402450	600	260	.965880
260	112.62	.418548	650	282	1.046370
270	116.96	.434646	700	303	1.126860
280	121.29	.450744	750	325	1.207350
290	125.62	.466842	800	346	1.287840
300	129.95	.482940	900	390	1.448820

When the Exact Head is found in the Table.

EXAMPLE—Have 100 foot head and 300 cubic feet of water. How many horse power have I?

From table—H. P. for 100 ft. head=.160980 for 1 cu. ft. of water, hence .160980×300=48.294 the H. P. for 300 cu. ft. per minute.

From table 36 we find that 300 cu. ft.=2244 gallons.

If a well having a flow of 2244 gallons per minute will, *while throwing* that amount, show a pressure of 43 lbs. per inch (=100 ft. head) then it will develop 48.29 effective horse power.

When Exact Head is not found in the Table.

Take the H. P. of 1 cu. ft. under 1 foot head and multiply by the number of ft. head given, then by the number of cu. ft given. The product will be the required H. P.

NOTE—The table is based upon an efficiency of 85 per cent.

Note the fact that a well shows *no pressure, or head*, when discharging its full volume. Turn it off a little so as to get some pressure, then measure volume and proceed according to above table to calculate the power.

See page 82.

WOONSOCKET MILL.

Northy and Duncan of the Woonsocket mill report as follows: Our well is 775 feet deep; 7 inches in diameter all the way; pressure 135 lbs. when closed; 62 lbs. with a 4-inch opening, 75 lbs. with a 3-inch opening. We use a 3 foot PELTON wheel, running at 275 revolutions per minute, the nozzle throwing a 1¾ inch stream. We have made 88 barrels of flour and 36 tons of good feed per day of 24 hours, and we figure on a saving of from $14 to $17 per day as compared with steam power of equal service. The element of safety being worth much that cannot be expressed in figures.

SPRINGFIELD MILL.

Mr. J. J. Kattleman of the Springfield mill reports as follows: Our well is 593 feet deep, and 8 inches all the way. The pressure, when closed, is 80 lbs., and when mill is running it is 40 lbs. We use a 16-inch turbine wheel, making about 800 revolutions per minute. The well cost $3,000, but could be drilled for less now. We put out about 60 barrels of flour per day, and figure on a saving of from $12 to $15 per day as against steam power. This item alone being a handsome profit or interest on the cost of the well. Repairs are very light and insurance much less than with steam. We get over 42 horse power from the well.

YANKTON—"FOUNTAIN" AND "EXCELSIOR" MILLS.

Mr. E. Miner of the Fountain Roller Mills of Yankton says: Well is 600 feet deep, 6 inches in diameter, pressure from 48 to 56 pounds per inch, and flows from 1600 to 2000 gallons per minute. We use a Dubuque turbine wheel 12 inches in diameter and of guaranteed 27 horse power. The cost of the power plant, complete to run, was about $4,000. We pay 3 per cent insurance and would pay 4½ or 5 if running by steam. I think we are saving over $8 per day as compared with an engine. Our mill is one of 40 barrel capacity.

F. L. Van Tassell of the Excelsior Mill Co., says: Our well is 500 ft. deep, pipe 8 inches to the bottom; pressure when closed 52 lbs., with 1 inch opening 48 lbs., with 2 inch opening 42 lbs., with 4 inch opening 20 lbs.; water clear and hard. We use a PELTON wheel 6 feet diameter with 2¾ inch nozzle, revolutions, 125 per minute. Power about 30 horse. We run our elevator and raise about 500 bushels of wheat per hour, shell 100 bushels of corn and grind 4000 lbs. of feed per hour. Will soon attach all the mill machinery to the well. The well flows 3000 gallons per minute, and, with wheel, power house, etc., cost about $4,000. Cost of running it practically nothing, so saving per year as compared with steam power is very great.

HITCHCOCK MILL.

Mr. M. B. Potter of the Hitchcock Milling Co., says: Size of well 4 inches at top, 3 inches at the bottom. Depth 960 feet. Volume 1240 gallons per minute. Pressure when closed 155 pounds. With 1 inch opening 140 pounds. With 2 inch opening 82 pounds. We get about 30 horse power from a wheel of our own design, it being 50 inches in diameter and runs at about 300 revolutions per minute. The well cost the town $4,500. We have had no expense for repairs since putting in the wheel in June, 1890 —nearly 3 years. The mill has a capacity of 50 barrels in 24 hours. Besides running the mill the well supplies water to the town, maintains water in an artificial lake, and waters an irrigated farm. The well has been running since 1886 and the volume is invariable and apparently inexhaustible and the pressure is uniform.

HORSE POWER.

A horse power is such a power as will raise 33,000 pounds one foot high in one minute of time. The term is one of mechanics and does not fairly represent the power of the average horse which is only about two-thirds as much.

To calculate the horse power of falling water multiply together the number of cubic feet of water falling per minute, the vertical distance (head) through which it falls, and the number 62.3 (approximate weight of 1 cubic foot of water) and divide the product by 33000.

EXAMPLE—A well discharges 800 cubic feet per minute from a pipe 16 feet above the surface, what is the horse power of the well?

$$\text{Here,} \quad \frac{800 \text{ cu. ft.} \times 16 \text{ ft.} \times 62.3 \text{ lbs,}}{33,000} = \frac{797440}{33000} = 24.17 \text{ H. P.}$$

This is the *theoretical* H. P. The actual H. P. as realized from machinery will be less because the wheel or motor does not realize the full efficiency of the water. The percentage of efficiency realized will depend on the form of the wheel and the skill of the makers. It will range from 25 to 90 per cent. of the full power. Turbine wheels realize from 75 to 85 per cent. of the power and impact wheels about the same amount.

The table on the next page will prove of value in this connection.

TO GET THE VELOCITY OF THE FLOW OF A WELL.

If the volume has been accurately measured.

Divide the volume of the flow, in gallons, by the volume in gallons contained in one foot of the pipe of the well (=the area of the cross section of the pipe). The answer will be the velocity in feet per minute.

Thus—Suppose a 6-inch well throws 1836 gallons per minute, what is its velocity of discharge in feet per minute? From table No. 26 we see that 1 foot of 6-inch pipe contains 1.469 gallons. How many feet, therefore, will it take to hold 1836 gallons? 1836÷1.469=1250=the number of feet necessary to hold 1836 gallons, *or* the length of the column of water thrown out each minute, *or* the velocity in feet per minute. 1250÷60=20.8, the velocity in feet per second.

This is the same as the rule for finding the velocity of any stream, viz: Divide volume per minute by area of section to get velocity per minute, and divide this quotient by 60 to get velocity per second.

To Compute the Volume of Discharge per Minute.

RULE—Multiply the area of the wet section in sq. ft. by the velocity in feet per second to get volume in cubic ft. per sec. Multiply this product by 60 to get the volume per min.

To Compute the Height of the Head in Feet.

RULE—Divide the volume in cu. ft. per second by the area, and the square of this quotient, divided by 64.33, will give the height of the head in feet.

TABLE NO. 33.

TABLE SHOWING FLOW PER MINUTE EQUAL TO A GIVEN FLOW PER DAY AND TOTAL FLOW PER DAY FROM A GIVEN FLOW PER MINUTE.

New.

Total gallons per day.	Equal gallons per minute.	Gallons per minute.	Equal gallons per day.
100	.07	.1	144
200	.14	.2	288
300	.21	.3	432
400	.28	.4	576
500	.35	.5	720
600	.42	.6	864
700	.49	.7	1 008
800	.56	.8	1 152
900	.63	.9	1 296
1 000	.7	1.	1 440
2 000	1.4	2.	2 880
3 000	2.1	3.	4 320
4 000	2.8	4.	5 760
5 000	3.5	5.	7 200
6 000	4.2	6.	8 640
7 000	4.9	7.	10 080
8 000	5.6	8.	11 520
9 000	6.3	9.	12 960
10 000	6.9	10	14 400
25 000	17.4	25	36 000
50 000	34.8	50	72 000
75 000	52.2	75	108 000
100 000	69.5	100	144 000
200 000	138.9	200	288 000
300 000	208.3	300	432 000
400 000	277.8	400	576 000
500 000	347.2	500	720 000
600 000	416.7	600	864 000
700 000	486.1	700	1 008 000
800 000	555.6	800	1 152 000
900 000	625.0	900	1 296 000
1 000 000	694.5	1000	1 440 000
2 000 000	1388.9	2000	2 880 000
3 000 000	2083.3	3000	4 320 000
4 000 000	2777.8	4000	5 760 000
5 000 000	4372.2	5000	7 200 000
6 000 000	4166.7	6000	8 640 000
7 000 000	4861.1	7000	10 080 000
8 000 000	5555.6	8000	11 520 000
9 000 000	6250.0	9000	12 960 000
10 000 000	6944.5	10000	14 400 000

This table will be most convenient in making quick comparisons as between different wells in Dakota and those elsewhere where, as a rule, the flow is reported as so much per day while in Dakota the flow is always so much per minute. The greatest wells outside of Dakota are those of Kern Co., California, which flow from 150,000 to 4,000,000 gallons per day *or* (see table) from 104.3 (69.5 + 34.8) to 2,777.8 gallons per minute. Of their 54 wells only 10 flow over 1,200,000 gallons per day or 833 4 gallons per minute. This table shows at a glance the superiority of the Dakota wells.

Example of use of table. How many gallons per minute flow from a well throwing 5,359,800 gals. per day?—Add the quantities in 2d. column 3,472.2 + 208.3 + 34.8 + 6.3 + .56 = 3,722.16 gallons per minute.

TABLE NO. 34.

New.

Area in Acres to be Flooded.	SECTION A. Cubic feet of water needed to flood the land to a depth of					SECTION B. Volume in Gals. if land is covered to a depth of 1 ft. (One Cu. Ft. = 7.4805 Gals.)	SECTION C. Approximate time required for Wells of different volumes per minute to throw the amount of water shown in Sec. B.									
							500 gall. well.				1000 gall. well.			2000 gall.		
	1 inch.	2 inches.	3 inches.	6 inches.	1 foot.		yr.	mo.	ds.	hr.	mo.	ds.	hr.	mo.	ds.	hr.
*	3 630	7 260	10 890	21 780	43 560	325 850				10			5			2.5
10	36 300	72 600	108 900	217 800	435 600	3 258 500			4	12		2	6		1	3
20	72 600	145 200	217 800	435 600	871 200	6 517 000			9	1		4	13		2	6
30	108 900	217 800	326 700	653 400	1 306 800	9 775 500			13	13		6	18		3	9
40	145 200	290 400	435 600	871 200	1 742 400	13 034 000			18	2		9	1		4	12
60	217 700	435 600	653 400	1 306 800	2 613 600	19 551 000		1	27	3		13	14		6	19
80	290 400	580 800	871 200	1 742 400	3 484 800	26 068 000		1	6	4		18	2		9	1
100	363 000	726 000	1 089 000	2 178 000	4 356 000	32 585 000		1	15	6		22	18		11	7
160-½ Sec.	580 800	1 161 600	1 742 400	3 484 800	6 969 600	52 136 000		2	12	10	1	6	5		18	6
320-½ "	1 161 600	2 323 200	3 484 800	6 969 600	13 939 200	104 272 000		4	24	20	2	12	10	1	6	5
480-¾ "	1 742 400	3 484 800	5 227 200	10 454 400	20 908 800	156 408 000		7	7	5	3	18	14	1	24	7
640-1 "	2 323 200	4 646 400	6 969 600	13 939 200	27 878 400	208 544 000		9	19	16	4	24	20	2	12	10
800-1¼ "	2 904 000	5 808 000	8 712 000	17 424 000	34 848 000	260 680 000	1		24	12	6	1	3	3		12
960-1½ "	3 484 800	6 969 600	10 454 400	20 908 800	41 817 600	312 816 000	1	2	14	12	7	7	5	3	18	15
1120-1¾ "	4 065 600	8 131 200	12 196 800	24 393 600	48 787 200	364 952 000	1	4	26	21	8	13	10	4	6	17
1240-2 "	4 646 400	9 292 800	13 939 200	27 878 400	55 756 800	417 090 742	1	6	20	8	9	10	4	4	20	3

* For further figures as to volume on one acre, see table 21.

This table will, at a glance, give one an idea as to the duty of a well of most any volume; that is, as to what area it will cover to a given depth in a given time. The amounts here given forming a basis for ready calculations for amounts *not* here given. See next page.

By interpolation other quantities may be readily taken from the foregoing table; thus—

To cover 10 acres 8½ inches deep,
Multiply 36,300 (amount for 1 inch) by 8 = 290,400
and add ½ of 36,300 " " " " = 18,150

Total = 308,550 cu. ft.

Where the required acres and the required depth are neither one in the table as—Required the cu. ft. to cover 17 acres 7 inches,—proceed thus—

Take out quantity for 1 acre and multiply by the given number of acres.

Thus — To cover 1 acre 6 inches = 21,780
" " 1 " 1 inch = 3,630
" " 1 " 7 inches = 25,410

25,410 × 17, the given number of acres = 431,970 cubic feet, OR if the inches cannot be taken from the table as in above case multiply the amount for one inch by the given number of inches, Thus, amount for 11 inches = 3630 (amount for one inch) × 11 = 39,930 cu. ft.

The volume in gallons may be found by multiplying the total cu. ft. by 7.48052, the number of gallons in one cu. ft.

or

by interpolation from Section B. How many gallons in 308,550 cu. ft. (amount to cover 10 acres 8½ inches deep)? From Section B. we find 3,258,500 as gals. to cover 10 acres 1 foot or 24 half inches; 8½ inches = 17 half inches, therefore, divide 3,258,500 by 24, to get amount for one half inch, and multiply this quotient by 17 to get gals. for 17 half inches.

OR see table No. 36

The time required for a well of given volume per minute to throw any given quantity of water is found by dividing the total volume by the volume of the well per minute and then reduce the number of minutes thus found to hours, days, weeks, &c. *or*

If the quantity is given in the foregoing table take out the time from Section C. or, if the quantity is not given in the table proceed as in the following. Example: 9 inches deep on 100 acres from a 500 gal. well will take—

2,178,000 cu. ft. = 6 inches.) Sec'n { 32,585,000 = gals. on 100 Ac. 1 ft. deep
1,089.000 " " = 3 " } A. { (Sec. B.) divided by 12 = 2.715,417 × 9
3,267,000 cu. ft. = 9 inches.) = 24,438,753 = gals. at 9 inches.

From Section C we find it takes a 500 gal. well 1 mo., 15 ds., 6 hrs., to cover 100 acres 12 inches deep, or 1,086 hours. Since 9 = ¾ of 12 take ¾ of 1,086 hours = 813 hours or 33 days and 21 hours. Ans.

From table 35 (next page) an approximation may be quickly taken. Thus, under head of 500 gal. well we see 21,600,000 = gals. thrown in 1 mo. and 720,000 = gals. in 1 day. 720,000 × 4 = 2,880,000 gals. which added to 21,600,000 gals. = 24,480,000 gals. in 34 days, or a little more than our estimated amount of 24,438,753 gals. From this it is shown that the amount will be thrown in a little less than 34 days (33 ds. 21 hours as above.)

For exact amounts and times one should figure exactly which may be done from the tables by using a few more figures.

TABLE NO. 35.

TABLE SHOWING VOLUME OF WATER THROWN IN DIFFERENT PERIODS OF TIME BY WELLS OF DIFFERENT VOLUMES PER MINUTE. *New.*

TIME.	VOLUME IN GALLONS THROWN.				
	100	**300**	**500**	**1 000**	**2 000**
MINUTE	100	300	500	1 000	2 000
Hour	6 000	18 000	30 000	60 000	120 000
Day	144 000	432 000	720 000	1 440 000	2 880 000
Week	1 008 000	3 024 000	5 040 000	10 080 000	20 160 000
One Month	4 320 000	12 960 000	21 600 000	43 200 000	86 400 000
Two Months	8 640 000	25 920 000	43 200 000	86 400 000	172 800 000
Three "	12 960 000	38 880 000	64 800 000	129 600 000	259 200 000
Four "	17 280 000	51 840 000	86 400 000	172 800 000	345 600 000
Six "	26 280 000	78 840 000	131 400 000	262 800 000	525 600 000
One Year.	52 560 000	157 680 000	262 800 000	525 600 000	1 051 200 000

From this table may be taken the approximate volume for a well with any flow not given in the table.

Thus—What will a well with a volume of 1250 gallons per minute throw in 3 months?

$$1000 \text{ gal. well} = 129,600,000.$$
$$200 \text{ " " } = 25,920,000 = 100 \times 2.$$
$$50 \text{ " " } = 6,480,000 = 100 \div 2.$$

or

$$1250 \text{ " " } = 162,000,000 = \text{Total.}$$

Take from table for 100 gals, for three months 12,960,000 and multiply by 12.50 and get the same result. Had the given flow been 763 gals. per minute multiply by 7.63 to get answer.

From table on opposite page any amount here given or estimated may be quickly converted into cubic feet, or multiply the gallons by .133679, the number of cubic feet in one gallon.

TABLE NO. 36.
TABLE SHOWING EQUIVALENCE OF CUBIC FEET AND GALLONS—AND GALLONS AND CUBIC FEET. *New.*

Cubic feet to gallons.		Gallons to cubic feet.	
Cubic feet. =	Gallons.	Gallons. =	Cubic feet.
1	7.48	1	.133679
2	14.96	2	.267358
3	22.44	3	.401037
4	29.92	4	.534716
5	37.40	5	.668395
6	44.88	6	.802074
7	52.36	7	.935753
8	59.84	8	1.069432
9	67.32	9	1.203111
10	74.80	10	1.336790
20	149.61	20	2.673580
30	224.41	30	4.010370
40	299.22	40	5.347160
50	374.02	50	6.683950
60	448.83	60	8.020740
70	523.63	70	9.357530
80	598.44	80	10.694320
90	673.24	90	12.031110
100	748.05	100	* 13.367
200	* 1 496	200	26.735
300	2 244	300	40.103
400	2 992	400	53.471
500	3 740	500	66.839
600	4 488	600	80.207
700	5 236	700	93.575
800	5 984	800	106.943
900	6 732	900	120.311
1 000	7 480	1 000	* 133
2 000	14 961	2 000	267
3 000	22 441	3 000	401
4 000	29 922	4 000	534
5 000	37 402	5 000	668
6 000	44'883	6 000	802
7 000	52'363	7 000	935
8 000	59'844	8 000	1 069
9 000	67'324	9 000	1 203
10 000	74'805	10 000	1 336
100 000	748.052	100 000	13 367
1 000 000	7 480 520	1 000 000	133 679
10 000 000	74 805 200	10 000 000	1 336 790
100 000 000	748 052 000	100 000 000	13 367 900

*Note change in location of decimal point at * * **

This table will be of great use in quickly converting cubic feet to gallons or vice versa.

Example, How many gallons in a reservoir containing 6,450,620 cu. ft.?

Take from the table the gallons for 1,000,000 cu. ft. and × it by 6, also the gallons for 100,000 cu. ft. and × it by 4, &c., as shown below.

7,480,520 × 6 =	44,883,120.	= gals for	6 000 000 cu ft		OR
748,052 × 4 =	2,992,208.	= " "	400 000 " "		Multiply the total
74,805 × 5 =	374,025.	= " "	50 000 " "		cubic feet by
600 =	4,488.	= " "	600 " "		7.48052, the gallons
20 =	149.61.	= " "	20 " "		in one cubic foot
					This requires
Total yards =	48,253,990.61. =	" "	6 450 620 " "		more figures.

TABLE NO. 37.

Table showing volume in gallons and in cubic feet thrown by wells of different volumes per minute, in periods of one month (30 days) and three months (90 days). *New.*

	ONE MONTH.		THREE MONTHS.	
Gallons per MINUTE thrown by well.	Total gallons thrown in 1 month. (30 ds.)	Equivalent volume in ucbic feet.	Total gallons thrown in 3 months. (90 ds.)	Equivalent volume in cubic feet.
1	43 200	5 775	129 600	17 325
5	216 000	28 873	648 00	86 619
10	432 000	57 748	1 296 000	173 244
20	864 000	115 497	2 592 000	346 491
25	1 080 000	144 373	3 240 000	433 119
30	1 296 000	173 247	3 888 000	519 741
40	1 728 000	230 996	5 184 000	692 988
50	2 160 000	288 745	6 480 000	866 235
60	2 592 000	346 495	7 776 000	1 039 485
70	3 024 000	404 244	9 072 000	1 212 732
80	3 456 000	461 993	10 368 000	1 385 979
90	3 888 000	519 743	11 664 000	1 559 229
100	4 320 000	577 492	12 960 000	1 732 476
200	8 640 000	1 154 986	25 920 000	3 464 958
300	12 960 000	1 732 479	38 880 000	5 197 437
400	17 280 000	2 309 972	51 840 000	6 929 916
500	21 600 000	2 887 466	64 800 000	8 662 398
600	25 920 000	3 464 959	77 760 000	10 394 877
700	30 240 000	4 042 452	90 720 000	12 127 356
800	34 560 000	4 619 945	103 680 000	13 859 835
900	38 880 000	5 197 439	116 640 000	15 592 317
1 000	43 200 000	5 774 932	129 600 000	17 324 796
1 100	47 520 000	6 352 425	142 560 000	19 057 275
1 200	51 840 000	6 929 919	155 5 0 000	20 789 757
1 300	56 160 000	7 507 411	168 480 000	22 522 233
1 400	60 480 000	8 084 905	181 440 000	24 254 715
1 500	64 800 000	8 662 399	194 400 000	25 987 197
1 600	69 120 000	9 239 891	207 360 000	27 719 673
1 700	73 440 000	9 817 385	220 320 000	29 452 155
1 800	77 760 000	10 394 878	233 280 000	31 184 634
1 900	82 080 000	10 972 372	246 240 000	32 917 116
2 000	86 400 000	11 549 865	259 200 000	34 649 595
2 100	90 720 000	12 127 358	272 160 000	36 382 074
2 200	95 040 000	12 704 852	285 120 00	38 114 556
2 300	99 360 000	13 282 344	298 080 000	39 847 032
2 400	103 680 000	13 859 838	311 040 000	41 579 514
2 500	108 000 000	14 437 332	324 000 000	43 311 996
3 000	129 600 000	17 324 796	388 800 000	51 974 394
3 500	151 200 000	20 212 264	453 600 000	60 636 792
4 000	172 800 000	23 099 731	518 400 000	69 299 193
4 500	194 400 000	25 987 197	583 200 000	77 961 591
5 000	216 000 000	28 874 664	648 000 000	86 623 992
5 500	237 600 000	31 762 130	712 800 000	95 286 390
6 000	259 200 000	34 649 596	777 600 000	103 948 788
7 000	302 400 000	40 424 529	907 200 000	121 273 587
8 000	345 600 000	46 199 562	1 036 800 000	138 598 686
9 000	388 800 000	51 974 395	1 166 400 000	155 923 185
10 000	432 000 000	57 749 328	1 296 000 000	173 247 984

See explanation on opposite page.

The table on opposite page is an extension of table on page 86, but changed to give two periods of time and wells of a greater range of volume per minute; and giving the volumes in both gallons and cubic feet. The irrigation season lasts about three months and is preceded in the spring and followed in the f ll by about equal periods of time, so that one month and three months are the periods assumed to be those upon which the greater number will desire to base estimates as to the volumes they can count on during these periods. By simple addition the volume of any well may be taken from the table.

EXAMPLE—What volume will a well with a volume of 3572 gals. per minute throw in 3 months?

3000 gal. well	=	388,800,000 gals.	—51,974,394 cu. ft.	
500 " "	=	64,800,000 "	— 8,662,398 "	
70 " "	=	9,072,000 "	— 1,212,732 "	
2 " "	=	259,200 "	— 34,650 "	

3572 " "	462,931,200	61,884,174 "

Having the amount for 3 months, the amount for any lesser or greater time may be found by division or addition. Thus: In above example the well, in 40 days, would throw $\frac{1}{3}+\frac{1}{9}$=(30 ds.+10 ds.) of the total amount or volume shown; or in 4½ months a well would throw, total $+\frac{1}{3}+\frac{1}{6}$=(3 Mo.+1 Mo +½ Mo) of the total volume shown.

The table will be found useful for taking out rapid approximations as to volumes and in this will answer the purpose of the preceeding table—table 37—thus, by inspection it is shown that a reservoir holding *about* 36,000,000 cu. ft. holds *about* 272,000,000 gals. and that a 2100 gal. well would be required in order to fill it in *about* 3 months.

TABLE NO. 38.

DISCHARGE OF JETS IN GALLONS PER MINUTE.

Head on Jet in Pounds.	Head on Jet in feet.	Discharge from Jets of following diameters.					
		¾	1 inch.	1⅛	1¼	1⅜	1½
20	46.16	70.4	125.2	158	196	237	282
25	57.70	78.7	140.0	177	219	265	315
30	69.24	86.3	153.4	194	240	290	345
40	92.32	99.6	177.1	224	277	335	398
50	115.40	111.4	198.0	251	309	374	445
60	138.48	121.9	216.8	274	339	410	488
70	161.56	131.8	234.3	297	366	443	527
80	184.64	140.8	250.3	317	391	473	563
90	207.72	149.4	265.6	336	415	502	598
100	230.80	157.5	280.0	354	437	529	630
110	253.88	....	293.6	372	459	555	661
120	276.96	....	306.7	388	479	580	690
130	300.04	....	319.2	404	499	604	718
140	323.12	....	331.2	419	518	626	745
150	346.20	....	....	434	536	649	772
160	369.28	....	....	448	553	670	797
170	392.36	....	....	....	570	690	823
180	415.44	....	....	....	....	710	845

This table is calculated from the formula given on page 73 except that H. (head) in feet is taken at 2.308 ft. per pound of head instead of 2.311 as given. The difference is not material.

WIND MILLS.

The following tables are from a circular issued by the U. S. Department of Agriculture, office of Irrigation Inquiry.

TABLE NO. 39.

SIZE AND CAPACITY OF WIND MILLS AT VARIOUS DEPTHS.

Diameter of wheel in feet	25 ft. Eelevation.		50 ft. Elevation.		100 ft. Elevation.	
	Size of pump in in.	Gallons per hour.	Size of pump, ins.	Gallons per hour.	Size of pump,ins	Gallons per hour.
10	3½	500	3	300	2½	200
12	4	750	3½	500	3	350
14	5	1150	4	800	3½	550
16	6	1500	5	1200	4	800

This table is only intended as a general guide and is subject to modification by reason of some mills having greater capacity, for given size, than other mills; and the same applies to the pump used and the manner of attachment.

TABLE NO. 40.

VOLUME OF WATER PUMPED PER MINUTE.

From 10 to 100 Feet.

Diameter of wheel	Vertical distance from water to point of delivery, in feet.					
	10	15	25	50	75	100
Feet	Gallons	Gallons	Gallons	Gallons	Gallons	Gallons
8.5	15.24	10.16	6.16	3.02	....	....
10	48.26	32.18	19.18	9.56	6.64	4.25
12	86.71	57.81	33.94	17.95	11.85	8.49
14	111.67	74.44	45.14	22.57	15.30	11.25
16	155.98	103.99	64.60	31.65	19.54	16.15
18	249.93	159.95	97.68	52.17	32.51	24.42
20	309.60	206.40	124.95	63.75	40.80	31.25
25	532.52	355.01	212.38	106.96	71.60	49.73
30	1080.11	728.83	430.85	216.17	146.61	107.71

VELOCITY OF WIND.

The average over the U. S., as determined by signal service examinations, is 5769 miles per month, or about 8 miles per hour. See page 91—table of wind velocity in Dakota. Experience has demonstrated that to operate a wind mill, there is required an average velocity of wind of 6 miles per hour.

TABLE NO. 41.

VELOCITY AND FORCE OF WIND.—*Haswell.*

Miles per hour.	Feet per minute.	Pressure per sq. ft. in lbs.	Description of the wind.
1 to 3	88—264	.005—.045	Just perceptible
6	440	.125	Pleasant wind
10	880	.5	Fresh breeze
20	1760	2.	Stiff breeze
30	2640	4.5	High wind
45	3960	10.125	Gale
60	5280	18.	Great storm
80	7040	32.	Hurricane
100	8800	50.	Tornado

The mean weight of the air will support a column of water 33.95 ft. high, at sea level. The velocity of sound in air at 60° = 1107 ft. ,in water about 49,000 ft. per second.

TABLE NO. 42.

WIND IN DAKOTA.

Average daily and hourly Wind Velocity for 9 years from 1882 to 1891, inclusive, at Huron, S. D., by Sam. W. Glenn, U. S. Weather Bureau.

Month.	Average daily velocity, miles.	Average hourly velocity, miles.
January	232.5	9.7
February	242.6	10.1
March	239.9	10.0
April	274.8	13.1
May	265.7	11.1
June	238.6	9.9
July	220.2	9.2
August	217.5	9.0
September	254.0	10.6
October	244.7	10.0
November	227.0	9.5
December	224.2	9.3

Average hourly velocity for 9 years = 10.1 miles.

TABLE NO. 43.

RAIN IN DAKOTA.

Total Rain Fall by months as recorded at Huron, S. D., from 1881 to 1892 by S. W. Glenn, U. S. Weather Bureau.

Year.	Jan	Feb	Mch	Apr.	May	June	July	Aug.	Sep.	Oct.	Nov.	Dec.	Tot'l
1881							3.58	6.31	3.11	2.10	.45	.06	.....
1882	.14	.25	.80	4.18	4.50	5.86	5.83	1.44	.86	3.37	.61	.23	28.12
1883	.17	.47	.42	2.14	4.45	4.33	5.20	1.77	1.68	1.96	.05	.61	23.25
1884	.09	.58	1.53	2.70	2.90	3.18	5.11	1.18	1.26	1.52	.17	.62	20.84
1885	.15	.22	.12	1.06	5.20	5.43	4.52	3.89	2.61	.98	1.50	.10	25.78
1886	.48	.16	.62	3.52	1.58	1.90	1.60	5.62	1.59	1.26	1.18	.74	20.25
1887	.33	1.11	.64	3.72	1.38	3.93	4.96	6.13	.15	.79	.25	2.09	25.54
1888	.78	.52	1.22	.88	4.98	1.10	3.11	3.46	.19	.29	.34	.18	17.05
1889	1.26	.93	.19	3.41	3.04	1.04	3.51	.66	3.89	.55	.16	1.53	20.17
1890	.66	.18	.32	.64	2.88	5.87	1.41	.73	.32	.61	.38	.68	14.68
1891	.07	1.32	1.64	3.45	.44	8.03	1.01	1.43	.47	.78	.94	.54	20.17
Mean	.41	.57	.72	2.57	3.14	4.03	3.63	2.96	1.46	1.29	.55	.67	21.58
1892	.28	.70	1.11	5.90	6.03	4.00	Total in 6 months=18.02						

Read carefully the note on the next page with reference to this table. Read it twice—and don't forget it.

PRECIPITATION FOR FIRST 6 MONTHS DURING THE FOLLOWING YEARS.

1882	15.73	1886	8.26	1890	10.55
1883	11.98	1887	11.16	1891	15.00
1884	10.98	1888	9.48	1892	18.02
1885	12.08	1889	9.87	Av'g.	12.10

(See also table No. 14.)

92

NOTE—As to precipitation table No. 43.

This table of rain-fall has much interest as it shows the distribution and amount of our rains by months and years.

1882 was Dakota's "boom" year in rain-fall, as in other respects, and was the most bountiful on record in consequence. 1883—'85 and '87 were good years, while 1888—'89 and '90 were years of almost total failure. It will be of special interest to note that 1889 and 1891 have *exactly* the same total rain-fall; whereas 1889 was a year of drouth and failure, while 1891 was a year of phenominally good crops. Note further that the record of 1891 followed a record of but 14.68 in 1890; whereas the equal record of 1889 followed a record of 17.08 for 1838, so that, so far as the records for the two-year periods are concerned, the period of '89 and '90 ought to have shown better results than the period of '90 and 91.

Note still further that the rain-fall of 1889 for the months from January to July was but 13.36 inches out of the total of 20.17; whereas in 1891 the rain-fall for these months was 16.01 out of the total of 20.17. Herein, then, lies the secret of the good year 1891—during the *growing months* of 1891 there was a rain fall of 2.65 inches *greater* than during these months of 1889—the *totals* for the two years being the same.

In 1889 the rain came too late, while in 1891 it came in the proper season.

A valuable lesson may therefore be drawn from the table—it is, that the 2 or 3 inches of timely rain in 1891 saved Dakota from a fourth year of failure, and enriched the people at the rate of

OVER $5,000,000 PER INCH.

There is the record!   There is the lesson!

From this draw the further lesson as to the true value of the water of a well the distribution of which you have in your absolute control both as to the quantity and the time when it shall be used.

If this lesson alone is well learned by a few then will that one table have made this little book well worth the cost of publishing.

Year	First Frost	Last Frost	Temperature.		Days			
			Highest	Lowest	Clear.	Fair	Cloudy	Rain
*1881	Sept 15	....	95.6°	− 6°	62	81	41	66
1882	" 20	May 22	93.7	−20	113	171	81	96
1883	July 17	April 30	99.2	−32	110	168	87	115
1884	Sept 11	May 13	95.9	−38	139	155	72	111
1885	" 1	June 8	98.2	−33	129	164	72	95
1886	Aug. 31	May 6	103.6	−33	121	180	64	118
1887	Sept. 15	" 3	99.2	−43	130	162	73	114
1888	" 12	" 18	101.7	−36	141	142	83	95
1889	" 5	" 2	104.0	−30	133	143	89	92
1890	Aug. 22	" 15	103.0	−28	151	150	64	90
1891	" 23	" 16	97.0	−24	135	136	94	92

Records from Huron, S. D., Signal Station.
*From July 1st 1881.

TO MEASURE THE HEIGHT OF A STREAM.

The following method will enable any one to easily and quickly measure the exact height of the stream thrown out by a well, without the use or instruments or of tables of tangents.

Referring to figure 11 let W be a well and EF the stream thrown. Carefully measure off a distance of say 100 feet and drive a stake S, to the level of the pipe if possible. Drive another 3 or 4 feet nearer and across the top nail a piece of board B; which set level. Measure off AC = 5 feet (or any other amount) and nail the stick H to this mark, and at right angles to AC. Now look over the point of the board at A and have some one mark on the stick H a point D in line with E the top of the stream EF. Measure the length CD, then may the height EF be found by simple proportion.

Example. AF = 100 ft. AC = 5 ft. CD = 4 ft. then,

AC : AF :: CD : FE or 5 : 100 :: 4 : (required height)

100 × 4 = 400, 400 ÷ 5 = 80 ft. = height of stream EF.

If the horizontal line AF will not strike the top of the pipe, as at Y, measure the distance YZ and subtract it from the total height found.

Although a rough method it is an easy one and sufficient accuracy may be obtained. If this is done by all wells, while throwing streams of different sizes, and a record made of the results it will be a vast improvement on the guess-work so freely indulged in heretofore.

Fig. 11.

Method of measuring height of a stream.

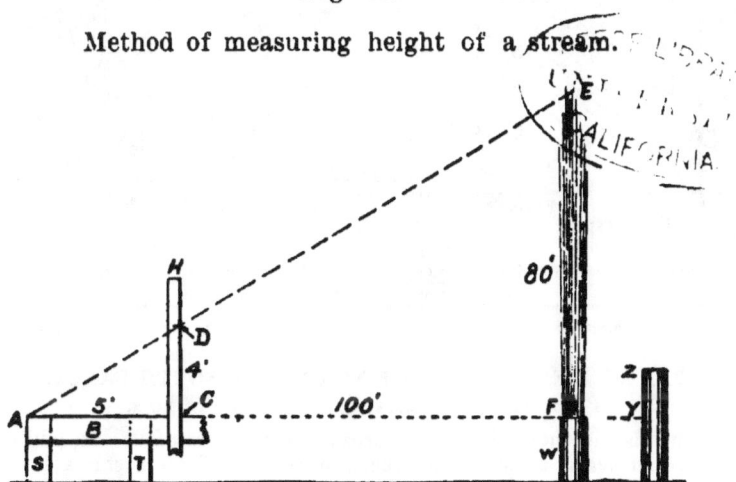

(See also page 147.)

From Harper's Magazine.

Copyright, 1889, by Harper & Brothers.

FIG 12. WEATHER MAP OF NORTH AND SOUTH DAKOTA.
By permission of Messrs. Harper & Brothers.

Showing isothermal lines and areas of varying-rainfall. It will be
seen that nearly all of the agricultural section of both states has a
range of rainfall of from 15—20 inches. This area should extend
farther to the South than shown on the map.

Fig. 13. View of Brick-Yard Well at Yankton, S. D.

From photograph by L. Janousek, Yankton.
By permission of Harper and Brothers.

Depth = 595 feet. Size of pipe = 6 inches.
Pressure = 48 to 57 lbs. per square inch.
Volume = 1620 to 2000 gallons per minute.
Location, on top of the Missouri river bluffs.
Use, for power. Cost, about $3,000.
The view as taken showed the well throwing a 6 inch stream about 6 feet above the top of a 20 foot stand-pipe. This well is one of a number of large wells in the southern portion of South Dakota having a comparatively low pressure and very large volume.

RESERVOIRS.

In the western states where irrigation by water taken from streams is the rule, and irrigation by well waters the exception, the waters are, in most cases, impounded at some place near their head waters where the topography is such as to admit of the construction of a dam which will create a reservoir in the valley wherein are stored the waters of the freshet season for use, many miles away, during the season of drouth. Such vast engineering works can only be entered upon by corporations possessing vast capital, for, in some cases, the dam, with flumes and ditches to convey the water to the irrigated districts, has cost over a million dollars.

The general government has already provided for the location, survey and reservation of all sites on the public domain where dams and reservoirs may, to advantage, be located in the future, and wise restrictions have been thrown around corporations securing such sites so as the best to protect the individual comsumers from corporate exactions

Vast tracts of the finest land in the world lie undeveloped and barren because the necessary capital has not yet been found to improve it by first constructing a dam and creating a reservoir for the storage of the necessary water.

· **IN DAKOTA** how different is all this?

There is not in the state a reservoir site worthy of the name and no money need be expended on great engineering works for the storage of water. Nor is there a stream that can, to advantage, be dammed. The Dakota reservoir will rarely if ever exceed 10 acres in area and in place of one covering many miles there may be several small ones on one mile.

When artesian irrigation was first agitated it was the popular belief that the well waters might be run directly into the ditches and thence distributed; but no thought was given to the fact that thereby the service of a well of but moderate volume would be very limited, for the water flowing within any given time would be insufficient, within that time, to cover any considerable area.

If, however, the waters could be stored in a reservoir during such periods as it was unnecessary to apply any to the land then when water *was* needed over a broad area, and within a brief period of time, the accumulated store could be made to do service which the well alone could not do in the same time. The necessity for small storage reservoirs being thus apparent they become as much a part of every irrigation plant as the well itself. In fact if the land under service of any particular well is quite rolling it may, and in many cases will, be necessary to have two or more small reservoirs on the farm in order to secure the best service to the land and the most economical storage and distribution.

Reservoirs being necessary, how and where shall they be built?

LOCATION.

The highest points will, of course, be the natural sites for reservoirs but the land may lay so as to make it not only better but cheaper not to locate the reservoir on the highest point. Such cases will be few and the conditions in mind will in all such cases be apparent to one on the ground. If a tract of land is divided into two or more parts by a gully or depression of any extent it may be best in such case to have two or three smaller reservoirs, one on each tract or division of the land. If but one large reservoir were built the other tracts or elevations would have to be served from flumes which would be larger and more expensive than one sufficient to feed the reservoir alone, and they might, at the critical time, fail to do proper service by reason of adverse winds or other causes thereby causing more loss than a reservoir would cost.

In ordinary cases the proper site for a reservoir may be selected by a farmer without the aid of an engineer but where any doubt exists as to the choice of locations then no chances should be taken and the services of one competent to judge should be secured.

FORM.

In most cases the circular form will be adopted because the greatest area is enclosed by a given amount of bank. Occasional departures from this form will be necessary by reason of the lay of the land.

Only the cicular form will be considered in the tables.

SIZE.

The matter of size will, in a few cases, be governed by the land but, as a rule, the *service* to be rendered by the waters stored will govern. If a township well is to be provided with storage then the volume of the well should be determined in order to know how small a reservoir would suffice not only to give service to the area to be irrigated but also to hold all the water the well will supply within the longest time it could be permitted to run without allowing the water in the reservoir to be drawn off. This would give all the necessary storage capacity without any waste of money in making it larger than needed.

Since most wells throw over 500 gallons per minute the time of impounding could not be long except with a very large reservoir. Table No. 37 taken in connection with tables 47 and 48 will quickly supply all needed information in this connection. From them it will be seen that a 500 gallon well will fill a 10-acre reservoir seven feet deep every 30 days, &c., &c. Where, as in case of a township well which will be used to serve several farmers, the volume used will be large the storage capacity should be as large as economy will warrant and each consumer might to his own advantage be supplied with a sub-reservoir. In case of special-service or sub-reservoirs which are designed to serve only a limited area as for example, a knoll of 10 or 15 acres then the water to be used on that area alone should be estimated and storage area provided only sufficient for that volume, allowance being made for seepage, evaporation and waste. Thus, assume a field of 10 acres to be supplied by a sub-reservoir and volume sufficient provided to flood the land 6 inches; what would be the size of reservoir required if the water be given a depth of 5 feet in the reservoir? Table 34 or table 21 gives the cubic feet of water required to flood 10 acres 6 inches deep as 217,800. Table 29, under head of water 5 feet deep, shows at a glance that a reservoir of 1½ acres will hold this volume and enough more to cover all waste. Table 45 gives the diameter, circumference and area of this reservoir.

These suggestions will show the importance of duly considering the elements of volume of well, time it may flow, area to be served, &c., in the laying out of a reservoir for either general or special service. The depth of water in the reservoir will always enter into the consideration.

Where any considerable volume is required it will be best to have the depth in excess of 4 feet, *first*, because if the water is deeper the reservoir will occupy less ground for a given capacity; *second*, the evaporation will be less, the exposed area being less, and the waste from seepage will be less; *third*, the wash of the banks will be less because the wind will have less sweep over the surface.

Table of sizes.

Table No. 45 shows the diameters, circumferences, and areas in sq. ft. of reservoirs from ⅛ acre to 10 acres, for each ¼ acre, and explanation follows as to calculating the elements for other sizes.

LAYING OUT.

The size having been determined the staking out follows. If the reservoir is to cover a given area the whole bank will be within that area and the foot of the outer slope will bound the given area. If the area is to *exclude* the bank the foot of the inner slope will bound the area. If the water is to cover a given area then the high water line or the point half way down the bank therefrom will bound the given area. Or the area may be bounded by the center line either of the *whole* bank or of the *top* of the bank.

Usually these considerations will not be of much importance, but in case of joint ownership or of contracting for the construction they may be important and should then be clearly understood and carefully specified. In staking out it will be best, for the convenience of graders, to drive stakes on the outer and inner lines of the bank. The line of the top follows as a result of the slopes.

The measurement may be made with a measured wire one end of which is fastened or held at the center while the outer end is carried around and stakes driven at convenient distances along the circle. If wire cannot be had then rope or even binding twine will answer the purpose.

If the land is uneven or covered with stubble, corn stalks, growing grain or other obstructions which prevent swinging the wire or line around the center point then two persons may manage the wire or line as follows.—A holds one end at the center while B drives stakes at the north points; *(At both the inner and outer slopes of the banks.)* both then walk south across the circle until B reaches the center when A drives the south stakes; they then walk back, B turning a little to the east or west, until A comes again to the center while B drives stakes at the outer end; A then, as before, walks straight across the circle and drives other stakes. Repeat this until the circuit of the circle has been made and all the stakes set. The result is the same but the walking a little more. Any farmer can thus lay out his own reservoir, if need be, in an hour's time and do it as well as it could be done by an engineer at an expense to the farmer of $5 to $10. The outlines having been staked out, and the stakes numbered, the levels should be taken to determine the height of the bank at each stake. If the ground is not fairly level the stakes will have to be set in or out to give the proper base line according to the length of the slope.

Where the ground is comparatively level any farmer can do his own leveling not only for reservoirs but for ditches, but where it is rolling the services of an engineer should be secured as a measure of economy. Better to pay for having the work properly done by responsible parties than to do it wrong and then be obliged to have it done over again.

See notes on leveling, page 128 and following pages.

THE BANKS.

The banks should be constructed of as firm earth as possible in order to give strength and prevent percolation and washing, and they should be thrown up by drag scrapers which results in a more solid and firmly packed bank than can be made by the use of wheel scrapers or graders unless the work with the latter be properly done. (See embankments and footings—under head of Ditches.) The outer slope may be one of 1½ horizontal to 1 vertical. The breadth of the top will depend upon the height and strength required. Most reservoirs will be 9 feet or less in height and for such heights a width of top of 5 feet will be sufficient. Where the bank exceeds 9 feet in height an additional foot in width may be added for each 2 feet of additional height, the slopes remaining the same.

Fig. 14, on the next page shows in sectional diagram the inner slopes of banks from 1 ft. to 14 ft. high and with slopes of 2 to 1. The horizontal lines indicate the water levels and the diagonal lines the slopes of the banks. The upper horizontal line of figures indicate the distances of the foot of the banks from the top (measured horizontally;) and the lower line of figures the amount the *diameter* of the reservoir is reduced by banks of the different heights. Thus, if the bank is 8 feet high and the water 4 ft. deep the shore line will be at A and the area of the water surface will have a diameter 21 feet less than that of the reservoir (measured to center line of top.) To get the volume, take the diameter half way down the bank, at C, which is 29 ft. less than the total diameter, and proceed as explained in the tables. The further use of the diagram will be apparent. Similar diagrams may easily be constructed for use with other slopes or for banks of greater height than here given.

As to construction of footings for banks see remarks under head of Ditches, on page 119, and as to cost of grading, &c., see "Excavation and Cost," P. 117.

Fig. 14.

Slope Diagram for Banks of Reservoirs.

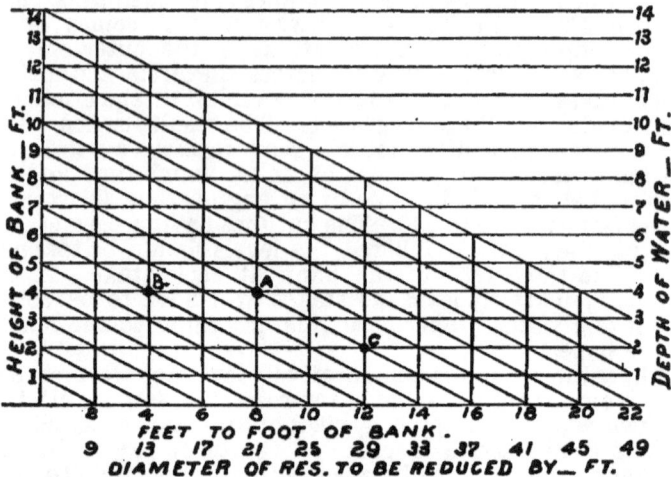

FEET TO FOOT OF BANK.

DIAMETER OF RES. TO BE REDUCED BY— FT.

Table No. 44 shows the cross sections of banks from 3 ft. to 10 ft. high; with area of cross sections and cubic yards of earth per lineal foot and per 100 feet.

This table will be of use to contractors and graders.

To find the cubic contents of a bank × the area of the cross section by the length of the bank in feet and then divide by 27. Thus, in first example given in the table, the area of the cross section = 6 × 10 = 60) Total
20 × 5 = 100 } = 235
15 × 5 = 75) sq. ft.

this × 1656 (the circumference of a 6 acre reservoir) = 389,160 cubic feet which ÷ 27 = 14,413 cu. yds.; by table—870.37. the cu. yds. in 100 ft- × 16.56 = 14.413 the same as by the other and longer method.

WASHING OF BANKS.

The washing down of the banks by the waves in the reservoir is a matter of much importance and yet little can be said as to the best means of preventing it. Where, as is the case in some sections, there are plenty of stone the water line may be partially protected by riprapping with them but this involves a large amount of labor. In most sections of the state there are no stone so other means must be used. In sections near the James, or other rivers, along which willows grow these willows may, at but little expense, be transplanted in the banks where they will form a self maintaining protection. Nor can this expedient be practiced by but few. The tough prairie sods taken from the surface of the ditch may be laid aside and be afterward laid along the water line. This has been tried and has worked well and, although much labor is involved it probably remains the best for general use. Where gravel may be had a shore line may be covered with it thus forming a natural water break. In some cases it may be best to construct a break-water of plank sharpened and driven into the bank or laid to posts set in the bank. The steeper the bank the greater of course will be the displacement of the earth by wave action.

Outlets and Gates—See P. 107.

TABLE NO. 44. CROSS SECTIONS OF RESERVOIR BANKS
WITH AREAS AND CUBIC CONTENTS.   New.

SECTIONS	Area of cross section Sq. ft.	Cu Yds perft of bank	Cu. Yds. per 100 ft. of bank.
	2.35	8.7037	870.37
	189.	7.0	700.0
	152.	5.6296	562.96
	122.5	4.5370	453.70
	93.	3.4444	344.44
	70.	2.5925	259.25
	48.	1.7777	177.77
	31.5	1.1666	116.66
	44.	1.6296	162.96
	28.5	1.0505	105.05

TABLE NO. 45.   RESERVOIR TABLE.

Diameters, Circumferences and Areas in square ft. of reservoirs from ⅛ acre to 10 acres in area — advancing by ¼ acre.

New.

Area in Acres.	Diameter in feet.	Circmuference in feet.	Area in Square feet.
⅛	83+	261	5 455
¼	118—	371	10 890
½	167—	525	21 780
¾	204—	641	32 670
1	235—	738	43 560
¼	263+	826	54 450
½	288+	905	65 340
¾	312—	980	76 230
2	333+	1046	87 120
¼	353+	1109	98 010
½	372+	1169	108 900
¾	391—	1228	119 790
3	408—	1282	130 680
¼	425—	1335	141 570
½	441—	1385	152 460
¾	456+	1433	163 350
4	471+	1480	174 240
¼	486—	1527	185 130
½	500—	1571	196 020
¾	513+	1612	206 910
5	527—	1656	217 800
¼	540—	1696	228 690
½	552+	1734	239 580
¾	565—	1775	250 470
6	577—	1813	261 360
¼	589—	1850	272 250
½	601—	1888	283 140
¾	612—	1923	294 030
7	623+	1957	304 920
¼	634+	1992	315 810
½	645—	2026	326 700
¾	656—	2061	337 590
8	666+	2092	348 480
¼	676+	2124	359 370
½	687—	2158	370 260
¾	697—	2189	381 150
9	707—	2221	392 040
¼	716+	2249	402 930
½	726—	2281	413 820
¾	735+	2309	424 710
10	745—	2340	435 600

NOTE—In the above table the diameters and circumferences are taken to the nearest foot. The area in square feet is correct for the given areas in acres. The signs of + and — after the diameters indicate whether the diameters given are too large or too small. Thus, 83 + indicates that a fraction of a foot, less than ½, must be added to 83 to give the true diameter; and 118 — indicates that a fraction less than ½ foot must be taken from 118 to give the true diameter; 83 is therefore a little too small and 118 a little too large—less than ½ foot in each case. See explanation on

Explanation as to table 45. Table No. 45 is constructed from table 72; the areas in square feet having first been calculated. The area in sq. ft. of a 5 acre res. being 217,800 enter table 72 in the column of areas and find 2181.28 as the area of a circle whose diameter is 52.7 and circumference 165.56. This tabular area agrees most nearly with the given area in sq. ft.

Therefore, for a circle of 527 ft. diam. the circumference would be 1655.6 ft. (*decimal point* **ONE** *place to the right.*) and the area 218,128.(*decimal point* **TWO** *places to the right.*) This area corresponds most nearly to the given area and hence the diameter and circumference are the ones most nearly corresponding to the given area. If diameter is less than 100 the area and circumf. may be taken directly from the table. If diameter is more than 100 and less than 1000 enter the table 72 and from the first column take the whole number and decimal corresponding to the given diameter; then, for the area, move the decimal point TWO places, and for the circumference ONE place, to the right. Example, required the circumference and area of a circle or reservoir having a diameter of 472 ft.? In table 72 opposite 47.2 (472) find circumf. = 1482.8 and area = 174 974.1 [*The decimal points having been moved as above described·*] The area in acres is found by dividing the area in sq. ft. by 43560.

If either the diameter, circumf. or area in sq. ft. or acres be given all the other elements may thus be found from table 72.

EVAPORATION AND FILTRATION.

Evaporation is the greatest during warm or windy weather; greater in shallow than in deep water and greater in running than in still water. The evaporation from a ditch or reservoir during June, July and Aug. will rarely exceed .3 to .4 inch per day. During the remaining months the average will be about .1 inch making for the year from 3 to 5 feet of loss by evaporation. To the loss by evaporation must be added the loss by seepage or filtration either into the earth or through the banks. The amount of seepage through the banks will depend not only upon the character of the soil of which they are made but also upon the solidity with which they have been thrown up. So with the seepage into the earth. If the soil is of soft loam, sand or gravel the percentage of loss will be much greater than if the sub-soil is of clay or hard-pan.

The loss from both evaporation and seepage from a properly constructed reservoir on average ground may be assumed to be about 1 inch per day after the reservoir has been in use for a season. The following table will show the approximate volume of loss per day in gallons from reservoirs of different areas.

	Area acres	Loss in Gallons.	Area acres	Loss in Gallons.
TABLE NO. 46.				
Showing loss in Reservoirs	1	27100	6	162000
from Evaporation and Filtration.	2	54300	7	190000
Approximate only.	3	81400	8	217000
	4	108600	9	244000
	5	135700	10	271000

TABLE NO. 47.

TABLE SHOWING AREA IN SQUARE FEET AND ACRES; ALSO DIAMETERS AND CIRCUMFERENCES OF RESERVOIRS FROM ONE ACRE TO TEN ACRES : ALSO CUBIC YARDS OF EARTH IN THE BANKS IF 4 6 OR 8 FEET HIGH.

Acres in Reservoirs	Area in square feet	Diam in ft to center line of bank	Circum in ft on center line of bank	Diam. at foot of bank 8 feet high, ft	Circum in feet on this line	Area in sq. feet within this line	Area in acres within this line	Diam. at foot of bank 6 feet high, ft	Circum in feet on this line	Area in sq. ft. within this line	Area in acres within this line	Cu. yds in bank 4 feet high	Cu. yds in bank 6 feet high	Cu. yds in bank 8 feet high
1	43 560	235	738	198	622	30 790	.70	206	647	33 329	.77	1 312	2 542	4 155
2	87 120	333	1 046	296	930	68 814	1.58	304	955	72 584	1.66	1 859	3 603	5 888
3	130 680	408	1 282	371	1 166	108 103	2.48	379	1190	112 816	2.59	2 279	4 419	7 217
4	174 240	471	1 480	434	1 363	147 935	3.39	442	1389	153 439	3.52	2 631	5 098	8 332
5	217 800	527	1 656	491	1 543	189 345	4.34	499	1568	195 565	4.49	2 944	5 704	9 323
6	261 360	577	1 813	540	1 696	229 022	5.26	548	1722	235 859	5.41	3 223	6 245	10 206
7	304 920	623	1 957	586	1 841	269 703	6.19	594	1866	277 117	6.36	3 479	6 741	11 017
8	348 480	666	2 092	629	1 976	310 736	7.13	637	2001	318 691	7.32	3 718	7 206	11 777
9	392 040	707	2 221	669	2 102	351 514	8.07	677	2127	359 972	8.26	3 948	7 650	12 502
10	435 600	745	2 340	708	2 224	393 693	9.04	716	2249	402 640	9.24	4 160	8 060	13 172

See table on next page.

In the above table the diameters and circumferences are given to the nearest foot. In the first section of the table it is assumed that the center of the top of the bank is on the line of the circumference of the area given. If it is desired to cover a given area with the reservoir then the circumference would be at the foot of the outer slope of the bank all of which would be *within* the given area. If the *water* is to cover a given area then the circumference would be half way between high water mark and the foot of the bank, and most of the bank would lie *outside* of the given area. In the 2d and 3d sections are given areas, etc., where the banks are 6 and 8 feet high and where the available water area is assumed to be the area within the *foot* of the bank. The 4th section shows the cubic yards of earth in the banks 4, 6 and 8 feet high and having sections as shown on page 101.

TABLE NO. 48.

RESERVOIR TABLE, SHOWING DIAMETER AND AREA OF WATER AREA, in reservoirs of different sizes; with Volume in Cubic feet and Gallons, with depths of 3, 5 and 7 feet; in reservoirs having banks 8 ft high. The water diameter is taken at a point half way between the water line and the foot of the bank.

Reservoir in Acres	Water 3 feet deep in reservoir				Water 5 ft. deep in reservoir				Water 7 ft. deep in reservoir			
	Diam. in feet.	Area in square feet.	Volume in Cubic ft.	Gallons.	Diam in feet	Area in square feet	Volume in Cubic ft.	Gallons.	Diam in feet	Area in square feet	Volume in Cubic ft.	Gallons.
1	204	32 635	98 055	733 500	208	33 980	169 900	1 270 939	212	35 300	247 100	1 848 435
2	302	71 632	214 896	1 607 533	306	73 542	367 710	2 750 661	310	75 477	528 339	3 952 250
3	377	111 628	334 884	2 505 105	381	114 009	570 045	4 264 233	385	116 416	814 912	6 095 961
4	440	152 053	456 159	3 412 306	444	154 831	774 155	5 791 082	448	157 633	1 103 431	8 254 237
5	496	193 220	579 660	4 336 156	500	196 350	983 750	7 358 960	504	199 504	1 386 528	10 446 754
6	546	234 140	702 420	5 254 467	550	237 584	1 187 920	8 886 257	554	241 052	1 687 364	12 622 359
7	592	275 254	825 762	6 177 128	596	278 987	1 394 935	10 434 838	600	282 744	1 979 208	14 805 504
8	635	316 693	950 079	7 107 085	639	320 695	1 603 475	11 994 826	643	324 723	2 273 061	17 003 678
9	676	358 909	1 076 727	8 054 477	680	363 169	1 815 845	13 583 464	684	367 454	2 572 178	19 241 229
10	714	400 394	1 201 182	8 985 465	718	404 893	2 024 465	15 144 051	722	409 416	2 865 912	21 438 511

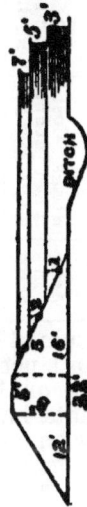

Fig. 15.

This table will be of great use but chiefly as a basis for other estimates. If the bank is but 6 feet high the inner slope will not be so long and the reservoir will be *larger* for any given depth of water. The difference in volume will not be great, however, and a close approximation may be taken from the table. So, too, for other depths it will do to take volumes intermediate to those here given. Example—What will be the capacity of a 5 acre reservoir with 6 ft. bank and water 4 ft. deep? From table—vol. in gal. for 5 ft. = 7,388,960 and for 3 ft. vol. = 5,847,558 and for 3 ft. vol. = 4,336,156. Difference = 3,022,804 which ÷ 2 = 1,511,402 which added to vol. for 3 ft. = 5,847,558 vol. for 4 ft. Assume the addition of 150,000 gals. for increased size of reservoir and we have 5,997,558 as the required approximate volume. The actual volume is 39,365 gals. greater, or a volume too small to be of importance in the calculation. In the table no account has been taken of the ditch or of any irregularity of the the surface. If irregularity exists take the *average* height of the bank as the height all around. Accompanying figure illustrates the table. Points 1, 2 and 3 are points from which diameters are measured.

TABLE NO. 49.

COST OF RESERVOIRS.

With banks 4, 6 and 8 feet high, and at rates of 6 and 8 cents per cubic yard for moving earth. (To cost of embankment add cost of outlets, gates, protection for banks, etc.)

New.

Area in Acres	Cu Yds in bank 4 feet high	Cost, at 6 cts per yd.	Cost, at 8 cts per yd.	Cu yds in bank 6 feet high	Cost, at 6 cts per yd	Cost, at 8 cts per yd.	Cu. yds in bank 8 feet high	Cost, at 6 cts per yd.	Cost, at 8 cts per yd.
1	1312	$79	$105	2542	$153	$203	4155	$249	$332
2	1859	112	149	3603	216	288	5888	353	471
3	2279	137	182	4419	265	354	7217	433	577
4	2631	158	210	5098	306	408	8332	500	657
5	2944	177	236	5704	342	456	9323	559	746
6	3223	193	258	6245	375	500	10206	612	816
7	3479	209	278	6741	404	539	11017	661	882
8	3718	223	297	7206	432	576	11777	707	942
9	3948	237	316	7650	459	608	12502	750	1000
10	4160	250	333	8060	484	645	13172	790	1054

NOTE—It is assumed that the price of moving earth will be from 6 to 8 cents per yard at which rate (8c) most of the sub-contract work on Dakota Ry. grades has been let, the lesser rate of 6 cents has, in some cases, been paid. If the cost is desired for an embankment of any other size or cross section the length may be taken directly from table 45, the cross section from table 44 and the cubic yards then quickly calculated and multiplied by the price agreed upon, in order to get the total cost. This table will answer most purposes and will be of value for ready reference.

Continued from page 100.

OUTLETS AND GATES.

OUTLETS. The outlets or culverts through the banks to the main ditches should be set before the bank is built and with refeference to the location of the ditches. The size of the outlet will be governed by the amount of water to be delivered to the ditch. If the ditch is small or short the size may be smaller than for a large or long ditch. In the latter case make the outlet large enough to deliver the requisite amount of water at a velocity not so great as to wash the banks of the ditch. The outlets may be made of plank or of sewer pipe, the latter being especially good, but, in most cases, not so readily obtainable. The earth should be well tamped about the box or pipe in order to make a water tight joint.

By reason of the difference in sizes of the outlets, the difference in length through banks of different breadths, and with the difference in the head due to constant lowering of the water in the reservoir, and the different methods of constructing the outlets, no precise data can be given as to the relative discharging capacities of different sizes of outlets but the following table will give the approximate volumes in cubic feet per minute discharged.

TABLE NO. 50.

FLOW OF WATER FROM RESERVOIRS.

New.

Head of water in feet.	Outlet 12×12 inches	Outlet 12×24 inches	Outlet 12×36 inches	Outlet 24×24 inches	Outlet 24×36 inches	
2	400	800	1200	1600	2400	
3	500	1000	1500	2000	3000	
4	575	1150	1725	2300	3450	Cubic ft.
5	650	1300	1950	2600	3900	per min.
6	720	1440	2160	2880	4320	

GATES. The gates should be set at the the inner end of the outlets and a plank walk built from the top of the bank leading out over the water to a point over the gate in order that the gate may be lifted. In construction the gate is most simple; any farmer or carpenter being competent to make them. A tightly fitting slide over the end of the box or pipe outlet being all that is necessary to shut off the water. The gate may be raised or lowered by a stick of 2×4 bolted to the front of the gate and leading up through slides or guide holes in the end of the walk. Simple means too, may be provided for fastening the gate either up or down. The pressure of the water against the gate will keep it in position and preserve a tight joint if the sliding surfaces have been properly dressed or surfaced. Guides should be provided in the sliding supports so as to make sure that the gate will return to its seat when it is desired to lower it. Modifications of detail are many and will suggest themselves to any one as the conditions of the work or the setting may require.

Fig. 16 shows a simple and common form of gate.

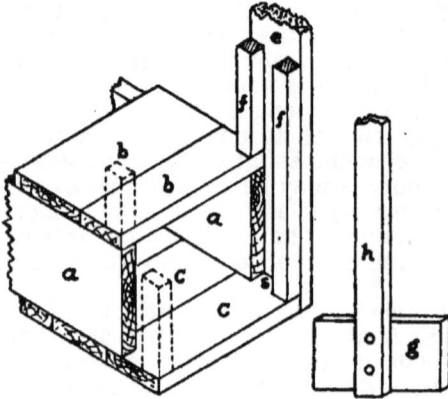

Fig. 16.

Simple form of gate. aa=side plank of outlet box. bb and cc = top and bottom plank of outlet box. e = upright plank supporting outer end of walk. ff = guides for gate. s = space in which gate slides. g=gate. h = hoisting timber.

Sub Reservoirs and Storage Ditches.

As previously stated it may be best to have two or more reservoirs on the same farm or under service by the same well. These may be on different ridges or knolls and may be directly connected with the well or with each other by piping, flumes or ditches. A sub reservoir may be provided to receive the waters elevated from lower ditches or pools by wind mills or water rams. In many cases storage ditches will be necessary to give proper service to areas at a considerable distance from the well or reservoir. A storage ditch is merely a *big ditch*, or one made higher and wider than the ordinary main ditch so as to hold in store a large volume of water ready for immediate service through lateral ditches to the adjacent lands. Such a ditch or canal along a quarter line might better serve adjacent farms than a reservoir of any other form, or if located along the top of a narrow ridge where a large circular reservoir would be impracticable or needlessly expensive.

For the volume of water stored a storage ditch requires a greater cubic capacity of embankment and hence a greater proportionate cost than a circular reservoir; but the economy of space, the lay of the land or the character of the service to be rendered may more than compensate for the increased proportionate cost.

DISTRIBUTION OF WATER BY DITCHES, FLUMES AND PIPES.

The water having been obtained and stored the next consideration is as to its conveyance from the well or reservoir to any desired place and then its distribution over the land to be irrigated.

The distinctive feature of the great irrigation systems of the west, and of other countries, is the great length, size, and expense of the ditches and flumes necessary to convey the water from the storage reservoirs or rivers to the low-lying irrigated lands. These ditches are often of great size and extend for many miles; the cost reaching tens or hundreds of thousands of dollars. Great viaducts of masonry, or trestles of timber or iron, to carry the canal over rivers or valleys, deep cuts along the mountain sides, flumes suspended over or along precipitous canyons, tunnels through the rock hills, and enormous dams and head gates are features of great interest, as well as of expense, common to the distribution of irrigation waters in regions less favored than our own.

How tame, in comparison, will be the means of distribution on the Dakota prairies and under the individual system of irrigation by wells. Our people may well forego the glory of being the possessors of world renowned works of engineering skill, for the sake of the greater economy and the honorable distinction of being the possessors of the largest and most fertile valley in America, wherein irrigation may be more cheaply inaugurated and maintained than in any other state·

All the leading features of other systems, such as dams, head-works, main canals, pipe lines, viaducts, &c., will not be known here. Probably few ditches will be larger than 10 feet at the bottom, and but few will be over 5 miles in length. Pipe lines will be small, and flumes will be low and short. In brief, there will be no heavy or expensive features attached to the distribution of water in this prairie country, and hence the great economy of an irrigation system in Dakota.

The *result* sought by all systems is the *bringing of water to the land.*

While it may sound well, or arouse in one the spirit of pride, to say that we have the largest dam, the largest or the longest ditch, the longest tunnel, or the highest flume in the world, it is a distinction the wary capitalist will willingly forego for the more humble statement that, *for a given outlay,* we have under water a larger number of acres than can be shown any where else. This will be the pride of the Dakota irrigator. He will point not to his towering masonry, not to his navigable canal system, not to his sky-scraping trestle-work, nor to the dismal depths of a hole through a hill, but with pride to his perennial fountain, to his simple ditches and to his broad expanse of fertile fields, where more that is of profit may be seen, as the result of a dollar spent, than can be shown by any of his neighbors in other states.

If this true picture does not soon attract the scrutinizing eye of capital, and Dakota ere long become their chosen pasture, then, indeed, will all signs fail.

Water is conveyed from point of supply to place of distribution in ditches, flumes, or pipes, and is distributed over the land through smaller, lateral-ditches or by plow furrows, by the actual flooding of the surface, or by means of sub-irrigation through lines of tile pipes; the latter system however, being confined almost exclusively to the irrigation of garden and orchard lands.

Volumes might be written on the subject of water distribution and allied subjects, but the limit of this little book will admit of but brief reference to some of the matters most likely to engage the attention of our farmers.

DITCHES.

Form and Size.

According to a classification adopted by the Census Department of Agriculture, irrigation ditches are divided into three classes.

First, those under 5 feet in width,

Second, those from 5 to 10 feet wide, and

Third, those over 10 feet wide on the bottom, the depth in a general way corresponding with these widths being 1 foot, 1½ feet, and 2½ feet and over. By reason of the comparatively small volumes of water to be carried, and the restricted area to be served from any one source, the Dakota irrigation ditches will be mostly small; few, it is safe to say, need be as large as 10 feet in width. A ditch need be only large enough to convey the water to the place whence it is to be distributed. By "large enough" is meant, of such a size as will deliver the volume of water needed, at a velocity not so great as to wash the banks of the ditch, and not so large as to present a needless excess of surface of bank, which will increase the percentage of seepage, or of surface to the air, which will increase the percentage of evaporation.

In large ditches much depends upon the form or sectional outline of the excavation and banks. In smaller ditches this is of less importance so long as the flow is not impeded by the roughness of the sides or by the abrupt changes of direction.

The same degree of care in the original construction and future maintenance of ditches cannot be secured in a section where irrigation is first practiced, and where the new irrigator has yet to learn the importance of close attention to details, as in a section where irrigation has long been practiced and where each detail of the operation has been reduced to a system.

The sooner attention is given to the careful and workmanlike construction of ditches, the sooner will the labor devoted to irrigation return a satisfactory profit. A channel, roughly scratched in the ground is not a ditch, and, however much the owner may believe in its sufficiency to give proper service, the flowing water cannot be deceived and will not do its full service until given the opportunity which the laws of of hydraulics have decreed.

The main distributing ditches should be built for permanent use. The smaller or distributing laterals may, in certain cases, be cheaply built to serve the purpose for a season. They may be thrown out by a double-mould-board plow or as a single plow furrow. The larger sections can be most cheaply built with ditching machines. The section of the ditch may have the form shown in Fig. 17, where the slope of the bank in the cut or excavation is one foot horizontal to one foot vertical. The excavated earth may, and usually will, be put into the banks as shown at *A*, or it may be placed as shown at *B*, where a berm, or ledge, b is left at the sides of the ditch. The slope of the banks in the embankment being 1½ to 1.

Fig. 17

If excess earth is required to build the bank higher or wider either the ditch may be made wider and deeper or the extra earth may be obtained from side ditches or borrow-pits *D*, or by both means. It is the province of the engineer to direct as to thse details of the work so we will here consider only such details as relate to the ordinary work which the farmer himself may be required to perform. For all ordinary purposes of distribution from the reservoirs to the more distant laterals, main ditches from 4 to 6 feet wide will suffice. (The width of ditch, as stated, is understood to be the width at the bottom.)

The construction should be workmanlike, the bottom even and free from sods, stones, lumps, of clay,or weeds; the sides smooth, even, and free from like obstructions to the even and free flow of the water.

Fig. 18 represents the cross section of a ditch 4 feet wide and having water 3 feet deep. The area of Fig. 18 the wet section of the ditch is equal to the average width multiplied by the depth. In this case

$$\frac{10 \text{ ft.} + 4 \text{ ft}}{2} = \frac{14}{2} = 7, \qquad 7 \times 3 = 21 \text{ sq. ft.} = \text{area of wet section}$$

The Wet Perimeter in the length of that portion of the surface of the cross-section which is covered by water, $A B$, BC, CD In order to determine this length, the length of the slopes $A B$ and $C D$ must be known. These may be found, for any depth of water or for any degree of slope—as follows: The slope is the hypothenuse of the right-angled triangle $A B E$, and its length is therefore equal to the square root of the sum of the squares of the other two sides. In this case the sides $A E$ and $E B$ are each equal (the slope being 1 to 1) to 3 feet. The sum of the squares of $A E$ & $E B$ $=9+9=18$. The square root of 18 (see table of roots)$=4.2$, which is therefore the length of $A B$. If the slope had been $1\frac{1}{2}$ to 1, $A E$ would $= 4.5$ feet which squared$=20.25$ which $+9$, the square of $E B$, $= 29.25$ the sq. rt. of which$=5.4=$ length of $A B$. So with any other depth or degree of slope. In this case the wet perimeter $- 4.2+4+4.2=12.4$ feet.

The *"mean radius," "hydraulic radius," "hydraulic mean depth"* and *"mean depth"* are synonymous terms for the

$$\frac{\text{area of wet cross section}}{\text{wet perimeter}} \quad \text{or} \quad \frac{\text{area } A\,B\,C\,D,}{(AB+BC+CD)} \text{ or, as in}$$

the above illustration, $\dfrac{21 \text{ sq. ft.}}{12.4} = 1.69 = \text{mean radius.}$

This term, "mean radius," is frequently used in the calculation of volumes, grades, and velocities, by Kutter's and other formulae and it is is therefore explained,

Since most slopes will be 1 to 1 or $1\frac{1}{2}$ to 1, and most depths from 1 to 5 feet, and most widths from 2 to 6 feet, the following table has been prepared to show at once the lengths of the slopes $A B$ and $C D$ for slopes of 1 to 1, and of $1\frac{1}{2}$ to 1, and for depths of 1 to 5 feet; also the wet areas of ditches, having bottom widths of 2 to 6 feet, and water from 2 to $2\frac{1}{2}$ feet deep; also the lengths of the wet perimeter, and the corresponding mean radii.

Application—The water in a ditch, having side slopes of 1 to 1, is $3\frac{1}{4}$ feet deep, what is the length of the wetted slope $A B$? In second column, opposite depth of $3\frac{1}{4}$, is $4.6=$ length in feet required. In third column is $5.8=$corresponding length when slope$=1\frac{1}{2}$ to 1. A ditch has $2\frac{1}{2}$ feet of water and a bottom width of 5 feet, what is area of wet section, length of wet perimeter and mean radius? Under head of depth of 2½ feet take width of 5 feet; in succeeding columns find $A+18.75$ sq. ft., $P=12$ ft., and $R=1.56$. The limits of the table will serve for the ordinary range of work and will no doubt save some time in making calculations.

TABLE NO. 51.

TABLE OF DEPTHS, SLOPES, WET AREAS, WET PERIMETERS AND MEAN RADII OF SMALL DITCHES. *New.*

Slope of bank 1 hor. to 1 vert. Depth of water in feet	Length of slope (ab) in ft	Slope of bk 1½ to 1 Length of slope (ab) in feet	Depth of water in ditches, ft.	Bottom width of ditch, ft.	Area of wet section, sq. feet.	Length of wet perimeter in ft	Mean Radius
1	1.4	1.8	D.	W.	A.	P.	R.
1¼	1.8	2.2	1	2	3.	4.8	.625
1½	2.1	2.7	1	3	4.	5.8	.690
1¾	2.5	3.2	1	4	5.	6.8	.735
2	2.8	3.6	1	5	6.	7.8	.76?
2¼	3.2	4.1	1½	2	5.25	6.2	.847
2½	3.5	4.5	1½	3	6.75	7.2	.937
2¾	3.9	4.9	1½	4	8.25	8.2	1.01
3	4.2	5.4	1½	5	9.75	9.2	1.06
3¼	4.6	5.8	2	2	8.	7.6	1.05
3½	4.9	6.3	2	3	10.	8.6	1.16
3¾	5.3	6.7	2	4	12.	9.6	1.25
4	5.7	7.2	2	5	14.	10.6	1.32
4¼	6.0	7.6	2	6	16.	11.6	1.38
4½	6.4	8.1	2½	3	13.75	10.	1.37
4¾	6.7	8.5	2½	4	16.25	11.	1.48
5	7.1	9.0	2½	5	18.75	12.	1.56
			2½	6	21.25	13.	1.63
			2½	7	23.75	14.	1.70

Flow of Water in Ditches.

This complex branch of dydraulics is treated exhaustively in several large works on the subject, it being of prime importance in countries where water is taken from rivers, or from large storage basins, and carried for miles in large canals or ditches. Important, because upon its proper treatment rests the accurate gauging of rivers and canals, or the measurement of the volume of water flowing in them. On a knowledge of the exact volume of the supply rests the matter of the volume of apportionment to different districts or ditches.

Many mechanical divices are used for measuring the velocities of running streams, and many formulae and rules are given for the calculation of the velocity and volume.

The Dakota system of irrigation being so entirely different, the necessity for the accurate measurement of water in ditches is almost entirely done away with; so but brief mention will be made of a few points in this connection. The measurement of most ditches and streams is in the unit of the cubic foot per second; or the number of cubic feet of water the stream will discharge in one second. The discharge—for a given depth of water in the ditch—will depend upon the slope or grade of the ditch, the area of the section, the condition of the bottom and banks, and upon the direction and force of the wind, which exerts a considerable effect upon the exposed surface of the water. [One-tenth of the width of surface being allowed for wind resistance.]

As above explained, the sectional area of any ditch, or of the wet section thereof, is equal to the average width × by the depth.

The velocity of a running stream is not the same at all points of the cross-section, it being least at the bottom and sides, where the friction is greatest, and less at the surface than at a point a short distance below it. The point of greatest velocity is therefore at the middle of the stream and just below the surface. To determine the velocity of any stream it becomes necessary, therefore, to determine the *mean velocity*, or such a velocity as would be common to all the threads of water of the stream if the discharge remained the same and all flowed at the same rate.

Current meters and other mechanical devices are used to determine the velocity of the current at several points in the cross-section. and from a reduction of these observations a mean is obtained for the whole section.

Intricate formulae are likewise employed to determine the velocity and discharge, mathematically; but their application, involving a considerable knowledge of mathematics and hydraulics, they are not popular with the average irrigator. The simplest way to determine the approximate mean velocity of a stream is to take a certain percentage of the ascertained *maximum surface velocity*. By experiment the *mean velocity* has been found to be from 80 to 85 per cent of the maximum surface velocity. In this country 80 per cent is usually taken as the standard. To determine the maximum surface velocity, select a straight section of ditch, in good repair, and stake out a section of 100 feet. Place in the current—at a short distance above the upper stake—a small block of wood, so that when it passes the upper stake it will have acquired the velocity of the water. Note carefully the exact time of its passage of both the upper and the lower stakes, and record the interval. Repeat this, say four or five times. and take an average of the intervals to get the nearest true interval.

Example,—1st. interval = 25 seconds.
        2d.   "   24   "
        3d.   "   25 . "
        4th.   "   26   "
                          100 which ÷ 4 = 25 sec. = average interval. If the current runs 100 feet in 25 seconds it runs $\frac{100}{25}$ = 4 feet per second, = *maximum surface velocity*. 80 per cent of 4 feet = 3.2 feet per second = the *mean* velocity of the stream.

The volume in cubic feet discharged will of course equal the wet area × by the mean velocity. Assume the ditch to be 5 feet wide and the water 2 feet deep. From table No. 51 we find the wet section to have an area of 14 square feet. Then 14 × 3.2 (area × mean vel.) = 44.8 = cubic feet per second discharged. Table 36 shows this to be equal to 335

gallons per second. The section of ditch should be in good
condition and fairly uniform in section.

The determination of the velocity and volume, as above
described, necessitates the *measurement* of the surface velocity. Where formulae are used this is not necessary.

As above stated, the use of formulae not being convenient
to the average irrigator, and the space within the limit of
this little book being insufficient to properly explain even
the simpler ones, the subject will not be considered. The
reader being referred to such standard works as Trautwine's
Engineer's Pocket Book—where the formula of Kutter is
fully explained and illustrated by examples and tables of
coefficients (P. 571 to 279b, in editions of 1888 or 1891); Wiesbach's Mechanics, where is found a much simpler formula,
and one more convenient, with table of coefficients; and to
the recent exhaustive work of P. J. Flynn on Irrigation, and
the Flow of Water in Open Canals. (See advertisement of
Irrigation Age); as well as to any of the many standard
works on hydraulics.

Grades.

A study of the details of the larger canals or ditches of
the west shows a great variety of sizes and grades, yet more
uniformity than some would expect. Ditches running from
20 to over 100 miles have widths from 20 to 80 feet, some being built with, and some without, berms; the grades ranging
from 1 foot to 7 feet per mile. The steeper grades are not
common and are for short distances only. The average
grades for main ditches, carrying from 2 to 6 feet of water,
are from 1½ to 2¾ feet per mile. Such low grades will answer only for the larger ditches carrying large volumes of
water and where the ratio of volume to resistance, or friction
on the sides, is large.

In smaller distributing ditches, where the volume is smaller, and the resistance proportionately much greater, a steeper grade must be allowed. It is frequently said by those who
are not informed that this country is too level to irrigate to
advantage.

Such is far from being the case. The writter has yet to
find a quarter section of land, in the most level portion of
the James river valley, that is too level to irrigate. The
gently rolling lands, or such as have a comparatively uniform slope, are the best located for irrigation.

The location of the well or reservoir, on or near the highest point, fixes the point of radiation of the ditches, their
lines being located according to the grades secured and the
lay of the land to be served. The aim will always be to
keep the water *up* as high as possible for it is useless to sac-
rifice grade or make a ditch run at a greater grade than is
necessary. It is an easy matter to let the water *down* but a
difficult thing to *raise* it. By keeping the grades up, a broad-
er area is kept within the range of service.

Grades of from 2 to 5 feet per mile will be ample to secure good delivery from the smaller main ditches, while the laterals will require steeper grades, which, in many cases, may be confined to the approximate level of the field, except on hill sides or quite abrupt slopes, in which case the grades will be carried around the slope as contours. The following table will show the grades per 100 feet corresponding to given grades per mile. If the grade per *rod* is required it may be taken *approximately* from the table by taking ¼ of the grade for 100 feet. If the grade is required *exactly* for any given distance, and corresponding to any given grade per mile, it may be found by simple proportion, thus:

grade per mile : one mile : : required grade : given distance.

Example,—What is the grade for 3,500 feet, corresponding to a grade of 10 feet per mile?

10 : 5280 : : (?) : 3500 = 35000 ÷ 5280 = 6.62 = Ans.

or 10 : 5280 : : 6.62 : 3500.

That is, the given distance multiplied by the grade per mile and the product divided by 5280, the number of feet in a mile, equals the required grade. In this way any grades, other than those given in the table, may be found. In like manner the grade per mile, corresponding to the grade for any given distance, would be found, thus:

grade per mile (?) : 5280 : : given grade : given distance.

TABLE NO. 52.

Table of Grades per Mile; or per 100 ft. measured horizontally.

From Trautwine.

Grade in ft. per mi.	Grade in feet per 100 feet.	NOTE.	Grade in ft. per mi.	Grade per 100 feet.
1	.01894	If the grade per mile con-	.05	.00094
2	.03788	sists of feet and tenths add	.1	.00189
3	.05682	to the grade per 100 ft. as	.15	.00283
4	.07576	given in the first table,	.2	.00379
5	.09470	the grade per 100 feet for	.25	.00473
6	.11364	the required tenths, as	.3	.00568
7	.13258	given in the second table.	.35	.00662
8	.15152	Example, Grade per mile	.4	.00758
9	.17045	= 12.85 ft. what is grade	.45	.00852
10	.18939	per 100 feet and in 725	.5	.00947
11	.20833	ft.? .22727 + .01609 =	.55	.01041
12	.22727	.24336 = grade in 100	.6	.01136
13	.24621	ft. .24336 × 7 = 1.70352	.65	.01230
14	.26515	= grade in 700 ft. and	.7	.01326
15	.28409	.24336 ÷ 4 = .06084 =	.75	.01420
16	.303 3	grade in 25 ft. 1.70352	.8	.01515
17	.32197	+ .06084 = 1.76436 =	.85	.01609
18	.34091	grade for 725 feet. OR	.9	.01705
19	.35985	.24336 × 7.25 = 1.76436	.95	.01799
20	.37879		1.0	.01894

117

Laying Out.

The laying out of the ditches is the provience of the engineer or surveyor, although the more intelligent farmers may do much of their own work and thus save considerable expense. In the arrangement of fields it may become necessary to change the location of a ditch or to lay out a new one. This work the farmer may do with simple means, although, in many cases, it will pay an intelligent farmer to own a drainage level. Its use on his own, and on his neighbors' work, will soon pay for it. Simple devices for small jobs will be described later on.

Something of a knowledge of leveling must be had in order to do the work, but sufficient may soon be acquired to permit of much home-work being done. If any doubt exists as to ones ability to lay out a piece of work it will be cheaper to hire some one to do it who knows how.

The running of preliminary lines, making of profiles. cross sectioning, calculation of sizes, carrying capacities, and grades, and the final location and construction are details of the work, each the proper subject of a chapter. The limit of this little book will not permit. however. of any special consideration of these purely technical details of the work. (See remarks on leveling, P. 132 to 134.)

Excavation and Cost.

The smaller ditches may be constructed by hand-shoveling, by plowing and scraping, or by plowing with a large double-mould-board plow. The larger ditches by plowing and scraping, or by grading or ditching machines. Hand work is of course most expensive but it will be necessary in some places. Simple piowed ditches are of course the cheapest, as they are also but temporary, and in the end the more expensive. Scraper woak will cover the greatest range of work and will fairly represent the average cost. Work done with a ditching machine is very satisfactory and far cheaper than other work.

The New Era grader and ditcher (see advertisement) is the leading machine of its class. It will place in the bank from 1000 to 1400 cubic yards of earth per day at a cost of about 2 cents per yard; or it will load from 600 to 800 wagons per day. It has been used in all states, in all soils. and on all classes of work with full satisfaction and great economy. Its use on reservoirs is especially recommended. Done with a ditcher, the ditches on a section of average land need not cost to exceed $200, or $50 per quarter section. Under favorable circumstances the work has been done for half this sum. (See also page 246.)

Dakota's soil and topography renders the operation of a grader easy, economical and altogether satisfactory.

No farmer can afford to buy a machine to do his own work alone, but when farmers become associated in the putting down of wells and construction of reservoirs and ditches, then it will pay to buy machines, for on a large job they will soon save their cost. The suggestion is made that townships or counties purchase not only drilling outfits but also ditching outfits. Each farmer could pay for its use on his work, at such a rate as would effect a great saving to himself, and, at the same time, soon return to the township the cost of the machine. An additional advantage of such an arrangement would be in the use of the grader on the public roads where much cost to the tax-payers could be saved thereby.

In this, as in all other fields, the machine has come to stay as against all other forms of labor.

The suggestion here made will bear careful consideration by associations of farmers or by townships and counties.

Most of the railway grading in the state has been sub-let to farme s and others at from 6 to 8 cents per yard, at which rate—and on large contracts, there is only fair wages.

Table No. 49 shows the cost of grading reservoir embankments at the rate of 6 and 8 cents per yard. A reservoir of 5 acres, having an 8 foot bank, would cost $746 at 8 cents per yard. Four such reservoirs on adjacent farms would cost about $3,000. If done with a grading machine, at a cost of even 3 cents per yard, there would, on that small job, be a clear saving of $1,500 over other work. Such conservative illustrations show the value of properly considering the *means* of doing the work. What applies to reservoirs applies likewise to ditches.

Embankments and Footings.

Under the head "Reservoirs," on page 99, the qualified statement is made that the use of drag-scrapers will result in a more solid bank than when scrapers or graders are used. This is commonly so; but not necessarily so, for if the grader-work is properly followed up with a harrow the earth is torn, mixed, and more thoroughly compacted than in any other way and the resulting embankment is as good as if done by any other means.

The object in any embankment is to have it sufficiently solid to hold water. Around gates and outlets the earth should be solidly tamped or puddled—wetted down—in order to make a tight joint. So, too, with the footings of high banks, they require special attention. If the dirt is thrown loosely on top of the sod the water may percolate through the loose, filter-like footing of grass and weeds and cause a leak, and possibly a wash-out of the bank.

To insure against this there should be, along the middle-line of every heavy bank, several plow furrows turned and the sod cast aside. The fresh earth of the bank settles into the trench and soon forms a tight joint with the solid surface. If the banks are but 6 or 8 feet high, this will suffice; but if they are higher the trench may better be doubleplowed and a bank of wet earth piled in and over it thus insuring a compact core for the bank.

Reference has been made to the slope of the banks. The slope in the excavation need not usually be more that 1 to 1, but if the cut is of any considerable depth, and the soil sandy or loose, then a slope of 1¼ to 1 will be better.

The slope in the fill or banks may usually be 1½ to 1, but if they are high a slope of 2 to 1, on the wet side, will be safer. The slopes of the reservoir banks are thus given in the diagrams and tables under head of reservoirs.

Cubic Contents of Excavations.

Tables giving the cubic contents, per unit of length, for ditches of different depths, widths, and slopes, would be convenient for reference, but they would necessarily be long in order to cover the whole ground. On this account they will be omitted and the simple rule given by which the calcluations may be made in any given case.

RULE: Multiply the area of the section of the ditch, in square feet, by the length of the ditch, in feet, and divide the product by 27 to get the cubic yards of earth in the ditch.

Determine the area of the section as explained in connection with table 51.

Example—How many cubic yards in a ditch 4 feet wide, 2¼ feet deep, and 1835 feet long?. Bottom width 4 feet+top width 8½ feet=12½ which÷2=6¼=average width. 6¼ ×2¼, the depth,=14.0625=area, and cubic yards in 1 ft. of ditch. 14.0625×1835, the length,=25,805 cu. ft. which÷27= 956=cubic yards.

To get the contents of the ditch in *gallons*, proceed as above, using the wet section—and multiply the volume in *cubic feet* by 7.48052 to get volume in gallons.

Gates. The gates or outlets from the main ditches to the laterals are too simple in construction to need illustration or special consideration. They may be made with more or less complication, but a simple frame of plank with a board or plank slide or gate, fitted to slide vertically within cleats will answer every purpose. When the gate is down—closed—the mud in the ditch may be drawn about the base and sides to aid in keeping it water tight.

In the working laterals, where it is desired either to cut off any further flow or to dam up the water for the flooding of a certain area, a small portable dam or stop of sheet iron or wood may be used. In case the water passing from the main ditch to the laterals is to be *measured* or gauged then the common gate will give place to the weir or to the spillbox shown in Fig. 6.

. One matter will be mentioned as to the *location* of ditches
—the same applying to both flumes and pipe-lines—which
is to locate them, as nearly as circumstances of economy,
grades, &c will permit, on such courses as will permit of the
proper working of the land. Rectangular areas are the
most convenient to cultivate, and sharp angular pieces the
most difficult. So, in locating water-ways some consideration should be given to the after convenience of handling
machinery in the cultivation of the land. A moderate increase of the first cost of the water-way would be justified
in an effort to secure an area more favorable in form to
convenient cultivation or access from other parts of the
land.

Flumes.

Flumes are boxes or troughs used to convey water where
ditches are impracticable or needlessly expensive either to
construct or to maintain. Where a ravine, valley, or any
considerable depression crosses the line of a ditch the water
may be turned into a flume, carried over the depression, and
then discharged into another ditch on the farther side. It
may, too, be advisable to carry the water in a flume over
loose, sandy soil, where the loss by percolation would be so
excessive as to render a sufficient delivery from an open
ditch either difficult or impossible.

Many cases will therefore arise where the use of flumes
will either save the farmer considerable expense or conserve
his greater convenience. Special forms of sheet iron, or
other sheet metal, flumes are much used in mountainous
sections because of their lightness, tightness, and economy,
and the facility of erecting them in difficult places.

As usually constructed flumes are merely wooden boxes,
open at the top, and of such size and strength as is necessary to carry and support the water supplied. Many in the
west are of large size, great strength, and traverse long
distances and at great height. Such as Dakota farmers will
use will be small, short and low. The grades may, if necessary, be somewhat lighter, and the size smaller, than those
of the ditches supplying them, because of the lesser friction
and the greater facility of flow. The volume of water to be
carried will regulate the size the same as in ditches and the
grade will, in the same way, regulate the carrying capacity
by increasing or decreasing the velocity of the current.

The effect of friction of the water upon the sides of the
flume, and of even a gentle wind upon the surface of the
water, will be quite noticeable—more so than in a ditch.
An instance is cited. A flume 12 x 18 inches by 800 feet
long, with a fall of 2 feet, ran to overflowing at the upper
end while discharging but 3 inches at the lower end. Wind
and friction prevented the water from running.

Since the delivery depends upon the velocity of flow, and since the velocity in an open water-way is due solely to gravity, and not to any confined head or pressure, the delivering capacity of a flume will be governed by the size and grade not by the size of a pipe delivering water to it under high pressure. The volume and relative velocities must be considered. If the volume to be carried is that of the well alone, as where the flume is used to carry the water from the well to the ditches or the reservoir, the size may be moderate as compared with that of a flume farther away and forming part of the waterway from a reservoir from which a much larger volume will flow at one time than would flow from the well alone.

The flume box may be made of 2 inch plank, selected as free from loose knots or cracks, closely spiked with 5 or 6 penny wire spikes (wire spikes will hold better than others and are less apt to split the wood in driving.)

If a small box is needed a single plank of 14 to 18 in. will do for the bottom, and similar ones for the sides. The addition of a second plank to the bottom, the sides remaining the same, will double the volume and a little more than double the carrying capacity of the flume, and at but slight increase of expense for the supports, braces, etc., may remain substantially the same. The construction of a flume is but a simple matter. Any carpenter or intelligent farmer can build one.

The supports may in many cases be a single line of heavy fence posts, which may be had in lengths as great as 12 or 14 feet. The buts set 2 or 3 feet in the ground, and well tamped, give a good foundation. The grade line for the tops is marked by leveling, and the tops then sawed to grade, the caps or cross bars spiked to the posts, and the flume then constructed on these. If of 6 feet or more in height the posts and cross bars had better be braced to prevent the rocking of the flume by heavy winds.

Where greater heights than 10 or 12 feet are met a trestle of timber posts, properly footed, braced, *and anchored,* will be used. The rigidity of the supporting posts should be carefully looked to in this country of almost constant and heavy winds, for upon this will depend very largely the tightness of the flume and its freedom from leakage.

The planks, before being spiked together, should be painted along the edges in contact, with a coat of very thick paint. This will not only aid in making a water tight joint but will preserve the wood at the joint. The edges of the planks should be dressed true so as to fit properly. As rough sawed by the mill they are often wavy or uneven. Cut out all warped or crooked pieces for they cannot be worked in to advantage.

If double widths of plank are used on the bottom or sides they should be tongued and grooved if possible, or at least carefully matched and secured in close contact by cross pieces. The joints of the plank at the *"bents"* or supports, will be protected by side strips or braces and the box, at intervals between the bents, will be surrounded by strips or wooden braces to give rigidity to the flume and prevent loosening of the joints.

The length of the space between the bents will depend somewhat on the style of the flume or upon the length of the lumber used. Where a single line of posts is used have the bents at the ends and middle of each length of 16 or 18 ft. plank (8 or 9 foot spaces.) If the flume is more solidly built 20 foot lumber may as well be used, leaving 10 foot spaces. If the ditch is large, and the flume correspondingly large, the trestles must be heavier and a line of stringers will support the flume between the bents.

The dressed surface of the lumber will be on the inside of the box to present as smooth a surface as possible to the running water. After the completion of the flume go over all the joints with a coat of thick paint applied with an old stiff brush. By so doing, and using care and plenty of nails, a box may be made that is perfectly watei tight. A small leak may often be stopped by filling the crack with stiff clay or mud. The details of construction will depend somewhat upon the builder and his means, but they are so simple as to render further suggestion unnecessary.

PIPES. The use of pipe-lines for conveying water, in the place of ditches or flumes, has increased much since the introduction of certain cheaper forms of pipe. In the west, pipes of wood, banded with iron, are extensively used as are pipes of spiral-riveted or welded iron or steel. These latter combining great strength with lightness and economy.

Where waters can be forced under heavy pressure, as from our wells, the use of surface pipe-lines of light pipe will find a broad field of usefulness and should receive such consideration as its merits deserve; especially where the work of constructing ditches or flumes is of any special magnitude. The pipe-line is intended to take the place of the main ditch or flume and not of the distributing laterals. The advantage of a pipe-line over a ditch lies in this—that the water supply is not reduced by seepage or evaporation and the duty of the well is thereby increased. The area of surface occupied by the pipe line is not nearly so great as the area occupied by the ditch and embankments and thus the area subject to cultivation in increased. The cost of maintenance is less, for a pipe-line will need but little attention, whereas, ditches, however well they may be made, will require an annual overhauling; especially if made of loose or sandy soil which in a windy country soon blows down. The matter of grade is of no importance for the water, being forced, will run up hill as well as down and the pipe may be laid to the grade of the surface and deliver water at a level higher than the well. The area under service from the well may thereby be increased by rendering it possible to reach areas to which gravity alone would not carry the water. In this way a well owner may be enabled to sell and deliver water to a neighbor whose land lies, or is controlled from a higher level. The advantage over a flume lies in the fact that evaporation and leakage are done· away with. The delivering capacity is greater because under pressure. The first cost may be less even than that of the flumes, and the cost of maintenance less. The matter of grade is eliminated and the line is on or near the surface where it may be more easily constructed or repaired and where less liable to damage from winds. The alignment, or location, too, may be accommodated to the circumstances of the surroundings more readily than that of either ditches or flumes.

It is here assumed that the pipe line connects with the well; otherwise there could be no pressure upon the pipe and it would stand, in relation to delivery, on a plane with the ditch or flume.

If the line is accommodated to the surface and there is any inverted or downward bend in the pipe there should be a valve set at the lowest point to permit of emptying or draining the pipe during the cold weather or for repairs. The pipe may be laid on or near the surface on low supports of such form and material as circumstances may suggest. It should, at suitable intervals, be fastened or anchored down in some suitable way to prevent displacement by the wind or by other means, and it should be painted to preserve it from rust.

The concluding remark as to location of ditches may be again referred to in this connection, and the suggestion made that the location of the lines of the water-ways be made as far as possible along the lines of the fields or along fences or roads. In the case of the smaller pipe-lines the fences themselves will often serve as sufficient and convenient supports for the pipe, intermediate supports being set if necessary. In view of the advantages possessed, under certain conditions, by pipe-lines over other forms of water-ways one should fully consider the advantages of each as well as the cost and maintenance before deciding which to adopt. On most lands there will be no use for either pipe-lines or flumes. Their service is justified only by the circumstances of the topography and service.

HYDRAULIC RAM.

The occasion will frequently arise where the area to be irrigated is divided by a water-course, gully, or other depression, the land on the side of the well and reservoir sloping gently toward the "*draw*," the opposite side of which is high and comparatively level. The well and reservoir being at a distance from the draw it will hardly pay to lay a pipe line to serve the other side and the water cannot be carried across by ditch or flume. How then can it be delivered into a ditch on the opposite and higher ground? By elevating it only. This could be done from the end of an open ditch on the low side by means of a steam or wind pump. The former way, by reason of fuel and attendance, would not prove profitable, and the latter way possibly ineffectual in spite of an abundant supply. A simple and inexpensive water elevator may be had in the hydraulic engine or ram which may be so set as to take the supply from the open ditch, with a fall of such an amount as the slope will permit, leaving drainage away from the ram.

By this means the water may be forced across the draw in a constant stream, working night and day, rain or shine, and without fuel, attention, cost, or care.

The Rife's Hydraulic Engine (See advertisement, P. 214) is such a machine and one of high efficiency. The No. 40 machine is fitted with a 4-inch supply pipe and a 2-inch discharge pipe, and, with a fall of from 4 to 6 feet, it will raise from 60 to 70 gallons per minute to a height of 20 feet or more, and lesser volumes to much greater heights. The machine will work under heads of but one or two feet and in such cases it could often be used to advantage along side slopes to raise a supply of water to a ditch at a higher level.

Such appliances, together with wind mills and steam pumps, will, in the near future, find a welcome place among Dakota irrigators, for, although a well will do almost anything within its immediate reach, there will be duties to perform in connection with a properly managed irrigation system which are outside of the sphere of the well itself, yet properly within the sphere of other appliances, all of which must be considered if the greatest good is desired and secured.

PUMPS.

While this little book is devoted most especially to a consideration of artesian wells as a source of water supply for irrigation, it must not be forgotten that there are other sources of supply. Dakota has few lakes or rivers from which any supply could be drawn, except of course the Missouri, the supply from which is practically inexhaustible.

There are many sections all over the states where large, shallow wells may be sunk into the sand and gravel beds from which an almost inexhaustible water supply may be obtained. It must of course be elevated by artificial means and the question will at once suggest itself as to whether it will pay to do this.

Yes, It Will Pay!

As to this there can be no question, and ere long this source of water supply will cut a very large figure in the irrigation of lands in Dakota.

Certain very erroneous and misleading statements have been made by government specialists and agents as to the relative value of these phreatic or sub-surface waters, and the true artesian waters; they claiming that by far the larger supply was the sub-surface supply. These statements and reports were founded upon observations elsewhere than in Dakota, and upon a woeful lack of personal knowledge as to our true artesian supply. The sub-surface supply, while no doubt of vast extent and importance, cannot be compared with the artesian supply in its extent, universality, volume, or the *ultimate* economy of obtaining it. In other words—a given volume, in a given time, may be obtained more cheaply from an artesian well than from any sub-surface source by whatever means it may be secured.

Notwithstanding this great percentage in favor of the artesian supply the other sources should by no means be neglected or overlooked. The value to the state of the phreatic supply will be beyond calculation if the people will but seek its development.

As before stated it must be secured by mechanical means; either by wind or by steam power. Many farmers—most of them—cannot raise the means necessary to put down an artesian well, but there are few who cannot raise enough to put in a pumping plant at an expense of but a few hundred dollars.

Reference must again be made to the west where the manufacture and use of water-elevating machinery is a very large and rapidly growing industry. Many sections of country cannot be supplied by water taken from streams by ditches, so the water must be elevated. Thousands of wells have been put down in the several western states and territories from which the water will not flow so it must be pumped. This industry is most fully developed in California and in Colorado. The following illustration will show the comparative economy and great value of such means.

A pumping plant, with a 50 horse-power engine, will raise 7,500,000 gallons of water to a height of 10 feet in 10 hours. This amount of water will cover 28 acres to a depth of one foot. The cost of the plant would be about $3000. One man can operate it with about one ton of coal per day. While so large a plant would not be in order except where the supply was very large, a plant of proportionately less capacity and cost would accomplish proportionate results. Many places may be found from which enough water may be pumped to irrigate a quarter section of land.

The question would follow as to the *means* to be used in raising the water to the surface in the greatest volume and at the least expense. The author knows of no better *means* than the use of the PULSOMETER or the NYE VACUUM steam pumps which possess features especially adapting them to such uses. They are both vacuum pumps, having no pistons or machinery to wear out or become deranged, are exceedingly simple, strong, and efficient, and, above all, are *standard* the world over; being used for irrigation purposes in many countries. All that is needed is the pump, a steam boiler, and a little pipe. There are hundreds of thresher engines in the state that could be used to supply steam, and straw being used as fuel the expense of running would be but nominal.

A No. 6 Pulsometer pump throwing 300 gallons per minute (18,000 gallons per hour) would cost about $225; an engine to supply steam could be rented during its period of idleness and could be run at an expense of but $2 or $3 per day for fuel and attendance. Surely, then, here is a most valuable auxiliary supply in the irrigation field of Dakota, and a means of utilizing it not heretofore presented to our people.

The cost of starting the plant—buying the pump, pipe and fittings, digging and connecting 2 or 3 large wells and getting the boiler need not cost over $1000, yet on such an outlay of capital enough may be easily made in any one year to pay the cost of installation and enough surplus very soon accumulated to warrant the sinking of an artesian well.

The increased service rendered by a well, as the result of a given outlay or cost, renders that means, or source of supply, cheaper in the long run, as it is otherwise the basis of more extensive operations; but if the greater source is beyond one's financial reach then by all means grasp at the lesser and use a pump.

WIND MILLS.

In the utilization of this sub-surface supply the agency of wind mills may be made to play an important part and this is especially true in this country of almost constant winds. A wind mill may supply water for a very considerable area of garden and orchard, and, if reinforced by a proper water-elevating device, as to which there are several good ones in the market, and also a storage reservoir, the area of service could be very greatly extended and the profit of the farm greatly increased. This *means*, too, deserves the careful consideration of our farmers.

Get the water from the most available source and by the most efficient means. Only get it! for to get it is to acquire a competency.

Wherever a deposit of sand or gravel is found, or where wells wherein there is a flow or current—in and out—are found, there is to be found, beyond much doubt, a supply which would abundantly serve the land upon which the supply is found. Every farmer should take some pains to investigate the extent and character of his sub-surface supply with a view to its future utilization.

Fig. 19.

Showing the Pulsometer Pump as set for taking water from a stream for the use of irrigation. The view shows the extreme simplicity of the plant which renders it especially applicable to use where skilled labor or attendance is lacking. Any man can run it or set it up.
[See next page and page 244.]

Fig. 20.

Fig. 20. Shows a No. 6 Pulsometer [capacity 18,000 gallons per hour] throwing a stream 46 feet high through 160 feet of 3½ inch pipe, into a flume on top of the bluff. The pump irrigates 1400 fruit trees, uses about ⅛ cord of soft wood per day and is operated by an Indain boy. The plant is in Idaho.

A No. 9 pump, on a lift of 102 feet, used ¾ cord of wood in 10 hours and delivered 60,000 gallons per hour. [See page 244.]

LEVELING.

It would require more space, diagrams, and illustrations than can be here given to fully treat of the different kinds of levels, their adjustment, use, and care; and to describe and illustrate the many nice points in the art of leveling. Much of this techincal information may be had from the pamphlets issued by level manufacturers and supplied with the instruments.

Enough will be given to convey to any person of average intelligence so much of a knowledge of the art as is necessary to aid in doing such work as may arise about the farm, and yet such as it would not pay to hire an engineer to do, even if one were to be had at call. The principle of leveling is to reduce the inequalities of the surface to a uniform plane, or to determine the position of a succession of points with reference to a uniform plane.

DATUM PLANE.

It is apparent from this that some plane of reference must be chosen which shall be that to which all other points are referred. Such an arbitrarily selected plane is called the *Datum Plane,* or plane of reference, and it is assumed to lie at a considerable distance below the surface in order that all points referred to it may have plus (+) elevations, instead of some plus (+) and some minus (—) as would be the case if some portion of the line to be run sank below the level of the datum plane.

In a rough or mountainous country 500 or 1000 feet is taken as the depth of the plane of reference. In this level country 100 feet will be sufficient. That is, in starting any piece of level work assume that the starting point is 100 feet above this plane, or at an elevation of 100; then proceed to get the elevations of all other points, whether higher or lower than the starting point. Before describing the operation of leveling let us very briefly consider the level or leveling instrument.

THE LEVEL.

The engineer's level is a telescopic tube carried in Ys or collars, and having a long level-bubble tube attached, mounted on a horizontally revolving cross-head which is adjusted and maintained in a level or horizontal position by four leveling-screws attached to the head of the tripod on which the instrument rests. Cross hairs in the tube give the exact center and the horizontal line of sight. Such are the main features of a level, and all are constructed on the same general plan.

Some instruments are made with a less powerful and shorter telescope, with fewer parts, lighter weight, and cheaper in price. Levels of this class known as contractors, builders or architects levels are far cheaper than larger engineer's levels but they are finely constructed and good for all classes of work.

A still cheaper grade of level is the so called "drainage level" which is made for the express purpose of farm use in laying out drains and ditches. In this special class of instruments there is a wide range of design and price, the latter ranging from $10 to $30. (The manufacturers, Buff and Berger, W. and L. E. Gurley, and Young and Sons, whose advertisements appear herein, are leading makers of the finest instruments and will supply anything in the level line.)

A $25 or $50 instrument will do good work and last a lifetime, if properly cared for. One who can use a level will soon pay the cost of a good one by home-work. If no good level is at hand a simple one, for rough work, may be made out of three pieces of board as shown in Fig. 21.

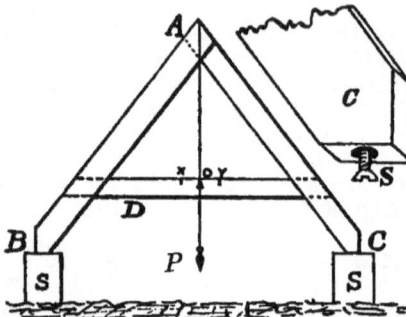

Take two pieces of narrow board, AB and AC, of exactly equal length and form as shown, and having a span from B to C of 10 feet [one of 16½ foot span—1 rod—may be more convenient.] At exactly equal distances from A, measured along the sides, attach the cross stick D. Fasten on the plumb line and bob P and then adjust the zero point O as follows: Drive two stakes in the ground, as supports for the level, having one of them 2 or 3 ins. higher than the other.

Fig. 21. A simple form of level.

Set the foot C on the higher stake and mark upon D the exact point where the line cuts the edge—as at x. Then reverse the level, end for end, so foot B is on the higher stake, and again mark the point where the line cuts D—as at y. Draw o just midway between these lines. Then whenever the plumb line cuts this o mark the feet B and C are on a level. In one foot a large screw may be set, as shown in the enlarged view at S. When screwed in flush the level is set for level work but when screwed out the level is set for running grades. Thus—if a ditch has a fall of 1 foot in 500 feet the screw would be turned out slightly over ¼ inch. The level would be set 50 times in the 500 feet (it having 10 foot span,) so $\frac{1}{80}$ of 1 foot would be the grade for each setting.

Such a tool is of course crude but, if well made and skillfully handled, it will yield quite good results. Other simple home-made levels are frequently described but this is as good as any. Get a good level if possible and learn to do good work with it. It will pay you if you do much irrigating.

The level rod is a rod of dry wood from 8 to 12 feet long, marked into feet, and tenths and hundredths of feet, measuring *upward* from the *bottom* of the rod. The rod may have a target or be what is called a "self-reading" rod. The target rod has the graduations cut into the wood and the distances indicated by figures as at A, Fig. 22, the feet in large red figures and the tenths by smaller black figures. The -leveler views the cross lines on the target and the rod-man takes the reading as indicated by the target. (In the Fig. the target reads 4 feet)

The self-reading rod needs no target, for the leveler takes the reading from sight at the instrument, the graduations being made visible by painting as shown at B, Fig. 22. Here only the feet are numbered, the smaller graduations not requiring it.

Thus, if the horizontal hair of the level cuts at the following points on the rod the reading would be as follows. Refer to B in the Fig.

1=1.0 feet.   4=1.5 feet.
2=1.05 "   5=1.75 "
3=1.3 "   6=1.85 " ·

The reading to .05 feet being easily made, and, on short sights, a finer reading may be approximated although a reading of less than .05 is not necessary except in very fine work.

Such rods can be easily and accurately made by any intelligent person, and at a cost of not over one dollar. The target may be made of sheet brass or of galvanized iron.

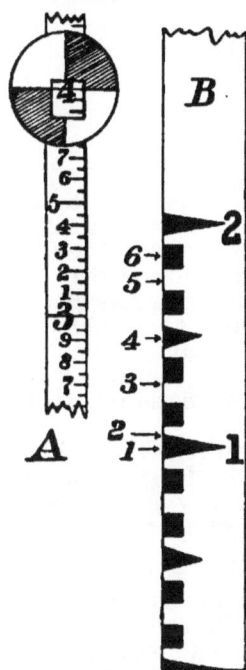

Fig. 22.
Leveling Rods.

LEVELING.

Leveling is very simple work, and the keeping and reduction of level notes equally so. The first thing to do is to set up and level the instrument and to select the HUB or starting point. The form of note-keeping and the order of procedure is shown on the next page. In this sample page from a note-book the following is the significance of the letters heading the several columns. Stn. = Station Number; B. S. = Back Sight [sometimes called + Sight]; H. I. = Height of Instrument; F. S. = Fore Sight [sometimes called − Sight]; Elev. or Ht. = Elevation or height of Station; Rem. = Remarks.

The hub, or starting point, which may be any permanent object, or a stake driven for the purpose, is assumed to have an elevation of 100 feet which fact is entered in the note-book as shown. The rod now being held on this hub the line of sight of the instrument, or the plane passing through its center, strikes the rod 4 feet from the bottom. Enter this under B. S. as shown. Now if the hub is 100 feet and the instrument reads 4 feet above it. the center of the instrument is evidently on a plane or level of 104 feet [so that Elev. added to B. S. = H. I. or 104 ft.] The H. I. being known the height of any other point is found thus—. The rodman goes to station 1 and the leveler reads a F. S. of 5.20, which he enters as shown under F. S.

SAMPLE PAGE FROM LEVELER'S NOTE BOOK.

Stn.	B. S.	H. I.	F. S.	Elev.	Rem.
Hub	4.00	104.00		100.00	Hub near well.
1			5.20	98.80	
3			6.00	98.	
3			7.55	96.45	T. P. [turning point.]
	• 7.35	103.80	8.80	95.	Hub, at barn.
4			2.60	101.20	
5			1.50	102.30	T. P.
6	1.20	103.50	8.60	94.90	
7			2.10	101.40	
			1.70	101.80	

If the instrument is on a level of 104 ft., and the reading
on the rod at Stn. 1 is 5.20, it is evident that Stn. 1 is 5.20 ft.
lower than the instrument. The level of Stn. 1 is therefore
found by merely subtracting the F. S. reading on that Stn.
(5.20) from the H. I. (104) = 98.80—which enter as shown.
In like manner readings are taken at Stns. 2 and 3 which result as shown in the notes. From where the instrument
now stands stn. 4 cannot be seen so the level is moved to a
new position from which stns. 4 and 5 may be seen. Set up
and adjust as before.

The rodman having staid at Stn. 3 the leveler now takes a
B. S. reading on that point. The reading of 7.35 is entered
as a B. S. Stn. 3 (T. P., or *turning point*) having an Elev. of
96.45 and the B. S. equaling 7.35 their sum, or 103.80, will
give a new H. I. or plane of reference.

Before proceeding to take the level of Stn. 4 the leveler
deems it best to take level on some new hub so that in case
the original hub is moved or destroyed he can relocate his
work from the new hub. The rodman sets up on the barn
floor and the leveler reads 8.80 which substracted from 103.80
=95 as the Elev. of the barn floor.

He then proceeds as before to take the elevations of other
stations and to set such other hubs as he may desire. From
this explanation may be drawn the whole secret of leveling
and note keeping.

The Elev. of *any* starting point *added* to the B. S. reading
on that point give the H. I. and *any* F. S. reading *subtracted*
from the H. I. gives the *Elev.* of the point on which the
reading is taken. Any number of F. S. readings may be
taken from one setting of the instrument so long as the
range of sight is clear. Thus, the instrument may be set at
or near the center of a reservoir and the levels taken at all
points about the bank without moving.

Aim, however, to have the lengths of B S and F S courses
as nearly equal as possible in order not to magnify any
slight error in the adjustment of the instrument.

Note especially one fact—as the grade or level runs *down*
the target or reading runs *up* on the rod; that is, it takes a
greatar length of rod to reach from the plane of the instru-

ment *down* to the surface. The reverse is also true—as the surface *rises* the reading on the rod *lowers*.

TO SET A LINE OF STAKES ON A LEVEL.

Set one stake at the level desired, set the rod on this stake and clamp the target on the reading. Proceed then to set other stakes, tapping each one down until the target—set on the stake—comes into the plane of the instrument.

TO SET A LINE OF STAKES ON ANY GRADE.

Set and get level on first stake. Suppose now that the grade runs *down* at the rate of .1 ft. in 50 feet and that the stakes are 25 feet apart. Move the target *up* on the rod .05 ft., clamp it, and set the second stake by it. Move it *up* 05. again and set the third stake; and so on to the end. Had the grade ran *up* then the target would have been set *down* at each setting.

If, instead of setting long stakes to the line of the grade, short ones are set, the level of each short stake may be taken and then from the notes the height of the grade-line *above* or *below* each stake may be estimated and indicated.

Many complications will arise in any extended practice but the principle is the same and the specimen notes given embrace the secret of the whole operation. If care and judgment are exercised fairly good work may be done by one not skilled in the work.

For still further illustration the notes are here given of the level-work in the laying out of a reservoir. A reservoir of but 1½ acres will be taken for illustration. Stake out the circumference, on the center line of the top of the bank, into sections of 50 feet each (except where otherwise stated in the notes)—circumference being 905 ft.

LEVEL NOTES —LAYING OUT A RESERVOIR.

Stn.	B. S.	H. I.	F. S.	Elev.	Height to Grade.
Hub	5.2	105.2		100.0	106.0
1			5.0	100.2	5.8
2			5.5	99.7	6.3
3			6.2	99.0	7.0
3+30			7.6	97.6	8.4
+60			10.2	95.0	11.0
+90			7.5	97.7	8.3
4			6.6	98.6	7.4
5			4.2	101.0	5.0
6			3.2	102.0	4.0
7			4.4	100.8	5.2
8			4.8	100.4	5.6
9			4.8	100.4	5.6
Stn = 105 ft					
1			5.0	100.2	5.8

Set up near the center and proceed to take the level of each stake; first having set a reference hub at some conven-

ient place *outside* of the reservoir, the height of which call
100 ft., which, added to the B S of 5.2=105.2=the H I. The
notes show a gradual descent from station 1 to a point 30 ft.
beyond stn. 3 at which point there is a sudden descent into a
shallow "draw", the bottom of which is at 3+60. Thence
there is a sudden rise to 30+90 and then a gradual rise to
stn. 6, where the highest point is reached, and thence a gradual fall to stn. 1 where, on a reading of 5.0, the level is
found to check with the beginning of the work.

In looking over either the F. S. readings or the Elev. results one may readily see, in the imagination, a profile of the
work without platting it on paper.

Assume, now, that the top of the bank will be 4 feet above
the highest point, at stn. 6—the elev. of which is 102 ft.,
then the grade-line will be on a level of 106. Enter this in
the last column as shown. It is apparent that the height of
the bank at each stn. will be the difference between the level
of that stn. and the level of the grade-line; therefore, subtract the height or elev. of each stn. from the grade-height
(106) and the remainder will be the height of the bank at
that stn., which enter as shown in the last column.

The staking out of the toe or base of the bank on the inside and outside may now be done since the height and
slopes are known. The inner slope being 2 to 1 and the
outer slope 1½ to 1 measure off from each stake, toward and
from the center of the reservoir the bottom widths occord-
ing to the height of the bank at that point *plus ½ the width
of the top of the bank*. Thus—at stn. 4. the height being
7.4 ft., the distance to the *inner* toe would be 7.4×2=14.8+
2.5 (½ top)=17.3 ft.   The distance to the *outer* toe would be
7.4×1.5=11.1+2.5=13.6 ft., a total width of 30.9 feet.

The estimate of the number of cubic yds. of earth in the
bank may be done with sufficient accuracy by assuming the
cross-section to be level and the height of the bank in each
section as a mean or average of the end heights. Thus, the
height at stn. 6 is 4 feet; and at stn. 7 it is 5.2 ft. The average height may be taken, therefore, as the height of the
full stn., 4.0+5.2=9.2÷2=4.6=average for 100 ft.

Get area of section of this height, and compute cu. yds.
for 100 feet as explained under head of " Reservoirs." Do
the same for each stn., add the sums to get the total cubic
contents.

This, it is believed, will make clear what is really a very
simple operation and will enable any farmer to do, or to aid
in doing, part or all of his own work.

With three sticks, a ball of binding twine, a few stakes,
and a hatchet, with a little good judgment and care thrown
in, any farmer may do in two hours what it would cost him
$5 to $10 to have done—and still not be overcharged. Do
some level practice, if only for exercise.

Fig.23.

DECIMAL AND DUODECIMAL SCALES.

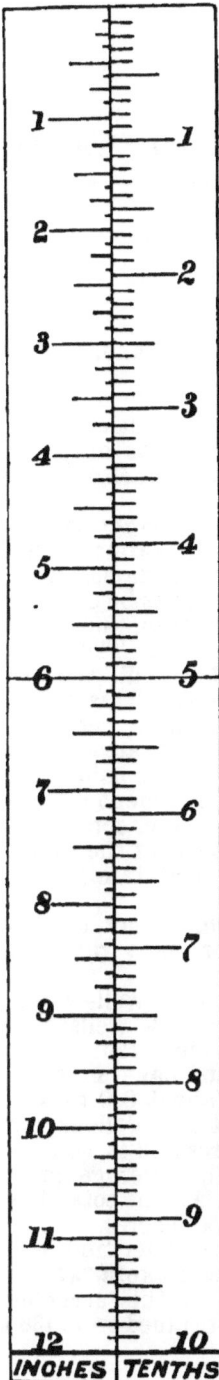

TRUE AND APPARENT LEVEL.

Brief mention only need be made of the difference between *true* and *apparent* level. In ordinary leveling operations no account is taken of the curvature of the earth.

True level is a water-level which is the true curvature of the earth.

Apparent level is a horizontal plane tangent to the plane of true level at any point and extending indefinitely into space.

In leveling the sights are short and constitute, therefore, a succession of tangent planes which closely approximate a curve of true level. The difference between a curve of true level and a plane of apparent level is about 8 inches per mile [7.98 ins. or .667 ft.] and increases as the square of the distance; being 4 times 8 inches in 2 miles, 9 times 8 inches in 3 miles, etc.

MEASUREMENTS.

Nearly all measurements in engineering work are made in feet and decimals —tenths and hundredths—instead of in feet and inches. This is especially necessary in leveling. Table No. 67, showing the decimals of a foot corresponding to each $\frac{1}{64}$ of an inch will be of convenience in the conversion of measurements from one unit to the other. For ordinary work the decimal corresponding to the nearest half or quarter inch will be close enough. To aid in getting this at a glance Fig. 23 has been prepared showing (in $\frac{1}{2}$ size) a foot measure divided into inches and eighths; and, on the opposite side the divisions to tenths and hundredths. This will be of much use to the leveler in certain work.

Examples.— 6 inches = 5 tenths.
         9   "   = 75 hundredths.
       10   "   = 83   "
  and   7 tenths = 8⅜ inches.
      25 hundredths = 3 inches, &c.

The scale may be more readily used than a table.

The unit of measurement used by the government in surveys of the public lands is the chain of 66 feet,—4 rods—this being divided into 100 links of 7.92 inches each. For rules as to the conversion of chains and links to feet, yards, &c., see " Mensuration " and table of multipliers.

VALUE OF WATER, VALUE OF LAND
AND SIZE OF FARMS UNDER A SYSTEM
OF IRRIGATION.

VALUE OF WATER.

Water for irrigation has a double value.

First. The first cost of getting it upon the land, or the value of the *Water right.*

Second. The annual rental value.

Table No. 53, on the opposite page, shows statistics as to values, etc., which are official and as accurate as only the Government could secure. The table contains much of value and deserves careful study.

The first cost of securing a water supply or *right* will depend upon the supply, the distance it must be brought, the manner of bringing, etc. All the expense of dams, headgates, ditches, flumes, pipe-lines, or tunnels must be born-by the area served, so all these expenses enter into, and form a part of, the first cost per acre of a water right. The value of the right being such an amount as will pay all the expenses and leave a proper margin of profit. This value ranges from a mere nominal price to $30 or more per acre, but averages as shown in the table. The right attaches to the land and passes with the title thereto. Once paid for it is perpetual as a right, but the continued enjoyment of that right is contingent upon the performance of other conditions —as the payment of an annual tax for the use of the water, or the performance of certain labors in maintaining the ditches.

The amount of the value of the water right may usually be considered as the value of the land, for, as a rule, the land has little or no value without the right.

As touching most directly upon the value of well–waters reference may be made to the Gage group of 29 wells near San Bernardino, California. They are within a radius of 1 mile, are from 4 to 10 inches in diameter and have an average daily flow of about 33 miner's inches, (about 300 gallons per minute) or a total of 954 inches, (about 8600 gallons per minute.) One inch is apportioned to 5 acres and is sold as high as $250 an acre, or $1250 an inch. The average price thereabouts being $1000 per inch. At this rate the total flow is worth $954,000 and it will water nearly 5000 acres.

Four good Dakota wells will throw more water and will serve more land. Such being the case one Dakota well of 2200 gallons per minute would, according to this accepted California estimate, be worth $238,500. (Continued on P. 138.)

TABLE NO. 53.

IRRIGATION STATISTICS.

ITEMS.	Arizona	New Mexico	Utah	Wyoming	Montana	Idaho	Nevada
Total irrigated acreage in crop, 1889	65,821	91,745	263,473	229,676	350,582	217,005	224,403
Total number of irrigators, 1889	1,075	3,085	9,724	1,917	3,706	4,323	1,167
Average size of irrigated crop areas, in acres, 1889	61	30	27	119	95	50	192
Average size of irrigated crop areas of 160 acres and upward, in acres	287	312	312	494	307	270	513
Per ct. of acreage of irrigated crop areas of 160 acres and upward to total irrigated.	34	21	10	65	50	26	79
Average size of irrigated crop areas under 160 acres, in acres	43	24	25	50	56	39	58
Average first cost of water per irrigated acre	$ 7.07	$ 5.58	$10.55	$ 3.62	$ 4.63	$ 4.74	$ 7.58
Average annual cost of water per irrigated "	" 1.55	" 1.54	" 0.91	" 0.44	" 0.95	" 0.80	" 0.84
Average first cost per acre of preparation for cultivation	" 8.60	" 11.71	" 14.85	" 8.23	" 8.29	" 9.31	" 10.57
Average value of irrigated land including buildings, etc., per acre	" 48.68	" 50.98	" 84.25	" 31.40	" 49.50	" 46.50	" 41.00
Average annual value of products per acre irrigated, 1889	" 13.92	" 12.80	" 18.03	" 8.25	" 12.96	" 12.93	" 12.92

Tabulated statistics as to irrigation in seven western states and territories, as reported by the U. S. Census Office in Bulletins 1 to 8 (Nos. 35, 60, 85; 107, 153, 157, 163.)

It is not the intention to place such values on wells that can be sunk for $3000 or $4000 yet such is their legitimate value as compared with values elsewhere.

Our wells possess values far in excess of their cost, and far greater than even their owners now dream of. A good well is really a fortune to its owner.

In Oregon, on one large tract, the annual charge is $3.00 per acre for 1 foot depth of water (1 acre foot) to be used in 3 irrigations. At this rate a Dakota well would pay its cost in two years, if not in one. In other states the annual charge per acre foot is about the same, but, inasmuch as the crop is a certainty and abundant in amount, this apparently high tax is not felt as at all burdensome.

The Dakota irrigator who would achieve success must abandon the false idea, which many farmers entertain, of getting someting for nothing. He must put in both money and labor, and considerable of each, in order to make a success of irrigation. Nor need he be discouraged; for all the advantage is on his side. It will cost less here to secure a water right than in almost any other section because a given volume may be had for a lesser outlay.

Again, the Dakota water-right is also a water-power which very largely increases its value. It is not subject to periodic fluctuations, prior rights of up-stream claimants, and such other uncertainties and annoyances as are experienced under other systems. It is perpetual, is under perfect controll, may be put to many uses and in all respects has a value not possessed by water rights in other sections or under other systems

The cost of reservoirs, ditches, gates, etc., is not a part of the water right, but a tax upon the land in its preparation for irrigation. In this respect also Dakota has a great advantage, for her gently rolling or nearly level lands require but little preparation as compared with the heavy work of terracing, checking, diking, ditching, leveling and otherwise treating the land, as so often necessary elsewhere.

Finally, as to the ANNUAL COST of water. Where, in other states, the annual cost is from 25 cents to $5 per acre —averaging over $1—the Dakota average will be but a few cents, and in most cases nothing, for the flow of the well being continuous, requires no attention or expense. Once obtained its volume comes free.

In every essential particular wherein an irrigation system burdens the irrigator with expense—first cost of water, annual cost of water, preparation of ground, future maintenance of plant—he who irrigates in Dakota bears the least burden; has the greatest advantage; the most valuable, controllable, and diverse right; to say nothing of the proximity to the best and largest markets.

A consideration of many details only tends to strengthen and confirm this conclusion that Dakota's artesian irrigation system will be the cheapest and the best of the many systems developed in this country.

The experience of the failure years, 1888-1889-1890, taken in connection with the results obtained by the great crop of 1891 (See table No. 43 and remarks in connection therewith) prove not only the enormous value of water in Dakota but substantiate the estimate of duty of water given in table 16. If the estimate there given is approximately correct, and the annual value of water be taken to be but $2 per acre then from table 16 it will appear that a well of 1350 gallons per minute would be worth $1950 per year or fully 40 per cent on its cost. This is assumed to be a *rental* value.

To the *owner* the actual value would be the *net value of all crops raised in excess of the average yield of non-irrigated lands in his neighborhood.* No reasonable person will estimate the probable average yield of irrigated wheat at less than 30 bushels per acre, which average would be fully 18 bushels more than the average without irrigation. Assuming a net return of but 50 cents per bushel, this would give to the water a value of $9 per acre to the owner; or an amount sufficient to pay the full cost of the well together with the cost of the land, in one year.

This is not an exaggerated estimated but rather an under-estimate as has been demonstrated by actual experience.

A parallel cannot fairly be drawn between the values either of water or of land as between the fruit growing lands of California and the grain fields of Dakota; but making all needful allowances for the character of the crops raised, and their value per acre, the value of water to our grass and grain fields is still actually far beyond the amount which even sanguine estimate would give to it.

A thousand gold mines would not be so valuable to our people as are these artesian waters. Hasten, therefore, to develope this pent-up wealth which awaits the opportunity to flow to the coffers of each enterprising claimant.

VALUE OF LAND.

One, in considering the relative values of irrigated and un-irrigated lands, may border closely upon the realm of the marvelous while yet not transgressing the bounds of cold facts, for it is truly marvelous that the worthless deserts of the arid west, have, within a few years, been clothed in semi-tropical luxuriance through the agency of irrigation, and have been raised in value from actual zero to as much as $2000 per acre. It is but a few years since California and Colorado were known only as great mining states. To-day, through the agency of the impounded waters of the mountain streams, they have been transformed into great agricultural states; the harvest of the golden fruit and of golden grain having long since superseded in value the harvest of the golden metal. Where then there were mining camps now there are prosperous cities, and where then vice reigned supreme, now peace and plenty bless the community.

Millions of acres of barren, sage-brush or of sand-flecked desert, of lava-beds and of sun-parched plains have been reclaimed and are to-day the most valuable and productive lands on the continent. It is true that the high values of $1000 per acre and upward are usually *fancy* prices, but many thousands of acres have ready market values of from $50 to $500 per acre.

Good lands, under water, the ditching and like preparation being done, are worth from $50 to $100 per acre, and find a ready market at these figures.

Any piece of property is truly worth such an amount as will represent the principal upon which a fair rate of interest can be permanently earned.

If land will produce annually a crop which will yield a *net* income of $10 per acre that land is worth $100 per acre to a man who demands a 10 per cent investment; or $200 per acre to a man who is content with 5 per cent. Such values, and only such, are legitimate.

The remarkable development of Southern California has been due almost solely to irrigation. As an illustration of the increase in property values may be cited the statistics relative to San Diego Co., which may be taken to represent that section of the state.

Real Estate.		*Improvements.*	
1880	1890	1880	1890
$1,307,302	$20,000,085	$341,948	$4,450,286

While no corresponding increase can be expected in any Dakota county there is still room for an increase in value far beyond the present values. Taking Brown Co., S. D., to fairly represent the two Dakotas, the average market value of the lands of the county would probably not exceed $6 per acre. An increase of $5 per acre would add over $6,000,000 to the valuation of the county and still leave the lands *far* below their *actual* value.

Such a change in the ready market value of these lands may be brought about within two years if, within that time it can be shown that these lands can be made to produce from 25 to 50 bushels of wheat to the acre, no matter what the season may be.

No doubt exists as to this being demonstrated—it has been already in Brown Co. and in other counties within the artesian basin.

As soon as the foreign land purchaser and investor learns of the wonderful possibilities of this artesian basin the present land owners will find a ready market for their surplus holdings at prices now beyond their fairest fancies. What is it that can do this magic act—the creation of millions of value where now little appears? What is it that can and will do for Dakota what irrigation has done for our sister states? What is it that can banish poverty, misfortune and ruin from our state and bring riches, prosperity and happiness in their place? That can quench the thirst of our once parched prairies with a perennial draught of nature's purest waters?

ARTESIAN WELLS!

No agency is so pregnant of promise for the welfare of the Dakotas and none deserves the same attention as the development of this great industry—artesian irrigation. It is not only a boon to him who puts it to practice but to the community in which he lives, for it shows to the world the possibilities awaiting all who choose to engage therein, and fixes to our lands a value *because of their latent possibilities for successful agricultural development.*

The author has heard it remarked, but recently, by a wealthy eastern man who owns (perforce) several thousand acres of Dakota lands, but possesses no knowledge of irrigation, that if artesian irrigation proves to be what it is claimed to be he would sink several wells and thus treble the value of the lands which today he would sell for what they cost.

No doubt there are scores of such cases, and it is to prove to such men the true value of their lands, and to still further interest them and their monied friends in schemes of development that every effort should be put forth to demonstrate to the world the true extent and value of the latent possibilities we have within our reach and control.

Every possible publicity should be given to every truth, to every demonstrated fact touching upon the well or irrigation interests, and, by reason of the approaching World's Fair and its resultant era of prosperity and commercial activity every possible effort should be made to push the business of irrigation at home and a knowledge of its results abroad; for no better time will ever come for Dakota to enthrone herself in the good will of the capitalists of the world and regain her lost prestige, than the immediate future.

The farmers and the business men of the state should organize and prepare in every legitimate way to promote this all important industry, for the success or failure of the state depends upon it, and all other interests pale before it in importance and the effect upon the general prosperity of all classes. If this appeal to the patriotic home enterprise of Dakotans shall result in creating any of that interest which the subject warrants, then will this little volume not have been issued in vain.

SIZES OF FARMS.

A word of caution as to over-irrigation, in point of area, will well-nigh be wasted inasmuch as the invariable tendency is to attempt to irrigate too large an area. A few unsuccessful attempts to irrigate too broad an area will convince the farmer that a lesser area, better served and cultivated, will yield better results.

In a fruit-growing country an area of 5 or 10 acres is enough for a single holding. As the crop is changed to vegetables, grass, or cereals the area which may be advantageously cultivated increases. It is assumed that the holding is worked on the plan of the average farm—by the farmer and his family, with the assistance of the average amount of hired help. As the number of hands, actively engaged in the farm labor, increases, so may the area treated be increased. The character of the land to be cultivated—whether it be easily managed or the reverse—will likewise determine the area which a given service of labor can properly manage; as will also, the character of the crops raised.

It will be well in starting out to thoroughly treat such an area as the supply of water, as well as of labor, can treat to the best advantage. In short, go only so far as you can go with thoroughness. The following year this area will require far less attention so the surplus of water and of labor may be expended in an extension of the area served, until the maximum shall have been reached. No other method of proceedure will prove satisfactory unless "bonanza" methods are adopted.   Table No. 53, of statistics, in the 3d, 4th, 5th and 6th lines, shows at a glance the results reached in 7 other states as to areas under irrigation.

What there is shown is true of all other states and countries, except that, as the country becomes older, and irrigation methods are improved, the duty of water increased, and more care and labor is given to a given area, the product of that area increases and a lesser holding is relied upon. So it will be in Dakota after the irrigation system is more general; the farms, instead of becoming larger will become smaller, and better and more thorough methods of cultivation will be practiced. From these smaller areas will be returned a larger yield and one as certain as the order of the seasons and as bounteous as the prosperity which will attend them.

"Bonanza" farms may be, and no doubt are, fine things for their owners, but they are of little use to any community. A community of small farms, all of which are prosperous and each of which supports in plenty a family, is the most truly a model in all the elements which enter into the general prosperity, wellfare and happiness of the people. So each farmer will do better by his own interests, and those of his neighbors, if he seeks to place his present holding under more thorough cultivation rather than to extend his holding and neglect the proper cultivation of the whole.

PHOTOGRAPHS.

Any good engraver can engrave a picture of an artesian well, and—so to speak—can doctor it up to show according to his own ideas of magnitude, or those of the person for whom he works, which ideas may far exceed the facts.

Not so, however, with a photograph or any picture having a photograph as its base—such as photo-engravings. The camera, with the quickness of light, makes a record true to nature, and of the smallest details; a record with which the enthusiast cannot tamper; which none can question.

The importance of photographing the wells of the state has but recently impressed itself upon the leading photographers. Already several of them have quite fine collections of views of the wells in their neighborhood and take pains to secure views of each new well. Some have made a considerable profit out of their views, for a fine view finds a ready sale at home and abroad. Ere long the sale of well views will form an important item in the income of Dakota artists. A photograph of a well needs no argument back of it; it tells its own story; is its own best witness as to its truthfulness to nature, and convices the skeptic who would not otherwise accept the facts, as shown, on the affidavit of a friend, without some misgivings.

Hence the importance of taking photographs and giving them a wide circulation. They are unimpeachable witnesses as to the volume and power of our wells and will command respectful attention where the most glowing verbal description will be wasted on skeptical ears.

The eastern man who has never seen a flowing well cannot comprehend the nature of one from a mere verbal description; and even an old well driller, unacquainted with such great wells, will laugh in his sleeve at the narrator or will, with his friend the capitalist, say "that is the biggest Dakota lie I have heard yet."

Show him a photograph, however, and his skepticism turns to wonder and amazement. No argument will prevail against the evidence of the light, and the capitalist whose interest, perchance, has been solicited will turn to investigate or to invest instead of turning away in disgust or in wonder at the stupendous lying abilities of the Dakota man.

Euthusiasm on the well subject is ligitmate and laudable and increases as one sees and learns more of this wonderful power and supply. Enthusiasm is still further heightened by a comparison of the Dakota wells with those of other sections of the country. Not a comparison of reports, set in cold type, but a comparison of lifelike photographs. It is this enthusiasm that should be fostered by every resident of Dakota, and especially by every photographer.

Every person and corporation should lend every possible aid to the photographer in his effort to secure good views; and the photographer in his turn should improve every opportunity to secure views, and then place them at a price such as will enable every one to secure a supply to send away.

There is no telling what one will find its way into the hands of some man who will invest thousands of dollars in wells and irrigation projects as the direct result of having seen, and been impressed with, a photograph of a well. Every person engaged in placing irrigation bonds, or the stocks of irrigation companies, should have a collection of the best views in the state and every eastern bond-negotiating agent should be similarly supplied.

Collections of well views could, to excellent advantage, be handsomely framed and placed in the lobbies of the leading eastern hotels and in other places of popular resort. Such exhibitions would be seen by thousands of wondering and admiring spectators. Thus would a knowledge of the vast possibilities of Dakota's great wells be spread among a class of people who could not be reached by other means.

Thousands of views could in this, and in other ways, be placed where they would be a greater advertisement to the state at large than any other that could be made.

A lithograph of a goddess, of an eagle, of a gapping crowd of emigrants, or of a chariot procession may be a work of art but it can be of little value to the people; but if an equal number of views of our great artesian wells were scattered over the land the result would be a large influx of people, seeking to share the undoubted benefits the artesian waters will confer, and of money to develop an industry upon which the agricultural success of this agricultural state depends. Every view sent out should have attached a full and ACCURATE description covering as many as possible of the following points:

Name, or location of the well.
When drilled, and by whom.
Depth, in feet.
Pipe, size in inches all the way, or at top and at bottom.

Volume, discharge in gallons per minute when opened and full size, and if possible, when discharging through smaller sized openings.

Pressure, in pounds per sq. inch, when closed, and, if possible, when streams of different sizes are being discharged.

Discharge, height of throw or discharge of streams of different sizes, or the horizontal distance to which the streams are thrown.

Temperature,

Character of water, hard, soft, clear, muddy, palatable, &c.
Use to which the supply is put.

If several views are had of one well note which view is
shown and what it is—whether it is the 4 inch stream or the
6 inch stream, &c.

Without this description the view has little value, and the
value even then rests largely on the exact TRUTHFUL-
NESS of the description given. It is poor policy, to say the
least, to exaggerate as to the volume, pressure, discharge, or
the size or height of the stream shown.

If an exceptionally fine negative is secured a duplicate
should be made, for some accident may befall the first one
or it may become gradually worn out through use.

The author was desirous of having, as a prominent feature of this little volume, a series of photogravure views of
the leading wells of the state but the expense would have
been greater than the circumstances of its issue would permit, so the idea was abandoned for the present edition.
Should the book meet with such favor as to warrant another
edition this feature will be added thereto. Through the
courtesy of the leading photographers of the state the author
has secured a collection of all the views of the wells thus far
photographed.

A list is added(on the next page)of the photographers having views, their addresses, and a list of the views they have
for sale. This will be a great boon to the general public
who will thus be informed as to what views may be had, and
where to secure them. By this means it is to be hoped a
large trade in views may be worked up and the photographers thereby stimulated to the work of taking all such views
as may be possible within their territory. The importance
of cultivating this mutual interest is far reaching and it is
hoped that added interest will be taken in well photography
because of the great good that may flow therefrom to the
people of all parts or the state.

.

The author with pleasure acknowledges the courtesy of
views received from the following:
S. W. Fergusson, Bakersfield, Cal. 5 Kern Co. wells.
Wm. Kennish, Wilmington, N. C. Ponce de Leon well, Fla.
H. C. Humphrey, North Yakima, Wash. Yakima wells.
And from all the photographers listed on page 146.

WHERE TO BUY WELL PHOTOGRAPHS.

Photographs of Dakota's famous artesian wells may be secured by writing to the following Photographers.

Photographer.	Address.	List of Views.	Grade.
B. W. Burnett. These views are among the best in the state.	Tyndall, S. D.	Springfield well, 6 inch stream. " " 4 " " " " and mill. Niobrara, Neb. well, 8 in. stream. " " " 2 derrick v'ws Zinnert well 3 in. stream. " " Shadeland farm	A A A A B A A
D. O. Root. City well views are the best in the state.	Woonsocket, S. D.	Large, of City well, 4 in. stream. 2 small " " " " Hinds well, vertical stream. " " horizontal & vert. s.	A A B B
L. Janousek.	Yankton, S. D.	Brick yard well. stand-pipe view. " " " boiler view.	A A
P. C. Anderson	Redfield, S. D.	Water works display view.	B
Quiggle & Johnson.	Rapid City, S. D.	Doland well 6 inch stream. " " 6 " "	A A
J. Q. Miller.	Aberdeen, S. D.	Railway well. Beard " 6 inch stream. " " 4 " " Williams " 4 " "	B . A A B
Chas. H. Newcombe. These views are also very nice.	Huron, S. D.	Day well, vertical stream. " " double " City " water works display. 10 views of irrigated farm. Risdon well, 8 in. derrick view. " " 4 " " " " " 2 " " " " " 6 " clear " " " 5 " " " " " 4 " " " " " 2½ " " " Kerr " 3 views.	A A A B A A A A A A A A

Note: In the above list A and B refer to the grade or relative values of the views. A indicates a view of special excellence or interest and B a view of lesser value.

EXPLANATION OF TABLE OF TANGENTS & COTANG'S. P.148

I. *Required the tangent of the angle 65° 20'?*

In the first column of degrees find 65, then pass horizontally across to the column headed 20' where find 2.17749 as the tang. required. If the number of minutes in the given angle is not found in the head of the table proceed as follows:

II. *Required the tangent of the angle 65 26'?*

Proceed as before to get the tangent for 65° 20', which is the next lowest number of minutes given at the head of the table. This leaves an excess of 6 minutes. At the right hand of the table under the head of " Prop. (Proportional) parts to 1' " find 169 in the same line with 65° at the left side. 169 × 6=1014 which added to 2.17749, the tang. for 65° 20', equals 2.18763 as the required tangent. (*This gives a sufficiently approximate Tangent for ordinary use. Exact Tangent=2.18755.*)

COTANGENTS are taken from the table by taking the degrees from the column of degrees at the right side and the minutes from those indicated at the foot of the table, thus—

III. *Required the cotangent of the angle 24° 40'?*

In the right hand column of degrees find 24°, then pass horizontally across the table—to the left—to column having 40' at the foot, and find 2.17749 as the cotang. required. From this it is seen that the tang. of any angle is the cotang. of the complement of that angle, for 65° 20'+24° 40'=90°. Proceeding as at II—

IV. *Required the cotangent of angle 24° 34'?*

(*The complement of 65° 26'.*)

Obtain cotangt. for 24° 30' which=2.19430 and from column of prop. parts find 169, which multiplied by 4, for the 4' we have in excess of 30',=676. Where, in finding the *tangent*, this correction was *added* it is now *subtracted*, in finding the *cotangent*. 2.19430 minus 676=2.18754 The exact cotangent = 2.18755.

USE OF TABLE OF TANGENTS.

Tangents are used principally in determining heights and distances by means of angles. Refering to Fig. 11. page 93, suppose a surveyor's transit to be set at A, so the angle FAE can be measured, and suppose that angle to be 38° 40'. The line EF is the tangent of the angle FAE. From the table we find the tangent of the angle 38° 40' to be .80020 which multiplied by 100, the distance from A to F,=80.02 or 80 ft. as the height of the stream.

Proceed in like manner, for any other angle, to multiply the horizontal distance by the tabular tangent to get the length of the tangent. Suppose a 2 ft. rule is used to measure the angle, as described on page 158, and

Fig. 24.

that the opening of the rule is 8 inches—which corresponds to an angle of 38° 57'—and that the joint is 100 feet from the well. We find from the following table that the tang. for 38° 57' =.80855 which×100 =80.85. In this simple way the height of a stream may be determined within a foot or less.

So, too, in measuring horizontal distances to inaccessible points, as across a stream. Suppose it is desired to measure the distance A B, Fig. 24, between points on opposite sides of a river, across which measurements cannot be carried. From A lay off a right angle BAC and measure A C any suitable length, say 350 feet. From C measure angle A C B which=60° 5'—then tang. of 60° 5'= 1.73805 which×350=608.3 ft , the distance from A to B

TABLE NO. 78.

See explanation of table on page 147.

NATURAL TANGENTS.

Deg.	0′	10′	20′	30′	40′	50′		Deg.	Prop parts to 1′
0	00000	00291	00582	00873	01164	01455	01746	89	29
1	01746	02036	02328	02619	02910	03201	03492	88	29
2	03492	03783	04075	04366	04658	04949	05241	87	29
3	05241	05533	05824	06116	06408	06700	06993	86	29
4	06993	.07285	07578	07870	08163	08456	08749	85	29
5	08749	09042	09335	09629	09923	10216	10510	84	29
6	10510	10805	11099	11394	11688	11983	12278	83	29
7	12278	12574	12869	13165	13461	13758	14054	82	30
8	14054	14351	14648	14945	15243	15540	15838	81	30
9	15838	16137	16435	16734	17033	17333	17633	80	30
10	17633	17933	18233	18534	18835	19136	19438	79	30
11	19438	19740	20042	20345	20648	20952	21256	78	30
12	21256	21560	21864	22169	22475	22781	23087	77	31
13	23087	23393	23700	24008	24316	24624	24933	76	31
14	24933	25242	25552	25862	26172	26483	26795	75	31
15	26795	27107	27419	27732	28046	28360	28675	74	31
16	28675	28990	29305	29621	29938	30255	30573	73	32
17	30573	30891	31210	31530	31850	32171	32492	72	32
18	32492	32814	33136	33460	33783	34108	34433	71	32
19	34433	34758	35085	35412	35740	36068	36397	70	33
20	36397	36727	37057	37388	37720	38053	38386	69	33
21	38386	38721	39055	39391	39727	40065	40403	68	34
22	40403	40741	41081	41421	41763	42105	42447	67	34
23	42447	42791	43136	43481	43828	44175	44523	66	34
24	44523	44872	45222	45573	45924	46277	46631	65	35
25	46631	46985	47341	47698	48055	48414	48773	64	36
26	48773	49134	49495	49858	50222	50587	50953	63	36
27	50953	51319	51688	52057	52427	52798	53171	62	37
28	53171	53545	53920	54296	54673	55051	55431	61	38
29	55431	55812	56194	56577	56962	57348	57735	60	38
30	57735	58124	58513	58905	59297	59691	60086	59	39
31	60086	60483	60681	61280	61681	62083	62487	58	40
32	62187	62892	63299	63707	64117	64528	64941	57	41
33	64941	65355	65771	66189	66608	67028	67451	56	42
34	67451	67875	68301	68728	69157	69588	70021	55	43
35	70021	70455	70891	71329	71769	72211	72654	54	44
36	72654	73100	73547	73996	74447	74900	75355	53	45
37	75355	75812	76272	76733	77196	77661	78129	52	46
38	78129	78598	79070	79544	80020	80498	80978	51	47
39	80978	81461	81946	82434	82923	83415	83910	50	49
40	83910	84407	84906	85408	85912	86419	86929	49	50
41	86929	87441	87955	88473	88992	89515	90040	48	52
42	90040	90569	91099	91633	92170	92709	93252	47	53
43	93252	93797	94345	94896	95451	96008	96569	46	55
44	96569	97133	97700	98270	98843	99420	1.00000	45	57
Deg.		50′	40′	30′	20′	10′	0′	Deg.	

NATURAL COTANGENTS.

149

TABLE NO. 79—Continued.

NATURAL TANGENTS.

Deg.	0'	10'	20'	30'	40'	50'		Deg.	Prop parts to 1'
45	1.00000	1.00583	1.01170	1.01761	1.02355	1.02952	1.03553	44	59
46	1.03553	1.04158	1.04766	1.05378	1.05994	1.06613	1.07237	43	61
47	1.07237	1.07864	1.08496	1.09131	1.09770	1.10414	1.11061	42	63
48	1.11061	1.11713	1.12369	1.13029	1.13694	1.14363	1.15037	41	66
49	1.15037	1.15715	1.16398	1.17085	1.17777	1.18474	1.19175	40	69
50	1.19175	1.19882	1.20593	1.21310	1.22031	1.22758	1.23490	39	72
51	1.23490	1.24227	1.24969	1.25717	1.26471	1.27230	1.27994	38	75
52	1.27994	1.28764	1.29541	1.30323	1.31110	1.31904	1.32704	37	78
53	1.32704	1.33511	1.34323	1.35142	1.35968	1.36800	1.37638	36	82
54	1.37638	1.38484	1.39336	1.40195	1.41061	1.41934	1.42815	35	86
55	1.42815	1.43703	1.44598	1.45501	1.46411	1.47330	1.48256	34	90
56	1.48256	1.49190	1.50133	1.51084	1.52043	1.53010	1.53987	33	95
57	1.53987	1.54972	1.55966	1.56969	1.57981	1.59002	1.60033	32	100
58	1.60033	1.61074	1.62125	1.63185	1.64256	1.65337	1.66428	31	107
59	1.66428	1.67530	1.68643	1.69766	1.70901	1.72047	1.73205	30	113
60	1.73205	1.74375	1.75556	1.76749	1.77955	1.79174	1.80405	29	120
61	1.80405	1.81649	1.82906	1.84177	1.85462	1.86760	1.88073	28	128
62	1.88073	1.89400	1.90741	1.92008	1.93470	1.94858	1.96261	27	136
63	1.96261	1.97680	1.99116	2.00569	2.02039	2.03526	2.05030	26	146
64	2.05030	2.06553	2.08094	2.09654	2.11233	2.12832	2.14451	25	157
65	2.14451	2.16090	2.17749	2.19430	2.21132	2.22857	2.24604	24	169
66	2.24604	2.26374	2.28167	2.29984	2.31826	2.33693	2.35585	23	183
67	2.35585	2.37504	2.39449	2.41421	2.43422	2.45451	2.47509	22	199
68	2.47509	2.49597	2.51715	2.53865	2.56046	2.58261	2.60509	21	217
69	2.60509	2.62791	2.65109	2.67462	2.69853	2.72281	2.74748	20	235
70	2.74748	2.77254	2.79802	2.82391	2.85023	2.87700	2.90421	19	261
71	2.90421	2.93189	2.96004	2.98868	3.01783	3.04749	3.07768	18	289
72	3.07768	3.10842	3.13972	3.17159	3.20406	3.23714	3.27085	17	322
73	3.27085	3.30521	3.34023	3.37594	3.41236	3.44951	3.48741	16	360
74	3.48741	3.52609	3.56557	3.60588	3.64705	3.68909	3.73205	15	407
75	3.73205	3.77595	3.82083	3.86671	3.91364	3.96165	4.01078	14	464
76	4.01078	4.06107	4.11256	4.16530	4.21933	4.27471	4.33148	13	534
77	4.33148	4.38969	4.44942	4.51071	4.57363	4.63825	4.70463	12	621
78	4.70463	4.77286	4.84300	4.91516	4.98940	5.06584	5.14455	11	732
79	5.14455	5.22566	5.30928	5.39552	5.48451	5.57638	5.67128	10	876
80	5.67128	5.76937	5.87080	5.97576	6.08444	6.19703	6.31375	9	1068
81	6.31375	6.43484	6.56055	6.69116	6.82694	6.96823	7.11537	8	1331
82	7.11537	7.26873	7.42871	7.59575	7.77035	7.95302	8.14435	7	1708
83	8.14435	8.34496	8.55555	8.77689	9.00963	9.25530	9.51436	6	2270
84	9.51436	9.78817	10.0780	10.3854	10.7119	11.0594	11.4301	5	3168
85	11.4301	11.8262	12.2505	12.7062	13.1969	13.7267	14.3007	4	4728
86	14.3007	14.9244	15.6048	16.3499	17.1693	18.0750	19.0811	3	7806
87	19.0811	20.2056	21.4704	22.9038	24.5418	26.4316	28.6363	2	
88	28.6363	31.2416	34.3678	38.1885	42.9641	49.1039	57.2900	1	
89	57.2900	68.7501	85.9398	114.589	171.885	343.774	∞	0	
Deg.		50'	40'	30'	20'	10'	0'	Deg	

NATURAL COTANGENTS.

MENSURATION.

WEIGHTS, MEASURES AND USEFUL NUMBERS.

AVOIRDUPOIS OR COMMERCIAL WEIGHT.
16 drachms = 1 ounce = 437.5 grains.
16 ounces   = 1 pound = 256 drachms = 7000 grains.
28 pounds   = 1 quarter = 448 ounces.
4 quarters = 1 cwt.   = 112 pounds.
20 cwts.   = 1 ton   = 2240 pounds (long ton.)
2000 pounds = 1 short or commercial ton.

APOTHECARIES WEIGHT.
20 grains   = 1 scruple.
3 scruples = 1 drachm =   60 grains.
8 drachms= 1 ounce   =   480 "   = 24 scru.
12 ounces = 1 pound = 5760 "   = 288 " = 96 drms.

LONG MEASURE.
12 inches = 1 foot.
3 feet   = 1 yard   =   36 inches.
16½ "   = 1 rod   =   198 "
160 rods   = ½ mile = 31680 "   = 2640 feet.
320 "   = 1 mile   = 63360 "   = 5280 "
3 miles   = 1 league.
A palm = 3 ins. A hand = 4 ins. A span = 9 ins.
A fathom = 6 ft.

GUNTER'S CHAIN.
7.92 inches = 1 link.
100 links   = 1 chain = 4 rods = 22 yards = 66 feet.
80 chains = 1 mile = 320 "   = 1760 "   = 5280 "

SQUARE MEASURE.
144   square inches = 1 square foot.
9   "   feet   = 1   "   yard.
100   "   "   = 1   "   (architects measure.)
30.25   "   yards   = 1   "   rod.
160   "   rods   = 1   "   acre.
16   "   "   = 1   "   chain.
10   "   chains = 1   "   acre.
640   "   acres   = 1   "   mile.
43,560 sq. ft. = 1 acre = 208.71 ft. on each side.
A circular acre is 235,504 ft. in diameter.

MEASURES OF VOLUMES.

LIQUID MEASURE.
(*See also Page 151.*)

4 gills   = 1 pint = 16 ounces.
2 pints   = 1 quart = 8 gills = 32 ounces.
4 quarts = 1 gallon = 32 "   = 8 quarts.
31½ gallons = 1 wine barrel.
63 "   = 1 hogshead.

DRY MEASURE.
2 pints   = 1 quart.
4 quarts = 1 gallon = 8 pints.
2 gallons = 1 peck = 16 "   = 8 quarts.
4 pecks = 1 bushel = 64 "   = 32 " = 8 gallons

MENSURATION, continued.

CUBIC MEASURE.

1728 cubic inches = 1 cubic foot.
  27 "   feet = 1 "   yard = 46,656 cu. in.
Note—A cubic foot contains 2200 cylindrical ins., 3300 spherical ins., or 6600 conical inches.

LIQUID MEASURES.

Giving approximate sizes of measures to contain given quantities of liquid.

	Diam. ins.	Height.		Diam. ins.	Height.
Gill	1¾	3	Gallon	7	6
Half pint	2¼	3⅝	2 gallons	7	12
Pint	3½	3	8 "	14	12
Quart	3½	6	10 "	14	15

A cylinder 1 ft. in diameter and 1 ft. high contains

.02909 cubic yards.	2.524 U. S. dry pecks.
.7854 " feet.	20.196 U. S. dry quarts.
1357.1712 " inches.	40.392 U. S. dry pints.
.6311 U. S. dry bushels.	23.50 U S. liquid quarts.

5.876 U. S. gallons = 48.96 lbs.

SQUARE BOX MEASURE.

A box 24 × 16 inches square and 28 inches deep contains a barrel.
  " 24 × 16 "   "   " 14 "   "   " ½ "
  " 16 × 16¾ "   "   " 8 "   "   " 1 bushel.
  " 12 × 11¼ "   "   " 8 "   "   " ½ "
  " 8¼ × 8¼ "   "   " 8 "   "   " 1 peck.
  " 8¼ × 8¼ "   "   " 4 "   "   " . 1 gallon.
  " 8¼ × 4⅛ "   "   " 4 "   "   " ½ "
  " 4 × 4¼ "   "   " 4 "   "   " 1 quart.

MISCELLANEOUS.

A CUBIC FOOT is Equal to

1728 cubic inches.
.037037 cubic yard.
7.48052 liquid gallons (of 231 cu. ins.)
6.42851 U. S. dry gallons.
.803564 U. S. bushels (of 2150.42 cu. in.)
3.31426 U. S. pecks.
3300.23 spherical inches.
.23748 U. S. liquid barrel of 31½ gals.
62.425 pounds of pure water (approximately 62½ lbs.)

A CUBIC YARD is Equal to

27 cubic feet.
46,656 cubic inches.
21.69623 U. S. bushels (struck.)
201.974 U. S. gallons.

A GALLON is Equal to

231 cubic inches.
8.3216 pounds of water (by some authorities 8.3333) 8⅓ lbs.
.13368 cubic foot.
A cylinder 7 inches in diam. and 6 inches high.
A cube 6.1358 inches on a side.

MENSURATION, continued.

OF SQUARES, RECTANGLES AND CUBES.

The area of any parallelogram = length × width.
Area of square = square of one side.

The side of a square equal ⎰ = ⎰ diameter × .88623, or
in area to a given circle ⎱   ⎱ circumference × .2821.

To find side of inscribed square × diameter by .7071.

Area of inscribed square = square of radius × 2.
The side of a square × 1.128 = diameter of an equal circle.
Side of square = square root of its area.

Side of square = square root of ½ the square of the diagonal.
The side of a square =the diagonal× .707107 or ÷ 1.41421
Side of square × 1.51967=side of equilateral triangle of equal area.
The diagonal = the sq. root of twice the square of a side.
The diagonal = side × 1.41421
The length of a rectangle = area ÷ breadth.
The 4 angles of any quadrilateral = 4 right angles.
Any two adjacent angles of any parallelogram = 2 right angles.
The contents of a cube = length × breadth × height.
The length of the side of a cube = the cube root of its contents.

OF TRIANGLES AND POLYGONS.

The area of any triangle = ⎰ base × ½ the altitude, or
⎱ altitude × ½ the base.

The "   "   " = ⎰ half the product of the 2 sides and
⎱ the natural sine of the contained angle.

The complement of an angle = its defect from a right angle (90°)
" supplement "   " = "   "   "   two right angles (180°)
The 3 angles of any triangle = 2 right angles.
Area of trapezoid = altitude × ½ the sum of the parallel sides.
Area of trapezium = divide into 2 triangles and and find their area.
Area of equilateral triangle = square of a side × .433.

Area of any regular polygon = ⎰ sum of its sides × perpendicular
⎨ from center to one side and product
⎱ divided by 2.

OF CIRCLES.

DIAMETER × 3.14159 = circumference.   (commonly, 3.1416)
"   × .88623 = side of equal square.
"   × .7071 = "   " inscribed square.
"   squared × .7854 = area of circle.
"   = circumference ÷ 3.14159 (3.1416).
"   = side of equal square ÷ .8862.
"   = "   " inscribed square ÷ .7071.

"   = √area ÷ .7854.
"   = circumference × 0.3183.
"   = "   × 7 and product ÷ 22.
"   =1.12837 × square root of the area.
"   = as 355 is to 113 so is circumference to diameter.
CIRCUMFERENCE ÷ 3.1416 = diameter.
'.   = diameter × 3.1416.
"   = 3.5446 × square root of area.
"   = as 113 is to 355 so is diameter to circumference.
AREA = square of diameter × .7854.
"   = "   " circumference × .07958.
"   = ½ diameter × ¼ circumference.
"   = square of radius × 3.1416.
".   = ⎰ areas of circles are to each other as the squares of their
⎱ diameters.

Continued on next page.

MERSURATION, continued.

Doubling the diameter of a circle increases the area 4 times.

To find diameter of cicle = } × side of given square by 1.12837.
in area to a given square }

Diameter of circle of equal priphery as square = side × 1.2732.
Side of square of equal periphery as circle = diameter × .7854.

Diameter × 1.3468 = side of an equilateral triangle of equal area.

Length of arc = number of degrees × .017453 × radius.

Area of circular ring = { From area of outer circle take the area of inner cicle, remainder = area.
OR
Sum of diameter × difference of diameters and product × .7854.

Area of sector of circle = length of arc × ½ radius.

Surface of cylinder equals circumf. × length + area of two ends.

Contents " " area of end × length.

Surface of sphere " diameter × circumf.

Contents " " cube of diam. × .5236.

  " of widge " area of base × ½ altitude.

  " pyramid " } area of base × ⅓ altitude.
    or cone

The square of the diam. of a sphere × 3.1416 = its surface.

The product of the two axes of an eclipse × .7854 = its area.

The sq. rt. of ½ the sum of the squares of the two diameters of an elipse × 3.1416 = its circumference.

USEFUL MULTIPLIERS.

Note: The converse is obtained by dividing instead of by multiplying.

Lineal feet	×	.00019	= miles.
" yards	×	.000568	= "
Square inches	×	.00695	= square feet.
" feet	×	.111	= " yards.
" yards	×	.0002067	= acres.
Acres	×	.4840	= square yards.
Cubic inches	×	.00058	= cubic feet.
" feet	×	.03704	= " yards.
Circular inches	×	.00546	= square feet.
Cylindrical inches	×	.0004546	= cubic "
" feet	×	.02909	= " yards.
Links	×	.22	= yards.
"	×	.66	= feet.
Feet	×	1.5151	= links.
Square feet	×	2.2957	= square links.
Width in chains	×	8.	= acres per mile.
Cubic feet	×	7.48052	= U. S. gallons.
" inches	×	.004329	= " "
Cylindrical feet	×	5.874	= " "
" inches	×	.0034	= " "
U. S. gallons	×	.133679	= cubic feet.
U. S. "	× 231.		= " inches.
Cubic feet	×	.8036	= U. S. bushels.
U. S. bushels	×	1.2446	= cubic feet.
lbs. avoirdupois	×	.00045	= tons (2240 lbs.)
Cu. ft. water	×	62.425	= lbs. avoir.
" "	×	62.37925	= lbs. (according to Haswell.)

268.8 gallons of water = 1 ton.
35.88 cu. ft. " " = 1 "

A column of water 12 inches high by 1 inch diameter = .341 lbs.

MISCELLANEOUS NOTES.

CORN AND HOGS.

A bushel of corn will make 10½ lbs. of pork, gross. Then:

When corn costs 12½ cents per bushel	Pork costs 1½ cents per pound.
17 " " "	2 " " "
25 " " "	3 " " "
35 " " "	4 " " "
42 " " "	5 " " "
50 " " "	6 " " "

Jones & Laughlin.

TABLE NO. 54.

TABLE OF TIME. *New.*

Time.	Days.	Hours.	Minutes.	Seconds.
1 minute =	....	....	....	60
1 hour =	....	....	60	3 600
1 day =	....	24	1 440	86 400
1 week =	7	168	10 080	604 800
1 civil month =	28	672	40 320	2 419 200
1 month =	30	720	43 200	2 592 000
1 month =	31	744	44 640	2 678 400
2 months =	60	1440	86 400	5 184 000
3 " =	90	2160	129 600	7 776 000
6 " =	180	4320	259 200	15 552 000
1 year =	365	8765	525 948	31 556 829

1 year = 365 ds., 5 hrs., 48 min., 49 7⁄50 sec.
1 year = 52 weeks, 1 day, 5 h., 48 m., 49 7⁄50 sec.
1 year = { 1 month of 28 or 29 days (Feb.)
{ 4 months of 30 days.
{ 7 "   " 31 "

"**A Solar Day** is the time between two successive solar noons, or transits (passages) of the sun over the meridian of a place. These intervals are not of equal length all the year around. The average length of all the solar days is called the **Mean Solar Day;** and is the same as the common civil day of 24 hours of clock time. Civil noon is at 12 o'clock; but solar, or apparent noon, may be about 14½ min. before; or 16¼ min. after 12 correct clock time. **A Siderial Day** is the interval between two passages of the same star past the range of two fixed objects; and is the precise time required for one complete revolution of the earth on its axis. The sideral day never varies; but is always equal to 23 hours, 56 minutes, 4.09 sec., so that a star will on any night appear to set, or to pass the range of any two fixed objects, 3 min., 55.91 sec. earlier by the clock than it did on the night before, so that the number of sideral days in a civil year is 1 greater than that of the civil days.

An Astronomical Day degins at *noon*, and its hours are counted from 0 to 24. In comparing it with the civil day, the last is supposed to begin at the midnight *before* the noon at which the first began."

Example: Nov. 15 (civil day) begins at midnight; while Nov. 15 (astronomical day) does not begin until 12 hours later, i. e. at noon of Nov. 15, civil day.

9 A. M. of civil day = 21 o'clock of artronomical day.
3 P. M. "   "   " = 3 "   "   "   "

TABLE NO. 55.

TABLES OF WAGES.

WAGES PER HOUR, AT DIFFERENT RATES PER DAY.
On basis of 10 hours to the day. _New._

TIME.	WAGES PER DAY.						
	1.50	1.75	2.00	2.25	2.50	3.00	4.25
½ hour.	.07	.08	.10	.11	.12	.15	.21
1 "	.15	.17	.20	.22	.25	.30	.42
2 "	.30	.35	.40	.45	.50	.60	.85
3 "	.45	.52	.60	.67	.75	.90	1.27
4 "	.60	.70	.80	.90	1.00	1.20	1.70
5 "	.75	.87	1.00	1.12	1.25	1.50	2.12
6 "	.90	1.05	1.20	1.35	1.50	1.80	2.55
7 "	1.05	1.22	1.40	1.57	1.75	2.10	2.97
8 "	1.20	1.40	1.60	1.80	2.00	2.40	3.40
9 "	1.35	1.57	1.80	2.02	2.25	2.70	3.82
1 Day.	1.50	1.75	2.00	2.25	2.50	3.00	4.25
2 "	3.00	3.50	4.00	4.50	5.00	6.00	8.50
3 "	4.50	5.25	6.00	6.75	7.50	9.00	12.75
4 "	6.00	7.00	8.00	9.00	10.00	12.00	17.00
5 "	7.50	8.75	10.00	11.25	12.50	15.00	21.25
6 "	9.00	10.50	12.00	13.50	15.00	18.00	25.50
7 "	10.50	12.25	14.00	15.75	17.50	21.00	29.75
¼ "	.38	.44	.50	.56	.62	.76	1.06
¾ "	1.12	1.31	1.50	1.68	1.87	2.25	3.18

By combination of rates given, amounts per hour at other rates may be quickly found.—amounts at 2.25 + 1.50 equal amount at 3.75 etc.

WAGES PER DAY, AT DIFFERENT RATES PER MONTH, AND ON BASIS OF DIFFERENT NUMBER OF DAYS IN THE MONTH.

Days in the mo.	Rate per day, at following rates per month.											
	$ 20	25	30	35	40	45	50	55	60	75	80	90	100
26	.77	.96	1.15	1.34	1.54	1.73	1.92	2.12	2.31	2.89	3.08	3.46	3.85
28	.71	.89	1.07	1.25	1.43	1.61	1.79	1.96	2.14	2.67	2.85	3.21	3.57
30	.67	.83	1.00	1.17	1.33	1.50	1.67	1.83	2.00	2.50	2.67	3.00	3.33
31	.65	.81	.97	1.13	1.29	1.45	1.62	1.78	1.94	2.42	2.58	2.90	3.23

It is the practice among most large mercantile conserns and corporations, and railway companies. to pay on the basis of 26 days to the month, ·that being the average number of working days. All government employees are paid on substantially the same basis.

WAGES PER HOUR, AT DIFFERENT RATES PER MONTH, AND ON BASIS OF 26 DAYS TO THE MONTH.

Time.	Rate per hour, at following rates per month.									
	20	25	30	35	40	45	50	60	75	90
1 hour.	.08	.10	.12	.14	.15	.17	.19	.23	.28	.34
2 hours.	.16	.19	.23	.28	.31	.34	.38	.46	.57	.69
3 "	.23	.29	.35	.42	.46	.51	.57	.69	.86	1.03
4 "	.31	.38	.46	.55	.61	.69	.76	.92	1.15	1.38
5 "	.39	.48	.58	.69	.77	.86	.96	1.15	1.44	1.73
6 "	.46	.57	.69	.82	.92	1.03	1.15	1.38	1.72	2.06
7 "	.54	.67	.81	.95	1.07	1.21	1.34	1.61	2.01	2.42
8 "	.62	.76	.92	1.08	1.23	1.38	1.53	1.84	2.30	2.76
9 "	.69	.86	1.04	1.21	1.38	1.55	1.72	2.07	2.59	3.11
1 day.	.77	.96	1.15	1.34	1.54	1.73	1.92	2.31	2.89	3.46

AREA OF FIELDS.

TABLE NO. 56.

SHOWING SIZES OF A ONE ACRE FIELD, THE WIDTH ADVANCING
BY 5 FEET. *New.*

Wide	Long	Wide	Long	Wide	Long	Wide	Long	Wide	Long
ft. 1	43560	45	968	90	484	135	322.7	180	242
5	8712	50	971.2	95	458.5	140	311.1	185	235.5
10	4356	55	792	100	435.6	145	300.4	190	229.3
15	2904	60	726	105	414.9	150	290.4	195	223.4
20	2178	65	670.2	110	396	155	281	200	217.8
25	1742.5	70	622.2	115	378.8	160	272.3	205	212.5
30	1452	75	580.8	120	363	165	264	208.71	208.71
35	1244.6	80	544.5	125	348.5	170	256.3	||
40	1089	85	512.4	130	335.1	175	248.9	A square acre.	

This table is near enough for all practical purposes. If
the *exact* size is required to a second decimal place, or the
length corresponding to any width not given in the table,
divide 43,560 (the number of sq. ft. in 1 acre) by the given
width. Thus: what will be the length of a field of one acre
the width being 183.7 ft. ?

43,560÷183.7=237.12 ft. long.

In like manner obtain the area of the size of any rectangular field. Had it been desired to find the length of a field of
17 acres the width of which was to be 183.7 ft. then 43,560
would be multiplied by 17 and the product divided by the
given width.

If the length and breadth are given and the area is wanted
divide the total area in square feet (the product of the
length×by the breadth) by 43,560 and the answer will be in
acres. In the above table the doubling of any *one* dimen-
sion doubles the area—1089 ft. long by 80 ft. wide would
contain 2 acres; but doubling *both* dimensions increases the
area 4 times—2178 long by 80 ft. wide=4 acres.

TABLE NO. 57.

SHOWING SQUARE FEET IN DIFFERENT AREAS. *New.*

Acres.	Square feet of area.	Acres.	Square feet of area.
½	21 780	60	2 613 600
1	43 560	80	3 484 800
2	87 120	100	4 356 000
3	130 680	120	5 227 200
4	174 240	160	6 969 600
5	217 800	240	10 454 400
6	261 360	320	13 939 200
7	304 920	480	20 908 800
8	348 480	640	27 878 400
9	392 040	800	34 848 000
10	435 600	960	41 817 600
20	871 200	1120	48 787 200
40	1 742 400	1280	55 756 800

AREA OF FIELDS, continued.

```
1 Acre             =   10     square chains.
1 square    acre   =  208.71  feet on a side.
1    "    ½   "    =  147.581   "     "     "
1    "    ¼   "    =  104.355   "     "     "
1 circular   "     =  235.50   "  in diameter.
1    "    ½   "    =  166.52    "     "     "
1    "    ¼   "    =  117.75    "     "     "
```

AREA OF RAILWAY RIGHT OF WAY.

```
50 feet wide contains   .1148 acres to 100 feet of length.
100   "    "      "      .2296    "    "  100   "     "     "
50    "    "      "     6.06      "    "  1 mile  "     "
100   "    "      "    12.12      "    "  1   "      "     "
```

If the field is of irregular form divide it up into smaller rectangular or triangular pieces, estimate the area of each in cu. ft., add these areas and divide the total by 43,560 to get the area in acres. The division may be made by platting the outline of the field on paper, then making the divisions desired, and taking the measurements of the parts from the scale of the drawing.

If the measurement has been made in chains and links point off 5 places from the right of the product obtained, to get the area. Example.—A field is 8 chains and 20 links wide and 10 chains and 45 links long—what is the area in acres?

8.20×10.45=8.56900. (5 places being pointed off.) Multiply the 5 figures cut off (.56900 in this case) by 4 and again point off 5 figures, the remainder is roods; multiply the 5 figures cut off by 4 and again cut off 5 figures to get a remainder in rods or perches. In the above example 56900×4 =2.27600 and 27600 ×4=1.10400. Therefore, above field equals 8 acres, 2 roods and1.103 rods in area.

TABLE NO. 58.

NUMBER OF HILLS ON ONE ACRE. *Haswell.*

Ft. apart	No.	Ft. apart	No.	Ft. apart	No.	Ft. apart	No.
1	43560	5	1742	9	538	16	171
1½	19360	5½	1440	9½	482	17	151
2	10890	6	1210	10	435	18	135
2½	6969	6½	1031	10½	361	20	108
3	4840	7	889	12	302	25	69
3½	3556	7½	775	13	258	30	48
4	2722	8	680	14	223	35	35
4½	2151	8½	692	15	193	40	27

PRISMOIDAL FORMULA.

A prismoid is a solid bounded by six plain surfaces only two of which are parallel.

To find the contents of a prismoid, add the areas of the two parallel sides and four times the area of a section taken midway between and parallel to them, and multiply this sum by ⅙ of the perpendicular distance between the parallel sides.

This formula is used in the calculation of quantities of excavation and embankment on railroads, canals, etc.

TABLE NO. 58½.
From Trautwine's "Civil Engineer's Pocket Book."

ANGLES.

Approximate Measurement of Angles.

(1) The four fingers of the hand, held at right angles to the arm and at arm's length from the eye, cover about 7 degrees. And an angle of 7° corresponds to about 12.2 feet in 100 feet; or to 36.6 feet in 100 yards; or to 645 feet in a mile.

(2) By means of a two-foot rule, either on a drawing or between distant objects in the field. If the inner edges of a common two-foot rule be opened to the extent shown in the column of inches, they will be inclined to each other at the angles shown in the column of angles. Since an opening of ⅛ inch (up to 19 inches or about 105°) corresponds to from about ½° to 1°, no great accuracy is to be expected, and beyond 105° still less; for the liability to error then increases very rapidly as the opening becomes greater. Thus, the last ⅛ inch corresponds to about 12°.

Angles for openings intermediate of those given may be calculated to the nearest minute or two, by simple proportion, up to 23 inches of opening, or about 147°.

Table of Angles corresponding to openings of a 2-foot rule.
(Original).

Correct.

Ins.	Deg. min.	Ins.	Deg. min.	Ins.	Deg. min.	Ins.	Deg. min.	Ins.	Deg. min.	Ins.	Deg. min.
¼	1 12	4¼	20 24	8¼	40 13	12¼	61 23	16¼	85 14	20¼	115 5
	1 48		21		40 51		62 5		86 3		116 12
½	2 24	½	21 37	½	41 29	½	62 47	½	86 52	½	117 20
	3 00		22 13		42 7		63 28		87 41		118 30
¾	3 36	¾	22 50	¾	42 46	¾	64 11	¾	88 31	¾	119 40
	4 11		23 27		43 24		64 53		89 21		120 52
1	4 47	5	24 3	9	44 3	13	65 35	17	90 12	21	122 6
	5 23		24 39		44 42		66 18		91 3		123 20
¼	5 58	¼	25 16	¼	45 21	¼	67 1	¼	91 54	¼	124 36
	6 34		25 53		45 59		67 44		92 46		125 54
½	7 10	½	26 30	½	46 38	½	68 28	½	93 38	½	127 14
	7 46		27 7		47 17		69 12		94 31		128 35
¾	8 22	¾	27 44	¾	47 56	¾	69 55	¾	95 24	¾	129 59
	8 58		28 21		48 35		70 38		96 17		131 25
2	9 34	6	28 58	10	49 15	14	71 22	18	97 11	22	132 53
	10 10		29 35		49 54		72 6		98 5		134 24
¼	10 46	¼	30 11	¼	50 34	¼	72 51	¼	99 00	¼	135 58
	11 22		30 49		51 13		73 36		99 55		137 35
½	11 58	½	31 26	½	51 53	½	74 21	½	100 51	½	139 16
	12 34		32 3		52 33		75 6		101 48		141 1
¾	13 10	¾	32 40	¾	53 13	¾	75 51	¾	102 45	¾	142 51
	13 46		33 17		53 53		76 36		103 43		144 46
3	14 22	7	33 54	11	54 34	15	77 22	19	104 41	23	146 48
	14 58		34 33		55 14		78 8		105 40		148 58
¼	15 34	¼	35 10	¼	55 55	¼	78 54	¼	106 39	¼	151 17
	16 10		35 47		56 35		79 40		107 40		153 48
½	16 46	½	36 25	½	57 16	½	80 27	½	108 41	½	156 34
	17 22		37 3		57 57		81 14		109 43		159 43
¾	17 59	¾	37 41	¾	58 38	¾	82 2	¾	110 46	¾	163 27
	18 35		38 19		59 19		82 49		111 49		168 18
4	19 12	8	38 57	12	60 00	16	83 37	20	112 53	24	180 00
	19 48		39 35		60 41		84 26		113 58		

(3) With the same table, using feet instead of inches. From any point measure 12 *feet* toward * each object, and place marks. Measure the distance in *feet* between these marks. Suppose the first column in the table to be *feet* instead of inches. Then opposite the distance in *feet* will be the angle.

⅛ foot = 1.5 inches.

1 in. = .083 ft.	4 ins. = .333 ft.	7 ins. = .583 ft.	10 ins. = .833 ft.
2 ins. = .167 ft.	5 ins. = .416 ft.	8 ins. = .667 ft.	11 ins. = .917 ft.
3 ins. = .25 ft.	6 ins. = .5 ft.	9 ins. = .75 ft.	12 ins. = 1.0 ft.

(4) Or, measure toward * each object 100 or any other number of feet, and place marks. Measure the distance in feet between the marks. Then

$$\text{Sine of } \frac{\text{half}}{\text{the angle}} = \frac{\text{half the distance between the marks}}{\text{the distance measured toward one of the objects}}.$$

*From a table of sines find this angle and multiply it by 2.

WEIGHT OF A CUBIC FOOT OF SUBSTANCES.

Trautwine.

Name of substances.	Average weight, lbs.
Aluminum,	162
Brick, best pressed	150
" common, hard	125
" " soft	100
Coal, Pennsylvania anthracite, solid	93
" " " broken, loose	54
" " " moderately shaken	58
" " " heaped ....bushel.... (77 to 83)	
" Bituminous, solid	84
" " broken, loose	49
" " heaped, loose...................bushel.... (74)	
Coke, loose	23 to 32
" heaped bushel	35 to 42
Cement, American Hydraulic, Rosendale	56
" " Louisville	50
" English " Portland	90
Clay, loose	63
Earth, common loam, dry, loose	76
" " " moderately rammed	95
" as soft mud	108
Flint	162
Glass	157
Gneiss	168
Granite	170
Gravel	90 to 106
Ice	58.7
Iron, cast	450
" wrought	480
Lead	711
Lime, loose or in small lumps	53
□ " ....struck bushel....[66]	
Limestone and marble	168
" loose, in fragments	96
Masonry of Granite or limestone, well dressed	165
" " mortar rubble	154
" " sandstone, well dressed	144
Mortar, hardened	103
Quartz	165
Salt, coarse	45
" fine	49
Sand, pure quartz, dry. loose	90 to 106
" well shaken	99 to 117
" wet	113 to 130
Sandstone	151
Shales	162
Silver	655
Snow, freshly fallen	5 to 12
" moistened and compacted	15 to 50
Steel	490
Water, pure. 62.425 [Fuller], 62.37925 [Haswell] approximately	62½
" sea	64.3

WOODS

Ash	47
Boxwood	60
Cherry	42
Cork	16
Elm	35
Hemlock	25
Hickory	53
Maple	35

Oak, live....59,	white....48,	red or black....32 to 45	
Pine, white....25	yellow....35,	southern....45	

Green timber usually weighs from ⅛ to ½ more than dry.

TABLE NO. 59.

NAILS AND SPIKES.

Carnegie, Phipps & Co.

Standard Steel Wire Nails.						Steel wire spikes.			Com'n. iron na'ls		
		Common.		Finishing.							
Size.	Long	Diam ins.	No. per lb	Diam ins.	No. per lb	Long	Diam ins.	No. per lb	Size.	Long	No. per lb
2 d	1 in.	.0524	1060	.0453	1558	3 in.	.1620	41	2 d	1 in.	800
3 d	1¼ "	.0588	640	.0508	913	3½ "	.1819	30	8 d	1¼ "	400
4 d	1½ "	.0720	380	.0508	761	4 "	.2043	23	4 d	1½ "	300
5 d	1¾ "	.0764	275	.0571	500	4½ "	.2294	17	5 d	1¾ "	200
6 d	2 "	.0808	210	.0641	350	5 "	.2576	13	6 d	2 "	150
7 d	2¼ "	.0858	160	.0641	315	5½ "	.2893	11	7 d	2¼ "	120
8 d	2½ "	.0935	115	.0720	214	6 "	.2893	10	8 d	2½ "	85
9 d	2¾ "	.0963	93	.0720	195	6½ "	.2249	7½	9 d	2¾ "	75
10 d	3 "	.1082	77	.0808	137	7 "	.2249	7	10 d	3 "	60
12 d	3¼ "	.1144	60	.0808	127	8 "	.3648	5	12 d	3¼ "	50
16 d	3½ "	.1285	48	.0907	90	9 "	.3648	4½	16 d	3½ "	40
20 d	4 "	.1620	31	.1019	62				20 d	4 "	20
30 d	4½ "	.1819	22						30 d	4½ "	16
40 d	5 "	.2043	17						40 d	5 "	14
50 d	5½ "	.2294	13						50 d	5½ "	11
60 d	6 "	.2576	11						60 d	6 "	8

TABLE NO. 60.

WROUGHT SPIKES.

Number to a keg of 150 pounds. *Carnegie, Phipps & Co.*

Length Ins.	¼ in. No.	5/16 in. No.	⅜ in. No.	Length Ins.	¼ in. No.	5/16 in. No.	⅜ in. No.	7/16 in. No.	½ in. No.
3	2250	......	......	7	1161	622	482	445	306
3½	1890	1208	......	8	......	635	455	384	256
4	1650	1135	......	9	......	573	424	300	240
4½	1464	1064	......	10	......	......	391	270	222
5	1380	930	742	11	......	......	....	249	203
6	1292	868	570	12	......	......	....	236	180

TABLE NO. 61.

TABLE OF MANILLA ROPE.

Trautwine.

Diameter Ins.	Circumference Inches.	Wt. per ft lbs.	Breaking load.		Diameter Inches.	Circumf. Ins.	Wt. per ft lbs.	Breaking load.	
			Tons.	Lbs.				Tons.	Lbs.
.239	¾	.019	.25	560	1.27	4	.528	5.16	11 558
.318	1	.033	.35	784	1.43	4½	.668	6.60	14 784
.477	1½	.074	.70	1 568	1.59	5	.825	8.20	18 368
.636	2	.132	1.21	2 733	1.75	5½	.998	9.80	21 952
.795	2½	.206	1.91	4 278	1.91	6	1.19	11.4	25 536
.955	3	.297	2.73	6 115	2.07	6½	1.39	13.0	29 120
1.11	3½	.404	3.81	8 534	2.23	7	1.62	14.6	32 704

TABLE NO. 62.   WELL DIGGING.

1 cubic yard = 201.95 gallons.   *Adapted from Trautwine.*

Diameter in feet.	Cubic yds. for each foot of depth.	Diameter in feet.	Cu. yds. for each foot of depth.	Diameter in feet.	Cubic yards for each foot in depth.
1	.0291	3½	.3563	6	1.047
¼	.0455	¾	.4091	¼	1.136
½	.0654	4	.4654	½	1.229
¾	.0891	¼	.5254	¾	1.325
2	.1164	½	.5890	7	1.425
¼	.1473	¾	.6563	½	1.636
½	.1818	5	.7272	8	1.862
¾	.2200	¼	.8018	½	2.102
3	.2618	½	.8799	9	2.356
¼	.3073	¾	.9617	½	2.625

For diameters twice as great as those given in the table, for the cu. yds. of digging, take out those opposite ½ of the greater diam., and×by 4. Thus, for the cu. yds. in each foot of a well 12 ft. in diam., take out the yds. for a well of 6 ft. diam. and×by 4....1.074×4=4.188=cu. yds. for a well of 12 feet diameter.

TABLE NO. 63.
CAPACITY OF CISTERNS IN GALLONS.
For each 10 inches in depth.   *Haswell.*

Diam.	Gallons.	Diam.	Gallons.	Diam.	Gallons.	Diam.	Gallons.
Feet.		Feet.		Feet.		Feet.	
2.	19.50	5.	122.40	8.	313.33	12	705.0
2.5	30.60	5.5	148.10	8.5	353.72	13	827.4
3.	44.60	6.	176.25	9.	396.56	14	959.6
3.5	59.97	6.5	206.85	9.5	461.40	15	1101.6
4.	78.33	7.	239.88	10.	489.60	20	1958.4
4.5	99.14	7.5	275.40	11.	592.40	25	3059.9

In this table the capacity being given for 10 inches it is but necessary to divide by 10 by moving the decimal point one place to the left, in order to get the capacity for 1 inch. Thus, the capacity for 6 ft. diam and 10 inches deep=176.25 gals., and for 1 inch deep it=17.625 gals. The capacity for any depths may be found by multiplying the capacity for 1 inch by the depths in inches. Example. How many gals. in a cistern 12 feet in diam. and 9 feet deep? 9 ft.=108 in. 70.5, gals. in one inch,×108=7614 gals. Ans.

TABLE NO. 64.
CAPACITY OF CISTERNS IN BARRELS. OF 31½ GALLONS.   *Leffel.*

Depth in feet.	Diameter in feet.									
	5	6	7	8	9	10	11	12	13	14
5	23.3	33.6	45.7	59.7	75.5	93.2	112.8	134.3	157.6	182.8
6	28.0	40.3	54.8	71.7	90.6	111.9	135.4	161.1	189.1	219.3
7	32.7	47.0	64.0	83.6	105.7	130.6	158.0	188.0	220.6	255.9
8	37.3	53.7	73.1	95.5	120.9	149.2	180.5	214.8	252.1	292.4
9	42.0	60.4	82.2	107.4	136.0	167.9	203.1	241.7	283.7	329.0
10	46.7	67.1	91.4	119.4	151.1	186.5	225.7	268.6	315.2	365.5
11	51.3	73.9	100.5	131.3	166.2	205.1	248.2	295.4	346.7	402.1
12	56.0	80.6	109.7	143.2	181.3	223.8	270.8	322.3	378.2	438.6
13	60.7	87.3	118.8	155.2	196.4	242.4	293.4	349.1	409.7	475.2
14	65.3	94.0	127.9	167.1	211.5	261.1	315.9	376.0	441.3	511.8

A BARREL.

The standard wine barrel contains 31½ gals. of 231 cu. in. In Pennsylvania a wine bbl.=32 gals. The standard wine bbl. contains 4.211 cu. ft. A hogshead=63 gals. The average size of the barrel used for oil or vinegar is about 19½ ins. diam. of head, 22¾ ins. diam. of bung, and 29 to 30 ins. long and contains from 48 to 52 gals. the contents being usually marked on the head.

In figuring on the barrel capacity of a cistern the size or volume of the barrel should be given or, in case of contract work, it should be specified. By reason of the size of the ordinary barrel being from 48 to 52 gals. it would, for convenience, be best to figure on the basis of 50 gals. to the bbl. The bbl. of 31½ gals., however, is the one commonly used.

MISCELLANEOUS.

Shingles. 1000 laid 4 inches to the weather will cover one square of 100 sq. ft. and 5 ℔s. of nails will lay them.

Lath. 1000 will cover 70 sq. yds. of surface and 11 ℔s. of nails will lay them.

Mortar. 8 bushels of lime, 16 of sand and 1 of hair will make mortar for 100 sq. yds. of surface.

Stone Wall. 1 cord of stone, 3 bushels of lime, and 1 cu. yd. of sand will lay 100 cu. ft. of wall.

Brick. 5 courses of brick will lay 1 foot high.

```
6 brick in a course will lay a flue  4 by 12 inches.
7   "      "      "      "    "    "     8  "  12   "
8   "      "      "      "    "    "     8  "  16   "
8   "      "      "      "    "    "    12  "  12   "
9   "      "      "      "    "    "    12  "  16   "
10  "      "      "      "    "    "    12  "  20   "
```

Thickness of wall.		No. to sq. ft. of wall.	
8 inches = 1	brick	14	
12 " 1½	"	21	No allowance being made for
16 " 2	"	28	mortar or extra thickness of
20 " 2½	"	35	brick. Brick 8 X 4 X 2 inches.
24 " 3	"	42	

Flooring & Siding. Add ⅛ to the area to be covered to allow for lap. This is the lumberman's rule in selling.

Hay. Get the number of cubic feet in the mow or stack; then, for new hay, divide by about 270 to get tons; for old hay, divide by about 230 to get tons; and for dry clover divide by about 310 to get tons. The weights of different grasses, in the different stages of dryness or compression, vary so greatly that any rule for weight by volume must be so purely arbitrary as to be of but little value.

Corn. Get the cubic feet and divide by 2¼ to get bushels.

Apples, Potatoes, & Grain in Bin. Get cu. ft. and ✕ by 8, then point off 1 place for decimals to get contents in bushels—or—from cubic ft. deduct ⅕ and the remainder =bushels in bin. (bush.=1.24445 cu. ft.) Example.— 100 cu. ft. ✕8=800, pointed off=80 bush.—or—100—⅕ (20) =80 bushels.

LUMBER TABLES.

TABLE NO. 65.

FEET, BOARD MEASURE, IN JOIST, SCANTLING AND TIMBER.

Length in feet. / Size in Inches.	10	12	14	16	18	20	22	24	26	28	30
	FEET, BOARD MEASURE.										
2 x 4	6⅔	8	9⅓	10⅔	12	13⅓	14⅔	16	17⅓	18⅔	20
2 x 6	10	12	14	16	18	20	22	24	26	28	30
2 x 8	13⅓	16	19⅔	21⅓	24	26⅔	29⅓	32	34⅔	37⅓	40
2 x 10	16⅔	20	23⅓	26⅔	30	33⅓	36⅔	40	43⅓	46⅔	50
2 x 12	20	24	28	32	36	40	44	48	52	56	60
2 x 14	23⅓	28	32⅔	37⅓	42	46⅔	51⅓	56	63⅔	65⅓	70
3 x 4	10	12	14	16	18	20	22	24	26	28	30
3 x 6	15	18	21	24	27	30	33	36	39	42	45
3 x 8	20	24	28	32	36	40	44	48	52	56	60
3 x 10	25	30	35	40	45	50	55	60	65	70	75
3 x 12	30	36	42	48	54	60	66	72	78	84	90
3 x 14	35	42	49	56	63	70	77	84	91	98	105
4 x 4	13⅓	16	18⅔	21⅓	24	26⅔	29⅓	32	34⅔	37⅓	40
4 x 6	20	24	28	32	36	40	44	48	52	56	60
4 x 8	26⅔	32	37⅓	42⅔	48	53⅓	58⅔	64	69⅓	74⅔	80
4 x 10	33⅓	40	46⅔	53⅓	60	66⅔	73⅓	80	86⅔	93⅓	100
4 x 12	40	48	56	64	72	80	88	96	104	112	120
6 x 6	30	36	42	48	54	60	66	72	78	84	90
6 x 8	40	48	56	64	72	80	88	96	104	112	120
6 x 10	50	60	70	80	90	100	110	120	130	140	150
6 x 12	60	72	84	96	108	120	132	144	156	168	180
8 x 8	53⅓	64	74⅔	85⅓	96	106⅔	117⅓	128	138⅔	149⅓	160
8 x 10	66⅔	89	93⅓	106⅔	120	133⅓	146⅔	160	173⅓	186⅔	200
8 x 12	80	96	112	128	144	160	176	192	208	224	240
10 x 10	83⅓	100	117	133	150	167	183	200	217	233	250
10 x 12	100	120	140	160	180	200	220	240	260	280	300
12 x 12	120	144	168	192	216	240	264	288	312	336	360
12 x 14	140	168	196	224	252	280	308	336	364	392	420
14 x 14	163⅓	196	228⅔	261⅓	294	326⅔	359⅓	392	424⅔	457⅓	490

TABLE NO. 66.

FEET—BOARD MEASURE, IN 1 INCH BOARDS. *New*

Width in inches.	Length in feet.								
	8	10	12	14	16	18	20	22	24
4	2⅔	3⅓	4	4⅔	5⅓	6	6⅔	7⅓	8
6	4	5	6	7	8	9	10	11	12
8	5⅓	6⅔	8	9⅓	10⅔	12	13⅓	14⅔	16
10	6⅔	8⅓	10	11⅔	13⅓	15	16⅔	18⅓	20
12	8	10	12	14	16	18	20	22	24
14	9⅓	11⅔	14	16⅓	18⅔	21	23⅓	25⅔	28
16	10⅔	13⅓	16	18⅔	21⅓	24	26⅔	29⅓	32
18	12	15	18	21	24	27	30	33	36
20	13⅓	16⅔	20	23⅓	26⅔	30	33⅓	36⅔	40

RULE for estimating ft. b. m. in any piece of board or timber.—[A foot b. m. = 12 × 12 inches by 1 inch thick, = 144 cubic inches.] Multiply the width by the thickness ÷ product by 12 and × quotient by length. Thus: A stick 8 by 10 inches by 10 feet equals 8 × 10 = 80 inches of sectional area which ÷ 12 = 6⅔ ft. b. m. per foot of length; this × 10 = 66⅔ ft.

3″ by 12″ by 10′ equals 3 × 12 = 36, 36 ÷ 12 = 3, 3 × 10 = 30 ft. B.M.

4″ by 6″ by 10′ equals 4 × 6 = 24, 24 ÷ 12 = 2, 2 × 10 = 20 ft. B.M. &c.

Lengths of a Degree of Longitude in different Latitudes, and at the level of the Sea.

These lengths are in common land or statute miles, of 5280 ft. Since the figure of the earth has never been *precisely* ascertained, these are but close approximations. Intermediate ones may be found correctly by simple proportion. 1° of longitude corresponds to 4 mins of civil or clock time; 1 min of longitude to 4 secs of time.

Deg of Lat.	Miles.	Deg of Lat.	Miles.	Deg of Lat.	Miles.	Deg of Lat.	Miles.	Deg of Lat.	Miles.	Deg of Lat.	Miles.
0	69.16	14	67.12	28	61.11	42	51.47	56	38.76	70	23.72
2	69.12	16	66.50	30	59.94	44	49.83	58	36.74	72	21.43
4	68.99	18	65.80	32	58.70	46	48.12	60	34.67	74	19.12
6	68.78	20	65.02	34	57.39	48	46.36	62	32.55	76	16.78
8	68.49	22	64.15	36	56.01	50	44.54	64	30.40	78	14.42
10	68.12	24	63.21	38	54.56	52	42.67	66	28.21	80	12.05
12	67.66	26	62.20	40	53.05	54	40.74	68	25.98	82	9.66

Inches reduced to Decimals of a Foot. No errors.

Ins.	Foot.	Ins.	Foot.	Ins.	Foot.	Ins.	Foot.	Ins.	Foot.	Ins.	Foot.
0	.0000	2	.1667	4	.3333	6	.5000	8	.6667	10	.8333
1-32	.0026		.1693		.3359		.5026		.6693		.8359
1-16	.0052		.1719		.3385		.5052		.6719		.8385
3-32	.0078		.1745		.3411		.5078		.6745		.8411
⅛	.0104	⅛	.1771	⅛	.3438	⅛	.5104	⅛	.6771	⅛	.8438
5-32	.0130		.1797		.3464		.5130		.6797		.8464
3-16	.0156		.1823		.3490		.5156		.6823		.8490
7-32	.0182		.1849		.3516		.5182		.6849		.8516
¼	.0208	¼	.1875	¼	.3542	¼	.5208	¼	.6875	¼	.8542
9-32	.0234		.1901		.3568		.5234		.6901		.8568
5-16	.0260		.1927		.3594		.5260		.6927		.8594
11-32	.0286		.1953		.3620		.5286		.6953		.8620
⅜	.0313	⅜	.1979	⅜	.3646	⅜	.5313	⅜	.6979	⅜	.8646
13-32	.0339		.2005		.3672		.5339		.7005		.8672
7-16	.0365		.2031		.3698		.5365		.7031		.8698
15-32	.0391		.2057		.3724		.5391		.7057		.8724
½	.0417	½	.2083	½	.3750	½	.5417	½	.7083	½	.8750
17-32	.0443		.2109		.3776		.5443		.7109		.8776
9-16	.0469		.2135		.3802		.5469		.7135		.8802
19-32	.0495		.2161		.3828		.5495		.7161		.8828
⅝	.0521	⅝	.2188	⅝	.3854	⅝	.5521	⅝	.7188	⅝	.8854
21-32	.0547		.2214		.3880		.5547		.7214		.8880
11-16	.0573		.2240		.3906		.5573		.7240		.8906
23-32	.0599		.2266		.3932		.5599		.7266		.8932
¾	.0625	¾	.2292	¾	.3958	¾	.5625	¾	.7292	¾	.8958
25-32	.0651		.2318		.3984		.5651		.7318		.8984
13-16	.0677		.2344		.4010		.5677		.7344		.9010
27-32	.0703		.2370		.4036		.5703		.7370		.9036
⅞	.0729	⅞	.2396	⅞	.4063	⅞	.5729	⅞	.7396	⅞	.9063
29-32	.0755		.2422		.4089		.5755		.7422		.9089
15-16	.0781		.2448		.4115		.5781		.7448		.9115
31-32	.0807		.2474		.4141		.5807		.7474		.9141
1	.0833	3	.2500	5	.4167	7	.5833	9	.7500	11	.9167
1-32	.0859		.2526		.4193		.5859		.7526		.9193
1-16	.0885		.2552		.4219		.5885		.7552		.9219
3-32	.0911		.2578		.4245		.5911		.7578		.9245
⅛	.0938	⅛	.2604	⅛	.4271	⅛	.5938	⅛	.7604	⅛	.9271
5-32	.0964		.2630		.4297		.5964		.7630		.9297
3-16	.0990		.2656		.4323		.5990		.7656		.9323
7-32	.1016		.2682		.4349		.6016		.7682		.9349
¼	.1042	¼	.2708	¼	.4375	¼	.6042	¼	.7708	¼	.9375
9-32	.1068		.2734		.4401		.6068		.7734		.9401
5-16	.1094		.2760		.4427		.6094		.7760		.9427
11-32	.1120		.2786		.4453		.6120		.7786		.9453
⅜	.1146	⅜	.2813	⅜	.4479	⅜	.6146	⅜	.7813	⅜	.9479
13-32	.1172		.2839		.4505		.6172		.7839		.9505
7-16	.1198		.2865		.4531		.6198		.7865		.9531
15-32	.1224		.2891		.4557		.6224		.7891		.9557
½	.1250	½	.2917	½	.4583	½	.6250	½	.7917	½	.9583
17-32	.1276		.2943		.4609		.6276		.7943		.9609
9-16	.1302		.2969		.4635		.6302		.7969		.9635
19-32	.1328		.2995		.4661		.6328		.7995		.9661
⅝	.1354	⅝	.3021	⅝	.4688	⅝	.6354	⅝	.8021	⅝	.9688
21-32	.1380		.3047		.4714		.6380		.8047		.9714
11-16	.1406		.3073		.4740		.6406		.8073		.9740
23-32	.1432		.3099		.4766		.6432		.8099		.9766
¾	.1458	¾	.3125	¾	.4792	¾	.6458	¾	.8125	¾	.9792
25-32	.1484		.3151		.4818		.6484		.8151		.9818
13-16	.1510		.3177		.4844		.6510		.8177		.9844
27-32	.1536		.3203		.4870		.6536		.8203		.9870
⅞	.1563	⅞	.3229	⅞	.4896	⅞	.6563	⅞	.8229	⅞	.9896
29-32	.1589		.3255		.4922		.6589		.8255		.9922
15-16	.1615		.3281		.4948		.6615		.8281		.9948
31-32	.1641		.3307		.4974		.6641		.8307		.9974

TABLE NO. 68.

DECIMALS OF AN INCH FOR EACH $_{64}$th. INCH.

$_{32}$ds.	$_{64}$ths.	Decimal.	Fraction.	$_{32}$ds.	$_{64}$ths.	Decimal.	Fraction.
	1	.015625			33	.515625	
1	2	.03125		17	34	.53125	
	3	.046875			35	.546875	
2	4	.0625	1-16	18	36	.5625	9-16
	5	.078125			37	.578125	
3	6	.09375		19	38	.59375	
	7	.109375			39	.609375	
4	8	.125	1-8	20	40	.625	5-8
	9	.140625			41	.640625	
5	10	.15625		21	42	.65625	
	11	.171875			43	.671875	
6	12	.1875	3-16	22	44	.6875	11-16
	13	.203125			45	.703125	
7	14	.21875		23	46	.71875	
	15	.234375			47	.734375	
8	16	.25	1-4	24	48	.75	3-4
	17	.265625			49	.765625	
9	18	.28125		25	50	.78125	
	19	.296875			51	.796875	
10	20	.3125	5-16	26	52	.8125	13-16
	21	.328125			53	.828125	
11	22	.34375		27	54	.84375	
	23	.359375			55	.859375	
12	24	.375	3-8	28	56	.875	7-8
	25	.390625			57	.890625	
13	26	.40625		29	58	.90625	
	27	.421875			59	.921875	
14	28	.4375	7-16	30	60	.9375	15-16
	29	.453125			61	.953125	
15	30	.46875		31	62	.96875	
	31	.484375			63	.984375	
16	32	.5	1-2	32	64	1.	1

HYDRAULICS.

TABLE **Of the square roots of the fifth powers of numbers.** In this table the numbers and the roots are supposed to be in the same dimensions; that is, both in inches, or both in feet, &c. See the next table.

No.	Sq. Rt. of 5th Power.	No.	Sq. Rt. of 5th Power.	No.	Sq. Rt. of 5th Power.	No.	Sq. Rt. of 5th Power.	No.	Sq. Rt. of 5th Power.	No.	Sq. Rt. of 5th Power.
.25	.031	7.	129.64	17.5	1281.1	31.	5351	49	16807	76	50354
.5	.177	7.25	141.53	18.	1374.6	31.5	5569	50	17675	77	52027
.75	.485	7.5	154.05	18.5	1472.1	32.	5793	51	18575	78	53732
1.	1.	7.75	167.21	19.	1573.6	32.5	6022	52	19499	79	55471
1.25	1.747	8.	181.02	19.5	1679.1	33.	6256	53	20450	80	57243
1.5	2.756	8.25	195.50	20.	1788.9	33.5	6496	54	21428	81	59049
1.75	4.051	8.5	210.64	20.5	1902.8	34.	6741	55	22434	82	60888
2.	5.657	8.75	226.48	21.	2020.9	34.5	6991	56	23468	83	62762
2.25	7.594	9.	243.	21.5	2143.4	35.	7247	57	24529	84	64669
2.5	9.882	9.25	260.23	22.	2270.2	35.5	7509	58	25620	85	66611
2.75	12.541	9.5	278.17	22.5	2401.4	36.	7746	59	26738	86	68593
3.	15.588	9.75	296.83	23.	2537.	36.5	8049	60	27886	87	70599
3.25	19.042	10.	316.23	23.5	2677.1	37.	8327	61	29062	88	72646
3.5	22.918	10.5	357.2	24.	2821.8	37.5	8611	62	30268	89	74727
3.75	27.232	11.	401.3	24.5	2971.1	38.	8901	63	31503	90	76843
4.	32.	11.5	448.5	25.	3125.	38.5	9197	64	32768	91	78996
4.25	37.24	12.	498.8	25.5	3283.6	39.	9498	65	34063	92	81184
4.5	42.96	12.5	552.4	26.	3446.9	39.5	9806	66	35388	93	83409
4.75	49.17	13.	609.3	26.5	3615.1	40.	10119	67	36744	94	85668
5.	55.90	13.5	669.6	27.	3788.	41.	10764	68	38131	95	87965
5.25	63.15	14.	733.4	27.5	3965.8	42.	11432	69	39548	96	90298
5.5	70.94	14.5	800.6	28.	4148.5	43.	12125	70	40996	97	92663
5.75	79.28	15.	871.4	28.5	4336.2	44.	12842	71	42476	98	95075
6.	88.18	15.5	945.9	29.	4528.9	45.	13584	72	43988	99	97519
6.25	97.66	16.	1024.	29.5	4726.7	46.	14351	73	45531	100	100000
6.5	107.72	16.5	1105.9	30.	4929.5	47.	15144	74	47106		
6.75	118.38	17.	1191.6	30.5	5138.	48.	15563	75	48714		

Numbers, in inches. Square roots of fifth powers, in feet.

Ins.	Sq. Rt. of 5th Pow. Feet.	Ins.	Sq. Rt. of 5th Pow. Feet.	Ins.	Sq. Rt. of 5th Pow. Feet.	Ins.	Sq. Rt. of 5th Pow. Feet.	Ins.	Sq. Rt. of 5th Pow. Feet.
1/4	.00006	3/4	.0547	12.	1.000	22 1/2	4.813	42	22.92
3/8	.00017	4.	.0641	1/2	1.108	23	5.086	43	24.31
1/2	.00035	1/4	.0731	13.	1.221	1/2	5.365	44	25.74
5/8	.00062	1/2	.0827	1/2	1.342	24	5.657	45	27.23
3/4	.00098	3/4	.0971	14.	1.470	25	6.264	46	28.77
7/8	.00144	5.	.1120	1/2	1.605	26	6.909	47	30.36
1.	.0020	1/4	.1271	15.	1.747	27	7.593	48	32.00
1/8	.0027	1/2	.1428	1/2	1.896	28	8.316	49	33.69
1/4	.0035	3/4	.1590	16.	2.053	29	9.079	50	35.44
3/8	.0044	6.	.1768	1/2	2.217	30	9.882	51	37.25
1/2	.0055	1/2	.2160	17.	2.389	31	10.73	52	39.13
5/8	.0067	7.	.2599	1/2	2.567	32	11.61	53	41.02
3/4	.0081	1/2	.3088	18.	2.756	33	12.54	54	42.96
7/8	.0096	8.	.3628	1/2	2.950	34	13.51	55	44.97
2.	.0113	1/2	.4228	19.	3.155	35	14.53	56	47.05
1/4	.0152	9.	.4871	1/2	3.365	36	15.59	57	49.17
1/2	.0196	1/2	.5577	20.	3.596	37	16.69	58	51.35
3/4	.0252	10.	.6339	1/2	3.813	38	17.84	59	53.60
3.	.0312	1/2	.7162	21.	4.051	39	19.04	60	55.90
1/4	.0383	11.	.8043	1/2	4.297	40	20.29	61	58.27
1/2	.0459	1/2	.8990	22.	4.551	41	21.58		

From Trautwine's "Civil Engineer's Pocket Book."

MENSURATION.

To find the length of a circular arc by the following table.

Knowing the rad of the circle, and the measure of the arc in deg, min, &c.
RULE. Add together the lengths in the table found respectively opposite to the deg, min, &c, of the arc. Mult the sum by the rad of the circle.
Ex. In a circle of 12.43 feet rad, is an arc of 13 deg, 27 min, 8 sec. How long is the arc?
Here, opposite 13 deg in the table, we find, .2268928
    "   27 min   "   "   "   .0078540
    "   8 sec   "   "   "   .0000388

Sum = .2347856

And .2347856 × 12.43 or rad = 2.918365 feet, the reqd length of arc.

LENGTHS OF CIRCULAR ARCS TO RAD 1.

No errors.

Deg.	Length.	Deg.	Length.	Deg.	Length.	Min.	Length.	Sec.	Length.
1	.0174533	61	1.0646508	121	2.1118484	1	.0002909	1	.0000048
2	.0349066	62	1.0821041	122	2.1293017	2	.0005818	2	.0000097
3	.0523599	63	1.0995574	123	2.1467550	3	.0008727	3	.0000145
4	.0698132	64	1.1170107	124	2.1642083	4	.0011636	4	.0000194
5	.0872665	65	1.1344640	125	2.1816616	5	.0014544	5	.0000242
6	.1047198	66	1.1519173	126	2.1991149	6	.0017453	6	.0000291
7	.1221730	67	1.1693706	127	2.2165682	7	.0020362	7	.0000339
8	.1396263	68	1.1868239	128	2.2340214	8	.0023271	8	.0000388
9	.1570796	69	1.2042772	129	2.2514747	9	.0026180	9	.0000436
10	.1745329	70	1.2217305	130	2.2689280	10	.0029089	10	.0000485
11	.1919862	71	1.2391838	131	2.2863813	11	.0031998	11	.0000533
12	.2094395	72	1.2566371	132	2.3038346	12	.0034907	12	.0000582
13	.2268928	73	1.2740904	133	2.3212879	13	.0037815	13	.0000630
14	.2443461	74	1.2915436	134	2.3387412	14	.0040724	14	.0000679
15	.2617994	75	1.3089969	135	2.3561945	15	.0043633	15	.0000727
16	.2792527	76	1.3264502	136	2.3736478	16	.0046542	16	.0000776
17	.2967060	77	1.3439035	137	2.3911011	17	.0049451	17	.0000824
18	.3141593	78	1.3613568	138	2.4085544	18	.0052360	18	.0000873
19	.3316126	79	1.3788101	139	2.4260077	19	.0055269	19	.0000921
20	.3490659	80	1.3962634	140	2.4434610	20	.0058178	20	.0000970
21	.3665191	81	1.4137167	141	2.4609142	21	.0061087	21	.0001018
22	.3839724	82	1.4311700	142	2.4783675	22	.0063995	22	.0001067
23	.4014257	83	1.4486233	143	2.4958208	23	.0066904	23	.0001115
24	.4188790	84	1.4660766	144	2.5132741	24	.0069813	24	.0001164
25	.4363323	85	1.4835299	145	2.5307274	25	.0072722	25	.0001212
26	.4537856	86	1.5009832	146	2.5481807	26	.0075631	26	.0001261
27	.4712389	87	1.5184365	147	2.5656340	27	.0078540	27	.0001309
28	.4886922	88	1.5358897	148	2.5830873	28	.0081449	28	.0001357
29	.5061455	89	1.5533430	149	2.6005406	29	.0084358	29	.0001406
30	.5235988	90	1.5707963	150	2.6179939	30	.0087266	30	.0001454
31	.5410521	91	1.5882496	151	2.6354472	31	.0090175	31	.0001503
32	.5585054	92	1.6057029	152	2.6529005	32	.0093084	32	.0001551
33	.5759587	93	1.6231562	153	2.6703538	33	.0095993	33	.0001600
34	.5934119	94	1.6406095	154	2.6878070	34	.0098902	34	.0001648
35	.6108652	95	1.6580628	155	2.7052603	35	.0101811	35	.0001697
36	.6283185	96	1.6755161	156	2.7227136	36	.0104720	36	.0001745
37	.6457718	97	1.6929694	157	2.7401669	37	.0107629	37	.0001794
38	.6632251	98	1.7104227	158	2.7576202	38	.0110538	38	.0001842
39	.6806784	99	1.7278760	159	2.7750735	39	.0113446	39	.0001891
40	.6981317	100	1.7453293	160	2.7925268	40	.0116355	40	.0001939
41	.7155850	101	1.7627825	161	2.8099801	41	.0119264	41	.0001988
42	.7330383	102	1.7802358	162	2.8274334	42	.0122173	42	.0002036
43	.7504916	103	1.7976891	163	2.8448867	43	.0125082	43	.0002085
44	.7679449	104	1.8151424	164	2.8623400	44	.0127991	44	.0002133
45	.7853982	105	1.8325957	165	2.8797933	45	.0130900	45	.0002182
46	.8028515	106	1.8500490	166	2.8972466	46	.0133809	46	.0002230
47	.8203047	107	1.8675023	167	2.9146999	47	.0136717	47	.0002279
48	.8377580	108	1.8849556	168	2.9321531	48	.0139626	48	.0002327
49	.8552113	109	1.9024089	169	2.9496064	49	.0142535	49	.0002376
50	.8726646	110	1.9198622	170	2.9670597	50	.0145444	50	.0002424
51	.8901179	111	1.9373155	171	2.9845130	51	.0148353	51	.0002473
52	.9075712	112	1.9547688	172	3.0019663	52	.0151262	52	.0002521
53	.9250245	113	1.9722221	173	3.0194196	53	.0154171	53	.0002570
54	.9424778	114	1.9896753	174	3.0368729	54	.0157080	54	.0002618
55	.9599311	115	2.0071286	175	3.0543262	55	.0159989	55	.0002666
56	.9773844	116	2.0245819	176	3.0717795	56	.0162897	56	.0002715
57	.9948377	117	2.0420352	177	3.0892328	57	.0165806	57	.0002763
58	1.0122910	118	2.0594885	178	3.1066861	58	.0168715	58	.0002812
59	1.0297443	119	2.0769418	179	3.1241394	59	.0171624	59	.0002860
60	1.0471976	120	2.0943951	180	3.1415927	60	.0174533	60	.0002909

168

EXPLAINATION OF TABLES OF CIRCLES.

It will be noticed that there are three tables of circles.

FIRST —Table giving diameters in units and **EIGHTHS.**
SECOND — " "   "   " " " **TENTHS**
THIRD — " "   "   " " " **TWELFTHS.**

The diameter in all cases extending to 100.

The following rules with reference to the table giving the diameters in TENTHS will also be of value.

To compute the area or circumference of a diameter greater than 100 and less than 1001:

Rule—Take out the area or circumference from the table as though the number had one decimal, and move the decimal point two places to the right for area and one place for the circumference.

Example—Wanted the area and circumference of 567. The tabular area for 56.7 is 2524.9687, and circumference 178.1283. Therefore area for 567=252496.87 and circumf.=1781.283.

To comptue the area or circumference of a diameter greater than 1000.

Rule—Divide by a factor 2, 3, 4, 5, etc., if practicable, that will leave a quotient to be found in the table; then multiply the tabular *area* of the quotient by the *square* of the factor, to get required area; and the tabular circumference by the factor to get the required circumference.

Example—Wanted the area and circumference of 2109. Dividing by 3 the quotient is 703, for which the area is 388,150.84 and the circumference 2208.54. Therefore area of 2109 = 388150.84 × 9 (9 = square of 3) = 3493357.56, and the circumference = 22 08.54 × 3 = 6625.62.

The following rules with reference to table giving the diameters in EIGHTHS will also be found of value.

If the required diameter is not in the table, separate it and take the circumference of each and add them.

Example—Wanted the circumference of 25½⅛ inches. Circumference of 25 in.=78.5398 and of ⅝=2.06167; adding these we get 80.60147 the required circumference. This process will not answer for the area, however. In case the area is wanted, reduce the given diameter to a decimal and multiply this by itself and the product by .7854 (area=square of diameter×.7854). Reduce to a decimal of a foot or of an inch by use of tables 67 and 68. See AREA P. 152.

Where the diameter contains more than one decimal, or where it contains fractions of an inch, see small tables following the tables giving diameters in TENTHS & TWELFTHS respectively, on pages 177 and 184.

See rules on page 152 for calculating diameters, circumferences, or areas, or the sides of equal squares, without the use of tables.

From Trautwine's "Civil Engineer's Pocket Book."

CIRCLES.

TABLE 1 OF CIRCLES.
Diameters in units and eighths, &c.

Circumferences or areas intermediate of those in this table, may be found by simple arithmetical proportion.   **No errors.**

Diam.	Circumf.	Area.	Diam.	Circumf.	Area.	Diam.	Circumf.	Area.	Diam.	Circumf.	Area.
1-64	.049087	.00019	½	10.9956	9.6211	10⅛	31.8086	80.516	19¼	60.4757	291.04
1-32	.098175	.00077	9-16	11.1919	9.9678	¼	32.2013	82.516	⅜	60.8684	294.83
3-64	.147262	.00173	⅝	11.3883	10.321	⅜	32.5940	84.541	½	61.2611	298.65
1-16	.196350	.00307	11-16	11.5846	10.690	½	32.9867	86.590	⅝	61.6538	302.49
3-32	.294524	.00690	¾	11.7810	11.045	⅝	33.3794	88.664	¾	62.0465	306.35
⅛	.392699	.01227	13-16	11.9773	11.416	¾	33.7721	90.763	⅞	62.4392	310.24
5-32	.490874	.01917	⅞	12.1737	11.793	⅞	34.1648	92.886	20.	62.8319	314.16
3-16	.589049	.02761	15-16	12.3700	12.177	11.	34.5575	95.033	⅛	63.2246	318.10
7-32	.687223	.03754	4.	12.5664	12.566	⅛	34.9502	97.205	¼	63.6173	322.06
¼	.785398	.04909	1-16	12.7627	12.962	¼	35.3429	99.402	⅜	64.0100	326.05
9-32	.883573	.06213	⅛	12.9591	13.364	⅜	35.7356	101.62	½	64.4027	330.06
5-16	.981748	.07670	3-16	13.1554	13.772	½	36.1283	103.87	⅝	64.7953	334.10
11-32	1.07992	.09281	¼	13.3518	14.186	⅝	36.5210	106.14	¾	65.1880	338.16
⅜	1.17810	.11045	5-16	13.5481	14.607	¾	36.9137	108.43	⅞	65.5807	342.25
13-32	1.27627	.12962	⅜	13.7445	15.033	⅞	37.3064	110.75	21.	65.9734	346.36
7-16	1.37445	.15031	7-16	13.9408	15.466	12.	37.6991	113.10	⅛	66.3661	350.50
15-32	1.47262	.17257	½	14.1372	15.904	⅛	38.0918	115.47	¼	66.7588	354.66
½	1.57080	.19635	9-16	14.3335	16.349	¼	38.4845	117.86	⅜	67.1515	358.84
17-32	1.66897	.22165	⅝	14.5299	16.800	⅜	38.8772	120.28	½	67.5442	363.05
9-16	1.76715	.24850	11-16	14.7262	17.257	½	39.2699	122.72	⅝	67.9369	367.29
19-32	1.86532	.27684	¾	14.9226	17.721	⅝	39.6626	125.19	¾	68.3296	371.54
⅝	1.96350	.30330	13-16	15.1189	18.190	¾	40.0553	127.68	⅞	68.7223	375.83
21-32	2.06167	.33824	⅞	15.3153	18.665	⅞	40.4480	130.19	22.	69.1150	380.13
11-16	2.15984	.37122	15-16	15.5116	19.147	13.	40.8407	132.73	⅛	69.5077	384.46
23-32	2.25802	.40574	5.	15.7080	19.635	⅛	41.2334	135.30	¼	69.9004	388.82
¾	2.35619	.44179	1-16	15.9043	20.129	¼	41.6261	137.89	⅜	70.2931	393.20
25-32	2.45437	.47937	⅛	16.1007	20.629	⅜	42.0188	140.50	½	70.6858	397.61
13-16	2.55254	.51843	3-16	16.2970	21.135	½	42.4115	143.14	⅝	71.0785	402.04
27-32	2.65072	.55914	¼	16.4934	21.648	⅝	42.8042	145.80	¾	71.4712	406.49
⅞	2.74889	.60132	5-16	16.6897	22.166	¾	43.1969	148.49	⅞	71.8639	410.97
29-32	2.84707	.64501	⅜	16.8861	22.691	⅞	43.5896	151.20	23.	72.2566	415.48
15-16	2.94524	.69023	7-16	17.0824	23.221	14.	43.9823	153.94	⅛	72.6493	420.00
31-32	3.04342	.73708	½	17.2788	23.758	⅛	44.3750	156.70	¼	73.0420	424.56
1.	3.14159	.78540	9-16	17.4751	24.301	¼	44.7677	159.48	⅜	73.4347	429.13
1-16	3.33794	.88661	⅝	17.6715	24.850	⅜	45.1604	162.30	½	73.8274	433.74
⅛	3.53429	.99402	11-16	17.8678	25.406	½	45.5531	165.13	⅝	74.2201	438.36
3-16	3.73064	1.1075	¾	18.0642	25.967	⅝	45.9458	167.99	¾	74.6128	443.01
¼	3.92699	1.2272	13-16	18.2605	26.535	¾	46.3385	170.87	⅞	75.0055	447.69
5-16	4.12334	1.3530	⅞	18.4569	27.109	⅞	46.7312	173.78	24.	75.3982	452.39
⅜	4.31969	1.4849	15-16	18.6532	27.688	15.	47.1239	176.71	⅛	75.7909	457.11
7-16	4.51604	1.6230	6.	18.8496	28.274	⅛	47.5166	179.67	¼	76.1836	461.86
½	4.71239	1.7671	⅛	19.2423	29.465	¼	47.9093	182.65	⅜	76.5763	466.64
9-16	4.90874	1.9175	¼	19.6350	30.680	⅜	48.3020	185.66	½	76.9690	471.44
⅝	5.10509	2.0739	⅜	20.0277	31.919	½	48.6947	188.69	⅝	77.3617	476.26
11-16	5.30144	2.2365	½	20.4204	33.183	⅝	49.0874	191.75	¾	77.7544	481.11
¾	5.49779	2.4053	⅝	20.8131	34.472	¾	49.4801	194.83	⅞	78.1471	485.98
13-16	5.69414	2.5802	¾	21.2058	35.785	⅞	49.8728	197.93	25.	78.5398	490.87
⅞	5.89049	2.7612	⅞	21.5984	37.122	16.	50.2655	201.06	⅛	78.9325	495.79
15-16	6.08684	2.9483	7.	21.9911	38.485	⅛	50.6582	204.22	¼	79.3252	500.74
2.	6.28319	3.1416	⅛	22.3838	39.871	¼	51.0509	207.39	⅜	79.7179	505.71
1-16	6.47953	3.3410	¼	22.7765	41.282	⅜	51.4436	210.60	½	80.1106	510.71
⅛	6.67588	3.5466	⅜	23.1692	42.718	½	51.8363	213.82	⅝	80.5033	515.72
3-16	6.87223	3.7583	½	23.5619	44.179	⅝	52.2290	217.08	¾	80.8960	520.77
¼	7.06858	3.9761	⅝	23.9546	45.664	¾	52.6217	220.35	⅞	81.2887	525.84
5-16	7.26493	4.2000	¾	24.3473	47.173	⅞	53.0144	223.65	26.	81.6814	530.93
⅜	7.46128	4.4301	⅞	24.7400	48.707	17.	53.4071	226.98	⅛	82.0741	536.05
7-16	7.65763	4.6664	8.	25.1327	50.265	⅛	53.7998	230.33	¼	82.4668	541.19
½	7.85398	4.9087	⅛	25.5254	51.849	¼	54.1925	233.71	⅜	82.8595	546.35
9-16	8.05033	5.1572	¼	25.9181	53.456	⅜	54.5852	237.10	½	83.2522	551.55
⅝	8.24668	5.4119	⅜	26.3108	55.088	½	54.9779	240.53	⅝	83.6449	556.76
11-16	8.44303	5.6727	½	26.7035	56.745	⅝	55.3706	243.98	¾	84.0376	562.00
¾	8.63938	5.9396	⅝	27.0962	58.426	¾	55.7633	247.45	⅞	84.4303	567.27
13-16	8.83573	6.2126	¾	27.4889	60.132	⅞	56.1560	250.95	27.	84.8230	572.56
⅞	9.03208	6.4918	⅞	27.8816	61.862	18.	56.5487	254.47	⅛	85.2157	577.87
15-16	9.22843	6.7771	9.	28.2743	63.617	⅛	56.9414	258.02	¼	85.6084	583.21
3.	9.42478	7.0686	⅛	28.6670	65.397	¼	57.3341	261.59	⅜	86.0011	588.57
1-16	9.62113	7.3662	¼	29.0597	67.201	⅜	57.7268	265.18	½	86.3938	593.96
⅛	9.81748	7.6699	⅜	29.4524	69.029	½	58.1195	268.80	⅝	86.7865	599.37
3-16	10.0138	7.9798	½	29.8451	70.882	⅝	58.5122	272.45	¾	87.1792	604.81
¼	10.2102	8.2958	⅝	30.2378	72.760	¾	58.9049	276.12	⅞	87.5719	610.27
5-16	10.4065	8.6179	¾	30.6305	74.662	⅞	59.2976	279.81	28.	87.9646	615.75
⅜	10.6029	8.9462	⅞	31.0232	76.589	19.	59.6903	283.53	⅛	88.3573	621.26
7-16	10.7992	9.2806	10.	31.4159	78.540	⅛	60.0830	287.27	¼	88.7500	626.80

From Trautwine's "Civil Engineer's Pocket Book."

CIRCLES.

TABLE 1 OF CIRCLES—(Continued).
Diameters in units and eighths, &c.

Diam.	Circumf.	Area.	Diam.	Circumf.	Area.	Diam.	Circumf.	Area.	Diam.	Circumf.	Area.
28⅜	89.1427	632.36	38.	119.381	1134.1	47⅝	149.618	1781.4	57¼	179.856	2574.2
½	89.5354	637.94	⅛	119.773	1141.6	¾	150.011	1790.8	⅜	180.249	2585.4
⅝	89.9281	643.55	¼	120.166	1149.1	⅞	150.404	1800.1	½	180.642	2596.7
¾	90.3208	649.18	⅜	120.559	1156.6	48	150.796	1809.6	⅝	181.034	2608.0
⅞	90.7135	654.84	½	120.951	1164.2	⅛	151.189	1819.0	¾	181.427	2619.4
29.	91.1062	660.52	⅝	121.344	1171.7	¼	151.582	1828.5	⅞	181.820	2630.7
⅛	91.4989	666.23	¾	121.737	1179.3	⅜	151.975	1837.9	58.	182.212	2642.1
¼	91.8916	671.96	⅞	122.129	1186.9	½	152.367	1847.5	⅛	182.605	2653.5
⅜	92.2843	677.71	39.	122.522	1194.6	⅝	152.760	1857.0	¼	182.998	2664.9
½	92.6770	683.49	⅛	122.915	1202.3	¾	153.153	1866.5	⅜	183.390	2676.4
⅝	93.0697	689.30	¼	123.308	1210.0	⅞	153.545	1876.1	½	183.783	2687.8
¾	93.4624	695.13	⅜	123.700	1217.7	49.	153.938	1885.7	⅝	184.176	2699.3
⅞	93.8551	700.98	½	124.093	1225.4	⅛	154.331	1895.4	¾	184.569	2710.9
30.	94.2478	706.86	⅝	124.486	1233.2	¼	154.723	1905.0	⅞	184.961	2722.4
⅛	94.6405	712.76	¾	124.878	1241.0	⅜	155.116	1914.7	59.	185.354	2734.0
¼	95.0332	718.69	⅞	125.271	1248.8	½	155.509	1924.4	⅛	185.747	2745.6
⅜	95.4259	724.64	40.	125.664	1256.6	⅝	155.902	1934.2	¼	186.139	2757.2
½	95.8186	730.62	⅛	126.056	1264.5	¾	156.294	1943.9	⅜	186.532	2768.8
⅝	96.2113	736.62	¼	126.449	1272.4	⅞	156.687	1953.7	½	186.925	2780.5
¾	96.6040	742.64	⅜	126.842	1280.3	50.	157.080	1963.5	⅝	187.317	2792.2
⅞	96.9967	748.69	½	127.235	1288.2	⅛	157.472	1973.3	¾	187.710	2803.9
31.	97.3894	754.77	⅝	127.627	1296.2	¼	157.865	1983.2	⅞	188.103	2815.7
⅛	97.7821	760.87	¾	128.020	1304.2	⅜	158.258	1993.1	60.	188.496	2827.4
¼	98.1748	766.99	⅞	128.413	1312.2	½	158.650	2003.0	⅛	188.888	2839.2
⅜	98.5675	773.14	41.	128.805	1320.3	⅝	159.043	2012.9	¼	189.281	2851.0
½	98.9602	779.31	⅛	129 198	1328.3	¾	159.436	2022.8	⅜	189.674	2862.9
⅝	99.3529	785.51	¼	129.591	1336.4	⅞	159.829	2032.8	½	190.066	2874.8
¾	99.7456	791.73	⅜	129.983	1344.5	51.	160.221	2042.8	⅝	190.459	2886.6
⅞	100.138	797.98	½	130.376	1352.7	⅛	160.614	2052.8	¾	190.852	2898.6
32.	100.531	804.25	⅝	130.769	1360.8	¼	161.007	2062.9	⅞	191.244	2910.5
⅛	100.924	810.54	¾	131.161	1369.0	⅜	161.399	2073.0	61.	191.637	2922.5
¼	101.316	816.86	⅞	131.554	1377.2	½	161.792	2083.1	⅛	192.030	2934.5
⅜	101.709	823.21	42.	131.947	1385.4	⅝	162.185	2093.2	¼	192.423	2946.5
½	102.102	829.58	⅛	132.340	1393.7	¾	162.577	2103.3	⅜	192.815	2958.5
⅝	102.494	835.97	¼	132.732	1402.0	⅞	162.970	2113.5	½	193.208	2970.6
¾	102.887	842.39	⅜	133.125	1410.3	52.	163.363	2123.7	⅝	193.601	2982.7
⅞	103.280	848.83	½	133.518	1418.6	⅛	163.756	2133.9	¾	193.993	2994.8
33.	103.673	855.30	⅝	133.910	1427.0	¼	164.148	2144.2	⅞	194.386	3006.9
⅛	104.065	861.79	¾	134.303	1435.4	⅜	164.541	2154.5	62.	194.779	3019.1
¼	104.458	868.31	⅞	134.696	1443.8	½	164.934	2164.8	⅛	195.171	3031.3
⅜	104.851	874.85	43.	135.088	1452.2	⅝	165.326	2175.1	¼	195.564	3043.5
½	105.243	881.41	⅛	135.481	1460.7	¾	165.719	2185.4	⅜	195.957	3055.7
⅝	105.636	888.00	¼	135.874	1469.1	⅞	166.112	2195.8	½	196.350	3068.0
¾	106.029	894.62	⅜	136.267	1477.6	53.	166.504	2206.2	⅝	196.742	3080.3
⅞	106.421	901.26	½	136.659	1486.2	⅛	166.897	2216.6	¾	197.135	3092.6
34.	106.814	907.92	⅝	137.052	1494.7	¼	167.290	2227.0	⅞	197.528	3104.9
⅛	107.207	914.61	¾	137.445	1503.3	⅜	167.683	2237.5	63.	197.920	3117.2
¼	107.600	921.32	⅞	137.837	1511.9	½	168.075	2248.0	⅛	198.313	3129.6
⅜	107.992	928.06	44.	138.230	1520.5	⅝	168.468	2258.5	¼	198.706	3142.0
½	108.385	934.82	⅛	138.623	1529.2	¾	168.861	2269.1	⅜	199.098	3154.5
⅝	108.778	941.61	¼	139.015	1537.9	⅞	169.253	2279.6	½	199.491	3166.9
¾	109.170	948.42	⅜	139.408	1546.6	54.	169.646	2290.2	⅝	199.884	3179.4
⅞	109.563	955.25	½	139.801	1555.3	⅛	170.039	2300.8	¾	200.277	3191.9
35.	109.956	962.11	⅝	140.194	1564.0	¼	170.431	2311.5	⅞	200.669	3204.4
⅛	110.348	969.00	¾	140 586	1572.8	⅜	170.824	2322.1	64.	201.062	3217.0
¼	110.741	975.91	⅞	140.979	1581.6	½	171.217	2332.8	⅛	201.455	3229.6
⅜	111.134	982.84	45.	141.372	1590.4	⅝	171.609	2343.5	¼	201.847	3242.2
½	111.527	989.80	⅛	141.764	1599.3	¾	172.002	2354.3	⅜	202.240	3254.8
⅝	111.919	996.78	¼	142.157	1608.2	⅞	172.395	2365.0	½	202.633	3267.5
¾	112.312	1003.8	⅜	142.550	1617.0	55.	172.788	2375.8	⅝	203.025	3280.1
⅞	112.705	1010.8	½	142.942	1626.0	⅛	173.180	2386.6	¾	203.418	3292.8
36.	113.097	1017.9	⅝	143.335	1634.9	¼	173.573	2397.5	⅞	203.811	3305.6
⅛	113.490	1025.0	¾	143.728	1643.9	⅜	173.966	2408.3	65.	204.204	3318.3
¼	113.883	1032 1	⅞	144.121	1652.9	½	174.358	2419.2	⅛	204.596	3331.1
⅜	114.275	1039.2	46.	144.513	1661.9	⅝	174.751	2430.1	¼	204.989	3343.9
½	114.668	1046.3	⅛	144.906	1670.9	¾	175.144	2441.1	⅜	205.382	3356.7
⅝	115.061	1053.5	¼	145.299	1680.0	⅞	175.536	2452.0	½	205.774	3369.6
¾	115.454	1060.7	⅜	145.691	1689.1	56.	175.929	2463.0	⅝	206.167	3382.4
⅞	115.846	1068.0	½	146.084	1698.2	⅛	176.322	2474.0	¾	206.560	3395.3
37.	116.239	1075.2	⅝	146.477	1707.4	¼	176.715	2485.0	⅞	206.952	3408.2
⅛	116.632	1082.5	¾	146.869	1716.5	⅜	177.107	2496.1	66.	207.345	3421.2
¼	117.024	1089.8	⅞	147.262	1725.7	½	177.500	2507.2	⅛	207.738	3434.2
⅜	117.417	1097.1	47.	147.655	1734.9	⅝	177.893	2518.3	¼	208.131	3447.2
½	117.810	1104.5	⅛	148.048	1744.2	¾	178.285	2529.4	⅜	208.523	3460.2
⅝	118.202	1111.8	¼	148.440	1753.5	⅞	178.678	2540.6	½	208.916	3473.2
¾	118.596	1119.2	⅜	148.833	1762.7	57.	179.071	2551.8	⅝	209.309	3486.3
⅞	118.988	1126.7	½	149.226	1772.1	⅛	179.463	2563.0	¾	209.701	3499.4

From Trautwine's "Civil Engineer's Pocket Book."

CIRCLES.

TABLE 1 OF CIRCLES—(Continued).
Diameters in units and eighths, &c.

Diam.	Circumf.	Area.	Diam.	Circumf.	Area.	Diam.	Circumf.	Area.	Diam.	Circumf.	Area.
⅞	210.094	3512.5	75¼	236.405	4447.4	83⅝	262.716	5492.4	92.	289.027	6647.6
67.	210.487	3525.7	⅜	236.798	4462.2	¾	263.108	5508.8	⅛	289.419	6665.7
⅛	210.879	3538.8	½	237.190	4477.0	⅞	263.501	5525.3	¼	289.812	6683.8
¼	211.272	3552.0	⅝	237.583	4491.8	84.	263.894	5541.8	⅜	290.205	6701.9
⅜	211.665	3565.2	¾	237.976	4506.7	⅛	264.286	5558.3	½	290.597	6720.1
½	212.058	3578.5	⅞	238.369	4521.5	¼	264.679	5574.8	⅝	290.990	6738.2
⅝	212.450	3591.7	76.	238.761	4536.5	⅜	265.072	5591.4	¾	291.383	6756.4
¾	212.843	3605.0	⅛	239.154	4551.4	½	265.465	5607.9	⅞	291.775	6774.7
⅞	213.236	3618.3	¼	239.546	4566.4	⅝	265.857	5624.5	93.	292.168	6792.9
68.	213.628	3631.7	⅜	239.939	4581.3	¾	266.250	5641.2	⅛	292.561	6811.2
⅛	214.021	3645.0	½	240.332	4596.3	⅞	266.643	5657.8	¼	292.954	6829.5
¼	214.414	3658.4	⅝	240.725	4611.4	85.	267.035	5674.5	⅜	293.346	6847.8
⅜	214.806	3671.8	¾	241.117	4626.4	⅛	267.428	5691.2	½	293.739	6866.1
½	215.199	3685.3	⅞	241.510	4641.5	¼	267.821	5707.9	⅝	294.132	6884.5
⅝	215.592	3698.7	77.	241.903	4656.6	⅜	268.213	5724.7	¾	294.524	6902.9
¾	215.984	3712.2	⅛	242.295	4671.8	½	268.606	5741.5	⅞	294.917	6921.3
⅞	216.377	3725.7	¼	242.688	4686.9	⅝	268.990	5758.4	94.	295.310	6939.8
69.	216.770	3739.3	⅜	243.081	4702.1	¾	269.392	5775.1	⅛	295.702	6958.2
⅛	217.163	3752.8	½	243.473	4717.3	⅞	269.784	5791.9	¼	296.095	6976.7
¼	217.555	3766.4	⅝	243.866	4732.5	86.	270.177	5808.8	⅜	296.488	6995.3
⅜	217.948	3780.0	¾	244.259	4747.8	⅛	270.570	5825.7	½	296.881	7013.8
½	218.341	3793.7	⅞	244.652	4763.1	¼	270.962	5842.6	⅝	297.273	7032.4
⅝	218.733	3807.3	78.	245.044	4778.4	⅜	271.355	5859.6	¾	297.666	7051.0
¾	219.126	3821.0	⅛	245.437	4793.7	½	271.748	5876.5	⅞	298.059	7069.6
⅞	219.519	3834.7	¼	245.830	4809.0	⅝	272.140	5893.5	95.	298.451	7088.2
70.	219.911	3848.5	⅜	246.222	4824.4	¾	272.533	5910.6	⅛	298.844	7106.9
⅛	220.304	3862.2	½	246.615	4839.8	⅞	272.926	5927.6	¼	299.237	7125.6
¼	220.697	3876.0	⅝	247.008	4855.2	87.	273.319	5944.7	⅜	299.629	7144.3
⅜	221.090	3889.8	¾	247.400	4870.7	⅛	273.711	5961.8	½	300.022	7163.0
½	221.482	3903.6	⅞	247.793	4886.2	¼	274.104	5978.9	⅝	300.415	7181.8
⅝	221.875	3917.5	79.	248.186	4901.7	⅜	274.497	5996.0	¾	300.807	7200.6
¾	222.268	3931.4	⅛	248.579	4917.2	½	274.889	6013.2	⅞	301.200	7219.4
⅞	222.660	3945.3	¼	248.971	4932.7	⅝	275.282	6030.4	96.	301.593	7238.2
71.	223.053	3959.2	⅜	249.364	4948.3	¾	275.675	6047.6	⅛	301.986	7257.1
⅛	223.446	3973.1	½	249.757	4963.9	⅞	276.067	6064.9	¼	302.378	7276.0
¼	223.838	3987.1	⅝	250.149	4979.5	88.	276.460	6082.1	⅜	302.771	7294.9
⅜	224.231	4001.1	¾	250.542	4995.2	⅛	276.853	6099.4	½	303.164	7313.8
½	224.624	4015.2	⅞	250.935	5010.9	¼	277.246	6116.7	⅝	303.556	7332.8
⅝	225.017	4029.2	80.	251.327	5026.5	⅜	277.638	6134.1	¾	303.949	7351.8
¾	225.409	4043.3	⅛	251.720	5042.3	½	278.031	6151.4	⅞	304.342	7370.8
⅞	225.802	4057.4	¼	252.113	5058.0	⅝	278.424	6168.8	97.	304.734	7389.8
72.	226.195	4071.5	⅜	252.506	5073.8	¾	278.816	6186.2	⅛	305.127	7408.9
⅛	226.587	4085.7	½	252.898	5089.6	⅞	279.209	6203.7	¼	305.520	7428.0
¼	226.980	4099.8	⅝	253.291	5105.4	89.	279.602	6221.1	⅜	305.913	7447.1
⅜	227.373	4114.0	¾	253.684	5121.2	⅛	279.994	6238.6	½	306.305	7466.2
½	227.765	4128.2	⅞	254.076	5137.1	¼	280.387	6256.1	⅝	306.698	7485.3
⅝	228.158	4142.5	81.	254.469	5153.0	⅜	280.780	6273.7	¾	307.091	7504.5
¾	228.551	4156.8	⅛	254.862	5168.9	½	281.173	6291.2	⅞	307.483	7523.7
⅞	228.944	4171.1	¼	255.254	5184.9	⅝	281.565	6308.8	98.	307.876	7543.0
73.	229.336	4185.4	⅜	255.647	5200.8	¾	281.958	6326.4	⅛	308.269	7562.2
⅛	229.729	4199.7	½	256.040	5216.8	⅞	282.351	6344.1	¼	308.661	7581.5
¼	230.122	4214.1	⅝	256.433	5232.8	90.	282.743	6361.7	⅜	309.054	7600.8
⅜	230.514	4228.5	¾	256.825	5248.9	⅛	283.136	6379.4	½	309.447	7620.1
½	230.907	4242.9	⅞	257.218	5264.9	¼	283.529	6397.1	⅝	309.840	7639.5
⅝	231.300	4257.4	82.	257.611	5281.0	⅜	283.921	6414.9	¾	310.232	7658.9
¾	231.692	4271.8	⅛	258.003	5297.1	½	284.314	6432.6	⅞	310.625	7678.3
⅞	232.085	4286.3	¼	258.396	5313.3	⅝	284.707	6450.4	99.	311.018	7697.7
74.	232.478	4300.8	⅜	258.789	5329.4	¾	285.100	6468.2	⅛	311.410	7717.1
⅛	232.971	4315.4	½	259.181	5345.6	⅞	285.492	6486.0	¼	311.803	7736.6
¼	233.263	4329.9	⅝	259.574	5361.8	91.	285.885	6503.9	⅜	312.196	7756.1
⅜	233.656	4344.5	¾	259.967	5378.1	⅛	286.278	6521.8	½	312.588	7775.6
½	234.049	4359.2	⅞	260.359	5394.3	¼	286.670	6539.7	⅝	312.981	7795.2
⅝	234.441	4373.8	83.	260.752	5410.6	⅜	287.063	6557.6	¾	313.374	7814.8
¾	234.834	4388.5	⅛	261.145	5426.9	½	287.456	6575.5	⅞	313.767	7834.4
⅞	235.227	4403.1	¼	261.538	5443.3	⅝	287.848	6593.5	100.	314.159	7854.0
75.	235.619	4417.9	⅜	261.930	5459.6	¾	288.241	6611.5			
⅛	236.012	4432.6	½	262.323	5476.0	⅞	288.634	6629.6			

CIRCLES.

TABLE 2 OF CIRCLES.
Diameters in units and tenths.

Dia.	Circumf.	Area.	Dia.	Circumf.	Area.	Dia.	Circumf.	Area.
0.1	.314159	.007854	6.3	19.79203	31.17245	12.5	39.26991	122.7185
.2	.628319	.031416	.4	20.10619	32.16991	.6	39.58407	124.6898
.3	.942478	.070686	.5	20.42035	33.18307	.7	39.89823	126.6769
.4	1.256637	.125664	.6	20.73451	34.21194	.8	40.21239	128.6796
.5	1.570796	.196350	.7	21.04867	35.25652	.9	40.52655	130.6981
.6	1.884956	.282743	.8	21.36283	36.31681	13.0	40.84070	132.7323
.7	2.199115	.384845	.9	21.67699	37.39281	.1	41.15486	134.7822
.8	2.513274	.502655	7.0	21.99115	38.48451	.2	41.46902	136.8478
.9	2.827433	.636173	.1	22.30531	39.59192	.3	41.78318	138.9291
1.0	3.141593	.785398	.2	22.61947	40.71504	.4	42.09734	141.0261
.1	3.455752	.950332	.3	22.93363	41.85387	.5	42.41150	143.1388
.2	3.769911	1.13097	.4	23.24779	43.00840	.6	42.72566	145.2672
.3	4.084070	1.32732	.5	23.56194	44.17865	.7	43.03982	147.4114
.4	4.398230	1.53938	.6	23.87610	45.36460	.8	43.35398	149.5712
.5	4.712389	1.76715	.7	24.19026	46.56626	.9	43.66814	151.7468
.6	5.026548	2.01062	.8	24.50442	47.78362	14.0	43.98230	153.9380
.7	5.340708	2.26980	.9	24.81858	49.01670	.1	44.29646	156.1450
.8	5.654867	2.54469	8.0	25.13274	50.26548	.2	44.61062	158.3677
.9	5.969026	2.83529	.1	25.44690	51.52997	.3	44.92477	160.6061
2.0	6.283185	3.14159	.2	25.76106	52.81017	.4	45.23893	162.8602
.1	6.597345	3.46361	.3	26.07522	54.10608	.5	45.55309	165.1300
.2	6.911504	3.80133	.4	26.38938	55.41769	.6	45.86725	167.4155
.3	7.225663	4.15476	.5	26.70354	56.74502	.7	46.18141	169.7167
.4	7.539822	4.52389	.6	27.01770	58.08805	.8	46.49557	172.0336
.5	7.853982	4.90874	.7	27.33186	59.44679	.9	46.80973	174.3662
.6	8.168141	5.30929	.8	27.64602	60.82123	15.0	47.12389	176.7146
.7	8.482300	5.72555	.9	27.96017	62.21139	.1	47.43805	179.0786
.8	8.796459	6.15752	9.0	28.27433	63.61725	.2	47.75221	181.4584
.9	9.110619	6.60520	.1	28.58849	65.03882	.3	48.06637	183.8539
3.0	9.424778	7.06858	.2	28.90265	66.47610	.4	48.38053	186.2650
.1	9.738937	7.54768	.3	29.21681	67.92909	.5	48.69469	188.6919
.2	10.05310	8.04248	.4	29.53097	69.39778	.6	49.00885	191.1345
.3	10.36726	8.55299	.5	29.84513	70.88218	.7	49.32300	193.5928
.4	10.68142	9.07920	.6	30.15929	72.38229	.8	49.63716	196.0668
.5	10.99557	9.62113	.7	30.47345	73.89811	.9	49.95132	198.5565
.6	11.30973	10.17876	.8	30.78761	75.42964	16.0	50.26548	201.0619
.7	11.62389	10.75210	.9	31.10177	76.97687	.1	50.57964	203.5831
.8	11.93805	11.34115	10.0	31.41593	78.53982	.2	50.89380	206.1199
.9	12.25221	11.94591	.1	31.73009	80.11847	.3	51.20796	208.6724
4.0	12.56637	12.56637	.2	32.04425	81.71282	.4	51.52212	211.2407
.1	12.88053	13.20254	.3	32.35840	83.32289	.5	51.83628	213.8246
.2	13.19469	13.85442	.4	32.67256	84.94867	.6	52.15044	216.4243
.3	13.50885	14.52201	.5	32.98672	86.59015	.7	52.46460	219.0397
.4	13.82301	15.20531	.6	33.30088	88.24734	.8	52.77876	221.6708
.5	14.13717	15.90431	.7	33.61504	89.92024	.9	53.09292	224.3176
.6	14.45133	16.61903	.8	33.92920	91.60884	17.0	53.40708	226.9801
.7	14.76549	17.34945	.9	34.24336	93.31316	.1	53.72123	229.6583
.8	15.07964	18.09557	11.0	34.55752	95.03318	.2	54.03539	232.3522
.9	15.39380	18.85741	.1	34.87168	96.76891	.3	54.34955	235.0618
5.0	15.70796	19.63495	.2	35.18584	98.52035	.4	54.66371	237.7871
.1	16.02212	20.42821	.3	35.50000	100.2875	.5	54.97787	240.5282
.2	16.33628	21.23717	.4	35.81416	102.0703	.6	55.29203	243.2849
.3	16.65044	22.06183	.5	36.12832	103.8689	.7	55.60619	246.0574
.4	16.96460	22.90221	.6	36.44247	105.6832	.8	55.92035	248.8456
.5	17.27876	23.75829	.7	36.75663	107.5132	.9	56.23451	251.6494
.6	17.59292	24.63009	.8	37.07079	109.3588	18.0	56.54867	254.4690
.7	17.90708	25.51759	.9	37.38495	111.2202	.1	56.86283	257.3043
.8	18.22124	26.42079	12.0	37.69911	113.0973	.2	57.17699	260.1553
.9	18.53540	27.33971	.1	38.01327	114.9901	.3	57.49115	263.0220
6.0	18.84956	28.27433	.2	38.32743	116.8987	.4	57.80530	265.9044
.1	19.16372	29.22467	.3	38.64159	118.8229	.5	58.11946	268.8025
.2	19.47787	30.19071	.4	38.95575	120.7628	.6	58.43362	271.7163

From Trautwine's "Civil Engineer's Pocket Book."

CIRCLES.

TABLE 2 OF CIRCLES—(Continued).

Diameters in units and tenths.

Dia.	Circumf.	Area.	Dia.	Circumf.	Area.	Dia.	Circumf.	Area.
18.7	58.74778	274.6459	24.9	78.22566	486.9547	31.1	97.70353	759.6450
.8	59.06194	277.5911	25.0	78.53982	490.8739	.2	98.01769	764.5380
.9	59.37610	280.5521	.1	78.85398	494.8087	.3	98.33185	769.4467
19.0	59.69026	283.5287	.2	79.16813	498.7592	.4	98.64601	774.3712
.1	60.00442	286.5211	.3	79.48229	502.7255	.5	98.96017	779.3113
.2	60.31858	289.5292	.4	79.79645	506.7075	.6	99.27433	784.2672
.3	60.63274	292.5530	.5	80.11061	510.7052	.7	99.58849	789.2388
.4	60.94690	295.5925	.6	80.42477	514.7185	.8	99.90265	794.2260
.5	61.26106	298.6477	.7	80 73893	518.7476	.9	100.2168	799.2290
.6	61.57522	301.7186	.8	81.05309	522.7924	32.0	100.5310	804.2477
.7	61.88938	304.8052	.9	81.36725	526.8529	.1	100.8451	809.2821
.8	62.20353	307.9075	26.0	81.68141	530.9292	.2	101.1593	814.3322
.9	62.51769	311.0255	.1	81.99557	535.0211	.3	101.4734	819.3980
20.0	62.83185	314.1593	.2	82.30973	539.1287	.4	101.7876	824.4796
.1	63.14601	317.3087	.3	82.62389	543.2521	.5	102.1018	829.5768
.2	63.46017	320.4739	.4	82.93805	547.3911	.6	102.4159	834.6898
.3	63.77433	323.6547	.5	83.25221	551.5459	.7	102.7301	839.8184
.4	64.08849	326.8513	.6	83.56636	555.7163	.8	103.0442	844.9628
.5	64.40265	330.0636	.7	83.88052	559.9025	.9	103.3584	850.1228
.6	64.71681	333.2916	.8	84.19468	564.1044	33.0	103.6726	855.2986
.7	65.03097	336.5353	.9	84.50884	568.3220	.1	103.9867	860.4901
.8	65.34513	339.7947	27.0	84.82300	572.5553	.2	104.3009	865.6973
.9	65.65929	343.0698	.1	85.13716	576.8043	.3	104.6150	870.9202
21.0	65.97345	346.3606	.2	85.45132	581.0690	.4	104.9292	876.1588
.1	66.28760	349.6671	.3	85.76548	585.3494	.5	105.2434	881.4131
.2	66.60176	352.9894	.4	86.07964	589.6455	.6	105.5575	886.6831
.3	66.91592	356.3273	.5	86.39380	593.9574	.7	105.8717	891.9688
.4	67.23008	359.6809	.6	86.70796	598.2849	.8	106.1858	897.2703
.5	67.54424	363.0503	.7	87.02212	602.6282	.9	106.5000	902.5874
.6	67.85840	366.4354	.8	87.33628	606.9871	34.0	106.8142	907.9203
.7	68.17256	369.8361	.9	87.65044	611.3618	.1	107.1283	913.2688
.8	68.48672	373.2526	28.0	87.96459	615.7522	.2	107.4425	918.6331
.9	68.80088	376.6848	.1	88.27875	620.1582	.3	107.7566	924.0131
22.0	69.11504	380.1327	.2	88.59291	624.5800	.4	108.0708	929.4088
.1	69.42920	383.5963	.3	88.90707	629.0175	.5	108.3849	934.8202
.2	69.74336	387.0756	.4	89.22123	633.4707	.6	108.6991	940.2473
.3	70.05752	390.5707	.5	89.53539	637.9397	.7	109.0133	945.6901
.4	70.37168	394.0814	.6	89.84955	642.4243	.8	109.3274	951.1486
.5	70.68583	397.6078	.7	90.16371	646.9246	.9	109.6416	956.6228
.6	70.99999	401.1500	.8	90.47787	651.4407	35.0	109.9557	962.1128
.7	71.31415	404.7078	.9	90.79203	655.9724	.1	110.2699	967.6184
.8	71.62831	408.2814	29.0	91.10619	660.5199	.2	110.5841	973.1397
.9	71.94247	411.8707	.1	91.42035	665.0830	.3	110.8982	978.6768
23.0	72.25663	415.4756	.2	91.73451	669.6619	.4	111.2124	984.2296
.1	72.57079	419.0963	.3	92.04866	674.2565	.5	111.5265	989.7980
.2	72.88495	422.7327	.4	92.36282	678.8668	.6	111.8407	995.3822
.3	73.19911	426.3848	.5	92.67698	683.4928	.7	112.1549	1000.9821
.4	73.51327	430.0526	.6	92.99114	688.1345	.8	112.4690	1006.5977
.5	73.82743	433.7361	.7	93.30530	692.7919	.9	112.7832	1012.2290
.6	74.14159	437.4354	.8	93.61946	697.4650	36.0	113.0973	1017.8760
.7	74.45575	441.1503	.9	93.93362	702.1538	.1	113.4115	1023.5387
.8	74.76991	444.8809	30.0	94.24778	706.8583	.2	113.7257	1029.2172
.9	75.08406	448.6273	.1	94.56194	711.5786	.3	114.0398	1034.9113
24.0	75.39822	452.3893	.2	94.87610	716.3145	.4	114.3540	1040.6212
.1	75.71238	456.1671	.3	95.19026	721.0662	.5	114.6681	1046.3467
.2	76.02654	459.9606	.4	95.50442	725.8336	.6	114.9823	1052.0880
.3	76.34070	463.7698	.5	95.81858	730.6166	.7	115.2965	1057.8449
.4	76.65486	467.5947	.6	96.13274	735.4154	.8	115.6106	1063.6176
.5	76.96902	471.4352	.7	96.44689	740.2299	.9	115.9248	1069.4060
.6	77.28318	475.2916	.8	96.76105	745.0601	37.0	116.2389	1075.2101
.7	77.59734	479.1636	.9	97.07521	749.9060	.1	116.5531	1081.0299
.8	77.91150	483.0513	31.0	97.38937	754.7676	.2	116.8672	1086.8654

TABLE NO. 72--CON.
From Trautwine's "Civil Engineer's Pocket Book."

CIRCLES.

TABLE 2 OF CIRCLES—(Continued).
Diameters in units and tenths.

Dia.	Circumf.	Area.	Dia.	Circumf.	Area.	Dia.	Circumf.	Area.
37.3	117.1814	1092.7166	43.5	136.6593	1486.1697	49.7	156.1372	1940.0041
.4	117.4956	1098.5835	.6	136.9734	1493.0105	.8	156.4513	1947.8189
.5	117.8097	1104.4662	.7	137.2876	1499.8670	.9	156.7655	1955.6493
.6	118.1239	1110.3645	.8	137.6018	1506.7393	50.0	157.0796	1963.4954
.7	118.4380	1116.2786	.9	137.9159	1513.6272	.1	157.3938	1971.3572
.8	118.7522	1122.2083	44.0	138.2301	1520.5308	.2	157.7080	1979.2348
.9	119.0664	1128.1538	.1	138.5442	1527.4502	.3	158.0221	1987.1280
38.0	119.3805	1134.1149	.2	138.8584	1534.3853	.4	158.3363	1995.0370
.1	119.6947	1140.0918	.3	139.1726	1541.3360	.5	158.6504	2002.9617
.2	120.0088	1146.0844	.4	139.4867	1548.3025	.6	158.9646	2010.9020
.3	120.3230	1152.0927	.5	139.8009	1555.2847	.7	159.2787	2018.8581
.4	120.6372	1158.1167	.6	140.1150	1562.2826	.8	159.5929	2026.8299
.5	120.9513	1164.1564	.7	140.4292	1569.2962	.9	159.9071	2034.8174
.6	121.2655	1170.2118	.8	140.7434	1576.3255	51.0	160.2212	2042.8206
.7	121.5796	1176.2830	.9	141.0575	1583.3706	.1	160.5354	2050.8395
.8	121.8938	1182.3698	45.0	141.3717	1590.4313	.2	160.8495	2058.8712
.9	122.2080	1188.4724	.1	141.6858	1597.5077	.3	161.1637	2066.9245
39.0	122.5221	1194.5906	.2	142.0000	1604.5999	.4	161.4779	2074.9905
.1	122.8363	1200.7246	.3	142.3141	1611.7077	.5	161.7920	2083.0723
.2	123.1504	1206.8742	.4	142.6283	1618.8313	.6	162.1062	2091.1697
.3	123.4646	1213.0396	.5	142.9425	1625.9705	.7	162.4203	2099.2829
.4	123.7788	1219.2207	.6	143.2566	1633.1255	.8	162.7345	2107.4118
.5	124.0929	1225.4175	.7	143.5708	1640.2962	.9	163.0487	2115.5563
.6	124.4071	1231.6300	.8	143.8849	1647.4826	52.0	163.3628	2123.7166
.7	124.7212	1237.8582	.9	144.1991	1654.6847	.1	163.6770	2131.8926
.8	125.0354	1244.1021	46.0	144.5133	1661.9025	.2	163.9911	2140.0843
.9	125.3495	1250.3617	.1	144.8274	1669.1360	.3	164.3053	2148.2917
40.0	125.6637	1256.6371	.2	145.1416	1676.3853	.4	164.6195	2156.5149
.1	125.9779	1262.9281	.3	145.4557	1683.6502	.5	164.9336	2164.7537
.2	126.2920	1269.2348	.4	145.7699	1690.9308	.6	165.2478	2173.0082
.3	126.6062	1275.5573	.5	146.0841	1698.2272	.7	165.5619	2181.2785
.4	126.9203	1281.8955	.6	146.3982	1705.5392	.8	165.8761	2189.5644
.5	127.2345	1288.2493	.7	146.7124	1712.8670	.9	166.1903	2197.8661
.6	127.5487	1294.6189	.8	147.0265	1720.2105	53.0	166.5044	2206.1834
.7	127.8628	1301.0042	.9	147.3407	1727.5697	.1	166.8186	2214.5165
.8	128.1770	1307.4052	47.0	147.6549	1734.9445	.2	167.1327	2222.8653
.9	128.4911	1313.8219	.1	147.9690	1742.3351	.3	167.4469	2231.2298
41.0	128.8053	1320.2543	.2	148.2832	1749.7414	.4	167.7610	2239.6100
.1	129.1195	1326.7024	.3	148.5973	1757.1635	.5	168.0752	2248.0059
.2	129.4336	1333.1663	.4	148.9115	1764.6012	.6	168.3894	2256.4175
.3	129.7478	1339.6458	.5	149.2257	1772.0546	.7	168.7035	2264.8448
.4	130.0619	1346.1410	.6	149.5398	1779.5237	.8	169.0177	2273.2879
.5	130.3761	1352.6520	.7	149.8540	1787.0086	.9	169.3318	2281.7466
.6	130.6903	1359.1786	.8	150.1681	1794.5091	54.0	169.6460	2290.2210
.7	131.0044	1365.7210	.9	150.4823	1802.0254	.1	169.9602	2298.7112
.8	131.3186	1372.2791	48.0	150.7964	1809.5574	.2	170.2743	2307.2171
.9	131.6327	1378.8529	.1	151.1106	1817.1050	.3	170.5885	2315.7386
42.0	131.9469	1385.4424	.2	151.4248	1824.6684	.4	170.9026	2324.2759
.1	132.2611	1392.0476	.3	151.7389	1832.2475	.5	171.2168	2332.8289
.2	132.5752	1398.6685	.4	152.0531	1839.8423	.6	171.5310	2341.3976
.3	132.8894	1405.3051	.5	152.3672	1847.4528	.7	171.8451	2349.9820
.4	133.2035	1411.9574	.6	152.6814	1855.0790	.8	172.1593	2358.5821
.5	133.5177	1418.6254	.7	152.9956	1862.7210	.9	172.4734	2367.1979
.6	133.8318	1425.3092	.8	153.3097	1870.3786	55.0	172.7876	2375.8294
.7	134.1460	1432.0086	.9	153.6239	1878.0519	.1	173.1018	2384.4767
.8	134.4602	1438.7238	49.0	153.9380	1885.7410	.2	173.4159	2393.1396
.9	134.7743	1445.4546	.1	154.2522	1893.4457	.3	173.7301	2401.8183
43.0	135.0885	1452.2012	.2	154.5664	1901.1662	.4	174.0442	2410.5126
.1	135.4026	1458.9635	.3	154.8805	1908.9024	.5	174.3584	2419.2227
.2	135.7168	1465.7415	.4	155.1947	1916.6543	.6	174.6726	2427.9485
.3	136.0310	1472.5352	.5	155.5088	1924.4218	.7	174.9867	2436.6899
.4	136.3451	1479.3446	.6	155.8230	1932.2051	.8	175.3009	2445.4471

From Trautwine's "Civil Engineer's Pocket Book."

CIRCLES.

TABLE 2 OF CIRCLES—(Continued).

Diameters in units and tenths.

Dia.	Circumf.	Area.	Dia.	Circumf.	Area.	Dia.	Circumf.	Area.
55.9	175.6150	2454.2200	62.1	195.0929	3028.8173	68.3	214.5708	3663.7960
56.0	175.9292	2463.0086	.2	195.4071	3038.5798	.4	214.8849	3674.5324
.1	176.2433	2471.8130	.3	195.7212	3048.3580	.5	215.1991	3685.2845
.2	176.5575	2480.6330	.4	196.0354	3058.1520	.6	215.5133	3696.0523
.3	176.8717	2489.4687	.5	196.3495	3067.9616	.7	215.8274	3706.8359
.4	177.1858	2498.3201	.6	196.6637	3077.7869	.8	216.1416	3717.6351
.5	177.5000	2507.1873	.7	196.9779	3087.6279	.9	216.4557	3728.4500
.6	177.8141	2516.0701	.8	197.2920	3097.4847	69.0	216.7699	3739.2807
.7	178.1283	2524.9687	.9	197.6062	3107.3571	.1	217.0841	3750.1270
.8	178.4425	2533.8830	63.0	197.9203	3117.2453	.2	217.3982	3760.9891
.9	178.7566	2542.8129	.1	198.2345	3127.1492	.3	217.7124	3771.8668
57.0	179.0708	2551.7586	.2	198.5487	3137.0688	.4	218.0265	3782.7603
.1	179.3849	2560.7200	.3	198.8628	3147.0040	.5	218.3407	3793.6695
.2	179.6991	2569.6971	.4	199.1770	3156.9550	.6	218.6548	3804.5944
.3	180.0133	2578.6899	.5	199.4911	3166.9217	.7	218.9690	3815.5350
.4	180.3274	2587.6985	.6	199.8053	3176.9042	.8	219.2832	3826.4913
.5	180.6416	2596.7227	.7	200.1195	3186.9023	.9	219.5973	3837.4633
.6	180.9557	2605.7626	.8	200.4336	3196.9161	70.0	219.9115	3848.4510
.7	181.2699	2614.8183	.9	200.7478	3206.9456	.1	220.2256	3859.4544
.8	181.5841	2623.8896	64.0	201.0619	3216.9909	.2	220.5398	3870.4736
.9	181.8982	2632.9767	.1	201.3761	3227.0518	.3	220.8540	3881.5084
58.0	182.2124	2642.0794	.2	201.6902	3237.1285	.4	221.1681	3892.5590
.1	182.5265	2651.1979	.3	202.0044	3247.2209	.5	221.4823	3903.6252
.2	182.8407	2660.3321	.4	202.3186	3257.3289	.6	221.7964	3914.7072
.3	183.1549	2669.4820	.5	202.6327	3267.4527	.7	222.1106	3925.8049
.4	183.4690	2678.6476	.6	202.9469	3277.5922	.8	222.4248	3936.9182
.5	183.7832	2687.8289	.7	203.2610	3287.7474	.9	222.7389	3948.0473
.6	184.0973	2697.0259	.8	203.5752	3297.9183	71.0	223.0531	3959.1921
.7	184.4115	2706.2386	.9	203.8894	3308.1049	.1	223.3672	3970.3526
.8	184.7256	2715.4670	65.0	204.2035	3318.3072	.2	223.6814	3981.5289
.9	185.0398	2724.7112	.1	204.5177	3328.5253	.3	223.9956	3992.7208
59.0	185.3540	2733.9710	.2	204.8318	3338.7590	.4	224.3097	4003.9284
.1	185.6681	2743.2466	.3	205.1460	3349.0085	.5	224.6239	4015.1518
.2	185.9823	2752.5378	.4	205.4602	3359.2736	.6	224.9380	4026.3908
.3	186.2964	2761.8448	.5	205.7743	3369.5545	.7	225.2522	4037.6456
.4	186.6106	2771.1675	.6	206.0885	3379.8510	.8	225.5664	4048.9160
.5	186.9248	2780.5058	.7	206.4026	3390.1633	.9	225.8805	4060.2022
.6	187.2389	2789.8599	.8	206.7168	3400.4913	72.0	226.1947	4071.5041
.7	187.5531	2799.2297	.9	207.0310	3410.8350	.1	226.5088	4082.8217
.8	187.8672	2808.6152	66.0	207.3451	3421.1944	.2	226.8230	4094.1550
.9	188.1814	2818.0165	.1	207.6593	3431.5695	.3	227.1371	4105.5040
60.0	188.4956	2827.4334	.2	207.9734	3441.9603	.4	227.4513	4116.8687
.1	188.8097	2836.8660	.3	208.2876	3452.3669	.5	227.7655	4128.2491
.2	189.1239	2846.3144	.4	208.6018	3462.7891	.6	228.0796	4139.6452
.3	189.4380	2855.7784	.5	208.9159	3473.2270	.7	228.3938	4151.0571
.4	189.7522	2865.2582	.6	209.2301	3483.6807	.8	228.7079	4162.4846
.5	190.0664	2874.7536	.7	209.5442	3494.1500	.9	229.0221	4173.9279
.6	190.3805	2884.2648	.8	209.8584	3504.6351	73.0	229.3363	4185.3868
.7	190.6947	2893.7917	.9	210.1725	3515.1359	.1	229.6504	4196.8615
.8	191.0088	2903.3343	67.0	210.4867	3525.6524	.2	229.9646	4208.3519
.9	191.3230	2912.8926	.1	210.8009	3536.1845	.3	230.2787	4219.8579
61.0	191.6372	2922.4666	.2	211.1150	3546.7324	.4	230.5929	4231.3797
.1	191.9513	2932.0563	.3	211.4292	3557.2960	.5	230.9071	4242.9172
.2	192.2655	2941.6617	.4	211.7433	3567.8754	.6	231.2212	4254.4704
.3	192.5796	2951.2828	.5	212.0575	3578.4704	.7	231.5354	4266.0394
.4	192.8938	2960.9197	.6	212.3717	3589.0811	.8	231.8495	4277.6240
.5	193.2079	2970.5722	.7	212.6858	3599.7075	.9	232.1637	4289.2243
.6	193.5221	2980.2405	.8	213.0000	3610.3497	74.0	232.4779	4300.8403
.7	193.8363	2989.9244	.9	213.3141	3621.0075	.1	232.7920	4312.4721
.8	194.1504	2999.6241	68.0	213.6283	3631.6811	.2	233.1062	4324.1195
.9	194.4646	3009.3395	.1	213.9425	3642.3704	.3	233.4203	4335.7827
62.0	194.7787	3019.0705	.2	214.2566	3653.0754	.4	233.7345	4347.4616

TABLE NO. 72—CON.

From Trautwine's "Civil Engineer's Pocket Book."

CIRCLES.

TABLE 2 OF CIRCLES—(Continued).
Diameters in units and tenths.

Dia.	Circumf.	Area.	Dia.	Circumf.	Area.	Dia.	Circumf.	Area.
74.5	234.0487	4359.1562	80.7	253.5265	5114.8977	86.9	273.0044	5931.0206
.6	234.3628	4370.8664	.8	253.8407	5127.5819	87.0	273.3186	5944.6787
.7	234.6770	4382.5924	.9	254.1548	5140.2818	.1	273.6327	5958.3525
.8	234.9911	4394.3341	81.0	254.4690	5152.9974	.2	273.9469	5972.0420
.9	235.3053	4406.0916	.1	254.7832	5165.7287	.3	274.2610	5985.7472
75.0	235.6194	4417.8647	.2	255.0973	5178.4757	.4	274.5752	5999.4681
.1	235.9336	4429.6535	.3	255.4115	5191.2384	.5	274.8894	6013.2047
.2	236.2478	4441.4580	.4	255.7256	5204.0168	.6	275.2035	6026.9570
.3	236.5619	4453.2783	.5	256.0398	5216.8110	.7	275.5177	6040.7250
.4	236.8761	4465.1142	.6	256.3540	5229.6208	.8	275.8318	6054.5088
.5	237.1902	4476.9659	.7	256.6681	5242.4463	.9	276.1460	6068.3082
.6	237.5044	4488.8332	.8	256.9823	5255.2876	88.0	276.4602	6082.1234
.7	237.8186	4500.7163	.9	257.2964	5268.1446	.1	276.7743	6095.9542
.8	238.1327	4512.6151	82.0	257.6106	5281.0173	.2	277.0885	6109.8008
.9	238.4469	4524.5296	.1	257.9248	5293.9056	.3	277.4026	6123.6631
76.0	238.7610	4536.4598	.2	258.2389	5306.8097	.4	277.7168	6137.5411
.1	239.0752	4548.4057	.3	258.5531	5319.7295	.5	278.0309	6151.4348
.2	239.3894	4560.3673	.4	258.8672	5332.6650	.6	278.3451	6165.3442
.3	239.7035	4572.3446	.5	259.1814	5345.6162	.7	278.6593	6179.2693
.4	240.0177	4584.3377	.6	259.4956	5358.5832	.8	278.9734	6193.2101
.5	240.3318	4596.3464	.7	259.8097	5371.5658	.9	279.2876	6207.1666
.6	240.6460	4608.3708	.8	260.1239	5384.5641	89.0	279.6017	6221.1389
.7	240.9602	4620.4110	.9	260.4380	5397.5782	.1	279.9159	6235.1268
.8	241.2743	4632.4669	83.0	260.7522	5410.6079	.2	280.2301	6249.1304
.9	241.5885	4644.5384	.1	261.0663	5423.6534	.3	280.5442	6263.1498
77.0	241.9026	4656.6257	.2	261.3805	5436.7146	.4	280.8584	6277.1849
.1	242.2168	4668.7287	.3	261.6947	5449.7915	.5	281.1725	6291.2356
.2	242.5310	4680.8474	.4	262.0088	5462.8840	.6	281.4867	6305.3021
.3	242.8451	4692.9818	.5	262.3230	5475.9923	.7	281.8009	6319.3843
.4	243.1593	4705.1319	.6	262.6371	5489.1163	.8	282.1150	6333.4822
.5	243.4734	4717.2977	.7	262.9513	5502.2561	.9	282.4292	6347.5958
.6	243.7876	4729.4792	.8	263.2655	5515.4115	90.0	282.7433	6361.7251
.7	244.1017	4741.6765	.9	263.5796	5528.5826	.1	283.0575	6375.8701
.8	244.4159	4753.8894	84.0	263.8938	5541.7694	.2	283.3717	6390.0309
.9	244.7301	4766.1181	.1	264.2079	5554.9720	.3	283.6858	6404.2073
78.0	245.0442	4778.3624	.2	264.5221	5568.1902	.4	284.0000	6418.3995
.1	245.3584	4790.6225	.3	264.8363	5581.4242	.5	284.3141	6432.6073
.2	245.6725	4802.8983	.4	265.1504	5594.6739	.6	284.6283	6446.8309
.3	245.9867	4815.1897	.5	265.4646	5607.9392	.7	284.9425	6461.0701
.4	246.3009	4827.4969	.6	265.7787	5621.2203	.8	285.2566	6475.3251
.5	246.6150	4839.8198	.7	266.0929	5634.5171	.9	285.5708	6489.5958
.6	246.9292	4852.1584	.8	266.4071	5647.8296	91.0	285.8849	6503.8822
.7	247.2433	4864.5128	.9	266.7212	5661.1578	.1	286.1991	6518.1843
.8	247.5575	4876.8828	85.0	267.0354	5674.5017	.2	286.5133	6532.5021
.9	247.8717	4889.2686	.1	267.3495	5687.8614	.3	286.8274	6546.8356
79.0	248.1858	4901.6699	.2	267.6637	5701.2367	.4	287.1416	6561.1848
.1	248.5000	4914.0871	.3	267.9779	5714.6277	.5	287.4557	6575.5498
.2	248.8141	4926.5199	.4	268.2920	5728.0345	.6	287.7699	6589.9304
.3	249.1283	4938.9685	.5	268.6062	5741.4569	.7	288.0840	6604.3268
.4	249.4425	4951.4328	.6	268.9203	5754.8951	.8	288.3982	6618.7388
.5	249.7566	4963.9127	.7	269.2345	5768.3490	.9	288.7124	6633.1666
.6	250.0708	4976.4084	.8	269.5486	5781.8185	92.0	289.0265	6647.6101
.7	250.3849	4988.9198	.9	269.8628	5795.3038	.1	289.3407	6662.0692
.8	250.6991	5001.4469	86.0	270.1770	5808.8048	.2	289.6548	6676.5441
9	251.0133	5013.9897	.1	270.4911	5822.3215	.3	289.9690	6691.0347
80.0	251.3274	5026.5482	.2	270.8053	5835.8539	.4	290.2832	6705.5410
.1	251.6416	5039.1225	.3	271.1194	5849.4020	.5	290.5973	6720.0630
.2	251.9557	5051.7124	.4	271.4336	5862.9659	.6	290.9115	6734.6008
.3	252.2699	5064.3180	.5	271.7478	5876.5454	.7	291.2256	6749.1542
.4	252.5810	5076.9394	.6	272.0619	5890.1407	.8	291.5398	6763.7233
.5	252.8982	5089.5764	.7	272.3761	5903.7516	.9	291.8540	6778.3082
.6	253.2124	5102.2292	.8	272.6902	5917.3783	93.0	292.1681	6792.9087

CIRCLES.

TABLE 2 OF CIRCLES—(Continued).
Diameters in units and tenths.

Dia.	Circumf.	Area.	Dia.	Circumf.	Area.	Dia.	Circumf.	Area.
93.1	292.4823	6807.5250	95.5	300.0221	7163.0276	97.8	307.2478	7512.2078
.2	292.7964	6822.1569	.6	300.3363	7178.0366	.9	307.5619	7527.5780
.3	293.1106	6836.8046	.7	300.6504	7193.0612	98.0	307.8761	7542.9640
.4	293.4248	6851.4680	.8	300.9646	7208.1016	.1	308.1902	7558.3656
.5	293.7389	6866.1471	.9	301.2787	7223.1577	.2	308.5044	7573.7830
.6	294.0531	6880.8419	96.0	301.5929	7238.2295	.3	308.8186	7589.2161
.7	294.3672	6895.5524	.1	301.9071	7253.3170	.4	309.1327	7604.6648
.8	294.6814	6910.2786	.2	302.2212	7268.4202	.5	309.4469	7620.1293
.9	294.9956	6925.0205	.3	302.5354	7283.5391	.6	309.7610	7635.6095
94.0	295.3097	6939.7782	.4	302.8495	7298.6737	.7	310.0752	7651.1054
.1	295.6239	6954.5515	.5	303.1637	7313.8240	.8	310.3894	7666.6170
.2	295.9380	6969.3406	.6	303.4779	7328.9901	.9	310.7035	7682.1444
.3	296.2522	6984.1453	.7	303.7920	7344.1718	99.0	311.0177	7697.6874
.4	296.5663	6998.9658	.8	304.1062	7359.3693	.1	311.3318	7713.2461
.5	296.8805	7013.8019	.9	304.4203	7374.5824	.2	311.6460	7728.8206
.6	297.1947	7028.6588	97.0	304.7345	7389.8113	.3	311.9602	7744.4107
.7	297.5088	7043.5214	.1	305.0486	7405.0559	.4	312.2743	7760.0166
.8	297.8230	7058.4047	.2	305.3628	7420.3162	.5	312.5885	7775.6382
.9	298.1371	7073.3037	.3	305.6770	7435.5922	.6	312.9026	7791.2754
95.0	298.4513	7088.2184	.4	305.9911	7450.8839	.7	313.2168	7806.9284
.1	298.7655	7103.1488	.5	306.3053	7466.1913	.8	313.5309	7822.5971
.2	299.0796	7118.0950	.6	306.6194	7481.5144	.9	313.8451	7838.2815
.3	299.3938	7133.0568	.7	306.9336	7496.8532	100.0	314.1593	7853.9816
.4	299.7079	7148.0343						

Circumferences when the diameter has more than one place of decimals.

Diam.	Circ.	Diam.	Circ.	Diam.	Circ.	Diam.	Circ.	Diam.	Circ.
.1	.314159	.01	.031416	.001	.003142	.0001	.000314	.00001	.000031
.2	.628319	.02	.062832	.002	.006283	.0002	.000628	.00002	.000063
.3	.942478	.03	.094248	.003	.009425	.0003	.000942	.00003	.000094
.4	1.256637	.04	.125664	.004	.012566	.0004	.001257	.00004	.000126
.5	1.570796	.05	.157080	.005	.015708	.0005	.001571	.00005	.000157
.6	1.884956	.06	.188496	.006	.018850	.0006	.001885	.00006	.000188
.7	2.199115	.07	.219911	.007	.021991	.0007	.002199	.00007	.000220
.8	2.513274	.08	.251327	.008	.025133	.0008	.002513	.00008	.000251
.9	2.827433	.09	.282743	.009	.028274	.0009	.002827	.00009	.000283

Examples.

Diameter = 3.12699
Circumference =   Sum of

Circ for dia of   3.1   = 9.738937
        "   .02   = .062832
        "   .006   = .018850
        "   .0009 = .002827
        "   .00009 = .000283
                                9.823729

Circumfce = 9.823729
Diameter =   Sum of

Dia for circ of   9.738937 = 3.1
                   .084792
        "   .062832 = .02
                   .021960
        "   .018850 = .006
                   .003110
        "   .002827 = .0009
                   .000283
        "   .000283 = .00009
                                3.12699

CIRCLES.

TABLE 3 OF CIRCLES.

Diams in units and twelfths; as in feet and inches.

Dia.	Circumf.	Area.	Dia.	Circumf.	Area.	Dia.	Circumf.	Area.
Ft.In.	Feet.	Sq. ft.	Ft.In.	Feet.	Sq. ft.	Ft.In.	Feet.	Sq. ft.
0 1	.261799	.005454	5 0	15.70796	19.63495	10 0	31.41593	78.53952
2	.523599	.021817	1	15.96976	20.29491	1	31.67773	79.85427
3	.785398	.049087	2	16.23156	20.96577	2	31.93953	81.17963
4	1.047198	.087266	3	16.49336	21.64754	3	32.20132	82.51589
5	1.308997	.136354	4	16.75516	22.34021	4	32.46312	83.86307
6	1.570796	.196350	5	17.01696	23.04380	5	32.72492	85.22115
7	1.832596	.267254	6	17.27876	23.75829	6	32.98672	86.59015
8	2.094395	.349066	7	17.54056	24.48370	7	33.24852	87.97005
9	2.356195	·441786	8	17.80236	25.22001	8	33.51032	89.36086
10	2.617994	.545415	9	18.06416	25.96723	9	33.77212	90.76253
11	2.879793	.659953	10	18.32596	26.72535	10	34.03392	92.17520
1 0	3.14159	.785398	11	18.58776	27.49439	11	34.29572	93.59874
1	3.40839	.921752	6 0	18.84956	28.27433	11 0	34.55752	95.03318
2	3.66519	1.06901	1	19.11136	29.06519	1	34.81932	96.47853
3	3.92699	1.22718	2	19.37315	29.86695	2	35.08112	97.93479
4	4.18879	1.39626	3	19.63495	30.67962	3	35.34292	99.40196
5	4.45059	1.57625	4	19.89675	31.50319	4	35.60472	100.8900
6	4.71239	1.76715	5	20.15855	32.33768	5	35.86652	102.3690
7	4.97419	1.96895	6	20.42035	33.18307	6	36.12832	103.8689
8	5.23599	2.18166	7	20.68215	34.03937	7	36.39011	105.3797
9	5.49779	2.40528	8	20.94395	34.90659	8	36.65191	106.9014
10	5.75959	2.63981	9	21.20575	35.78470	9	36.91371	108.4340
11	6.02139	2.88525	10	21.46755	36.67373	10	37.17551	109.9776
2 0	6.28319	3.14159	11	21.72935	37.57367	11	37.43731	111.5320
1	6.54498	3.40885	7 0	21.99115	38.48451	12 0	37.69911	113.0973
2	6.80678	3.68701	1	22.25295	39.40626	1	37.96091	114.6736
3	7.06858	3.97608	2	22.51475	40.33892	2	38.22271	116.2607
4	7.33038	4.27606	3	22.77655	41.28249	3	38.48451	117.8588
5	7.59218	4.58694	4	23.03885	42.23697	4	38.74631	119.4678
6	7.85398	4.90874	5	23.30015	43.20235	5	39.00811	121.0877
7	8.11578	5.24144	6	23.56194	44.17865	6	39.26991	122.7185
8	8.37758	5.58505	7	23.82374	45.16585	7	39.53171	124.3602
9	8.63938	5.93957	8	24.08554	46.16396	8	39.79351	126.0128
10	8.90118	6.30500	9	24.34734	47.17298	9	40.05531	127.6763
11	9.16298	6.68134	10	24.60914	48.19290	10	40.31711	129.3507
3 0	9.42478	7.06858	11	24.87094	49.22374	11	40.57891	131.0360
1	9.68658	7.46674	8 0	25.13274	50.26548	13 0	40.84070	132.7323
2	9.94838	7.87580	1	25.39454	51.31813	1	41.10250	134.4394
3	10.21018	8.29577	2	25.65634	52.38169	2	41.36430	136.1575
4	10.47198	8.72665	3	25.91814	53.45616	3	41.62610	137.8865
5	10.73377	9.16843	4	26.17994	54.54154	4	41.88790	139.6263
6	10.99557	9.62113	5	26.44174	55.63782	5	42.14970	141.3771
7	11.25737	10.08473	6	26.70354	56.74502	6	42.41150	143.1388
8	11.51917	10.55924	7	26.96534	57.86312	7	42.67330	144.9114
9	11.78097	11.04466	8	27.22714	58.99213	8	42.93510	146.6949
10	12.04277	11.54099	9	27.48894	60.13205	9	43.19690	148.4893
11	12.30457	12.04823	10	27.75074	61.28287	10	43.45870	150.2947
4 0	12.56637	12.56637	11	28.01253	62.44461	11	43.72050	152.1109
1	12.82817	13.09542	9 0	28.27433	63.61725	14 0	43.98230	153.9386
2	13.08997	13.63538	1	28.53613	64.80080	1	44.24410	155.7761
3	13.35177	14.18625	2	28.79793	65.99526	2	44.50590	157.6250
4	13.61357	14.74803	3	29.05973	67.20063	3	44.76770	159.4849
5	13.87537	15.32072	4	29.32153	68.41691	4	45.02949	161.3557
6	14.13717	15.90431	5	29.58333	69.64409	5	45.29129	163.2374
7	14.39897	16.49882	6	29.84513	70.88218	6	45.55309	165.1300
8	14.66077	17.10423	7	30.10693	72.13119	7	45.81489	167.0335
9	14.92257	17.72055	8	30.36873	73.39110	8	46.07669	168.9479
10	15.18436	18.34777	9	30.63053	74.66191	9	46.33849	170.8732
11	15.44616	18.98591	10	30.89233	75.94364	10	46.60029	172.8094
			11	31.15413	77.23627	11	46.86209	174.7565

From Trautwine's "Civil Engineer's Pocket Book."

CIRCLES.

TABLE 3 OF CIRCLES—(Continued).

Diams in units and twelfths; as in feet and inches.

Dia.	Circumf.	Area.	Dia.	Circumf.	Area.	Dia.	Circumf.	Area.
Ft.In	Feet	Sq. ft.	Ft.In	Feet	Sq. ft.	Ft.In	Feet	Sq. ft.
15 0	47.12389	176.7146	20 0	62.83185	314.1593	25 0	78.53982	490.8739
1	47.38569	178.6835	1	63.09365	316.7827	1	78.80162	494.1518
2	47.64749	180.6634	2	63.35545	319.4171	2	79.06342	497.4407
3	47.90929	182.6542	3	63.61725	322.0623	3	79.32521	500.7404
4	48.17109	184.6558	4	63.87905	324.7185	4	79.58701	504.0511
5	48.43289	186.6684	5	64.14085	327.3856	5	79.84881	507.3727
6	48.69469	188.6919	6	64.40265	330.0636	6	80.11061	510.7052
7	48.95649	190.7263	7	64.66445	332.7525	7	80.37241	514.0486
8	49.21828	192.7716	8	64.92625	335.4523	8	80.63421	517.4029
9	49.48008	194.8278	9	65.18805	338.1630	9	80.89601	520.7681
10	49.74188	196.8950	10	65.44985	340.8846	10	81.15781	524.1442
11	50.00368	198.9730	11	65.71165	343.6172	11	81.41961	527.5312
16 0	50.26548	201.0619	21 0	65.97345	346.3606	26 0	81.68141	530.9292
1	50.52728	203.1618	1	66.23525	349.1149	1	81.94321	534.3380
2	50.78908	205.2725	2	66.49704	351.8802	2	82.20501	537.7578
3	51.05088	207.3942	3	66.75884	354.6564	3	82.46681	541.1884
4	51.31268	209.5268	4	67.02064	357.4434	4	82.72861	544.6300
5	51.57448	211.6703	5	67.28244	360.2414	5	82.99041	548.0825
6	51.83628	213.8246	6	67.54424	363.0503	6	83.25221	551.5459
7	52.09808	215.9899	7	67.80604	365.8701	7	83.51400	555.0202
8	52.35988	218.1662	8	68.06784	368.7008	8	83.77580	558.5054
9	52.62168	220.3533	9	68.32964	371.5424	9	84.03760	562.0015
10	52.88348	222.5513	10	68.59144	374.3949	10	84.29940	565.5085
11	53.14528	224.7602	11	68.85324	377.2584	11	84.56120	569.0264
17 0	53.40708	226.9801	22 0	69.11504	380.1327	27 0	84.82300	572.5553
1	53.66887	229.2108	1	69.37684	383.0180	1	85.08480	576.0950
2	53.93067	231.4525	2	69.63864	385.9141	2	85.34660	579.6457
3	54.19247	233.7050	3	69.90044	388.8212	3	85.60840	583.2072
4	54.45427	235.9685	4	70.16224	391.7392	4	85.87020	586.7797
5	54.71607	238.2429	5	70.42404	394.6680	5	86.13200	590.3631
6	54.97787	240.5282	6	70.68583	397.6078	6	86.39380	593.9574
7	55.23967	242.8244	7	70.94763	400.5585	7	86.65560	597.5626
8	55.50147	245.1315	8	71.20943	403.5201	8	86.91740	601.1787
9	55.76327	247.4495	9	71.47123	406.4926	9	87.17920	604.8057
10	56.02507	249.7784	10	71.73302	409.4761	10	87.44100	608.4436
11	56.28687	252.1183	11	71.99483	412.4704	11	87.70279	612.0924
18 0	56.54867	254.4690	23 0	72.25663	415.4756	28 0	87.96459	615.7522
1	56.81047	256.8307	1	72.51843	418.4918	1	88.22639	619.4228
2	57.07227	259.2032	2	72.78023	421.5188	2	88.48819	623.1044
3	57.33407	261.5867	3	73.04203	424.5568	3	88.74999	626.7968
4	57.59587	263.9810	4	73.30383	427.6057	4	89.01179	630.5002
5	57.85766	266.3863	5	73.56563	430.6654	5	89.27359	634.2145
6	58.11946	268.8025	6	73.82743	433.7361	6	89.53539	637.9397
7	58.38126	271.2296	7	74.08923	436.8177	7	89.79719	641.6758
8	58.64306	273.6676	8	74.35103	439.9102	8	90.05899	645.4228
9	58.90486	276.1165	9	74.61283	443.0137	9	90.32079	649.1807
10	59.16666	278.5764	10	74.87442	446.1280	10	90.58259	652.9495
11	59.42846	281.0471	11	75.13642	449.2532	11	90.84439	656.7292
19 0	59.69026	283.5287	24 0	75.39822	452.3893	29 0	91.10619	660.5199
1	59.95206	286.0213	1	75.66002	455.5364	1	91.36799	664.3214
2	60.21386	288.5247	2	75.92182	458.6943	2	91.62979	668.1339
3	60.47566	291.0391	3	76.18362	461.8632	3	91.89159	671.9572
4	60.73746	293.5644	4	76.44542	465.0430	4	92.15338	675.7915
5	60.99926	296.1006	5	76.70722	468.2337	5	92.41518	679.6367
6	61.26106	298.6477	6	76.96902	471.4352	6	92.67698	683.4928
7	61.52286	301.2056	7	77.23082	474.6477	7	92.93878	687.3591
8	61.78466	303.7746	8	77.49262	477.8711	8	93.20058	691.2377
9	62.04645	306.3544	9	77.75442	481.1055	9	93.46238	695.1264
10	62.30825	308.9451	10	78.01622	484.3507	10	93.72418	699.0261
11	62.57005	311.5467	11	78.27802	487.6068	11	93.98598	702.9364

TABLE NO. 73—CON.

From Trautwine's "Civil Engineer's Pocket Book."

CIRCLES.

TABLE 3 OF CIRCLES—(Continued).
Diams in units and twelfths; as in feet and inches.

Dia.	Circumf.	Area.	Dia.	Circumf.	Area.	Dia.	Circumf.	Area.
Ft.In.	Feet.	Sq. ft.	Ft.In.	Feet.	Sq. ft.	Ft.In.	Feet.	Sq. ft.
30 0	94.24778	706.8583	35 0	109.9557	962.1128	40 0	125.6637	1256.6371
1	94.50958	710.7908	1	110.2175	966.6997	1	125.9255	1261.8785
2	94.77138	714.7341	2	110.4793	971.2975	2	126.1873	1267.1309
3	95.03318	718.6884	3	110.7411	975.9063	3	126.4491	1272.3941
4	95.29498	722.6536	4	111.0029	980.5260	4	126.7109	1277.6683
5	95.55678	726.6297	5	111.2647	985.1566	5	126.9727	1282.9534
6	95.81858	730.6166	6	111.5265	989.7980	6	127.2345	1288.2493
7	96.08038	734.6145	7	111.7883	994.4504	7	127.4963	1293.5562
8	96.34217	738.6233	8	112.0501	999.1137	8	127.7581	1298.8740
9	96.60397	742.6431	9	112.3119	1003.7879	9	128.0199	1304.2027
10	96.86577	746 6737	10	112.5737	1008.4731	10	128.2817	1309.5424
11	97.12757	750.7152	11	112.8355	1013.1691	11	128.5435	1314.8929
31 0	97.38937	754.7676	36 0	113.0973	1017.8760	41 0	128.8053	1320.2543
1	97.65117	758.8310	1	113.3591	1022.5939	1	129.0671	1325.6267
2	97.91297	762.9052	2	113.6209	1027.3226	2	129.3289	1331.0099
3	98.17477	766.9904	3	113.8827	1032.0623	3	129.5907	1336.4041
4	98.43657	771.0865	4	114.1445	1036.8128	4	129.8525	1341.8091
5	98.69837	775.1934	5	114.4063	1041.5743	5	130.1143	1347.2251
6	98.96017	779.3113	6	114.6681	1046.3467	6	130.3761	1352.6520
7	99.22197	783.4401	7	114.9299	1051.1300	7	130.6379	1358.0898
8	99.48377	787.5798	8	115.1917	1055.9242	8	130.8997	1363.5385
9	99.74557	791.7304	9	115.4535	1060.7293	9	131.1615	1368.9981
10	100.0074	795.8920	10	115.7153	1065.5453	10	131.4233	1374.4686
11	100.2692	800.0644	11	115.9771	1070.3723	11	131.6851	1379.9500
32 0	100.5310	804.2477	37 0	116.2389	1075.2101	42 0	131.9469	1385.4424
1	100.7928	808.4420	1	116.5007	1080.0588	1	132.2087	1390.9456
2	101.0546	812.6471	2	116.7625	1084.9185	2	132.4705	1396.4598
3	101.3164	816.8632	3	117.0243	1089.7890	3	132.7323	1401.9848
4	101.5782	821.0901	4	117.2861	1094.6705	4	132.9941	1407.5208
5	101.8400	825.3280	5	117.5479	1099.5629	5	133.2559	1413.0676
6	102.1018	829 5768	6	117.8097	1104.4662	6	133.5177	1418.6254
7	102.3636	833.8365	7	118.0715	1109.3804	7	133.7795	1424.1941
8	102.6254	838.1071	8	118.3333	1114.3055	8	134.0413	1429.7737
9	102.8872	842.3886	9	118.5951	1119.2415	9	134.3031	1435.3642
10	103.1490	846.6810	10	118.8569	1124.1884	10	134.5649	1440.9656
11	103.4108	850.9844	11	119.1187	1129.1462	11	134.8267	1446.5780
33 0	103.6726	855.2986	38 0	119.3805	1134.1149	43 0	135.0885	1452.2012
1	103.9344	859.6237	1	119.6423	1139.0946	1	135.3503	1457.8353
2	104.1962	863.9598	2	119.9041	1144.0851	2	135.6121	1463.4804
3	104.4580	868.3068	3	120.1659	1149.0866	3	135.8739	1469.1364
4	104.7198	872.6646	4	120.4277	1154.0990	4	136.1357	1474.8032
5	104.9816	877.0334	5	120.6895	1159.1222	5	136.3975	1480.4810
6	105.2434	881.4131	6	120.9513	1164.1564	6	136.6593	1486.1697
7	105.5052	885.8037	7	121.2131	1169.2015	7	136.9211	1491.8693
8	105.7670	890.2052	8	121.4749	1174.2575	8	137.1829	1497.5798
9	106.0288	894.6176	9	121.7367	1179.3244	9	137.4447	1503.3012
10	106.2906	899 0409	10	121.9985	1184.4022	10	137.7065	1509.0335
11	106.5524	903.4751	11	122.2603	1189.4910	11	137.9683	1514.7767
34 0	106.8142	907.9203	39 0	122.5221	1194.5906	44 0	138.2301	1520.5308
1	107.0759	912.3763	*1	122.7839	1199.7011	1	138.4919	1526.2959
2	107.3377	916.8433	2	123.0457	1204.8226	2	138.7537	1532.0718
3	107.5995	921.3211	3	123.3075	1209.9550	3	139.0155	1537.8587
4	107.8613	925.8099	4	123.5693	1215.0982	4	139.2773	1543.6565
5	108.1231	930.3096	5	123.8311	1220.2524	5	139.5391	1549.4651
6	108.3849	934.8202	6	124.0929	1225.4175	6	139.8009	1555.2847
7	108.6467	939.3417	7	124.3547	1230.5935	7	140.0627	1561.1152
8	108.9085	943.8741	8	124.6165	1235.7804	8	140.3245	1566.9566
9	109.1703	948.4174	9	124.8783	1240.9782	9	140.5863	1572.8089
10	109.4321	952.9716	10	125.1401	1246.1869	10	140.8481	1578.6721
11	109.6939	957.5367	11	125.4019	1251.4065	11	141.1099	1584.5462

From Trautwine's "Civil Engineer's Pocket Book."

CIRCLES.

TABLE 3 OF CIRCLES—(Continued).

Diams in units and twelfths; as in feet and inches.

Dia.	Circumf.	Area.	Dia.	Circumf.	Area.	Dia.	Circumf.	Area.
Ft.In.	Feet.	Sq. ft.	Ft.In.	Feet.	Sq. ft.	Ft.In.	Feet.	Sq. ft.
45 0	141.3717	1590.4313	50 0	157.0796	1963.4954	55 0	172.7876	2375.8294
1	141.6335	1596.3272	1	157.3414	1970.0458	1	173.0494	2383.0344
2	141.8953	1602.2341	2	157.6032	1976.6072	2	173.3112	2390.2502
3	142.1571	1608.1518	3	157.8650	1983.1794	3	173.5730	2397.4770
4	142.4189	1614.0805	4	158.1268	1989.7626	4	173.8348	2404.7146
5	142.6807	1620.0201	5	158.3886	1996.3567	5	174.0966	2411.9632
6	142.9425	1625.9705	6	158.6504	2002.9617	6	174.3584	2419.2227
7	143.2043	1631.9319	7	158.9122	2009.5776	7	174.6202	2426.4931
8	143.4661	1637.9042	8	159.1740	2016.2044	8	174.8820	2433.7744
9	143.7279	1643.8874	9	159.4358	2022.8421	9	175.1438	2441.0666
10	143.9897	1649.8816	10	159.6976	2029.4907	10	175.4056	2448.3697
11	144.2515	1655.8866	11	159.9594	2036.1502	11	175.6674	2455.6837
46 0	144.5133	1661.9025	51 0	160.2212	2042.8206	56 0	175.9292	2463.0086
1	144.7751	1667.9294	1	160.4830	2049.5020	1	176.1910	2470.3445
2	145.0369	1673.9671	2	160.7448	2056.1942	2	176.4528	2477.6912
3	145.2987	1680.0158	3	161.0066	2062.8974	3	176.7146	2485.0489
4	145.5605	1686.0753	4	161.2684	2069.6114	4	176.9764	2492.4174
5	145.8223	1692.1458	5	161.5302	2076.3364	5	177.2382	2499.7969
6	146.0841	1698.2272	6	161.7920	2083.0723	6	177.5000	2507.1873
7	146.3459	1704.3195	7	162.0538	2089.8191	7	177.7618	2514.5886
8	146.6077	1710.4227	8	162.3156	2096.5768	8	178.0236	2522.0008
9	146.8695	1716.5368	9	162.5774	2103.3454	9	178.2854	2529.4239
10	147.1313	1722.6618	10	162.8392	2110.1249	10	178.5472	2536.8579
11	147.3931	1728.7977	11	163.1010	2116.9153	11	178.8090	2544.3028
47 0	147.6549	1734.9445	52 0	163.3628	2123.7166	57 0	179.0708	2551.7586
1	147.9167	1741.1023	1	163.6246	2130.5289	1	179.3326	2559.2254
2	148.1785	1747.2709	2	163.8864	2137.3520	2	179.5944	2566.7030
3	148.4403	1753.4505	3	164.1482	2144.1861	3	179.8562	2574.1916
4	148.7021	1759.6410	4	164.4100	2151.0310	4	180.1180	2581.6910
5	148.9639	1765.8423	5	164.6718	2157.8869	5	180.3798	2589.2014
6	149.2257	1772.0546	6	164.9336	2164.7537	6	180.6416	2596.7227
7	149.4875	1778.2778	7	165.1954	2171.6314	7	180.9034	2604.2549
8	149.7492	1784.5119	8	165.4572	2178.5200	8	181.1652	2611.7980
9	150.0110	1790.7569	9	165.7190	2185.4195	9	181.4270	2619.3520
10	150.2728	1797.0128	10	165.9808	2192.3299	10	181.6888	2626.9169
11	150.5346	1803.2796	11	166.2426	2199.2512	11	181.9506	2634.4927
48 0	150.7964	1809.5574	53 0	166.5044	2206.1834	58 0	182.2124	2642.0794
1	151.0582	1815.8460	1	166.7662	2213.1266	1	182.4742	2649.6771
2	151.3200	1822.1456	2	167.0280	2220.0806	2	182.7360	2657.2856
3	151.5818	1828.4560	3	167.2898	2227.0456	3	182.9978	2664.9051
4	151.8436	1834.7774	4	167.5516	2234.0214	4	183.2596	2672.5354
5	152.1054	1841.1096	5	167.8134	2241.0082	5	183.5214	2680.1767
6	152.3672	1847.4528	6	168.0752	2248.0059	6	183.7832	2687.8289
7	152.6290	1853.8069	7	168.3370	2255.0145	7	184.0450	2695.4920
8	152.8908	1860.1719	8	168.5988	2262.0340	8	184.3068	2703.1659
9	153.1526	1866.5478	9	168.8606	2269.0644	9	184.5686	2710.8508
10	153.4144	1872.9346	10	169.1224	2276.1057	10	184.8304	2718.5467
11	153.6762	1879.3324	11	169.3842	2283.1579	11	185.0922	2726.2534
49 0	153.9380	1885.7410	54 0	169.6460	2290.2210	59 0	185.3540	2733.9710
1	154.1998	1892.1605	1	169.9078	2297.2951	1	185.6158	2741.6995
2	154.4616	1898.5910	2	170.1696	2304.3800	2	185.8776	2749.4390
3	154.7234	1905.0323	3	170.4314	2311.4759	3	186.1394	2757.1893
4	154.9852	1911.4846	4	170.6932	2318.5826	4	186.4012	2764.9506
5	155.2470	1917.9478	5	170.9550	2325.7003	5	186.6630	2772.7228
6	155.5088	1924.4218	6	171.2168	2332.8289	6	186.9248	2780.5058
7	155.7706	1930.9068	7	171.4786	2339.9684	7	187.1866	2788.2998
8	156.0324	1937.4027	8	171.7404	2347.1188	8	187.4484	2796.1047
9	156.2942	1943.9095	9	172.0022	2354.2801	9	187.7102	2803.9205
10	156.5560	1950.4273	10	172.2640	2361.4523	10	187.9720	2811.7472
11	156.8178	1956.9559	11	172.5258	2368.6354	11	188.2338	2819.5849

TABLE NO. 73—CON.

From Trautwine's "Civil Engineer's Pocket Book."

CIRCLES.

TABLE 3 OF CIRCLES—(Continued).
Diams in units and twelfths; as in feet and inches.

Dia.	Circumf.	Area.	Dia.	Circumf.	Area.	Dia.	Circumf.	Area.
Ft.In.	Feet.	Sq. ft.	Ft.In.	Feet.	Sq. ft.	Ft.In.	Feet.	Sq. ft.
60 0	188.4956	2827.4334	65 0	204.2035	3318.3072	70 0	219.9115	3848.4510
1	188.7574	2835.2928	1	204.4653	3326.8212	1	220.1733	3857.6194
2	189.0192	2843.1682	2	204.7271	3335.3460	2	220.4351	3866.7988
3	189.2810	2851.0444	3	204.9889	3343.8818	3	220.6969	3875.9890
4	189.5428	2858.9366	4	205.2507	3352.4284	4	220.9587	3885.1902
5	189.8046	2866.8397	5	205.5125	3360.9860	5	221.2205	3894.4022
6	190.0664	2874.7536	6	205.7743	3369.5545	6	221.4823	3903.6252
7	190.3282	2882.6785	7	206.0361	3378.1339	7	221.7441	3912.8591
8	190.5900	2890.6143	8	206.2979	3386.7241	8	222.0059	3922.1039
9	190.8518	2898.5610	9	206.5597	3395.3253	9	222.2677	3931.3596
10	191.1136	2906.5186	10	206.8215	3403.9375	10	222.5295	3940.6262
11	191.3754	2914.4871	11	207.0833	3412.5605	11	222.7913	3949.9037
61 0	191.6372	2922.4666	66 0	207.3451	3421.1944	71 0	223.0531	3959.1921
1	191.8990	2930.4569	1	207.6069	3429.8392	1	223.3149	3968.4915
2	192.1608	2938.4581	2	207.8687	3438.4950	2	223.5767	3977.8017
3	192.4226	2946.4703	3	208.1305	3447.1616	3	223.8385	3987.1229
4	192.6843	2954.4934	4	208.3923	3455.8392	4	224.1003	3996.4549
5	192.9461	2962.5273	5	208.6541	3464.5277	5	224.3621	4005.7979
6	193.2079	2970.5722	6	208.9159	3473.2270	6	224.6239	4015.1518
7	193.4697	2978.6280	7	209.1777	3481.9373	7	224.8857	4024.5165
8	193.7315	2986.6947	8	209.4395	3490.6585	8	225.1475	4033.8922
9	193.9933	2994.7723	9	209.7013	3499.3906	9	225.4093	4043.2788
10	194.2551	3002.8608	10	209.9631	3508.1336	10	225.6711	4052.6763
11	194.5169	3010.9602	11	210.2249	3516.8875	11	225.9329	4062.0848
62 0	194.7787	3019.0705	67 0	210.4867	3525.6524	72 0	226.1947	4071.5041
1	195.0405	3027.1918	1	210.7485	3534.4281	1	226.4565	4080.9343
2	195.3023	3035.3239	2	211.0103	3543.2147	2	226.7183	4090.3755
3	195.5641	3043.4670	3	211.2721	3552.0123	3	226.9801	4099.8275
4	195.8259	3051.6209	4	211.5339	3560.8207	4	227.2419	4109.2905
5	196.0877	3059.7858	5	211.7957	3569.6401	5	227.5037	4118.7643
6	196.3495	3067.9616	6	212.0575	3578.4704	6	227.7655	4128.2491
7	196.6113	3076.1483	7	212.3193	3587.3116	7	228.0273	4137.7448
8	196.8731	3084.3459	8	212.5811	3596.1637	8	228.2891	4147.2514
9	197.1349	3092.5544	9	212.8429	3605.0267	9	228.5509	4156.7689
10	197.3967	3100.7738	10	213.1047	3613.9006	10	228.8127	4166.2973
11	197.6585	3109.0041	11	213.3665	3622.7854	11	229.0745	4175.8366
63 0	197.9203	3117.2453	68 0	213.6283	3631.6811	73 0	229.3363	4185.3868
1	198.1821	3125.4974	1	213.8901	3640.5877	1	229.5961	4194.9479
2	198.4489	3133.7605	2	214.1519	3649.5053	2	229.8599	4204.5200
3	198.7057	3142.0344	3	214.4137	3658.4337	3	230.1217	4214.1029
4	198.9675	3150.3193	4	214.6755	3667.3731	4	230.3835	4223.6968
5	199.2293	3158.6151	5	214.9373	3676.3234	5	230.6458	4233.3016
6	199.4911	3166.9217	6	215.1991	3685.2845	6	230.9071	4242.9172
7	199.7529	3175.2393	7	215.4609	3694.2566	7	231.1689	4252.5438
8	200.0147	3183.5678	8	215.7227	3703.2396	8	231.4307	4262.1813
9	200.2765	3191.9072	9	215.9845	3712.2335	9	231.6925	4271.8297
10	200.5383	3200.2575	10	216.2463	3721.2383	10	231.9543	4281.4890
11	200.8001	3208.6188	11	216.5081	3730.2540	11	232.2161	4291.1592
64 0	201.0619	3216.9909	69 0	216.7699	3739.2807	74 0	232.4779	4300.8403
1	201.3237	3225.3739	1	217.0317	3748.3182	1	232.7397	4310.5324
2	201.5855	3233.7679	2	217.2935	3757.3666	2	233.0015	4320.2353
3	201.8473	3242.1727	3	217.5553	3766.4260	3	233.2633	4329.9492
4	202.1091	3250.5885	4	217.8171	3775.4962	4	233.5251	4339.6739
5	202.3709	3259.0151	5	218.0789	3784.5774	5	233.7869	4349.4096
6	202.6327	3267.4527	6	218.3407	3793.6695	6	234.0487	4359.1562
7	202.8945	3275.9012	7	218.6025	3802.7725	7	234.3105	4368.9136
8	203.1563	3284.3606	8	218.8643	3811.8864	8	234.5723	4378.6820
9	203.4181	3292.8309	9	219.1261	3821.0112	9	234.8341	4388.4613
10	203.6799	3301.3121	10	219.3879	3830.1469	10	235.0959	4398.2515
11	203.9417	3309.8042	11	219.6497	3839.2935	11	235.3576	4408.0526

CIRCLES.

TABLE 3 OF CIRCLES—(Continued).

Diams in units and twelfths; as in feet and inches.

Dia.	Circumf.	Area.	Dia.	Circumf.	Area.	Dia.	Circumf.	Area.
Ft.In.	Feet.	Sq. ft.	Ft.In.	Feet.	Sq. ft.	Ft.In.	Feet.	Sq. ft.
75 0	235.6194	4417.8647	80 0	251.3274	5026.5482	85 0	267.0354	5674.5017
1	235.8812	4427.6576	1	251.5892	5037.0257	1	267.2972	5685.6337
2	236.1430	4437.5214	2	251.8510	5047.5140	2	267.5590	5696.7765
3	236.4048	4447.3662	3	252.1128	5058.0133	3	267.8208	5707.9302
4	236.6666	4457.2218	4	252.3746	5068.5234	4	268.0826	5719.0919
5	236.9284	4467.0884	5	252.6364	5079.0445	5	268.3444	5730.2705
6	237.1902	4476.9659	6	252.8982	5089.5764	6	268.6062	5741.4569
7	237.4520	4486.8543	7	253.1600	5100.1193	7	268.8680	5752.6543
8	237.7138	4496.7536	8	253.4218	5110.6731	8	269.1298	5763.8626
9	237.9756	4506.6637	9	253.6836	5121.2378	9	269.3916	5775.0818
10	238.2374	4516.5849	10	253.9454	5131.8134	10	269.6534	5786.3119
11	238.4992	4526.5169	11	254.2072	5142.3999	11	269.9152	5797.5529
76 0	238.7610	4536.4598	81 0	254.4690	5152.9974	86 0	270.1770	5808.8048
1	239.0228	4546.4136	1	254.7308	5163.6057	1	270.4388	5820.0676
2	239.2846	4556.3784	2	254.9926	5174.2249	2	270.7006	5831.3414
3	239.5464	4566.3540	3	255.2544	5184.8551	3	270.9624	5842.6260
4	239.8082	4576.3406	4	255.5162	5195.4961	4	271.2242	5853.9216
5	240.0700	4586.3380	5	255.7780	5206.1481	5	271.4860	5865.2280
6	240.3318	4596.3464	6	256.0398	5216.8110	6	271.7478	5876.5454
7	240.5936	4606.3657	7	256.3016	5227.4847	7	272.0096	5887.8737
8	240.8554	4616.3959	8	256.5634	5238.1694	8	272.2714	5899.2129
9	241.1172	4626.4370	9	256.8252	5248.8650	9	272.5332	5910.5630
10	241.3790	4636.4890	10	257.0870	5259.5715	10	272.7950	5921.9240
11	241.6408	4646.5519	11	257.3488	5270.2889	11	273.0568	5933.2959
77 0	241.9026	4656.6257	82 0	257.6106	5281.0173	87 0	273.3186	5944.6787
1	242.1644	4666.7104	1	257.8724	5291.7565	1	273.5804	5956.0724
2	242.4262	4676.8061	2	258.1342	5302.5066	2	273.8422	5967.4771
3	242.6880	4686.9126	3	258.3960	5313.2677	3	274.1040	5978.8926
4	242.9498	4697.0301	4	258.6578	5324.0396	4	274.3658	5990.3191
5	243.2116	4707.1584	5	258.9196	5334.8225	5	274.6276	6001.7564
6	243.4734	4717.2977	6	259.1814	5345.6162	6	274.8894	6013.2047
7	243.7352	4727.4479	7	259.4432	5356.4209	7	275.1512	6024.6639
8	243.9970	4737.6090	8	259.7050	5367.2365	8	275.4130	6036.1340
9	244.2588	4747.7810	9	259.9668	5378.0630	9	275.6748	6047.6149
10	244.5206	4757.9639	10	260.2286	5388.9004	10	275.9366	6059.1068
11	244.7824	4768.1577	11	260.4904	5399.7487	11	276.1984	6070.6097
78 0	245.0442	4778.3624	83 0	260.7522	5410.6079	88 0	276.4602	6082.1234
1	245.3060	4788.5781	1	261.0140	5421.4781	1	276.7220	6093.6480
2	245.5678	4798.8046	2	261.2758	5432.3591	2	276.9838	6105.1835
3	245.8296	4809.0420	3	261.5376	5443.2511	3	277.2456	6116.7300
4	246.0914	4819.2904	4	261.7994	5454.1539	4	277.5074	6128.2873
5	246.3532	4829.5497	5	262.0612	5465.0677	5	277.7692	6139.8556
6	246.6150	4839.8198	6	262.3230	5475.9923	6	278.0809	6151.4348
7	246.8768	4850.1009	7	262.5848	5486.9279	7	278.2927	6163.0048
8	247.1386	4860.3929	8	262.8466	5497.8744	8	278.5545	6174.6258
9	247.4004	4870.6958	9	263.1084	5508.8318	9	278.8163	6186.2377
10	247.6622	4881.0096	10	263.3702	5519.8001	10	279.0781	6197.8605
11	247.9240	4891.3343	11	263.6320	5530.7793	11	279.3399	6209.4942
79 0	248.1858	4901.6699	84 0	263.8938	5541.7694	89 0	279.6017	6221.1389
1	248.4476	4912.0165	1	264.1556	5552.7705	1	279.8635	6232.7944
2	248.7094	4922.3739	2	264.4174	5563.7824	2	280.1253	6244.4608
3	248.9712	4932.7423	3	264.6792	5574.8053	3	280.3871	6256.1382
4	249.2330	4943.1215	4	264.9410	5585.8390	4	280.6489	6267.8264
5	249.4948	4953.5117	5	265.2028	5596.8837	5	280.9107	6279.5256
6	249.7566	4963.9127	6	265.4646	5607.9392	6	281.1725	6291.2356
7	250.0184	4974.3247	7	265.7264	5619.0057	7	281.4343	6302.9566
8	250.2802	4984.7476	8	265.9882	5630.0831	8	281.6961	6314.6885
9	250.5420	4995.1814	9	266.2500	5641.1714	9	281.9579	6326.4313
10	250.8038	5005.6261	10	266.5118	5652.2706	10	282.2197	6338.1850
11	251.0656	5016.0817	11	266.7736	5663.3807	11	282.4815	6349.9496

TABLE NO. 73—CONCL.

From Trautwine's "Civil Engineer's Pocket Book."

CIRCLES.

TABLE 3 OF CIRCLES—(Continued).

Diams in units and twelfths; as in feet and inches.

Dia.	Circumf.	Area.	Dia.	Circumf.	Area.	Dia.	Circumf.	Area.
Ft.In.	Feet.	Sq. ft.	Ft.In.	Feet.	Sq. ft.	Ft.In.	Feet.	Sq. ft.
90 0	282.7433	6361.7251	93 5	293.4771	6853.9134	96 9	303.9491	7351.7686
1	283.0051	6373.5116	6	293.7389	6866.1471	10	304.2109	7364.4386
2	283.2669	6385.3089	7	294.0007	6878.3917	11	304.4727	7377.1195
3	283.5287	6397.1171	8	294.2625	6890.6472	97 0	304.7345	7389.8113
4	283.7905	6408.9363	9	294.5243	6902.9135	1	304.9963	7402.5140
5	284.0523	6420.7663	10	294.7861	6915.1908	2	305.2581	7415.2277
6	284.3141	6432.6073	11	295.0479	6927.4791	3	305.5199	7427.9522
7	284.5759	6444.4592	94 0	295.3097	6939.7782	4	305.7817	7440.6877
8	284.8377	6456.3220	1	295.5715	6952.0882	5	306.0435	7453.4340
9	285.0995	6468.1957	2	295.8333	6964.4091	6	306.3053	7466.1913
10	285.3613	6480.0803	3	296.0951	6976.7410	7	306.5671	7478.9595
11	285.6231	6491.9758	4	296.3569	6989.0837	8	306.8289	7491.7385
91 0	285.8849	6503.882?	5	296.6187	7001.4874	9	307.0907	7504.5285
1	286.1467	6515.7995	6	296.8805	7013.8019	10	307.3525	7517.3294
2	286.4085	6527.7278	7	297.1423	7026.1774	11	307.6143	7530.1412
3	286.6703	6539.6669	8	297.4041	7038.5638	98 0	307.8761	7542.9640
4	286.9321	6551.6169	9	297.6659	7050.9611	1	308.1379	7555.7976
5	287.1939	6563.5779	10	297.9277	7063.3693	2	308.3997	7568.6421
6	287.4557	6575.5498	11	298.1895	7075.7884	3	308.6615	7581.4976
7	287.7175	6587.5325	95 0	298.4513	7088.2184	4	308.9233	7594.3639
8	287.9793	6599.5262	1	298.7131	7100.6598	5	309.1851	7607.2412
9	288.2411	6611.5308	2	298.9749	7113.1112	6	309.4469	7620.1293
10	288.5029	6623.5163	3	299.2367	7125.5739	7	309.7087	7633.0284
11	288.7647	6635.5727	4	299.4985	7138.0476	8	309.9705	7645.9384
92 0	289.0265	6647.6101	5	299.7603	7150.5321	9	310.2323	7658.8593
1	289.2883	6659.6583	6	300.0221	7163.0276	10	310.4941	7671.7911
2	289.5501	6671.7174	7	300.2839	7175.5340	11	310.7559	7684.7338
3	289.8119	6683.7875	8	300.5457	7188.0513	99 0	311.0177	7697.6874
4	290.0737	6695.8684	9	300.8075	7200.5794	1	311.2795	7710.6519
5	290.3355	6707.9603	10	301.0693	7213.1185	2	311.5413	7723.6274
6	290.5973	6720.0630	11	301.3311	7225.6686	3	311.8031	7736.6137
7	290.8591	6732.1767	96 0	301.5929	7238.2295	4	312.0649	7749.6109
8	291.1209	6744.3013	1	301.8547	7250.8013	5	312.3267	7762.6191
9	291.3827	6756.4368	2	302.1165	7263.3840	6	312.5885	7775.6382
10	291.6445	6768.5832	3	302.3783	7275.9777	7	312.8503	7788.6681
11	291.9063	6780.7405	4	302.6401	7288.5822	8	313.1121	7801.7090
93 0	292.1681	6792.9087	5	302.9019	7301.1977	9	313.3739	7814.7608
1	292.4299	6805.0878	6	303.1637	7313.8240	10	313.6357	7827.8235
2	292.6917	6817.2779	7	303.4255	7326.4613	11	313.8975	7840.8971
3	292.9535	6829.4788	8	303.6873	7339.1095	100 0	314.1593	7853.9816
4	293.2153	6841.6907						

Circumferences in feet, when the diam contains fractions of an inch. See similar process, p 177

Diam, inch.	Circumf. foot	Diam, inch	Circumf foot	Diam, inch	Circumf. foot	Diam. inch.	Circumf. foot	Diam, inch	Circumf. foot
1-64	.004091	7-32	.057269	27-64	.110447	5-8	.163625	53-64	.216803
1-32	.008181	15-64	.061359	7-16	.114537	41-64	.167715	27-32	.220893
3-64	.012272	1/4	.065450	29-64	.118628	21-32	.171806	55-64	.224984
1-16	.016362	17-64	.069540	15-32	.122718	43-64	.175896	7-8	.229074
5-64	.020453	9-32	.073631	31-64	.126809	11-16	.179987	57-64	.233165
3-32	.024544	19-64	.077722	1/2	.130900	45-64	.184078	29-32	.237256
7-64	.028634	5-16	.081812	33-64	.134990	23-32	.188168	59-64	.241346
1/8	.032725	21-64	.085903	17-32	.139081	47-64	.192259	15-16	.245437
9-64	.036816	11-32	.089994	35-64	.143172	3/4	.196350	61-64	.249528
5-32	.040906	23-64	.094084	9-16	.147262	49-64	.200440	31-32	.253618
11-64	.044997	3/8	.098175	37-64	.151353	25-32	.204531	63-64	.257709
3-16	.049087	25-64	.102265	19-32	.155443	51-64	.208621	1	.261799
13-64	.053178	13-32	.106356	39-64	.159534	13-16	.212712		

SQUARE AND CUBE ROOTS.

Square Roots and Cube Roots of Numbers from .1 to 28.

No errors.

No.	Square.	Cube.	Sq. Rt.	C. Rt.	No.	Sq. Rt.	C. Rt.	No.	Sq. Rt.	C. Rt.
.1	.01	.001	.316	.464	.7	2.387	1.786	.4	3.661	2.375
.15	.0225	.0034	.387	.531	.8	2.408	1.797	.6	3.688	2.387
.2	.04	.008	.447	.585	.9	2.429	1.807	.8	3.715	2.399
.25	.0625	.0156	.500	.630	6.	2.449	1.817	14.	3.742	2.410
.3	.09	.027	.548	.669	.1	2.470	1.827	.2	3.768	2.422
.35	.1225	.0429	.592	.705	.2	2.490	1.837	.4	3.795	2.433
.4	.16	.064	.633	.737	.3	2.510	1.847	.6	3.821	2.444
.45	.2025	.0911	.671	.766	.4	2.530	1.857	.8	3.847	2.455
.5	.25	.125	.707	.794	.5	2.550	1.866	15.	3.873	2.466
.55	.3025	.1664	.742	.819	.6	2.569	1.876	.2	3.899	2.477
.6	.36	.216	.775	.843	.7	2.588	1.885	.4	3.924	2.488
.65	.4225	.2746	.806	.866	.8	2.608	1.895	.6	3.950	2.499
.7	.49	.343	.837	.888	.9	2.627	1.904	.8	3.975	2.509
.75	.5625	.4219	.866	.909	7.	2.646	1.913	16.	4.	2.520
.8	.64	.512	.894	.928	.1	2.665	1.922	.2	4.025	2.530
.85	.7225	.6141	.922	.947	.2	2.683	1.931	.4	4.050	2.541
.9	.81	.729	.949	.965	.3	2.702	1.940	.6	4.074	2.551
.95	.9025	.8574	.975	.983	.4	2.720	1.949	.8	4.099	2.561
1.	1.000	1.000	1.000	1.000	.5	2.739	1.957	17.	4.123	2.571
.05	1.103	1.158	1.025	1.016	.6	2.757	1.966	.2	4.147	2.581
1.1	1.210	1.331	1.049	1.032	.7	2.775	1.975	.4	4.171	2.591
.15	1.323	1.521	1.072	1.048	.8	2.793	1.983	.6	4.195	2.601
1.2	1.440	1.728	1.095	1.063	.9	2.811	1.992	.8	4.219	2.611
.25	1.563	1.953	1.118	1.077	8.	2.828	2.000	18.	4.243	2.621
1.3	1.690	2.197	1.140	1.091	.1	2.846	2.008	.2	4.266	2.630
.35	1.823	2.460	1.162	1.105	.2	2.864	2.017	.4	4.290	2.640
1.4	1.960	2.744	1.183	1.119	.3	2.881	2.025	.6	4.313	2.650
.45	2.103	3.049	1.204	1.132	.4	2.898	2.033	.8	4.336	2.659
1.5	2.250	3.375	1.225	1.145	.5	2.915	2.041	19.	4.359	2.668
.55	2.403	3.724	1.245	1.157	.6	2.933	2.049	.2	4.382	2.678
1.6	2.560	4.096	1.265	1.170	.7	2.950	2.057	.4	4.405	2.687
.65	2.723	4.492	1.285	1.182	.8	2.966	2.065	.6	4.427	2.696
1.7	2.890	4.913	1.304	1.193	.9	2.983	2.072	.8	4.450	2.705
.75	3.063	5.359	1.323	1.205	9.	3.	2.080	20.	4.472	2.714
1.8	3.240	5.832	1.342	1.216	.1	3.017	2.088	.2	4.494	2.723
.85	3.423	6.332	1.360	1.226	.2	3.033	2.095	.4	4.517	2.732
1.9	3.610	6.859	1.378	1.239	.3	3.050	2.103	.6	4.539	2.741
.95	3.803	7.415	1.396	1.249	.4	3.066	2.110	.8	4.561	2.750
2.	4.000	8.000	1.414	1.260	.5	3.082	2.118	21.	4.583	2.759
.1	4.410	9.261	1.449	1.281	.6	3.098	2.125	.2	4.604	2.768
.2	4.840	10.65	1.483	1.301	.7	3.114	2.133	.4	4.626	2.776
.3	5.290	12.17	1.517	1.320	.8	3.130	2.140	.6	4.648	2.785
.4	5.760	13.82	1.549	1.339	.9	3.146	2.147	.8	4.669	2.794
.5	6.250	15.63	1.581	1.357	10.	3.162	2.154	22.	4.690	2.802
.6	6.760	17.58	1.612	1.375	.1	3.178	2.162	.2	4.712	2.810
.7	7.290	19.68	1.643	1.392	.2	3.194	2.169	.4	4.733	2.819
.8	7.840	21.95	1.673	1.409	.3	3.209	2.176	.6	4.754	2.827
.9	8.410	24.39	1.703	1.426	.4	3.225	2.183	.8	4.775	2.836
3.	9.	27.	1.732	1.442	.5	3.240	2.190	23.	4.796	2.844
.1	9.61	29.79	1.761	1.458	.6	3.256	2.197	.2	4.817	2.852
.2	10.24	32.77	1.789	1.474	.7	3.271	2.204	.4	4.837	2.860
.3	10.89	35.94	1.817	1.489	.8	3.286	2.210	.6	4.858	2.868
.4	11.56	39.30	1.844	1.504	.9	3.302	2.217	.8	4.879	2.876
.5	12.25	42.88	1.871	1.518	11.	3.317	2.224	24.	4.899	2.884
.6	12.96	46.66	1.897	1.533	.1	3.332	2.231	.2	4.919	2.892
.7	13.69	50.65	1.924	1.547	.2	3.347	2.237	.4	4.940	2.900
.8	14.44	54.87	1.949	1.560	.3	3.362	2.244	.6	4.960	2.908
.9	15.21	59.32	1.975	1.574	.4	3 376	2.251	.8	4.980	2.916
4.	16.	64.	2.	1.587	.5	3.391	2.257	25.	5.	2.924
.1	16.81	68.92	2.025	1.601	.6	3.406	2.264	.2	5 020	2.932
.2	17.64	74.09	2.049	1 613	.7	3.421	2.270	.4	5.040	2.940
.3	18.49	79.51	2.074	1.626	.8	3.435	2.277	.6	5.060	2.947
.4	19.36	85.18	2.098	1.639	.9	3.450	2.283	.8	5.079	2.955
.5	20.25	91.13	2.121	1.651	12.	3.464	2 289	26.	5.099	2.962
.6	21.16	97.34	2.145	1.663	.1	3 479	2.296	.2	5.119	2.970
.7	22.09	103.8	2.168	1.675	.2	3.493	2.302	4	5.138	2.978
.8	23.04	110.6	2.191	1.687	.3	3.507	2.308	.6	5.158	2.985
.9	24.01	117.6	2.214	1.698	.4	3.521	2.315	.8	5.177	2.993
5.	25.	125.	2.236	1.710	.5	3.536	2.321	27.	5.196	3.000
.1	26.01	132.7	2.258	1.721	.6	3.550	2.327	.2	5.215	3.007
.2	27.04	140.6	2.280	1.732	.7	3.564	2.333	.4	5.235	3.015
.3	28.09	148.9	2.302	1.744	.8	3.578	2 339	.6	5.254	3.022
.4	29.16	157.5	2.324	1.754	.9	3.592	2.345	.8	5.273	3.029
.5	30.25	166.4	2.345	1.765	13.	3.606	2.351	28.	5.292	3.037
.6	31.36	175.6	2.366	1.776	.2	3 633	2.363	.2	5.310	3.044

To find roots by logarithms see Pages 200 and 202.

TABLE NO. 75.

From Trautwine's "Civil Engineer's Pocket Book."

SQUARES, CUBES, AND ROOTS.

TABLE of Squares, Cubes, Square Roots, and Cube Roots, of Numbers from 1 to 1000.

REMARK ON THE FOLLOWING TABLE. Wherever the effect of a fifth decimal in the roots would be to add 1 to the fourth and final decimal in the table, the addition has been made. No errors.

No.	Square.	Cube.	Sq. Rt.	C. Rt.	No.	Square.	Cube.	Sq. Rt.	C. Rt.
1	1	1	1.0000	1.0000	61	3721	226981	7.8102	3.9365
2	4	8	1.4142	1.2599	62	3844	238328	7.8740	3.9579
3	9	27	1.7321	1.4422	63	3969	250047	7.9373	3.9791
4	16	64	2.0000	1.5874	64	4096	262144	8.0000	4.
5	25	125	2.2361	1.7100	65	4225	274625	8.0623	4.0207
6	36	216	2.4495	1.8171	66	4356	287496	8.1240	4.0412
7	49	343	2.6458	1.9129	67	4489	300763	8.1854	4.0615
8	64	512	2.8284	2.0000	68	4624	314432	8.2462	4.0817
9	81	729	3.0000	2.0801	69	4761	328509	8.3066	4.1016
10	100	1000	3.1623	2.1544	70	4900	343000	8.3666	4.1213
11	121	1331	3.3166	2.2240	71	5041	357911	8.4261	4.1408
12	144	1728	3.4641	2.2894	72	5184	373248	8.4853	4.1602
13	169	2197	3.6056	2.3513	73	5329	389017	8.5440	4.1793
14	196	2744	3.7417	2.4101	74	5476	405224	8.6023	4.1983
15	225	3375	3.8730	2.4662	75	5625	421875	8.6603	4.2172
16	256	4096	4.0000	2.5198	76	5776	438976	8.7178	4.2358
17	289	4913	4.1231	2.5713	77	5929	456533	8.7750	4.2543
18	324	5832	4.2426	2.6207	78	6084	474552	8.8318	4.2727
19	361	6859	4.3589	2.6684	79	6241	493039	8.8882	4.2908
20	400	8000	4.4721	2.7144	80	6400	512000	8.9443	4.3089
21	441	9261	4.5826	2.7589	81	6561	531441	9.	4.3267
22	484	10648	4.6904	2.8020	82	6724	551368	9.0554	4.3445
23	529	12167	4.7958	2.8439	83	6889	571787	9.1104	4.3621
24	576	13824	4.8990	2.8845	84	7056	592704	9.1652	4.3795
25	625	15625	5.0000	2.9240	85	7225	614125	9.2195	4.3968
26	676	17576	5.0990	2.9625	86	7396	636056	9.2736	4.4140
27	729	19683	5.1962	3.0000	87	7569	658503	9.3274	4.4310
28	784	21952	5.2915	3.0366	88	7744	681472	9.3808	4.4480
29	841	24389	5.3852	3.0723	89	7921	704969	9.4340	4.4647
30	900	27000	5.4772	3.1072	90	8100	729000	9.4868	4.4814
31	961	29791	5.5678	3.1414	91	8281	753571	9.5394	4.4979
32	1024	32768	5.6569	3.1748	92	8464	778688	9.5917	4.5144
33	1089	35937	5.7446	3.2075	93	8649	804357	9.6437	4.5307
34	1156	39304	5.8310	3.2396	94	8836	830584	9.6954	4.5468
35	1225	42875	5.9161	3.2711	95	9025	857375	9.7468	4.5629
36	1296	46656	6.0000	3.3019	96	9216	884736	9.7980	4.5789
37	1369	50653	6.0828	3.3322	97	9409	912673	9.8489	4.5947
38	1444	54872	6.1644	3.3620	98	9604	941192	9.8995	4.6104
39	1521	59319	6.2450	3.3912	99	9801	970299	9.9499	4.6261
40	1600	64000	6.3246	3.4200	100	10000	1000000	10.	4.6416
41	1681	68921	6.4031	3.4482	101	10201	1030301	10.0499	4.6570
42	1764	74088	6.4807	3.4760	102	10404	1061208	10.0995	4.6723
43	1849	79507	6.5574	3.5034	103	10609	1092727	10.1489	4.6875
44	1936	85184	6.6332	3.5303	104	10816	1124864	10.1980	4.7027
45	2025	91125	6.7082	3.5569	105	11025	1157625	10.2470	4.7177
46	2116	97336	6.7823	3.5830	106	11236	1191016	10.2956	4.7326
47	2209	103823	6.8557	3.6088	107	11449	1225043	10.3441	4.7475
48	2304	110592	6.9282	3.6342	108	11664	1259712	10.3923	4.7622
49	2401	117649	7.0000	3.6593	109	11881	1295029	10.4403	4.7769
50	2500	125000	7.0711	3.6840	110	12100	1331000	10.4881	4.7914
51	2601	132651	7.1414	3.7084	111	12321	1367631	10.5357	4.8059
52	2704	140608	7.2111	3.7325	112	12544	1404928	10.5830	4.8203
53	2809	148877	7.2801	3.7563	113	12769	1442897	10.6301	4.8346
54	2916	157464	7.3485	3.7798	114	12996	1481544	10.6771	4.8488
55	3025	166375	7.4162	3.8030	115	13225	1520875	10.7238	4.8629
56	3136	175616	7.4833	3.8259	116	13456	1560896	10.7703	4.8770
57	3249	185193	7.5498	3.8485	117	13689	1601613	10.8167	4.8910
58	3364	195112	7.6158	3.8709	118	13924	1643032	10.8628	4.9049
59	3481	205379	7.6811	3.8930	119	14161	1685159	10.9087	4.9187
60	3600	216000	7.7460	3.9149	120	14400	1728000	10.9545	4.9324

SQUARES, CUBES, AND ROOTS.

TABLE of Squares, Cubes, Square Roots, and Cube Roots, of Numbers from 1 to 1000 — (CONTINUED.)

No.	Square.	Cube.	Sq. Rt.	C. Rt.	No.	Square.	Cube.	Sq. Rt.	C. Rt.
121	14641	1771561	11.	4.9461	186	34596	6434856	13.6382	5.7083
122	14884	1815848	11.0454	4.9597	187	34969	6539203	13.6748	5.7185
123	15129	1860867	11.0905	4.9732	188	35344	6644672	13.7113	5.7287
124	15376	1906624	11.1355	4.9866	189	35721	6751269	13.7477	5.7388
125	15625	1953125	11.1803	5.	190	36100	6859000	13.7840	5.7489
126	15876	2000376	11.2250	5.0133	191	36481	6967871	13.8203	5.7590
127	16129	2048383	11.2694	5.0265	192	36864	7077888	13.8564	5.7690
128	16384	2097152	11.3137	5.0397	193	37249	7189057	13.8924	5.7790
129	16641	2146689	11.3578	5.0528	194	37636	7301384	13.9284	5.7890
130	16900	2197000	11.4018	5.0658	195	38025	7414875	13.9642	5.7989
131	17161	2248091	11.4455	5.0788	196	38416	7529536	14.	5.8088
132	17424	2299968	11.4891	5.0916	197	38809	7645373	14.0357	5.8186
133	17689	2352637	11.5326	5.1045	198	39204	7762392	14.0712	5.8285
134	17956	2406104	11.5758	5.1172	199	39601	7880599	14.1067	5.8383
135	18225	2460375	11.6190	5.1299	200	40000	8000000	14.1421	5.8480
136	18496	2515456	11.6619	5.1426	201	40401	8120601	14.1774	5.8578
137	18769	2571353	11.7047	5.1551	202	40804	8242408	14.2127	5.8675
138	19044	2628072	11.7473	5.1676	203	41209	8365427	14.2478	5.8771
139	19321	2685619	11.7898	5.1801	204	41616	8489664	14.2829	5.8868
140	19600	2744000	11.8322	5.1925	205	42025	8615125	14.3178	5.8964
141	19881	2803221	11.8743	5.2048	206	42436	8741816	14.3527	5.9059
142	20164	2863288	11.9164	5.2171	207	42849	8869743	14.3875	5.9155
143	20449	2924207	11.9583	5.2293	208	43264	8998912	14.4222	5.9250
144	20736	2985984	12	5.2415	209	43681	9129329	14.4568	5.9345
145	21025	3048625	12.0416	5.2536	210	44100	9261000	14.4914	5.9439
146	21316	3112136	12.0830	5.2656	211	44521	9393931	14.5258	5.9538
147	21609	3176523	12.1244	5.2776	212	44944	9528128	14.5602	5.9627
148	21904	3241792	12.1655	5.2896	213	45369	9663597	14.5945	5.9721
149	22201	3307949	12.2066	5.3015	214	45796	9800344	14.6287	5.9814
150	22500	3375000	12.2474	5.3133	215	46225	9938375	14.6629	5.9907
151	22801	3442951	12.2882	5.3251	216	46656	10077696	14.6969	6.
152	23104	3511808	12.3288	5.3368	217	47089	10218313	14.7309	6.0092
153	23409	3581577	12.3693	5.3485	218	47524	10360232	14.7648	6.0185
154	23716	3652264	12.4097	5.3601	219	47961	10503459	14.7986	6.0277
155	24025	3723875	12.4499	5.3717	220	48400	10648000	14.8324	6.0368
156	24336	3796416	12.4900	5.3832	221	48841	10793861	14.8661	6.0459
157	24649	3869893	12.5300	5.3947	222	49284	10941048	14.8997	6.0550
158	24964	3944312	12.5698	5.4061	223	49729	11089567	14.9332	6.0641
159	25281	4019679	12.6095	5.4175	224	50176	11239424	14.9666	6.0732
160	25600	4096000	12.6491	5.4288	225	50625	11390625	15.	6.0822
161	25921	4173281	12.6886	5.4401	226	51076	11543176	15.0333	6.0912
162	26244	4251528	12.7279	5.4514	227	51529	11697083	15.0665	6.1002
163	26569	4330747	12.7671	5.4626	228	51984	11852352	15.0997	6.1091
164	26896	4410944	12.8062	5.4737	229	52441	12008989	15.1327	6.1180
165	27225	4492125	12.8452	5.4848	230	52900	12167000	15.1658	6.1269
166	27556	4574296	12.8841	5.4959	231	53361	12326391	15.1987	6.1358
167	27889	4657463	12.9228	5.5069	232	53824	12487168	15.2315	6.1446
168	28224	4741632	12.9615	5.5178	233	54289	12649337	15.2643	6.1534
169	28561	4826809	13.	5.5288	234	54756	12812904	15.2971	6.1622
170	28900	4913000	13.0384	5.5397	235	55225	12977875	15.3297	6.1710
171	29241	5000211	13.0767	5.5505	236	55696	13144256	15.3623	6.1797
172	29584	5088448	13.1149	5.5613	237	56169	13312053	15.3948	6.1885
173	29929	5177717	13.1529	5.5721	238	56644	13481272	15.4272	6.1972

TABLE NO. 75—CON.
From Trautwine's "Civil Engineer's Pocket Book."

SQUARES, CUBES, AND ROOTS.

TABLE of Squares, Cubes, Square Roots, and Cube Roots, of Numbers from 1 to 1000—(CONTINUED.)

No.	Square.	Cube.	Sq. Rt.	C. Rt.	No.	Square.	Cube.	Sq. Rt.	C. Rt.
511	261121	133432831	22.6053	7.9948	576	331776	191102976	24.	8.3203
512	262144	134217728	22.6274	8.	577	332929	192100033	24.0208	8.3251
513	263169	135005897	22.6495	8.0052	578	334084	193100552	24.0416	8.3300
514	264196	135796744	22.6716	8.0104	579	335241	194104539	24.0624	8.3348
515	265225	136590875	22.6936	8.0156	580	336400	195112000	24.0832	8.3396
516	266256	137388096	22.7156	8.0208	581	337561	196122941	24.1039	8.3443
517	267289	138188413	22.7376	8.0260	582	338724	197137368	24.1247	8.3491
518	268324	138991832	22.7596	8.0311	583	339889	198155297	24.1454	8.3539
519	269361	139798359	22.7816	8.0363	584	341056	199176704	24.1661	8.3587
520	270400	140608000	22.8035	8.0415	585	342225	200201625	24.1868	8.3634
521	271441	141420761	22.8254	8.0466	586	343396	201230056	24.2074	8.3682
522	272484	142236648	22.8473	8.0517	587	344569	202262003	24.2281	8.3730
523	273529	143055667	22.8692	8.0569	588	345744	203297472	24.2487	8.3777
524	274576	143877824	22.8910	8.0620	589	346921	204336469	24.2693	8.3825
525	275625	144703125	22.9129	8.0671	590	348100	205379000	24.2899	8.3872
526	276676	145531576	22.9347	8.0723	591	349281	206425071	24.3105	8.3919
527	277729	146363183	22.9565	8.0774	592	350464	207474688	24.3311	8.3967
528	278784	147197952	22.9783	8.0825	593	351649	208527857	24.3516	8.4014
529	279841	148035889	23.	8.0876	594	352836	209584584	24.3721	8.4061
530	280900	148877000	23.0217	8.0927	595	354025	210644875	24.3926	8.4108
531	281961	149721291	23.0434	8.0978	596	355216	211708736	24.4131	8.4155
532	283024	150568768	23.0651	8.1028	597	356409	212776173	24.4336	8.4202
533	284089	151419437	23.0868	8.1079	598	357604	213847192	24.4540	8.4249
534	285156	152273304	23.1084	8.1130	599	358801	214921799	24.4745	8.4296
535	286225	153130375	23.1301	8.1180	600	360000	216000000	24.4949	8.4343
536	287296	153990656	23.1517	8.1231	601	361201	217081801	24.5153	8.4390
537	288369	154854153	23.1733	8.1281	602	362404	218167208	24.5357	8.4437
538	289444	155720872	23.1948	8.1332	603	363609	219256227	24.5561	8.4484
539	290521	156590819	23.2164	8.1382	604	364816	220348864	24.5764	8.4530
540	291600	157464000	23.2379	8.1433	605	366025	221445125	24.5967	8.4577
541	292681	158340421	23.2594	8.1483	606	367236	222545016	24.6171	8.4623
542	293764	159220088	23.2809	8.1533	607	368449	223648543	24.6374	8.4670
543	294849	160103007	23.3024	8.1583	608	369664	224755712	24.6577	8.4716
544	295936	160989184	23.3238	8.1633	609	370881	225866529	24.6779	8.4763
545	297025	161878625	23.3452	8.1683	610	372100	226981000	24.6982	8.4809
546	298116	162771336	23.3666	8.1733	611	373321	228099131	24.7184	8.4856
547	299209	163667323	23.3880	8.1783	612	374544	229220928	24.7386	8.4902
548	300304	164566592	23.4094	8.1833	613	375769	230346397	24.7588	8.4948
549	301401	165469149	23.4307	8.1882	614	376996	231475544	24.7790	8.4994
550	302500	166375000	23.4521	8.1932	615	378225	232608375	24.7992	8.5040
551	303601	167284151	23.4734	8.1982	616	379456	233744896	24.8193	8.5086
552	304704	168196608	23.4947	8.2031	617	380689	234885113	24.8395	8.5132
553	305809	169112377	23.5160	8.2081	618	381924	236029032	24.8596	8.5178
554	306916	170031464	23.5372	8.2130	619	383161	237176659	24.8797	8.5224
555	308025	170953875	23.5584	8.2180	620	384400	238328000	24.8998	8.5270
556	309136	171879616	23.5797	8.2229	621	385641	239483061	24.9199	8.5316
557	310249	172808693	23.6008	8.2278	622	386884	240641848	24.9399	8.5362
558	311364	173741112	23.6220	8.2327	623	388129	241804367	24.9600	8.5408
559	312481	174676879	23.6432	8.2377	624	389376	242970624	24.9800	8.5453
560	313600	175616000	23.6643	8.2426	625	390625	244140625	25.	8.5499
561	314721	176558481	23.6854	8.2475	626	391876	245314376	25.0200	8.5544
562	315844	177504328	23.7065	8.2524	627	393129	246491883	25.0400	8.5590
563	316969	178453547	23.7276	8.2573	628	394384	247673152	25.0599	8.5635
564	318096	179406144	23.7487	8.2621	629	395641	248858189	25.0799	8.5681
565	319225	180362125	23.7697	8.2670	630	396900	250047000	25.0998	8.5726
566	320356	181321496	23.7908	8.2719	631	398161	251239591	25.1197	8.5772
567	321489	182284263	23.8118	8.2768	632	399424	252435968	25.1396	8.5817
568	322624	183250432	23.8328	8.2816	633	400689	253636137	25.1595	8.5862
569	323761	184220009	23.8537	8.2865	634	401956	254840104	25.1794	8.5907
570	324900	185193000	23.8747	8.2913	635	403225	256047875	25.1992	8.5952
571	326041	186169411	23.8956	8.2962	636	404496	257259456	25.2190	8.5997
572	327184	187149248	23.9165	8.3010	637	405769	258474853	25.2389	8.6043
573	328329	188132517	23.9374	8.3059	638	407044	259694072	25.2587	8.6088
574	329476	189119224	23.9583	8.3107	639	408321	260917119	25.2784	8.6132

SQUARES, CUBES, AND ROOTS.

TABLE of Squares, Cubes, Square Roots, and Cube Roots, of Numbers from 1 to 1000 — (CONTINUED.)

No.	Square.	Cube.	Sq. Rt.	C. Rt	No.	Square.	Cube.	Sq. Rt.	C. Rt.
251	63001	15813251	15.8430	6.3040	316	99856	31554496	17.7764	6.8113
252	63504	16003008	15.8745	6.3164	317	100489	31855013	17.8045	6.8185
253	64009	16194277	15.9060	6.3247	318	101124	32157432	17.8326	6.8256
254	64516	16387064	15.9374	6.3330	319	101761	32461759	17.8606	6.8329
255	65025	16581375	15.9687	6.3413	320	102400	32768000	17.8885	6.8399
256	65536	16777216	16.	6.3496	321	103041	33076161	17.9165	6.8470
257	66049	16974593	16.0312	6.3579	322	103684	33386248	17.9444	6.8541
258	66564	17173512	16.0624	6.3661	323	104329	33698267	17.9722	6.8612
259	67081	17373979	16.0935	6.3743	324	104976	34012224	18.	6.8683
260	67600	17576000	16.1245	6.3825	325	105625	34328125	18.0278	6.8753
261	68121	17779581	16.1555	6.3907	326	106276	34645976	18.0555	6.8824
262	68644	17984728	16.1864	6.3988	327	106929	34965783	18.0831	6.8894
263	69169	18191447	16.2173	6.4070	328	107584	35287552	18.1108	6.8964
264	69696	18399744	16.2481	6.4151	329	108241	35611289	18.1384	6.9034
265	70225	18609625	16.2788	6.4232	330	108900	35937000	18.1659	6.9104
266	70756	18821096	16.3095	6.4312	331	109561	36264691	18.1934	6.9174
267	71289	19034163	16.3401	6.4393	332	110224	36594368	18.2209	6.9244
268	71824	19248832	16.3707	6.4473	333	110889	36926037	18.2483	6.9313
269	72361	19465109	16.4012	6.4553	334	111556	37259704	18.2757	6.9382
270	72900	19683000	16.4317	6.4633	335	112225	37595375	18.3030	6.9451
271	73441	19902511	16.4621	6.4713	336	112896	37933056	18.3303	6.9521
272	73984	20123648	16.4924	6.4792	337	113569	38272753	18.3576	6.9589
273	74529	20346417	16.5227	6.4872	338	114244	38614472	18.3848	6.9658
274	75076	20570824	16.5529	6.4951	339	114921	38958219	18.4120	6.9727
275	75625	20796875	16.5831	6.5030	340	115600	39304000	18.4391	6.9795
276	76176	21024576	16.6132	6.5108	341	116281	39651821	18.4662	6.9864
277	76729	21253933	16.6433	6.5187	342	116964	40001688	18.4932	6.9932
278	77284	21484952	16.6733	6.5265	343	117649	40353607	18.5203	7.
279	77841	21717639	16.7033	6.5343	344	118336	40707584	18.5472	7.0068
280	78400	21952000	16.7332	6.5421	345	119025	41063625	18.5742	7.0136
281	78961	22188041	16.7631	6.5499	346	119716	41421736	18.6011	7.0203
282	79524	22425768	16.7929	6.5577	347	120409	41781923	18.6279	7.0271
283	80089	22665187	16.8226	6.5654	348	121104	42144192	18.6548	7.0338
284	80656	22906304	16.8523	6.5731	349	121801	42508549	18.6815	7.0406
285	81225	23149125	16.8819	6.5808	350	122500	42875000	18.7083	7.0473
286	81796	23393656	16.9115	6.5885	351	123201	43243551	18.7350	7.0540
287	82369	23639903	16.9411	6.5962	352	123904	43614208	18.7617	7.0607
288	82944	23887872	16.9706	6.6039	353	124609	43986977	18.7883	7.0674
289	83521	24137569	17.	6.6115	354	125316	44361864	18.8149	7.0740
290	84100	24389000	17.0294	6.6191	355	126025	44738875	18.8414	7.0807
291	84681	24642171	17.0587	6.6267	356	126736	45118016	18.8680	7.0873
292	85264	24897088	17.0880	6.6343	357	127449	45499293	18.8944	7.0940
293	85849	25153757	17.1172	6.6419	358	128164	45882712	18.9209	7.1006
294	86436	25412184	17.1464	6.6494	359	128881	46268279	18.9473	7.1072
295	87025	25672375	17.1756	6.6569	360	129600	46656000	18.9737	7.1138
296	87616	25934336	17.2047	6.6644	361	130321	47045881	19.	7.1204
297	88209	26198073	17.2337	6.6719	362	131044	47437928	19.0263	7.1269
298	88804	26463592	17.2627	6.6794	363	131769	47832147	19.0526	7.1335
299	89401	26730899	17.2916	6.6869	364	132496	48228544	19.0788	7.1400
300	90000	27000000	17.3205	6.6943	365	133225	48627125	19.1050	7.1466
301	90601	27270901	17.3494	6.7018	366	133956	49027896	19.1311	7.1531
302	91204	27543608	17.3781	6.7092	367	134689	49430863	19.1572	7.1596
303	91809	27818127	17.4069	6.7166	368	135424	49836032	19.1833	7.1661
304	92416	28094464	17.4356	6.7240	369	136161	50243409	19.2094	7.1726
305	93025	28372625	17.4642	6.7313	370	136900	50653000	19.2354	7.1791
306	93636	28652616	17.4929	6.7387	371	137641	51064811	19.2614	7.1855
307	94249	28934443	17.5214	6.7460	372	138384	51478848	19.2873	7.1920
308	94864	29218112	17.5499	6.7533	373	139129	51895117	19.3132	7.1984
309	95481	29503629	17.5784	6.7606	374	139876	52313624	19.3391	7.2048
310	96100	29791000	17.6068	6.7679	375	140625	52734375	19.3649	7.2112
311	96721	30080231	17.6352	6.7752	376	141376	53157376	19.3907	7.2177
312	97344	30371328	17.6635	6.7824	377	142129	53582633	19.4165	7.2240
313	97969	30664297	17.6918	6.7897	378	142884	54010152	19.4422	7.2304
314	98596	30959144	17.7200	6.7969	379	143641	54439939	19.4679	7.2368
315	99225	31255875	17.7482	6.8041	380	144400	54872000	19.4936	7.2432

From Trautwine's "Civil Engineer's Pocket Book."

SQUARES, CUBES, AND ROOTS.

TABLE of Squares, Cubes, Square Roots, and Cube Roots, of Numbers from 1 to 1000—(CONTINUED.)

No.	Square.	Cube.	Sq. Rt.	C. Rt.	No.	Square.	Cube.	Sq. Rt.	C. Rt.
381	145161	55306341	19.5192	7.2495	446	198916	88716536	21.1187	7.6403
382	145924	55742968	19.5448	7.2558	447	199809	89314623	21.1424	7.6460
383	146689	56181887	19.5704	7.2622	448	200704	89915392	21.1660	7.6517
384	147456	56623104	19.5959	7.2685	449	201601	90518849	21.1896	7.6574
385	148225	57066625	19.6214	7.2748	450	202500	91125000	21.2132	7.6631
386	148996	57512456	19.6469	7.2811	451	203401	91733851	21.2368	7.6688
387	149769	57960603	19.6723	7.2874	452	204304	92345408	21.2603	7.6744
388	150544	58411072	19.6977	7.2936	453	205209	92959677	21.2838	7.6801
389	151321	58863869	19.7231	7.2999	454	206116	93576664	21.3073	7.6857
390	152100	59319000	19.7484	7.3061	455	207025	94196375	21.3307	7.6914
391	152881	59776471	19.7737	7.3124	456	207936	94818816	21.3542	7.6970
392	153664	60236268	19.7990	7.3186	457	208849	95443993	21.3776	7.7026
393	154449	60698457	19.8242	7.3248	458	209764	96071912	21.4009	7.7082
394	155236	61162984	19.8494	7.3310	459	210681	96702579	21.4243	7.7138
395	156025	61629875	19.8746	7.3372	460	211600	97336000	21.4476	7.7194
396	156816	62099136	19.8997	7.3434	461	212521	97972181	21.4709	7.7250
397	157609	62570773	19.9249	7.3496	462	213444	98611128	21.4942	7.7306
398	158404	63044792	19.9499	7.3558	463	214369	99252847	21.5174	7.7362
399	159201	63521199	19.9750	7.3619	464	215296	99897344	21.5407	7.7418
400	160000	64000000	20.	7.3681	465	216225	100544625	21.5639	7.7473
401	160801	64481201	20.0250	7.3742	466	217156	101194696	21.5870	7.7529
402	161604	64964808	20.0499	7.3803	467	218089	101847563	21.6102	7.7584
403	162409	65450827	20.0749	7.3864	468	219024	102503232	21.6333	7.7639
404	163216	65939264	20.0998	7.3925	469	219961	103161709	21.6564	7.7695
405	164025	66430125	20.1246	7.3986	470	220900	103823000	21.6795	7.7750
406	164836	66923416	20.1494	7.4047	471	221841	104487111	21.7025	7.7805
407	165649	67419143	20.1742	7.4108	472	222784	105154048	21.7256	7.7860
408	166464	67917312	20.1990	7.4169	473	223729	105823817	21.7486	7.7915
409	167281	68417929	20.2237	7.4229	474	224676	106496424	21.7715	7.7970
410	168100	68921000	20.2485	7.4290	475	225625	107171875	21.7945	7.8025
411	168921	69426531	20.2731	7.4350	476	226576	107850176	21.8174	7.8079
412	169744	69934528	20.2978	7.4410	477	227529	108531333	21.8403	7.8134
413	170569	70444997	20.3224	7.4470	478	228484	109215352	21.8632	7.8188
414	171396	70957944	20.3470	7.4530	479	229441	109902239	21.8861	7.8243
415	172225	71473375	20.3715	7.4590	480	230400	110592000	21.9089	7.8297
416	173056	71991296	20.3961	7.4650	481	231361	111284641	21.9317	7.8352
417	173889	72511713	20.4206	7.4710	482	232324	111980168	21.9545	7.8406
418	174724	73034632	20.4450	7.4770	483	233289	112678587	21.9773	7.8460
419	175561	73560059	20.4695	7.4829	484	234256	113379904	22.	7.8514
420	176400	74088000	20.4939	7.4889	485	235225	114084125	22.0227	7.8568
421	177241	74618461	20.5183	7.4948	486	236196	114791256	22.0454	7.8622
422	178084	75151448	20.5426	7.5007	487	237169	115501303	22.0681	7.8676
423	178929	75686967	20.5670	7.5067	488	238144	116214272	22.0907	7.8730
424	179776	76225024	20.5913	7.5126	489	239121	116930169	22.1133	7.8784
425	180625	76765625	20.6155	7.5185	490	240100	117649000	22.1359	7.8837
426	181476	77308776	20.6398	7.5244	491	241081	118370771	22.1585	7.8891
427	182329	77854483	20.6640	7.5302	492	242064	119095488	22.1811	7.8944
428	183184	78402752	20.6882	7.5361	493	243049	119823157	22.2036	7.8998
429	184041	78953589	20.7123	7.5420	494	244036	120553784	22.2261	7.9051
430	184900	79507000	20.7364	7.5478	495	245025	121287375	22.2486	7.9105
431	185761	80062991	20.7605	7.5537	496	246016	122023936	22.2711	7.9158
432	186624	80621568	20.7846	7.5595	497	247009	122763473	22.2935	7.9211
433	187489	81182737	20.8087	7.5654	498	248004	123505992	22.3159	7.9264
434	188356	81746504	20.8327	7.5712	499	249001	124251499	22.3383	7.9317
435	189225	82312875	20.8567	7.5770	500	250000	125000000	22.3607	7.9370
436	190096	82881856	20.8806	7.5828	501	251001	125751501	22.3830	7.9423
437	190969	83453453	20.9045	7.5886	502	252004	126506008	22.4054	7.9476
438	191844	84027672	20.9284	7.5944	503	253009	127263527	22.4277	7.9528
439	192721	84604519	20.9523	7.6001	504	254016	128024064	22.4499	7.9581
440	193600	85184000	20.9762	7.6059	505	255025	128787625	22.4722	7.9634
441	194481	85766121	21.	7.6117	506	256036	129554216	22.4944	7.9686
442	195364	86350888	21.0238	7.6174	507	257049	130323843	22.5167	7.9739
443	196249	86938307	21.0476	7.6232	508	258064	131096512	22.5389	7.9791
444	197136	87528384	21.0713	7.6289	509	259081	131872229	22.5610	7.9843
445	198025	88121125	21.0950	7.6346	510	260100	132651000	22.5832	7.9896

SQUARES, CUBES, AND ROOTS.

TABLE of Squares, Cubes, Square Roots, and Cube Roots, of Numbers from 1 to 1000 — (CONTINUED.)

No.	Square.	Cube.	Sq. Rt.	C. Rt.	No.	Square.	Cube.	Sq. Rt.	C. Rt.
641	410881	263374721	25.3180	8.6222	706	498436	351895816	26.5707	8.9043
642	412164	264609288	25.3377	8.6267	707	499849	353393243	26.5895	8.9085
643	413449	265847707	25.3574	8.6312	708	501264	354894912	26.6083	8.9127
644	414736	267089984	25.3772	8.6357	709	502681	356400829	26.6271	8.9169
645	416025	268336125	25.3969	8.6401	710	504100	357911000	26.6458	8.9211
646	417316	269586136	25.4165	8.6446	711	505521	359425431	26.6646	8.9253
647	418609	270840023	25.4362	8.6490	712	506944	360944128	26.6833	8.9295
648	419904	272097792	25.4558	8.6535	713	508369	362467097	26.7021	8.9337
649	421201	273359449	25.4755	8.6579	714	509796	363994344	26.7208	8.9378
650	422500	274625000	25.4951	8.6624	715	511225	365525875	26.7395	8.9420
651	423801	275894451	25.5147	8.6668	716	512656	367061696	26.7582	8.9462
652	425104	277167808	25.5343	8.6713	717	514089	368601813	26.7769	8.9503
653	426409	278445077	25.5539	8.6757	718	515524	370146232	26.7955	8.9545
654	427716	279726264	25.5734	8.6801	719	516961	371694959	26.8142	8.9587
655	429025	281011375	25.5930	8.6845	720	518400	373248000	26.8328	8.9628
656	430336	282300416	25.6125	8.6890	721	519841	374805361	26.8514	8.9670
657	431649	283593393	25.6320	8.6934	722	521284	376367048	26.8701	8.9711
658	432964	284890312	25.6515	8.6978	723	522729	377933067	26.8887	8.9752
659	434281	286191179	25.6710	8.7022	724	524176	379503424	26.9072	8.9794
660	435600	287496000	25.6905	8.7066	725	525625	381078125	26.9258	8.9835
661	436921	288804781	25.7099	8.7110	726	527076	382657176	26.9444	8.9876
662	438244	290117528	25.7294	8.7154	727	528529	384240583	26.9629	8.9918
663	439569	291434247	25.7488	8.7198	728	529984	385828352	26.9815	8.9959
664	440896	292754944	25.7682	8.7241	729	531441	387420489	27.	9.
665	442225	294079625	25.7876	8.7285	730	532900	389017000	27.0185	9.0041
666	443556	295408296	25.8070	8.7329	731	534361	390617891	27.0370	9.0082
667	444889	296740963	25.8263	8.7373	732	535824	392223168	27.0555	9.0123
668	446224	298077632	25.8457	8.7416	733	537289	393832837	27.0740	9.0164
669	447561	299418309	25.8650	8.7460	734	538756	395446904	27.0924	9.0205
670	448900	300763000	25.8844	8.7503	735	540225	397065375	27.1109	9.0246
671	450241	302111711	25.9037	8.7547	736	541696	398688256	27.1293	9.0287
672	451584	303464448	25.9230	8.7590	737	543169	400315553	27.1477	9.0328
673	452929	304821217	25.9422	8.7634	738	544644	401947272	27.1662	9.0369
674	454276	306182024	25.9615	8.7677	739	546121	403583419	27.1846	9.0410
675	455625	307546875	25.9808	8.7721	740	547600	405224000	27.2029	9.0450
676	456976	308915776	26.	8.7764	741	549081	406869021	27.2213	9.0491
677	458329	310288733	26.0192	8.7807	742	550564	408518488	27.2397	9.0532
678	459684	311665752	26.0384	8.7850	743	552049	410172407	27.2580	9.0572
679	461041	313046839	26.0576	8.7893	744	553536	411830784	27.2764	9.0613
680	462400	314432000	26.0768	8.7937	745	555025	413493625	27.2947	9.0654
681	463761	315821241	26.0960	8.7980	746	556516	415160936	27.3130	9.0694
682	465124	317214568	26.1151	8.8023	747	558009	416832723	27.3313	9.0735
683	466489	318611987	26.1343	8.8066	748	559504	418508992	27.3496	9.0775
684	467856	320013504	26.1534	8.8109	749	561001	420189749	27.3679	9.0816
685	469225	321419125	26.1725	8.8152	750	562500	421875000	27.3861	9.0856
686	470596	322828856	26.1916	8.8194	751	564001	423564751	27.4044	9.0896
687	471969	324242703	26.2107	8.8237	752	565504	425259008	27.4226	9.0937
688	473344	325660672	26.2298	8.8280	753	567009	426957777	27.4408	9.0977
689	474721	327082769	26.2488	8.8323	754	568516	428661064	27.4591	9.1017
690	476100	328509000	26.2679	8.8366	755	570025	430368875	27.4773	9.1057
691	477481	329939371	26.2869	8.8408	756	571536	432081216	27.4955	9.1098
692	478864	331373888	26.3059	8.8451	757	573049	433798093	27.5136	9.1138
693	480249	332812557	26.3249	8.8493	758	574564	435519512	27.5318	9.1178
694	481636	334255384	26.3439	8.8536	759	576081	437245479	27.5500	9.1218
695	483025	335702375	26.3629	8.8578	760	577600	438976000	27.5681	9.1258
696	484416	337153536	26.3818	8.8621	761	579121	440711081	27.5862	9.1298
697	485809	338608873	26.4008	8.8663	762	580644	442450728	27.6043	9.1338
698	487204	340068392	26.4197	8.8706	763	582169	444194947	27.6225	9.1378
699	488601	341532099	26.4386	8.8748	764	583696	445943744	27.6405	9.1418
700	490000	343000000	26.4575	8.8790	765	585225	447697125	27.6586	9.1458
701	491401	344472101	26.4764	8.8833	766	586756	449455096	27.6767	9.1498
702	492804	345948408	26.4953	8.8875	767	588289	451217663	27.6948	9.1537
703	494209	347428927	26.5141	8.8917	768	589824	452984832	27.7128	9.1577
704	495616	348913664	26.5330	8.8959	769	591361	454756609	27.7308	9.1617
705	497025	350402625	26.5518	8.9001	770	592900	456533000	27.7489	9.1657

SQUARES, CUBES, AND ROOTS.

TABLE of Squares, Cubes, Square Roots, and Cube Roots, of Numbers from 1 to 1000 — (CONTINUED.)

No.	Square.	Cube.	Sq. Rt.	C. Rt.	No.	Square.	Cube.	Sq. Rt.	C. Rt.
771	594441	458314011	27.7669	9.1696	836	698896	584277056	28.9137	9.4204
772	595984	460099648	27.7849	9.1736	837	700569	586376253	28.9310	9.4241
773	597529	461889917	27.8029	9.1775	838	702244	588480472	28.9482	9.4279
774	599076	463684824	27.8209	9.1815	839	703921	590589719	28.9655	9.4316
775	600625	465484375	27.8388	9.1855	840	705600	592704000	28.9828	9.4354
776	602176	467288576	27.8568	9.1894	841	707281	594823321	29.	9.4391
777	603729	469097433	27.8747	9.1933	842	708964	596946488	29.0172	9.4429
778	605284	470910952	27.8927	9.1973	843	710649	599077107	29.0345	9.4466
779	606841	472729139	27.9106	9.2012	844	712336	601211584	29.0517	9.4503
780	608400	474552000	27.9285	9.2052	845	714025	603351125	29.0689	9.4541
781	609961	476379541	27.9464	9.2091	846	715716	605495736	29.0861	9.4578
782	611524	478211768	27.9643	9.2130	847	717409	607645423	29.1033	9.4615
783	613089	480048687	27.9821	9.2170	848	719104	609800192	29.1204	9.4652
784	614656	481890304	28.	9.2209	849	720801	611960049	29.1376	9.4690
785	616225	483736625	28.0179	9.2248	850	722500	614125000	29.1548	9.4727
786	617796	485587656	28.0357	9.2287	851	724201	616295051	29.1719	9.4764
787	619369	487443403	28.0535	9.2326	852	725904	618470208	29.1890	9.4801
788	620944	489303872	28.0713	9.2365	853	727609	620650477	29.2062	9.4838
789	622521	491169069	28.0891	9.2404	854	729316	622835864	29.2233	9.4875
790	624100	493039000	28.1069	9.2443	855	731025	625026375	29.2404	9.4912
791	625681	494913671	28.1247	9.2482	856	732736	627222016	29.2575	9.4949
792	627264	496793088	28.1425	9.2521	857	734449	629422793	29.2746	9.4986
793	628849	498677257	28.1603	9.2560	858	736164	631628712	29.2916	9.5023
794	630436	500566184	28.1780	9.2599	859	737881	633839779	29.3087	9.5060
795	632025	502459875	28.1957	9.2638	860	739600	636056000	29.3258	9.5097
796	633616	504358336	28.2135	9.2677	861	741321	638277381	29.3428	9.5134
797	635209	506261573	28.2312	9.2716	862	743044	640503928	29.3598	9.5171
798	636804	508169592	28.2489	9.2754	863	744769	642735647	29.3769	9.5207
799	638401	510082399	28.2666	9.2793	864	746496	644972544	29.3939	9.5244
800	640000	512000000	28.2843	9.2832	865	748225	647214625	29.4109	9.5281
801	641601	513922401	28.3019	9.2870	866	749956	649461896	29.4279	9.5317
802	643204	515849608	28.3196	9.2909	867	751689	651714363	29.4449	9.5354
803	644809	517781627	28.3373	9.2948	868	753424	653973032	29.4618	9.5391
804	646416	519718464	28.3549	9.2986	869	755161	656234909	29.4788	9.5427
805	648025	521660125	28.3725	9.3025	870	756900	658503000	29.4958	9.5464
806	649636	523606616	28.3901	9.3063	871	758641	660776311	29.5127	9.5501
807	651249	525557943	28.4077	9.3102	872	760384	663054848	29.5296	9.5537
808	652864	527514112	28.4253	9.3140	873	762129	665338617	29.5466	9.5574
809	654481	529475129	28.4429	9.3179	874	763876	667627624	29.5635	9.5610
810	656100	531441000	28.4605	9.3217	875	765625	669921875	29.5804	9.5647
811	657721	533411731	28.4781	9.3255	876	767376	672221376	29.5973	9.5683
812	659344	535387328	28.4956	9.3294	877	769129	674526133	29.6142	9.5719
813	660969	537367797	28.5132	9.3332	878	770884	676836152	29.6311	9.5756
814	662596	539353144	28.5307	9.3370	879	772641	679151439	29.6479	9.5792
815	664225	541343375	28.5482	9.3408	880	774400	681472000	29.6648	9.5828
816	665856	543338496	28.5657	9.3447	881	776161	683797841	29.6816	9.5865
817	667489	545338513	28.5832	9.3485	882	777924	686128968	29.6985	9.5901
818	669124	547344432	28.6007	9.3523	883	779689	688465387	29.7153	9.5937
819	670761	549353259	28.6182	9.3561	884	781456	690807104	29.7321	9.5973
820	672400	551368000	28.6356	9.3599	885	783225	693154125	29.7489	9.6010
821	674041	553387661	28.6531	9.3637	886	784996	695506456	29.7658	9.6046
822	675684	555412248	28.6705	9.3675	887	786769	697864103	29.7825	9.6082
823	677329	557441767	28.6880	9.3713	888	788544	700227072	29.7993	9.6118
824	678976	559476224	28.7054	9.3751	889	790321	702595369	29.8161	9.6154
825	680625	561515625	28.7228	9.3789	890	792100	704969000	29.8329	9.6190
826	682276	563559976	28.7402	9.3827	891	793881	707347971	29.8496	9.6226
827	683929	565609283	28.7576	9.3865	892	795664	709732288	29.8664	9.6262
828	685584	567663552	28.7750	9.3902	893	797449	712121957	29.8831	9.6298
829	687241	569722789	28.7924	9.3940	894	799236	714516984	29.8998	9.6334
830	688900	571787000	28.8097	9.3978	895	801025	716917375	29.9166	9.6370
831	690561	573856191	28.8271	9.4016	896	802816	719323136	29.9333	9.6406
832	692224	575930368	28.8444	9.4053	897	804609	721734273	29.9500	9.6442
833	693889	578009537	28.8617	9.4091	898	806404	724150792	29.9666	9.6477
834	695556	580093704	28.8791	9.4129	899	808201	726572699	29.9833	9.6513
835	697225	582182875	28.8964	9.4166	900	810000	729000000	30.	9.6549

From Trautwine's "Civil Engineer's Pocket Book."

SQUARES, CUBES, AND ROOTS.

TABLE of Squares, Cubes, Square Roots, and Cube Roots, of Numbers from 1 to 1000 —(CONTINUED.)

No.	Square.	Cube.	Sq. Rt.	C. Rt.	No.	Square.	Cube.	Sq. Rt.	C. Rt.
901	811801	731432701	30.0167	9.6585	951	904401	860085351	30.8383	9.8339
902	813604	733870408	30.0333	9.6620	952	906304	862801408	30.8545	9.8374
903	815409	736314327	30.0500	9.6656	953	908209	865523177	30.8707	9.8408
904	817216	738763264	30.0666	9.6692	954	910116	868250664	30.8869	9.8443
905	819025	741217625	30.0832	9.6727	955	912025	870983875	30.9031	9.8477
906	820836	743677416	30.0998	9.6763	956	913936	873722816	30.9192	9.8511
907	822649	746142643	30.1164	9.6799	957	915849	876467493	30.9354	9.8546
908	824464	748613312	30.1330	9.6834	958	917764	879217912	30.9516	9.8580
909	826281	751089429	30.1496	9.6870	959	919681	881974079	30.9677	9.8614
910	828100	753571000	30.1662	9.6905	960	921600	884736000	30.9839	9.8648
911	829921	756058031	30.1828	9.6941	961	923521	887503681	31.	9.8683
912	831744	758550528	30.1993	9.6976	962	925444	890277128	31.0161	9.8717
913	833569	761048497	30.2159	9.7012	963	927369	893056347	31.0322	9.8751
914	835396	763551944	30.2324	9.7047	964	929296	895841344	31.0483	9.8785
915	837225	766060875	30.2490	9.7082	965	931225	898632125	31.0644	9.8819
916	839056	768575296	30.2655	9.7118	966	933156	901428696	31.0805	9.8854
917	840889	771095213	30.2820	9.7153	967	935089	904231063	31.0966	9.8888
918	842724	773620632	30.2985	9.7188	968	937024	907039232	31.1127	9.8922
919	844561	776151559	30.3150	9.7224	969	938961	909853209	31.1288	9.8956
920	846400	778688000	30.3315	9.7259	970	940900	912673000	31.1448	9.8990
921	848241	781229961	30.3480	9.7294	971	942841	915498611	31.1609	9.9024
922	850084	783777448	30.3645	9.7329	972	944784	918330048	31.1769	9.9058
923	851929	786330467	30.3809	9.7364	973	946729	921167317	31.1929	9.9092
924	853776	788889024	30.3974	9.7400	974	948676	924010424	31.2090	9.9126
925	855625	791453125	30.4138	9.7435	975	950625	926859375	31.2250	9.9160
926	857476	794022776	30.4302	9.7470	976	952576	929714176	31.2410	9.9194
927	859329	796597983	30.4467	9.7505	977	954529	932574833	31.2570	9.9227
928	861184	799178752	30.4631	9.7540	978	956484	935441352	31.2730	9.9261
929	863041	801765089	30.4795	9.7575	979	958441	938313739	31.2890	9.9295
930	864900	804357000	30.4959	9.7610	980	960400	941192000	31.3050	9.9329
931	866761	806954491	30.5123	9.7645	981	962361	944076141	31.3209	9.9363
932	868624	809557568	30.5287	9.7680	982	964324	946966168	31.3369	9.9396
933	870489	812166237	30.5450	9.7715	983	966289	949862087	31.3528	9.9430
934	872356	814780504	30.5614	9.7750	984	968256	952763904	31.3688	9.9464
935	874225	817400375	30.5778	9.7785	985	970225	955671625	31.3847	9.9497
936	876096	820025856	30.5941	9.7819	986	972196	958585256	31.4006	9.9531
937	877969	822656953	30.6105	9.7854	987	974169	961504803	31.4166	9.9565
938	879844	825293672	30.6268	9.7889	988	976144	964430272	31.4325	9.9598
939	881721	827936019	30.6431	9.7924	989	978121	967361669	31.4484	9.9632
940	883600	830584000	30.6594	9.7959	990	980100	970299000	31.4643	9.9666
941	885481	833237621	30.6757	9.7993	991	982081	973242271	31.4802	9.9699
942	887364	835896888	30.6920	9.8028	992	984064	976191488	31.4960	9.9733
943	889249	838561807	30.7083	9.8063	993	986049	979146657	31.5119	9.9766
944	891136	841232384	30.7246	9.8097	994	988036	982107784	31.5278	9.9800
945	893025	843908625	30.7409	9.8132	995	990025	985074875	31.5436	9.9833
946	894916	846590536	30.7571	9.8167	996	992016	988047936	31.5595	9.9866
947	896809	849278123	30.7734	9.8201	997	994009	991026973	31.5753	9.9900
948	898704	851971392	30.7896	9.8236	998	996004	994011992	31.5911	9.9933
949	900601	854670349	30.8058	9.8270	999	998001	997002999	31.6070	9.9967
950	902500	857375000	30.8221	9.8305	1000	1000000	1000000000	31.6228	10.

To find the square or cube of any whole number ending with ciphers. First, omit all the final ciphers. Take from the table the square or cube (as the case may be) of the rest of the number. To this square add twice as many ciphers as there were final ciphers in the original number. To the cube add three times as many as in the original number. Thus, for 90500²; 905²=819025. Add twice 2 ciphers, obtaining 8190250000. For 90500³, 905³=741217625. Add 3 times 2 ciphers, obtaining 741217625000000.

TABLE NO. 76.

From Trautwine's "Civil Engineer's Pocket Book."

SQUARE AND CUBE ROOTS.

Square Roots and Cube Roots of Numbers from 1000 to 10000.

No errors.

Num.	Sq. Rt.	Cu. Rt.	Num.	Sq. Rt.	Cu. Rt.	Num.	Sq. Rt.	Cu. Rt.	Num.	Sq. Rt.	Cu. Rt.
1005	31.70	10.02	1405	37.48	11.20	1805	42.49	12.18	2205	46.96	13.02
1010	31.78	10.03	1410	37.55	11.21	1810	42.54	12.19	2210	47.01	13.03
1015	31.86	10.05	1415	37.62	11.23	1815	42.60	12.20	2215	47.06	13.04
1020	31.94	10.07	1420	37.68	11.24	1820	42.66	12.21	2220	47.12	13.05
1025	32.02	10.08	1425	37.75	11.25	1825	42.72	12.22	2225	47.17	13.05
1030	32.09	10.10	1430	37.82	11.27	1830	42.78	12.23	2230	47.22	13.06
1035	32.17	10.12	1435	37.88	11.28	1835	42.84	12.24	2235	47.28	13.07
1040	32.25	10.13	1440	37.95	11.29	1840	42.90	12.25	2240	47.33	13.08
1045	32.33	10.15	1445	38.01	11.31	1845	42.95	12.26	2245	47.38	13.09
1050	32.40	10.16	1450	38.08	11.32	1850	43.01	12.28	2250	47.43	13.10
1055	32.48	10.18	1455	38.14	11.33	1855	43.07	12.29	2255	47.49	13.11
1060	32.56	10.20	1460	38.21	11.34	1860	43.13	12.30	2260	47.54	13.12
1065	32.63	10.21	1465	38.28	11.36	1865	43.19	12.31	2265	47.59	13.13
1070	32.71	10.23	1470	38.34	11.37	1870	43.24	12.32	2270	47.64	13.14
1075	32.79	10.24	1475	38.41	11.38	1875	43.30	12.33	2275	47.70	13.15
1080	32.86	10.26	1480	38.47	11.40	1880	43.36	12.34	2280	47.75	13.16
1085	32.94	10.28	1485	38.54	11.41	1885	43.42	12.35	2285	47.80	13.17
1090	33.02	10.29	1490	38.60	11.42	1890	43.47	12.36	2290	47.85	13.18
1095	33.09	10.31	1495	38.67	11.43	1895	43.53	12.37	2295	47.91	13.19
1100	33.17	10.32	1500	38.73	11.45	1900	43.59	12.39	2300	47.96	13.20
1105	33.24	10.34	1505	38.79	11.46	1905	43.65	12.40	2305	48.01	13.21
1110	33.32	10.35	1510	38.86	11.47	1910	43.70	12.41	2310	48.06	13.22
1115	33.39	10.37	1515	38.92	11.49	1915	43.76	12.42	2315	48.11	13.23
1120	33.47	10.38	1520	38.99	11.50	1920	43.82	12.43	2320	48.17	13.24
1125	33.54	10.40	1525	39.05	11.51	1925	43.87	12.44	2325	48.22	13.25
1130	33.62	10.42	1530	39.12	11.52	1930	43.93	12.45	2330	48.27	13.26
1135	33.69	10.43	1535	39.18	11.54	1935	43.99	12.46	2335	48.32	13.27
1140	33.76	10.45	1540	39.24	11.55	1940	44.05	12.47	2340	48.37	13.28
1145	33.84	10.46	1545	39.31	11.56	1945	44.10	12.48	2345	48.43	13.29
1150	33.91	10.48	1550	39.37	11.57	1950	44.16	12.49	2350	48.48	13.30
1155	33.99	10.49	1555	39.43	11.59	1955	44.22	12.50	2355	48.53	13.30
1160	34.06	10.51	1560	39.50	11.60	1960	44.27	12.51	2360	48.58	13.31
1165	34.13	10.52	1565	39.56	11.61	1965	44.33	12.53	2365	48.63	13.32
1170	34.21	10.54	1570	39.62	11.62	1970	44.38	12.54	2370	48.68	13.33
1175	34.28	10.55	1575	39.69	11.63	1975	44.44	12.55	2375	48.73	13.34
1180	34.35	10.57	1580	39.75	11.65	1980	44.50	12.56	2380	48.79	13.35
1185	34.42	10.58	1585	39.81	11.66	1985	44.55	12.57	2385	48.84	13.36
1190	34.50	10.60	1590	39.87	11.67	1990	44.61	12.58	2390	48.89	13.37
1195	34.57	10.61	1595	39.94	11.68	1995	44.67	12.59	2395	48.94	13.38
1200	34.64	10.63	1600	40.00	11.70	2000	44.72	12.60	2400	48.99	13.39
1205	34.71	10.64	1605	40.06	11.71	2005	44.78	12.61	2405	49.04	13.40
1210	34.79	10.66	1610	40.12	11.72	2010	44.83	12.62	2410	49.09	13.41
1215	34.86	10.67	1615	40.19	11.73	2015	44.89	12.63	2415	49.14	13.42
1220	34.93	10.69	1620	40.25	11.74	2020	44.94	12.64	2420	49.19	13.43
1225	35.00	10.70	1625	40.31	11.76	2025	45.00	12.65	2425	49.24	13.43
1230	35.07	10.71	1630	40.37	11.77	2030	45.06	12.66	2430	49.30	13.44
1235	35.14	10.73	1635	40.44	11.78	2035	45.11	12.67	2435	49.35	13.45
1240	35.21	10.74	1640	40.50	11.79	2040	45.17	12.68	2440	49.40	13.46
1245	35.28	10.76	1645	40.56	11.80	2045	45.22	12.69	2445	49.45	13.47
1250	35.36	10.77	1650	40.62	11.82	2050	45.28	12.70	2450	49.50	13.48
1255	35.43	10.79	1655	40.68	11.83	2055	45.33	12.71	2460	49.60	13.50
1260	35.50	10.80	1660	40.74	11.84	2060	45.39	12.72	2470	49.70	13.52
1265	35.57	10.82	1665	40.80	11.85	2065	45.44	12.73	2480	49.80	13.54
1270	35.64	10.83	1670	40.87	11.86	2070	45.50	12.74	2490	49.90	13.55
1275	35.71	10.84	1675	40.93	11.88	2075	45.55	12.75	2500	50.00	13.57
1280	35.78	10.86	1680	40.99	11.89	2080	45.61	12.77	2510	50.10	13.59
1285	35.85	10.87	1685	41.05	11.90	2085	45.66	12.78	2520	50.20	13.61
1290	35.92	10.89	1690	41.11	11.91	2090	45.72	12.79	2530	50.30	13.63
1295	35.99	10.90	1695	41.17	11.92	2095	45.77	12.80	2540	50.40	13.64
1300	36.06	10.91	1700	41.23	11.93	2100	45.83	12.81	2550	50.50	13.66
1305	36.12	10.93	1705	41.29	11.95	2105	45.88	12.82	2560	50.60	13.68
1310	36.19	10.94	1710	41.35	11.96	2110	45.93	12.83	2570	50.70	13.70
1315	36.26	10.96	1715	41.41	11.97	2115	45.99	12.84	2580	50.79	13.72
1320	36.33	10.97	1720	41.47	11.98	2120	46.04	12.85	2590	50.89	13.73
1325	36.40	10.98	1725	41.53	11.99	2125	46.10	12.86	2600	50.99	13.75
1330	36.47	11.00	1730	41.59	12.00	2130	46.15	12.87	2610	51.09	13.77
1335	36.54	11.01	1735	41.65	12.02	2135	46.21	12.88	2620	51.19	13.79
1340	36.61	11.02	1740	41.71	12.03	2140	46.26	12.89	2630	51.28	13.80
1345	36.67	11.04	1745	41.77	12.04	2145	46.31	12.90	2640	51.38	13.82
1350	36.74	11.05	1750	41.83	12.05	2150	46.37	12.91	2650	51.48	13.84
1355	36.81	11.07	1755	41.89	12.06	2155	46.42	12.92	2660	51.58	13.86
1360	36.88	11.08	1760	41.95	12.07	2160	46.48	12.93	2670	51.67	13.87
1365	36.95	11.09	1765	42.01	12.09	2165	46.53	12.94	2680	51.77	13.89
1370	37.01	11.11	1770	42.07	12.10	2170	46.58	12.95	2690	51.87	13.91
1375	37.08	11.12	1775	42.13	12.11	2175	46.64	12.96	2700	51.96	13.92
1380	37.15	11.13	1780	42.19	12.12	2180	46.69	12.97	2710	52.06	13.94
1385	37.22	11.15	1785	42.25	12.13	2185	46.74	12.98	2720	52.15	13.96
1390	37.28	11.16	1790	42.31	12.14	2190	46.80	12.99	2730	52.25	13.98
1395	37.35	11.17	1795	42.37	12.15	2195	46.85	13.00	2740	52.35	13.99
1400	37.42	11.19	1800	42.43	12.16	2200	46.90	13.01	2750	52.44	14.01

From Trautwine's "Civil Engineer's Pocket Book."

SQUARE AND CUBE ROOTS.

Square Roots and Cube Roots of Numbers from 1000 to 10000
—(CONTINUED.)

Num.	Sq. Rt.	Cu. Rt.	Num.	Sq. Rt.	Cu. Rt.	Num.	Sq. Rt.	Cu. Rt.	Num.	Sq. Rt.	Cu. Rt.
2760	52.54	14.03	3550	59.58	15.25	4340	65.88	16.31	5130	71.62	17.25
2770	52.63	14.04	3560	59.67	15.27	4350	65.95	16.32	5140	71.69	17.26
2780	52.73	14.06	3570	59.75	15.28	4360	66.03	16.34	5150	71.76	17.27
2790	52.82	14.08	3580	59.83	15.30	4370	66.11	16.35	5160	71.83	17.28
2800	52.92	14.09	3590	59.92	15.31	4380	66.18	16.36	5170	71.90	17.29
2810	53.01	14.11	3600	60.00	15.33	4390	66.26	16.37	5180	71.97	17.30
2820	53.10	14.13	3610	60.08	15.34	4400	66.33	16.39	5190	72.04	17.31
2830	53.20	14.14	3620	60.17	15.35	4410	66.41	16.40	5200	72.11	17.32
2840	53.29	14.16	3630	60.25	15.37	4420	66.48	16.41	5210	72.18	17.34
2850	53.39	14.18	3640	60.33	15.38	4430	66.56	16.42	5220	72.25	17.35
2860	53.48	14.19	3650	60.42	15.40	4440	66.63	16.44	5230	72.32	17.36
2870	53.57	14.21	3660	60.50	15.41	4450	66.71	16.45	5240	72.39	17.37
2880	53.67	14.23	3670	60.58	15.42	4460	66.78	16.46	5250	72.46	17.38
2890	53.76	14.24	3680	60.66	15.44	4470	66.86	16.47	5260	72.53	17.39
2900	53.85	14.26	3690	60.75	15.45	4480	66.93	16.49	5270	72.59	17.40
2910	53.94	14.28	3700	60.83	15.47	4490	67.01	16.50	5280	72.66	17.41
2920	54.04	14.29	3710	60.91	15.48	4500	67.08	16.51	5290	72.73	17.42
2930	54.13	14.31	3720	60.99	15.49	4510	67.16	16.52	5300	72.80	17.44
2940	54.22	14.33	3730	61.07	15.51	4520	67.23	16.53	5310	72.87	17.45
2950	54.31	14.34	3740	61.16	15.52	4530	67.31	16.55	5320	72.94	17.46
2960	54.41	14.36	3750	61.24	15.54	4540	67.38	16.56	5330	73.01	17.47
2970	54.50	14.37	3760	61.32	15.55	4550	67.45	16.57	5340	73.08	17.48
2980	54.59	14.39	3770	61.40	15.56	4560	67.53	16.58	5350	73.14	17.49
2990	54.68	14.41	3780	61.48	15.58	4570	67.60	16.59	5360	73.21	17.50
3000	54.77	14.42	3790	61.56	15.59	4580	67.68	16.61	5370	73.28	17.51
3010	54.86	14.44	3800	61.64	15.60	4590	67.75	16.62	5380	73.35	17.52
3020	54.95	14.45	3810	61.73	15.62	4600	67.82	16.63	5390	73.42	17.53
3030	55.05	14.47	3820	61.81	15.63	4610	67.90	16.64	5400	73.48	17.54
3040	55.14	14.49	3830	61.89	15.65	4620	67.97	16.66	5410	73.55	17.55
3050	55.23	14.50	3840	61.97	15.66	4630	68.04	16.67	5420	73.62	17.57
3060	55.32	14.52	3850	62.05	15.67	4640	68.12	16.68	5430	73.69	17.58
3070	55.41	14.53	3860	62.13	15.69	4650	68.19	16.69	5440	73.76	17.59
3080	55.50	14.55	3870	62.21	15.70	4660	68.26	16.70	5450	73.82	17.60
3090	55.59	14.57	3880	62.29	15.71	4670	68.34	16.71	5460	73.89	17.61
3100	55.68	14.58	3890	62.37	15.73	4680	68.41	16.73	5470	73.96	17.62
3110	55.77	14.60	3900	62.45	15.74	4690	68.48	16.74	5480	74.03	17.63
3120	55.86	14.61	3910	62.53	15.75	4700	68.56	16.75	5490	74.09	17.64
3130	55.95	14.63	3920	62.61	15.77	4710	68.63	16.76	5500	74.16	17.65
3140	56.04	14.64	3930	62.69	15.78	4720	68.70	16.77	5510	74.23	17.66
3150	56.12	14.66	3940	62.77	15.79	4730	68.77	16.79	5520	74.30	17.67
3160	56.21	14.67	3950	62.85	15.81	4740	68.85	16.80	5530	74.36	17.68
3170	56.30	14.69	3960	62.93	15.82	4750	68.92	16.81	5540	74.43	17.69
3180	56.39	14.71	3970	63.01	15.83	4760	68.99	16.82	5550	74.50	17.71
3190	56.48	14.72	3980	63.09	15.85	4770	69.07	16.83	5560	74.57	17.72
3200	56.57	14.74	3990	63.17	15.86	4780	69.14	16.85	5570	74.63	17.73
3210	56.66	14.75	4000	63.25	15.87	4790	69.21	16.86	5580	74.70	17.74
3220	56.75	14.77	4010	63.32	15.89	4800	69.28	16.87	5590	74.77	17.75
3230	56.83	14.78	4020	63.40	15.90	4810	69.35	16.88	5600	74.83	17.77
3240	56.92	14.80	4030	63.48	15.91	4820	69.43	16.89	5610	74.90	17.77
3250	57.01	14.81	4040	63.56	15.93	4830	69.50	16.90	5620	74.97	17.78
3260	57.10	14.83	4050	63.64	15.94	4840	69.57	16.92	5630	75.03	17.79
3270	57.18	14.84	4060	63.72	15.95	4850	69.64	16.93	5640	75.10	17.80
3280	57.27	14.86	4070	63.80	15.97	4860	69.71	16.94	5650	75.17	17.81
3290	57.36	14.87	4080	63.87	15.98	4870	69.79	16.95	5660	75.23	17.82
3300	57.45	14.89	4090	63.95	15.99	4880	69.86	16.96	5670	75.30	17.83
3310	57.53	14.90	4100	64.03	16.01	4890	69.93	16.97	5680	75.37	17.84
3320	57.62	14.92	4110	64.11	16.02	4900	70.00	16.98	5690	75.43	17.85
3330	57.71	14.93	4120	64.19	16.03	4910	70.07	17.00	5700	75.50	17.86
3340	57.79	14.95	4130	64.27	16.04	4920	70.14	17.01	5710	75.56	17.87
3350	57.88	14.96	4140	64.34	16.06	4930	70.21	17.02	5720	75.63	17.88
3360	57.97	14.98	4150	64.42	16.07	4940	70.29	17.03	5730	75.70	17.89
3370	58.05	14.99	4160	64.50	16.08	4950	70.36	17.04	5740	75.76	17.90
3380	58.14	15.01	4170	64.58	16.10	4960	70.43	17.05	5750	75.83	17.92
3390	58.22	15.02	4180	64.65	16.11	4970	70.50	17.07	5760	75.89	17.93
3400	58.31	15.04	4190	64.73	16.12	4980	70.57	17.08	5770	75.96	17.94
3410	58.40	15.05	4200	64.81	16.13	4990	70.64	17.09	5780	76.03	17.95
3420	58.48	15.07	4210	64.88	16.15	5000	70.71	17.10	5790	76.09	17.96
3430	58.57	15.08	4220	64.96	16.16	5010	70.78	17.11	5800	76.16	17.97
3440	58.65	15.10	4230	65.04	16.17	5020	70.85	17.12	5810	76.22	17.98
3450	58.74	15.11	4240	65.12	16.19	5030	70.92	17.13	5820	76.29	17.99
3460	58.82	15.12	4250	65.19	16.20	5040	70.99	17.15	5830	76.35	18.00
3470	58.91	15.14	4260	65.27	16.21	5050	71.06	17.16	5840	76.42	18.01
3480	58.99	15.15	4270	65.35	16.22	5060	71.13	17.17	5850	76.49	18.02
3490	59.08	15.17	4280	65.42	16.24	5070	71.20	17.18	5860	76.55	18.03
3500	59.16	15.18	4290	65.50	16.25	5080	71.27	17.19	5870	76.62	18.04
3510	59.25	15.20	4300	65.57	16.26	5090	71.34	17.20	5880	76.68	18.05
3520	59.33	15.21	4310	65.65	16.27	5100	71.41	17.21	5890	76.75	18.06
3530	59.41	15.23	4320	65.73	16.29	5110	71.48	17.22	5900	76.81	18.07
3540	59.50	15.24	4330	65.80	16.30	5120	71.55	17.24	5910	76.88	18.08

SQUARE AND CUBE ROOTS.

Square Roots and Cube Roots of Numbers from 1000 to 10000 — (Continued.)

Num.	Sq. Rt.	Cu. Rt.	Num.	Sq. Rt.	Cu. Rt.	Num.	Sq. Rt.	Cu. Rt.	Num.	Sq. Rt.	Cu. Rt
5920	76.94	18.09	6710	81.91	18.86	7500	86.60	19.57	8290	91.05	20.24
593C	77.01	18.10	6720	81.98	18.87	7510	86.66	19.58	8300	91.10	20.25
5840	77.07	18.11	6730	82.04	18.88	7520	86.72	19.59	8310	91.16	20.26
5950	77.14	18.12	6740	82.10	18.89	7530	86.78	19.60	8320	91.21	20.26
5960	77.20	18.13	6750	82.16	18.90	7540	86.83	19.61	8330	91.27	20.27
5970	77.27	18.14	6760	82.22	18.91	7550	86.89	19.62	8340	91.32	20.28
5980	77.33	18.15	6770	82.28	18.92	7560	86.95	19.63	8350	91.38	20.29
5990	77.40	18.16	6780	82.34	18.93	7570	87.01	19.64	8360	91.43	20.30
6000	77.46	18.17	6790	82.40	18.94	7580	87.06	19.64	8370	91.49	20.30
6010	77.52	18.18	6800	82.46	18.95	7590	87.12	19.65	8380	91.54	20.31
6020	77.59	18.19	6810	82.52	18.95	7600	87.18	19.66	8390	91.60	20.32
6030	77.65	18.20	6820	82.58	18.96	7610	87.24	19.67	8400	91.65	20.33
6040	77.72	18.21	6830	82.64	18.97	7620	87.29	19.68	8410	91.71	20.34
6050	77.78	18.22	6840	82.70	18.98	7630	87.35	19.69	8420	91.76	20.34
6060	77.85	18.23	6850	82.76	18.99	7640	87.41	19.70	8430	91.82	20.35
6070	77.91	18.24	6860	82.83	19.00	7650	87.46	19.70	8440	91.87	20.36
6080	77.97	18.25	6870	82.89	19.01	7660	87.52	19.71	8450	91.92	20.37
6090	78.04	18.26	6880	82.95	19.02	7670	87.58	19.72	8460	91.98	20.38
6100	78.10	18.27	6890	83.01	19.03	7680	87.64	19.73	8470	92.03	20.38
6110	78.17	18.28	6900	83.07	19.04	7690	87.69	19.74	8480	92.09	20.39
6120	78.23	18.29	6910	83.13	19.05	7700	87.75	19.75	8490	92.14	20.40
6130	78.29	18.30	6920	83.19	19.06	7710	87.81	19.76	8500	92.20	20.41
6140	78.36	18.31	6930	83.25	19.07	7720	87.86	19.76	8510	92.25	20.42
6150	78.42	18.32	6940	83.31	19.07	7730	87.92	19.77	8520	92.30	20.42
6160	78.49	18.33	6950	83.37	19.08	7740	87.98	19.78	8530	92.36	20.43
6170	78.55	18.34	6960	83.43	19.09	7750	88.03	19.79	8540	92.41	20.44
6180	78.61	18.35	6970	83.49	19.10	7760	88.09	19.80	8550	92.47	20.45
6190	78.68	18.36	6980	83.55	19.11	7770	88.15	19.81	8560	92.52	20.46
6200	78.74	18.37	6990	83.61	19.12	7780	88.20	19.81	8570	92.57	20.46
6210	78.80	18.38	7000	83.67	19.13	7790	88.26	19.82	8580	92.63	20.47
6220	78.87	18.39	7010	83.73	19.14	7800	88.32	19.83	8590	92.68	20.48
6230	78.93	18.40	7020	83.79	19.15	7810	88.37	19.84	8600	92.74	20.49
6240	78.99	18.41	7030	83.85	19.16	7820	88.43	19.85	8610	92.79	20.50
6250	79.06	18.42	7040	83.90	19.17	7830	88.49	19.86	8620	92.84	20.50
6260	79.12	18.43	7050	83.96	19.17	7840	88.54	19.87	8630	92.90	20.51
6270	79.18	18.44	7060	84.02	19.18	7850	88.60	19.87	8640	92.95	20.52
6280	79.25	18.45	7070	84.08	19.19	7860	88.66	19.88	8650	93.01	20.53
6290	79.31	18.46	7080	84.14	19.20	7870	88.71	19.89	8660	93.06	20.54
6300	79.37	18.47	7090	84.20	19.21	7880	88.77	19.90	8670	93.11	20.54
6310	79.44	18.48	7100	84.26	19.22	7890	88.83	19.91	8680	93.17	20.55
6320	79.50	18.49	7110	84.32	19.23	7900	88.88	19.92	8690	93.22	20.56
6330	79.56	18.50	7120	84.38	19.24	7910	88.94	19.92	8700	93.27	20.57
6340	79.62	18.51	7130	84.44	19.25	7920	88.99	19.93	8710	93.33	20.57
6350	79.69	18.52	7140	84.50	19.26	7930	89.05	19.94	8720	93.38	20.58
6360	79.75	18.53	7150	84.56	19.26	7940	89.11	19.95	8730	93.43	20.59
6370	79.81	18.54	7160	84.62	19.27	7950	89.16	19.96	8740	93.49	20.60
6380	79.87	18.55	7170	84.68	19.28	7960	89.22	19.97	8750	93.54	20.61
6390	79.94	18.56	7180	84.73	19.29	7970	89.27	19.97	8760	93.59	20.61
6400	80.00	18.57	7190	84.79	19.30	7980	89.33	19.98	8770	93.65	20.62
6410	80.06	18.58	7200	84.85	19.31	7990	89.39	19.99	8780	93.70	20.63
6420	80.12	18.59	7210	84.91	19.32	8000	89.44	20.00	8790	93.75	20.64
6430	80.19	18.60	7220	84.97	19.33	8010	89.50	20.01	8800	93.81	20.65
6440	80.25	18.60	7230	85.03	19.34	8020	89.55	20.02	8810	93.86	20.65
6450	80.31	18.61	7240	85.09	19.35	8030	89.61	20.02	8820	93.91	20.66
6460	80.37	18.62	7250	85.15	19.35	8040	89.67	20.03	8830	93.97	20.67
6470	80.44	18.63	7260	85.21	19.36	8050	89.72	20.04	8840	94.02	20.68
6480	80.50	18.64	7270	85.26	19.37	8060	89.78	20.05	8850	94.07	20.68
6490	80.56	18.65	7280	85.32	19.38	8070	89.83	20.06	8860	94.13	20.69
6500	80.62	18.66	7290	85.38	19.39	8080	89.89	20.07	8870	94.18	20.70
6510	80.68	18.67	7300	85.44	19.40	8090	89.94	20.07	8880	94.23	20.71
6520	80.75	18.68	7310	85.50	19.41	8100	90.00	20.08	8890	94.29	20.72
6530	80.81	18.69	7320	85.56	19.42	8110	90.06	20.09	8900	94.34	20.72
6540	80.87	18.70	7330	85.62	19.43	8120	90.11	20.10	8910	94.39	20.73
6550	80.93	18.71	7340	85.67	19.43	8130	90.17	20.11	8920	94.45	20.74
6560	80.99	18.72	7350	85.73	19.44	8140	90.22	20.12	8930	94.50	20.75
6570	81.06	18.73	7360	85.79	19.45	8150	90.28	20.12	8940	94.55	20.75
6580	81.12	18.74	7370	85.85	19.46	8160	90.33	20.13	8950	94.60	20.76
6590	81.18	18.75	7380	85.91	19.47	8170	90.39	20.14	8960	94.66	20.77
6600	81.24	18.76	7390	85.97	19.48	8180	90.44	20.15	8970	94.71	20.78
6610	81.30	18.77	7400	86.02	19.49	8190	90.50	20.16	8980	94.76	20.79
6620	81.36	18.78	7410	86.08	19.50	8200	90.55	20.17	8990	94.82	20.79
6630	81.42	18.79	7420	86.14	19.50	8210	90.61	20.17	9000	94.87	20.80
6640	81.49	18.80	7430	86.20	19.51	8220	90.66	20.18	9010	94.92	20.81
6650	81.55	18.81	7440	86.26	19.52	8230	90.72	20.19	9020	94.97	20.82
6660	81.61	18.81	7450	86.31	19.53	8240	90.77	20.20	9030	95.03	20.82
6670	81.67	18.82	7460	86.37	19.54	8250	90.83	20.21	9040	95.08	20.83
6680	81.73	18.83	7470	86.43	19.55	8260	90.88	20.21	9050	95.13	20.84
6690	81.79	18.84	7480	86.49	19.56	8270	90.94	20.22	9060	95.18	20.85
6700	81.85	18.85	7490	86.54	19.57	8280	90.99	20.23	9070	95.24	20.85

SQUARE AND CUBE ROOTS.

Square Roots and Cube Roots of Numbers from 9000 to 10000
— (CONTINUED.)

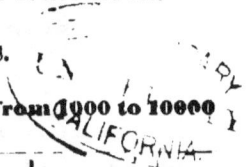

Num.	Sq. Rt.	Cu. Rt.	Num.	Sq. Rt.	Cu. Rt.	Num.	Sq. Rt.	Cu. Rt.	Num.	Sq. Rt.	Cu. Rt.
9080	95.29	20.86	9320	96.54	21.04	9550	97.72	21.22	9780	98.89	21.39
9090	95.34	20.87	9330	96.59	21.05	9560	97.78	21.22	9790	98.94	21.39
9100	95.39	20.88	9340	96.64	21.06	9570	97.83	21.23	9800	98.99	21.40
9110	95.45	20.89	9350	96.70	21.07	9580	97.88	21.24	9810	99.05	21.41
9120	95.50	20.89	9360	96.75	21.07	9590	97.93	21.25	9820	99.10	21.41
9130	95.55	20.90	9370	96.80	21.08	9600	97.98	21.25	9830	99.15	21.42
9140	95.60	20.91	9380	96.85	21.09	9610	98.03	21.26	9840	99.20	21.43
9150	95.66	20.92	9390	96.90	21.10	9620	98.08	21.27	9850	99.25	21.44
9160	95.71	20.92	9400	96.95	21.10	9630	98.13	21.28	9860	99.30	21.44
9170	95.76	20.93	9410	97.01	21.11	9640	98.18	21.28	9870	99.35	21.45
9180	95.81	20.94	9420	97.06	21.12	9650	98.23	21.29	9880	99.40	21.46
9190	95.86	20.95	9430	97.11	21.13	9660	98.28	21.30	9890	99.45	21.47
9200	95.92	20.95	9440	97.16	21.13	9670	98.34	21.30	9900	99.50	21.47
9210	95.97	20.96	9450	97.21	21.14	9680	98.39	21.31	9910	99.55	21.48
9220	96.02	20.97	9460	97.26	21.15	9690	98.44	21.32	9920	99.60	21.49
9230	96.07	20.98	9470	97.31	21.16	9700	98.49	21.33	9930	99.65	21.49
9240	96.12	20.98	9480	91.37	21.16	9710	98.54	21.33	9940	99.70	21.50
9250	96.18	20.99	9490	97.42	21.17	9720	98.59	21.34	9950	99.75	21.51
9260	96.23	21.00	9500	97.47	21.18	9730	98.64	21.35	9960	99.80	21.52
9270	96.28	21.01	9510	97.52	21.19	9740	98.69	21.36	9970	99.85	21.52
9280	96.33	21.01	9520	97.57	21.19	9750	98.74	21.36	9980	99.90	21.53
9290	96.38	21.02	9530	97.62	21.20	9760	98.79	21.37	9990	99.95	21.54
9300	96.44	21.03	9540	97.67	21.21	9770	98.84	21.38	10000	100.00	21.54
9310	96.49	21.04									

To find Square or Cube Roots of large numbers not contained in the column of numbers of the table.

Such roots may sometimes be taken at once from the table, by merely regarding the columns of powers as being columns of numbers; and those of numbers as being those of roots. Thus, if the sq rt of 25281 is reqd, first find that number in the column of *squares*; and opposite to it, in the column of numbers, is its sq rt 159. For the *cube* rt of 857375, find that number in the column of *cubes*; and opposite to it, in the col of numbers, is its cube rt 95. When the exact number is not contained in the column of squares, or cubes, as the case may be, we may use instead the number nearest to it, if no great accuracy is reqd. But when a considerable degree of accuracy is necessary, the following very correct methods may be used.

For the square root.

This rule applies both to whole numbers, and to those which are *partly* (not wholly) decimal. First, in the foregoing manner, take out the tabular number, which is nearest to the given one; and also its tabular sq rt. Mult this tabular number by 3; to the prod add the given number. Call the sum A. Then mult the given number by 3; to the prod add the tabular number. Call the sum B. Then

$$A : B : : \text{Tabular root} : \text{Reqd root.}$$

Ex. Let the given number be 946.53. Here we find the nearest tabular number to be 947; and its tabular sq rt 30.7734. Hence,

$$\begin{array}{r} 947 = \text{tab num} \\ 3 \\ \hline 2841 \\ 946.53 = \text{given num.} \\ \hline 3787.53 = A. \end{array} \quad \text{and} \quad \begin{array}{r} 946.53 = \text{given num.} \\ 3 \\ \hline 2839.59 \\ 947 = \text{tab num.} \\ \hline 3786.59 = B. \end{array}$$

Then
$$\begin{array}{cccc} A. & B. & \text{Tab root.} & \text{Reqd root.} \\ 3787.53 & : 3786.59 & : : 30.7734 & : 30.7657 \text{ +.} \end{array}$$

The root as found by actual mathematical process is also 30.7657 +.

For the cube root.

This rule applies both to whole numbers, and to those which are *partly* decimal. First take out the tabular number which is nearest to the given one; and also its tabular cube rt. Mult this tabular number by 2; and to the prod add the given number. Call the sum A. Then mult the given number by 3; and to the prod add the tabular number. Call the sum B. Then

$$A : B : : \text{Tabular root} : \text{Reqd root.}$$

Ex. Let the given number be 7368. Here we find the nearest tabular number (in the column of *cubes*) to be 6859; and its tabular cube rt 19. Hence,

$$\begin{array}{r} 6859 = \text{tab num.} \\ 2 \\ \hline 13718 \\ 7368 = \text{given num.} \\ \hline 21086 = A. \end{array} \quad \text{and} \quad \begin{array}{r} 7368 = \text{given num.} \\ 2 \\ \hline 14736 \\ 6859 = \text{tab num.} \\ \hline 21595 = B. \end{array}$$

From Trautwine's "Civil Engineer's Pocket Book."

SQUARE AND CUBE ROOTS.

this degree of accuracy; for his purposes, therefore, this process is greatly preferable to the ordinary laborious one.

To find the square root of a number which is wholly decimal.

Very simple, and correct to the third numeral figure inclusive. If the number does not contain at least five figures, *counting from the first numeral, and including it,* add one or more ciphers to make five. If, after that, the *whole number* is not separable into twos, add another cipher to make it so. Then beginning at the first numeral figure, and including it, assume the number to be a whole one. In the table find the number nearest to this assumed one; take out its tabular sq rt; move the decimal point of this tabular root to the left, *half* as many places as the finally modified *decimal* number has figures.

Ex. What is the sq rt of the decimal .002? Here, in order to have at least five decimal figures, counting from the first numeral (2), and including it, add ciphers thus, .00,20,00,0. But, as it is not now separable into twos, add another cipher. thus, .00,20,00,00. Then beginning at the first numeral (2), assume this decimal to be the whole number 200000. The nearest to this in the table is 199809; and the sq rt of this is 447. Now, the decimal number as finally modified, namely, .00,20,00,00, has eight figures; one-half of which is 4; therefore, move the decimal point of the root 447, four places to the left; making it .0447. This is the reqd sq rt of .002, correct to the third numeral 7 included.

To find the cube root of a number which is wholly decimal.

Very simple, and correct to the third numeral inclusive.

If the number does not contain at least five figures, counting from the first numeral, and including it, add one or more ciphers to make five. If, after that, the number is not separable into threes, add one or more ciphers to make it so. Then beginning at the first numeral, and including it, assume the number to be a whole one. In the table find the number nearest to this assumed one, and take out its tabular cub rt. Move the decimal point of this rt to the left, one-third as many places as the finally modified *decimal* number has figures.

Ex. What is the cube rt of the decimal .002? Here, in order to have at least five figures, counting from the first numeral (2), and including it, add ciphers thus, .002,000,0. But as it is not now separable into threes, add two more ciphers to make it so; thus, .002,000,000. Then beginning with the first numeral (2), assume the decimal to be the whole number 2000000. The nearest cube to this in the table in the column of cubes, is 2000376; and its tabular cube rt as found in the col of numbers, is 126. Now, the decimal number as finally modified, namely, .002 000 000, has nine figures; one-third of which is 3; therefore, move the decimal point of the root 126, three places to the left, making it .126. This is the reqd cube rt of the decimal .002, correct to the third numeral 6 included.

To find roots by logarithms, } See pages 200 & 202.

For tables of sq. rts. of 5th powers see table 69, page 166.

To find the sq. or cu. rt. of a number consisting of intigers and decimals.

Multiply the difference between the root of the intiger part of the given number, and the root of the next higher number, by the decimal part of the given number, and add the product to the root of the given intiger. The sum is the root required.

Ex.—Required the sq. rt. of 20.321—square root of 21 = 4.5825
" " " 20 = 4.4721
Difference = .1104

.1104 × .321 = .354384, add to rt. of 20, 4.4721, and get 4.5075384=rt. required.

Ex.—Required the cu. rt. of 16.42—cube root of 17 = 2.5712
" " " 16 = 2.5198
Difference = .0514

.0514 × .42 = .021588, add to rt. of 16, 2.5198, and get 2.541388 = rt. required.

To find the sq. or cu. rt. of a higher number than is contained in the table, when the number is divisib'e by 4 or 8 without leaving a remainder.

RULE.—Divide the number by 4 or 8 respectively, as the sq. or cu. rt. is required; take the rt. of the quotient in the table, multiply it by 2, and the product will be the root required.

Ex.—What are the square and cube roots of 2400?
2400 ÷ 4 = 600   and   2400 ÷ 8 = 300.
Then the sq. rt. of 600, per table, = 24.4949, which, being × 2 = 48.9898 = sq. rt. required.
Then the cu. rt. of 300, per table, = 6.6943, which, being × 2 = 13.3886 = cu. rt. required.

To find the 4th root of any number.

Take the square root of its square root.

To find the 6th root of any number.

Take the cube root of its square root.
To find *any root* or *any power* by logarithms see pages 200 and 202.

Logarithms of Numbers, from 0 to 1000.*

No.	0	1	2	3	4	5	6	7	8	9	Prop.
0	0	00000	30103	47712	60206	69897	77815	84510	90309	95424	
10	00000	00432	00860	01283	01703	02118	02530	02938	03342	03742	415
11	04139	04532	04921	05307	05690	06069	06445	06818	07188	07554	379
12	07918	08278	08636	08990	09342	09691	10037	10380	10721	11059	349
13	11394	11727	12057	12385	12710	13033	13353	13672	13987	14301	323
14	14613	14921	15228	15533	15836	16136	16435	16731	17026	17318	300
15	17609	17897	18184	18469	18752	19033	19312	19590	19865	20139	281
16	20412	20682	20951	21218	21484	21748	22010	22271	22530	22788	264
17	23045	23299	23552	23804	24054	24303	24551	24797	25042	25285	249
18	25527	25767	26007	26245	26481	26717	26951	27184	27415	27646	236
19	27875	28103	28330	28555	28780	29003	29225	29446	29666	29885	223
20	30103	30319	30535	30749	30963	31175	31386	31597	31806	32014	212
21	32222	32428	32633	32838	33041	33243	33445	33646	33845	34044	202
22	34242	34439	34635	34830	35024	35218	35410	35602	35793	35983	194
23	36173	36361	36548	36735	36921	37106	37291	37474	37657	37839	185
24	38021	38201	38381	38560	38739	38916	39093	39269	39445	39619	177
25	39794	39967	40140	40312	40483	40654	40824	40993	41162	41330	171
26	41497	41664	41830	41995	42160	42324	42488	42651	42813	42975	164
27	43136	43296	43456	43616	43775	43933	44090	44248	44404	44560	158
28	44716	44870	45024	45178	45331	45484	45636	45788	45939	46089	153
29	46240	46389	46538	46686	46834	46982	47129	47275	47421	47567	148
30	47712	47856	48000	48144	48287	48430	48572	48713	48855	48995	143
31	49136	49276	49415	49554	49693	49831	49968	50105	50242	50379	138
32	50515	50650	50785	50920	51054	51188	51321	51454	51587	51719	134
33	51851	51982	52113	52244	52374	52504	52633	52763	52891	53020	130
34	53148	53275	53402	53529	53655	53781	53907	54033	54157	54282	126
35	54407	54530	54654	54777	54900	55022	55145	55266	55388	55509	122
36	55630	55750	55870	55990	56110	56229	56348	56466	56584	56702	119
37	56820	56937	57054	57170	57287	57403	57518	57634	57749	57863	116
38	57978	58092	58206	58319	58433	58546	58658	58771	58883	58995	113
39	59106	59217	59328	59439	59549	59659	59769	59879	59988	60097	110
40	60206	60314	60422	60530	60638	60745	60852	60959	61066	61172	107
41	61278	61384	61489	61595	61700	61804	61909	62013	62118	62221	104
42	62325	62428	62531	62634	62786	62838	62941	63042	63144	63245	102
43	63347	63447	63548	63648	63749	63848	63948	64048	64147	64246	99
44	64345	64443	64542	64640	64738	64836	64933	65030	65127	65224	98
45	65321	65417	65513	65609	65705	65801	65896	65991	66086	66181	96
46	66276	66370	66464	66558	66651	66745	66838	66931	67024	67117	94
47	67210	67302	67394	67486	67577	67669	67760	67851	67942	68033	92
48	68124	68214	68304	68394	68484	68574	68663	68752	68842	68930	90
49	69020	69108	69196	69284	69372	69460	69548	69635	69722	69810	88
50	69897	69983	70070	70156	70243	70329	70415	70500	70586	70671	86
51	70757	70842	70927	71011	71096	71180	71265	71349	71433	71516	84
52	71600	71683	71767	71850	71933	72015	72098	72181	72263	72345	82
53	72428	72509	72591	72672	72754	72835	72916	72997	73078	73158	81
54	73239	73319	73399	73480	73559	73639	73719	73798	73878	73957	80
55	74036	74115	74193	74272	74351	74429	74507	74585	74663	74741	78
56	74818	74896	74973	75050	75127	75204	75281	75358	75434	75511	77
57	75587	75663	75739	75815	75891	75966	76042	76117	76192	76267	75
58	76342	76417	76492	76566	76641	76715	76789	76863	76937	77011	74
59	77085	77158	77232	77305	77378	77451	77524	77597	77670	77742	73
60	77815	77887	77959	78031	78103	78175	78247	78318	78390	78461	72
61	78533	78604	78675	78746	78816	78887	78958	79028	79098	79169	71
62	79239	79309	79379	79448	79518	79588	79657	79726	79796	79865	70
63	79934	80002	80071	80140	80208	80277	80345	80413	80482	80550	69
64	80618	80685	80753	80821	80888	80956	81023	81090	81157	81224	68
65	81291	81358	81424	81491	81557	81624	81690	81756	81822	81888	67

* Each log is supposed to have the decimal sign before it. An error of less than 1 in the final decimal exists in a number of the logs of this table, it will not, however, be material in ordinary computations.

Logarithms of Numbers, from 0 to 1000*—(Continued.)

No.	0	1	2	3	4	5	6	7	8	9	Prop.
66	81954	82020	82085	82151	82216	82282	82347	82412	82477	82542	66
67	82607	82672	82736	82801	82866	82930	82994	83058	83123	83187	65
68	83250	83314	83378	83442	83505	83569	83632	83695	83758	83821	64
69	83884	83947	84010	84073	84136	84198	84260	84323	84385	84447	63
70	84509	84571	84633	84695	84757	84818	84880	84941	85003	85064	62
71	85125	85187	85248	85309	85369	85430	85491	85551	85612	85672	61
72	85733	85793	85853	85913	85973	86033	86093	86153	86213	86272	60
73	86332	86391	86451	86510	86569	86628	86687	86746	86805	86864	59
74	86923	86981	87040	87098	87157	87215	87273	87332	87390	87448	58
75	87506	87564	87621	87679	87737	87794	87852	87909	87966	88024	57
76	88081	88138	88195	88252	88309	88366	88422	88479	88536	88592	56
77	88649	88705	88761	88818	88874	88930	88986	89042	89098	89153	56
78	89209	89265	89320	89376	89431	89487	89542	89597	89652	89707	55
79	89762	89817	89872	89927	89982	90036	90091	90145	90200	90254	54
80	90309	90363	90417	90471	90525	90579	90633	90687	90741	90794	54
81	90848	90902	90955	91009	91062	91115	91169	91222	91275	91328	53
82	91381	91434	91487	91540	91592	91645	91698	91750	91803	91855	53
83	91907	91960	92012	92064	92116	92168	92220	92272	92324	92376	52
84	92427	92479	92531	92582	92634	92685	92737	92788	92839	92890	51
85	92941	92993	93044	93095	93146	93196	93247	93298	93348	93399	51
86	93449	93500	93550	93601	93651	93701	93751	93802	93852	93902	50
87	93951	94001	94051	94101	94151	94200	94250	94300	94349	94398	49
88	94448	94497	94546	94596	94645	94694	94743	94792	94841	94890	49
89	94939	94987	95036	95085	95133	95182	95230	95279	95327	95376	48
90	95424	95472	95520	95568	95616	95664	95712	95760	95808	95856	48
91	95904	95951	95999	96047	96094	96142	96189	96236	96284	96331	48
92	96378	96426	96473	96520	96567	96614	96661	96708	96754	96801	47
93	96848	96895	96941	96988	97034	97081	97127	97174	97220	97266	47
94	97312	97359	97405	97451	97497	97543	97589	97635	97680	97726	46
95	97772	97818	97863	97909	97954	98000	98045	98091	98136	98181	46
96	98227	98272	98317	98362	98407	98452	98497	98542	98587	98632	45
97	98677	98721	98766	98811	98855	98900	98945	98989	99033	99078	45
98	99122	99166	99211	99255	99299	99343	99387	99431	99475	99519	44
99	99563	99607	99651	99694	99738	99782	99825	99869	99913	99956	44

*See foot note on page 199.

The log of 2870 is 3.45788	The log of .287 is — 1.45788
" " " 287 is 2.45788	" " " .028 is — 2.44716
" " " 28.7 is 1.45788	" " " .002 is — 3.30103
" " " 2.87 is 0.45788	" " " .0002 is — 4.30103

What is the log of 2873?

Here, log of 2870 = 3.45788

And prop 153 × 3 =   459

3.458339

To find roots divide the log (with its index) of the given number, by that number which expresses the kind of root. The quotient will be the log of the required root.

Example. What is the cube root of 2870?

Here, the log of 2870, with its index, is 3.45788. And $\dfrac{3.45788}{3} = 1.15263$. Hence the cube root is 14.2.

The Hyperbolic, or Napierian logarithm is the common log of the table multiplied by 2.3025851.

Sq. rt. 6925=Log 3.84042÷2=log 1.92021, corresponding No.=83.2138=sq. rt·
Cu-rt. 6925= "   3.84042÷3= " 1.28014,   " =19.0669=cu. rt.
4th rt. 6925= "   3.84042÷4= " ·96010,   "   " = 9.1222=4th rt.

Proceed in like manner for any other root required. This method of extracting roots is more rapid and simple than any other.

EXPLANATION AS TO TABLES OF LOGARITHMS.

LOGARITHMS are the exponents with which a *fixed* number must be affected in order to produce a *given* number. The fixed number is called the **BASE**. The base of the common system of logarithms is 10.

Since $10^0 = $ 1 the logarithm of 1 is 0.
" $10^1 = $ 10 " " " 10 " 1.
" $10^2 = $ 100 " " " 100 " 2.

Thus, the logarithms of all powers of the base are *integral numbers*, while the logarithms of numbers intervening between exact powers of the base are composed of an integer and a fractional or decimal part—called the **MANTISSA.** The integral part of the logarithm being called the

INDEX or **CHARACTERISTIC**

NOTE WELL THE FOLLOWING RULES.

I. The log. of any exact power of 10 is a positive $(+)$ intiger one *less* than the number of places in the number.

Thus—See figures at foot of table on page 200—
Log of 2870 has 3 for its index, there being 4 figures in the number.
" " 287 " 2 " " " " 3 " " "
" " 28 " 1 " " " " 2 " " "
" " 2 " 0 " " " " 1 " " "

II. The characteristic of any *decimal* number is negative $(-)$ and numerically one *more* than the number of zeros immediately following the decimal point.

Thus—See figures on page 200 (2d column.)
Log of decimal .287 (being no zeros) $= -1.$ (Negative, and 1 in excess of
" " " .028 (" 1 zero) $= -2.$ ⟨ the number of zeros immedi-
" " " .002 (" 2 zeros] $= -3.$ (ately following deci'al point.

{ The minus sign instead of being placed *befori* the index, as }
{ here shown, is usually placed *above* thei ndex, thus, $\overline{3}$. }

USE OF TABLE. The logarithms of numbers from 1 to 9 are taken from the top horizontal line of the table, Log of 9 being .95424; and logs of numbers from 11 to 99 are taken from the first column, headed by O, the index 1 being added as above explained [I]. Thus—the log of 91 = 1.95904, Log of 80 = 1.90309. Logs of numbers from 100 to 1000 are taken from the table as follows—required the log of 915; find 91 in first column and then run horizontally across the table to the column headed 5 where is found the log .96142 to which add an index of 2, as above explained, making 2.96142 the log required. Log of 800 would in like manner be 2.90309, log of 801 = 2.90363. *Since the decimal part of the logarithm is not changed by multiplying or dividing the number by any power of 10* the logarithm of a number of 4 or 5 places may also be taken from the table as shown at the foot of the table. The log of 287 = 2.45788 and log of 2870 = 3.45788—the index only being changed. If, however, the 4th figure is other than O, as 2873, then proceed as follows:—find the log of the 3 left hand figures and in the same horizontal line, at its intersection with the last vertical column, headed " Prop." [Proportionate parts] take the number indicated and multiply it by the last figure of the given number. Exclude one figure from the product and add the remainder to the log first found. In case as shown at foot of table log is taken for 2870 then in last column is found 153 which × 3, the last number of the given number 2873, exclude the right hand figure from the product of 459 and add the remainder, 45, to the log first found.

What is the log of 28735?
Here log of 28700 = 4.45788
And prop 153×35 = 53.55
Log of 28735 = 4.45841

Here 2 figures are cast off because there are 2 figures in the multiplier [35]. With numbers of 5 figures this may be in error 1 in the last decimal.

In the use of logarithms it is not only necessary to find the log corresponding to a given number but also to find the number corresponding to any given log.

III. Given any log to find the corresponding number.

A.—*Where the mantissa is found in the table.*

Look in the table for the given log, take out the corresponding number and place the decimal point according to the given index.
Example—Given log 4.96142, what is the corresponding number?
Look in table for log 96142 and find it corresponds to the number 915. The given index 4 indicates a number of 5 places therefore point off the number obtained to have 5 places and to read 91500.
Log of 2.90309 corresponds to 800; Log .30103 to 2. &c.

B.—*Where the mantissa is not found in the table.*

Take from the table the next *lesser* mantissa and its corresponding number. Then subtract this mantissa from the given one and divide the remainder by the number opposite in the column " Prop." Annex the quotient so found to the tabular number taken out and then point off as indicated by the given index.
Example—Given the log 1.96166 to find the corresponding number.
From table we find .96142 to be the nearest *lesser* mantissa and 915 to be the corresponding number. .96166, the given mantissa, minus .96142 the lesser one = difference of 24 which being divided by 48, the number found in column " Prop." = .5. This being annexed to the tabular number 915= 9155. The given index 1 indicates a number of 2 places, so 91.55 becomes the required number,

THE USE OF LOGARITHMS.

The **ADDITION** of logarithms corresponds to ordinary **MULTIPLICA-TION** and any number of given numbers either integral, decimal or mixed, may be multiplied together by one operation.
Thus: multiply together 166, 71.5, 8.25 and .078 (=7637.7).

Log 166.   =   2.22010
"   71.5   =   1.85430   Note. The *index* of the last log being
"   8.25   =   0.91645   minus it is subtracted from the sum of the
"   .078   =   —2.89209   + indices, 5, leaving 3 the index of the sum.
                ———————
" of product = 3.88294

By method B, above given, the log 3.88294 is found to correspond to the number 7637.7 which is the required product.

The **SUBTRACTION** of logarithms corresponds to ordinary **DIVISION**. The log of the divisor being subtracted from the log of the dividend gives, as a remainder, the log of the quotient.
Thus—Divide 86.32 by 6.85 (=12.601).

Log 86.32   =   1.93611
"   6.85   =   0.83569
                 ———————
" quotient=   1.10042, which, by method " B," = 12.601 = quotient.

TO RAISE A NUMBER TO A POWER.

Rule.—Multiply the log of the number by the exponent of the power and find the number corresponding to the product.
Thus—What is the 5th power of 7.65?
Log of 7.65 = .88366 which × 5 = 4.41830 the number corresponding to which is 26200.

TO FIND ANY ROOT BY LOGARITHMS.

See explanation at foot of table on page 200. The cube root 14.2 being the number corresponding to log 1.15263. Proceed in like manner for any other root required.

The foregoing explanations as to the use of logarithms are chiefly for the benefit of those who have, by disuse, become "rusty" in the use of the tables; although any one may in a day or two become familliar with them and may, by their use, greatly lessen the drudgery of mathematical calculations. Such uses only have been explained as pertain to the simpler mathematical operations.

EXPLANATION OF CHARACTERS.

The following brief explanation is given of a few of the more common characters used in calculations, etc. and which are so frequently met with in mathematical and similar works.

=	Signifies	*Equality.*	as $2 + 2 = 4$.
+	"	*Plus,*	as $2 + 2 = 4$.
×	"	*Multiplied* by,	as $2 \times 4 = 8$.
—	"	*Minus,*	as $8 - 2 = 6$.
÷	"	*Divided by,*	as $8 \div 2 = 4$.
: & ::	"	*Proportion,*	as $2 : 8 :: 4 : 16$ reads....as 2 is to 8

so is 4 to 16, or, 2 is to 8 as 4 is to 16.

———— *The Vinculum or Bar* indicates that all the numbers over which it is placed are to be considered as one quantity, thus, $\overline{2 + 8} + 2 = 5$; or $5 \times \overline{8 - 2} = 30$.

( ) [ ] *Parenthesis or Brackets* indicate, as in above, that all included figures are to be considered as one quantity, thus, $(3 \times 5) + 10 = 25$; or $3 \times [5 + 10] = 45$.

. *Decimal Point.*

$\sqrt{}$ *The Radical or Root sign* when placed before a number indicates that the *square root* of the number is required, $\sqrt{16} = 4$; $\sqrt{15 + 10} = 5$.   The *degree* of the root, other than the *square root,* is indicated by a figure placed above the radical, which figure is called the *Index.* $\sqrt[3]{} = $ *Cube root*; $\sqrt[4]{} = $ *4th. root* etc.

∠	Signifies	*Angle.*	
⊥	"	*Perpendicular.*	
△	"	*Triangle. or triangular*	as △ iron or inches.
☐	"	*Square,*	as ☐ " " "
○	"	*Circle or Circular,*	as ○ " " "
∴	"	*Therefore or Hence.*	
∵	"	*Because.*	
π	"	The *Ratio* of the circumference of a circle to its diameter, which $= 3.1416$.	
> <	"	*Greater and Less,* $a > b$ reads - *a* greater than *b*.	
∞	"	*Infinity.*	
° ′ ″	"	*Degrees. Minutes, and Seconds of arc.*	
′ ″	"	*Feet and Inches.*	

½ ⅓ &c.   "   when set *superior* to a number, that the *square or cube root* etc. is wanted, thus 25$^{\frac{1}{2}}$ indicates the sq. rt.of 25.

⅔ ⅖ ⅙ &c. "   when set *superior* to a number, respectively, the *sq. rt. of the cube;* the *sq. rt. of the 5th. power;* and the *cube root of the 6th. power* etc.

² ³ ⁴ &c. "   when set *superior* to a number, the *power* to which the number is to be raised, thus $2^2 = 4$; $2^3 = 8$; $2^5 = 32$ &c.

CONCLUSION.

The public may claim that the author owes to them an apology for having presented an irrigation manual wherein no direction is given as to the detail workings of an irrigation plant, or any direction as to when, and how often, to irrigate, how to prepare the soil, &c. Such was not the object, as stated in the preface, but rather to present certain items of technical information, and such other matter as would tend to show the importance and practicability of irrigation in the Dakotas. The subject is one too vast to be treated fully in one volume, or in a score of volumes, such as this. More has been omitted than has been included, and much which was of value, and which it was desired to include, has been omitted because of the limited means and space, and the circumstances under which this little book was made. Should it become advisable to issue a second edition many additional features of interest and of value will be included. A start has, however, been made which it is to be hoped others will more successfully emulate until all of the people of these states shall have become imbued with the vital importance to themselves and to their children of this matter of irrigation; and until the thousands of acres of our now waste paradise shall have put on that cloak of perrennial verdure which is their due and their destiny.

No more fitting conclusion can be made than to quote from the eloquent words of the late Hon. S. S. Cox, congressman from New York, delivered in his oration at Huron on July 4th, 1889. Words as poetic in sentiment as they are prophetic of truth. He said:

"But yesterday your fruitful valley was whitened with the bones of the buffalo. Now it is an ideal farming area. It is a lesser Nile region, without its overflow. Artesian Wells give water where the sun once made drouth perrennial. The water power of your matchless valley is as yet immeasurable by ordinary mechanical standards. It is so prevalent that your people will utilize its specific gravity for the diversity of their industries. When its undiminished flow and steady pressure from the bosom of the earth are properly harnessed by mechanism, it will give its lucid lymph to make grasses for stock and lawns for beautiful homes. Its sunless currents, through the ingenuity of man, will enhance the rich soil by quenching its thirst. Fabulous are the wasted energies of your water power. as we count it by the standard horse power of mechanics; but still more marvellous are the real energies of the soil which it would fructify.

The beautiful and fruitful valley of the James may not be as redolent of historic association and traditions as another James River of the colonial days; but deeper than historical or traditional incident are Dakota's pure springs under a magic more enchanting than that of Aladdin, which leap from your modern Artesium.

THE END.

www.ingramcontent.com/pod-product-compliance
Lightning Source LLC
Chambersburg PA
CBHW030825270326
41928CB00007B/896